GENDERED (IN)JUSTICE

Theory and Practice in Feminist Criminology

Pamela J. Schram
California State University, San Bernardino

Barbara Koons-Witt
University of South Carolina

Long Grove, Illinois

For information about this book, contact:
Waveland Press, Inc.
4180 IL Route 83, Suite 101
Long Grove, IL 60047-9580
(847) 634-0081
info@waveland.com
www.waveland.com

ISBN 1-57766-328-4

Printed in the United States of America

7 6 5 4 3 2 1

To Jeremy Alan, Trent Douglas, and Lindsay Paige

—Aunt Pam

To Ron Witt—my biggest supporter

—Barbara Koons-Witt

Contents

Section II: Understanding Women and the Crimes They Commit 93

Section III: Laws and Policies Affecting Women Offenders 195

INTRODUCTION

In the 1950 movie, *All About Eve*, Karen Richards (played by Celeste Holm) is having an argument with her husband, Lloyd Richards (played by Hugh Marlowe). In this particular scene, Lloyd comments to his wife, "That bitter cynicism of yours is something you've acquired since you left Radcliff." Karen responds by stating, "That cynicism you refer to I acquired the day I discovered I was different from little boys." Why would a girl's discovery that she is different from little boys evoke feelings of cynicism? Some argue that these feelings of cynicism are not necessarily due to little girls' realization that they are different from little boys. Rather, this cynicism may develop when one realizes that this difference is evaluated in terms of socially constructed negative and positive attributes; this evaluation can eventually lead to privilege and power for those whose differences are associated with positive attributes.

Trying to understand how gender shapes every aspect of our lives has been the major focus of feminist theory. While feminism is over one hundred years old, it was not until the 1960s that feminist discourses began shaping criminology, especially in the United States (Klein, 1995; Schwendinger & Schwendinger, 1991). Feminist scholars have argued that traditionally science has reflected the social values and concerns of dominant, privileged social groups such as white, upper class males (Eichler, 1979; Harding, 1987; Keller, 1978; McHugh, Koeske, & Frieze, 1986; Nielsen, 1990; Stanley & Wise, 1979; Westkott, 1979). Thus, research has often ignored, marginalized, or made women invisible, especially when studying female offenders (Belknap, 2001).

In 1977, Carol Smart argued that women had not been *entirely* ignored in the study of crime and deviance. The quality of work, however, was questionable at best. She stressed the importance of contextualizing female criminality within a broader framework: moral, political, economic, and gendered spheres (p. 185). Susan Okin (1989) questioned theories of social justice and the lack of attention given to issues pertaining to gender:

> [M]ajor contemporary theorists of justice . . . have displayed little interest in or knowledge of the findings of feminism. They have largely bypassed the fact that the society to which their theories are supposed

> to pertain is heavily and deeply affected by gender, and faces difficult issues of justice stemming from its gendered past and present assumptions. Since theories of justice are centrally concerned with whether, how, and why persons should be treated differently from one another, this neglect seems inexplicable. (p. 8)

Anne Edwards (1989) maintained that traditional academic research focused on different factors of criminality when studying females as compared to males. When studying men, "masculinity" or "maleness" was rarely considered as a significant variable. Instead, various factors were deemed essential in studying criminality and males. When studying females, however, criminality usually emphasized "female characteristics" (e.g., biological determinism).

Kathleen Daly and Meda Chesney-Lind (1988) argued that gender differences in crime "challenge us to see that in the lives of women, men have a great deal more to learn" (p. 527). They identified five elements that distinguish feminist thought from other forms of social and political thought:

- Gender is not a natural fact but a complex social, historical, and cultural product; it is related to, but not simply derived from, biological sex differences and reproductive capacities.
- Gender and gender relations order social life and social institutions in fundamental ways.
- Gender relations and constructs of masculinity and femininity are not symmetrical but are based on an organizing principle of men's superiority and social and political-economic dominance over women.
- Systems of knowledge reflect men's views of the natural and social world; the production of knowledge is gendered.
- Women should be at the center of intellectual inquiry, not peripheral, invisible, or appendages of men (p. 504).

When exploring the future impact and development of feminist thinking in criminology, Dorie Klein (1995) attempted to evoke a re-envisioning of feminist perspectives on crime and justice in the United States that could represent both an intellectual and socio-political perspective. She concluded by asking the following:

> The challenge for us is: can we create a criminology inspired by feminist questions—a homegrown feminist criminology that does not quite yet exist—that can make an intellectual and political difference? (p. 234)

In this vein, an essential goal of feminist research is to have a liberating or emancipating purpose (Acker, Barry, & Esseveld, 1983; Allen & Baber, 1992; Fonow & Cook, 1991):

> Because the feminist goal is to do research that is *for* women rather than *about* women, we suggest that priority be given to research that will provide information that women want and need to change the conditions of their lives. (Allen & Baber, 1992, p. 9)

Joan Acker, Kate Barry, and Johanna Esseveld (1983) argued that by producing knowledge, feminist research can contribute to women's liberation; this knowledge can be used by them to enhance their lives. Edwards (1989) also emphasized how feminist analyses can, and should, be directed toward an emancipating goal:

> In a particular society, where structurally-based inequalities (and particularly power inequalities) characterise the relationships between women and men, all institutions and practices will reflect and reinforce these inequalities. . . . Even if we are persuaded that the forces of male domination are less than absolute, feminists' own theory puts major limitations on any possibilities for change. *But at least in raising these questions the whole problem is put on the agenda and political strategies and further research can be directed at these fundamental issues* [emphasis added]. (p. 179)

Focus of the Book

This book is intended to provide students, scholars, and practitioners a "glimpse" of how feminist thinking has developed in criminology and criminal justice over the last few decades. Feminists have accumulated, and continue to accumulate, an increasing body of knowledge. To continue enhancing this body of knowledge, it is essential to appreciate how this knowledge has developed and consider the complexities and scope of the work by feminist criminologists today. With this in mind, articles were selected that would provide readers with the intellectual tools to understand and critique feminist knowledge. Our initial motivation for developing this book was to explore how feminist criminology has developed over the last few decades. Subsequently, we wanted to examine how feminist criminology has not only been *about* women but *for* women as well. Specifically, we wanted to explore how feminist criminology has influenced research on women offenders, laws, and policies as well as programming involving women offenders.

The first section of this text, "Feminist Theory and Criminology," provides readers with a brief overview of how feminist thought has developed in the field of criminology. The articles selected for this section also highlight some essential issues facing feminist criminologists today. One interesting debate pertains to epistemology. Epistemology has been defined as "a theory of knowledge" (Harding, 1987) or "the study of assumptions about how to know the social and apprehend its meaning" (Fonow & Cook, 1991, p. 1). These epistemological debates illustrate that it is essential to move beyond "grappling with the mainstream" to "grappling" with the effect of feminist scholarship on the production of knowledge (Smart, 1995). Further, there are many forms of feminism; discourses and debates between these various forms are productive. However, Smart (1995) emphasizes that engagements between the various forms may also be painful (p. 11).

As mentioned previously, we initially wanted to select articles that provide readers with a general overview of how feminist theory has developed in criminology over the last few decades. We have attempted to reveal some of these developments in the remaining sections of this book. The second section, "Understanding Women and the Crimes They Commit," includes articles that have continued to further our understanding of female criminality. There have been interesting advances—and challenges—in this area of study. For instance, Kathleen Daly and Lisa Maher (1998) have argued that it is essential, when studying female offenders, that one recognizes the need to cross the traditional boundaries of "victim" and "offender." Research needs to move beyond these boundaries, especially since many women offenders have also been victims of physical and sexual abuse.

In the third section, "Laws and Policies Affecting Women Offenders," we have selected articles that illustrate how laws and policies have the potential to control, and negatively affect, the lives of female offenders. Frances Heidensohn (1985) argued that social policies are one form of social control; she maintained that some of these policies are founded on stereotypes and assumptions regarding gender:

> Of all the subtler constraints on the way women act and are supposed to act, few are more complex than the workings of social policies.
>
> Social policies are not usually regarded as instruments whose prime purpose is the definition and enforcement of prescriptions about gender roles, especially women, but a growing body of analyses shows that such prescriptions underpin, or are an effective part of certain policies. (p. 191)

Specifically, we have selected articles on sentencing guidelines, "war on drugs" policies, and welfare reform efforts.

The final section of the book, "Programming for Women Offenders," illustrates how feminist perspectives have provided a critical framework that allows scholars and practitioners to re-assess programming for female offenders. For instance, the need for such re-assessment was emphasized at a 1999 national symposium sponsored by the Office of Justice Programs in the U.S. Department of Justice:

> . . . we do know what works well for women; programs that take into account [women's] different needs. Programs should be based on supporting women in relationships, providing them with good role models and mentors, helping them work through their problems with sexual abuse and trauma, providing them with job training and education they need to find productive work, and helping them gain increased feelings of self-esteem. *Equality for women does not mean sameness in programs for men and women. Instead, programs should be tailored to women's lives and reflect the cultures from which they come* [emphasis added]. (p. 25)

The articles selected for this section illustrate these efforts. The first two articles discuss general issues pertaining to programming for women prisoners. The remaining two articles specifically focus on two types of programs for women—substance abuse treatment and boot camps.

References

Acker, J., Barry, K., & Esseveld, J. (1983). Objectivity and truth: Problems in doing feminist research. *Women's Studies International Forum, 6*, 423–435.

Allen, K. R., & Baber, K. M. (1992). Ethical and epistemological tensions in applying a postmodern perspective to feminist research. *Psychology of Women Quarterly, 16*, 1–15.

Belknap, J. (2001). *The invisible woman: Gender, crime and justice* (2nd ed.). Belmont, CA: Wadsworth.

Daly, K., & Chesney-Lind, M. (1988). Feminism and criminology. *Justice Quarterly, 5*, 497–535.

Daly, K., & Maher, L. (Eds.). (1988). *Criminology at the crossroads: Feminist readings in crime and justice.* New York: Oxford.

Edwards, A. R. (1989). Sex/gender, sexism and criminal justice. Some theoretical considerations. *International Journal of the Sociology of Law, 17*, 165–184.

Eichler, M. (1979). *The double standard: A feminist critique of feminist social science.* New York: St. Martin's Press.

Fonow, M. M., & Cook, J. A. (1991). Back to the future: A look at the second wave of feminist epistemology. In M. M. Fonow & J. A. Cook (eds.), *Beyond methodology: Feminist scholarship as lived research* (pp. 1–15). Bloomington: Indiana University Press.

Harding, S. (1987). "Introduction." In S. Harding (ed.), *Feminism and methodology* (pp. 1–14). Bloomington: Indiana University Press.

Heidensohn, F. (1985). *Women and crime.* London: Macmillan.

Keller, E. F. (1978). Gender and science. *Psychoanalysis and Contemporary Thought: A Quarterly of Integrative and Interdisciplinary Studies, 1*, 409–433.

Klein, D. (1995). Crime through gender's prism: Feminist criminology in the United States. In N. H. Rafter & F. Heidensohn (eds.), *International feminist perspectives in criminology: Engendering a discipline* (pp. 216–240). Buckingham, UK: Open University Press.

McHugh, M. D., Koeske, R. D., & Frieze, I. H. (1986). Issues to consider in conducting nonsexist psychological research. *American Psychologist, 41*, 879–890.

National Symposium on Women Offenders (1999). Plenary III: Effective Interventions—Looking at Gender-Responsive Programming.

Nielsen, J. M. (1990). *Feminist research methods: Exemplary readings in the social sciences*. Boulder, CO: Westview Press.

Okin, S. M. (1989). *Justice, gender, and the family.* New York: Basic Books.

Schwendinger, H., & Schwendinger, J. (1991). Feminism, criminology and complex variations. In B. MacLean & D. Milovanovic (eds.), *Directions in critical criminology.* Vancouver: The Collective Press.

Smart, C. (1977). Criminology theory: Its ideology and implications concerning women. *British Journal of Sociology, 28*, 89–100.

Smart, C. (1995). *Law, Crime, and Sexuality: Essays in Feminism.* Thousand Oaks, CA: Sage Publications.

Stanley, L., & Wise, S. (1979). Feminist research, feminist consciousness, and experiences of sexism. *Women's Studies International Quarterly, 2*, 359–374.

Westkott, M. (1979). Feminist criticism of the social sciences. *Harvard Educational Review, 49*, 422–430.

SECTION I

Feminist Theory and Criminology

Traditional criminological theories have been based on negative, stereotypical perspectives of female offenders. These theories restrict an understanding of female criminality to a biological or psychological realm and ignore a broader understanding that includes the economic, social, and political realities of women offenders. The articles selected for this section highlight some of the issues pertaining to feminism and criminology. The first article introduces readers to key elements and issues central to feminist thought. The remaining two articles provide a historical overview of the development of feminist perspectives in criminology and briefly highlight some concerns that have been raised regarding this ongoing development.

Although Kathleen Daly and Meda Chesney-Lind's article, "Feminism and Criminology," was published over 15 years ago, it continues to be an intriguing essay that introduces readers, unfamiliar with feminism, key components and issues central to feminist thought. First, they address three myths about feminism: a lack of objectivity, the narrow focus on women, and the feminist analysis. Second, the authors attempt to disentangle the complexities involved in defining feminism. Third, Daly and Chesney-Lind engage the readers to consider the relevance of feminist thought to criminology. Specifically, they begin this section with an insightful, yet difficult question: "What can feminist thought bring to studies of crime and justice?" In the next section the authors provide readers with a broad overview of how feminist scholarhsip has been "incorporated" in the field of cirminology. The final section reviews three pivotal areas of study for feminism and criminology: approaches to building theories of gender and cirme, controlling men's violence toward women, and gender equlity in the criminal justice system. Daly and Chesney-Lind conclude by noting that they have "attempted to make feminist thought accessible to criminologists and to show its significance for criminology."

In her article, "Feminism in Criminology: Engendering the Outlaw," Dana Britton maintains that criminology continues to be one of the most masculinized of all the social sciences. Despite this critical problem, there have been efforts to incorporate feminism in criminology. Britton provides a brief overview of theory and research in this area during the last 25 years. She summarizes theory and research in the areas of women as offenders, as victims, and as workers. Britton concludes by providing some emerging issues in feminist criminology. For instance, some feminist criminologists have argued that the traditional boundaries between offenders and victims are, for many women, "blurred boundaries." Another emerging issue is recognizing that "women" cannot be categorized simplistically as a unitary group. Rather, feminist criminologists need to develop various dimensions fully, including race, ethnicity, social class, and sexual orientation. Finally, feminist criminologists need to re-think their relationship with the state. Specifically, they need to re-visit, re-assess, and re-evaluate the liberal strategy of strict legal equality.

As with Britton's work, Jeanne Flavin's article, "Feminism for the Mainstream Criminologist: An Invitation," discusses similar issues pertaining to feminism and criminology. A theme throughout Flavin's essay is that feminism is not just "about women"; rather, feminism focuses on understanding how gender, race, and social class influence research and policy in the field of criminal justice. She concludes that feminist criminologists *generally* agree for a transformation in the criminal justice discipline. There is less agreement, however, as to how this transformation should come about. For instance, do feminist criminologists continue to develop a "special niche" for themselves by publishing in specialized journals and books? Using this strategy, Flavin argues that feminists risk further marginalization in the discipline. Flavin attempts to present an alternative strategy. She invites both feminists and "mainstream" criminologists to meet midway in an effort to explain the strength and diversity of feminist perspectives and how these perspectives can enhance the field of criminal justice.

1

Feminism and Criminology

Kathleen Daly & Meda Chesney-Lind

The last decade has seen an outpouring of feminist scholarship in the academy. Theories, research methods, and pedagogies have been challenged across the disciplines (e.g., Abel and Abel 1983; Bowles and Klein 1983; Culley and Portuges 1985; DuBois, Kelly, Kennedy, Korsmeyer, and Robinson 1985; Griffin and Hoffman 1986; Harding and Hintikka 1983; Klein 1987; Sherman and Beck 1979; Spender 1981; Stanley and Wise 1983). Feminist thought has deepened and broadened. Whereas in the early years of second-wave feminism[1] there was a collective sense of a "we" to feminist theorizing, today postmodern thought and "fractured identities" have decentered feminism (Ackoff 1988; Flax 1987; Harding 1986). Previously the emphasis was on women gaining equality with men within existing social institutions, but today feminist thought emphasizes a new vision of the social order in which women's experiences and ways of knowing are brought to the fore, not suppressed (Gross 1986). Theories and concepts rooted in men's experience formerly monopolized intellectual inquiry, but today disciplinary debates in some fields reflect the impact of feminist thought, albeit uneven, across the disciplines (Stacey and Thorne 1985).

How has criminology been affected by these developments? With the exception of feminist treatments of rape and intimate violence, the field remains essentially untouched. The time has come for criminologists to step into the world of feminist thought and for feminist scholars to move more boldly into all areas of criminology. This task will not be easy; we write as feminists interested in problems of crime and justice, and find that we lead a double life. As feminists,[2] we grapple with the many strands of feminist thought and activism, educate ourselves and others about the

Justice Quarterly, Vol. 5 No. 4, December 1988 © 1988 Academy of Criminal Justice Sciences.

impact of gender relations on social life, and ponder our role as academics in a social movement. As criminologists, we grapple with the field's many theoretical and policy strands, educate ourselves and others on the conditions and social processes that make crime normal and deviant, and ponder the state's role in creating and reducing crime. All the while we wonder if it is possible to reconcile these double lives.

This essay is a step toward reconciliation. We want to expose our colleagues to feminist works and debates, and to demonstrate their significance for criminology.[3] Because of the magnitude of this task, we decided at the outset to examine only a selected set of issues. We invite others to address gaps and to see in our speculative passages an opportunity for dialogue and exchange. Because we write for those untutored in feminist thought, we start by discussing three myths about feminism. Then we turn to related questions about defining feminism. These sections lay a foundation for our analysis of the relevance of contemporary feminist thought to criminology.

Myths About Feminism

One difficulty in educating students and colleagues about feminism is that myths about the subject abound. We address three of these myths: feminist analyses are not objective, feminist analyses focus narrowly on women, and there is only one feminist perspective.

Myth 1: Lack of Objectivity

A major element of feminist thought centers on how gender constructs—the network of behaviors and identities associated with masculinity and femininity—are socially constructed from relations of dominance and inequality between men and women. Different natures, talents, and interests that define Western notions of manhood and womanhood rest on a number of male-centered oppositions to and negations of women and femininity. Masculinity and men are not only defined as not feminine, but also as superior to femininity and to women.

We will not discuss *why* gender relations took this form,[4] but instead will sketch some of the effects. In Western thought, depictions of men's and women's natures have been made almost exclusively by men (specifically by white, privileged men). As a consequence, these men's experience and intellectual stance have dominated explanations of gender difference and men's superiority. This situation led Poulain de la Barre, a seventeenth-century writer, to observe, "All that has been written about women by men should be suspect, for the men are at once judge and party to the lawsuit" (cited in de Beauvoir 1961:xxi). It is plain that men can be no more objective than women (and nonfeminist views no more objective than feminist) about the character of gender relations, the qualities of gender difference, or the organization of social life. In fact, some thinkers argue that women's marginality affords them keener insights (Collins 1986; Rohrlich-Leavitt, Sykes, and Weatherford 1975; Smith 1979), a perspective reminiscent of sociologists' (or other outsiders') claims to greater understanding because of their marginal status.

One consequence of male-centered (or androcentric) systems of knowledge is inaccurate readings of human history, evolution, and behavior, although these are presented as objective and authoritative depictions of the human condition. The central problem is that men's experiences are taken as the norm and are generalized to the population. For example, theories of the evolution of "mankind" are precisely that: theories of how bipedalism and expanded brain size resulted from men's cooperation, toolmaking, and tool use in the hunting of large game. This approach led feminist anthropologists to ask, "Have only men evolved?" (Hubbard 1982; Slocum 1975). Similarly, feminist historians questioned the basis for historical periodization by asking, "Did women have a Renaissance?" (Kelly-Gadol 1977).

Some scholars propose a way to legitimate women's claims to knowledge with the concept of "women's standpoint," which Jaggar (1983:370) argues is "epistemologically advantageous" and "provides the basis for a view of reality that is more impartial than that of the ruling class." Other forms of knowledge seeking are used or advocated (see Harding 1986), but a major feminist project today is to expose the distortions and assumptions of androcentric science (e.g., Bleier 1984; Fee 1981; Keller 1984). These efforts reveal that an ideology of objectivity can serve to mask men's gender loyalties as well as loyalties to other class or racial groups. Thus when feminist analyses are dismissed because they are said to lack objectivity or to be biased toward women's viewpoints, we are bewildered and vexed. Bemused by other people's apparent inability to hear alternate accounts of social life, we wonder whether feminists can even be heard. Such frustration is compounded by knowing that the dominant paradigms and modes of inquiry are *a priori* accorded greater legitimacy.

Myth 2: The Narrow Focus on Women

When feminists analyze women's situation and the ways in which gender relations structure social life, they do not ignore men and masculinity, although they may displace men as the central (or sole) actors and may give more attention to women. This approach spawns a perception by men that they are being neglected, misunderstood, or cast as the ignominious "other," a reaction akin to that of white people toward critical analyses of race or ethnic relations. Both perceptions express a sense of entitlement about *whose* social reality is worthy of description and explanation, and *who* can be trusted to get it right.

Much feminist attention has been devoted to the ways in which men think, theorize, and collect and marshal evidence. It is impossible to understand women's situation and gender relations without examining masculinity, men's lives, and men's viewpoints. The irony is that feminist scholarship is characterized as being only about women or as hopelessly biased toward women, when in fact the project is to describe and change both men's and women's lives. By contrast, nonfeminist scholarship is more narrow, focusing as it does on the lives and concerns of men without problematizing gender relations or men as a social group. Moreover, *all* social institutions and social phenomena are "women's issues" and thus subject to feminist inquiry. Furthermore, as we will argue, not all feminist analyses are put forth by women, nor is all research conducted on women or on gender difference *ipso facto* feminist.

Myth 3: The Feminist Analysis

To talk of *the* feminist analysis of a given social phenomenon is to talk nonsense. To assume that there is only one feminist analysis reveals a speaker's naiveté about the diverse views that characterize contemporary feminist thinking and strategies for social change. A more accurate way to describe feminist thought is as a *set of perspectives*, which are linked in turn to different assumptions about the causes of gender inequality. These perspectives (or frameworks) include liberal, radical, Marxist, and socialist feminist. Drawing from Andersen (1983), Donovan (1985), Jaggar (1983), and Jaggar and Rothenberg (1984), we sketch the core features of each perspective in the appendix. (The appendix also shows a traditional perspective; although not feminist, it is often found in gender-related research.) There are other ways to categorize feminist thought (e.g., Banks 1981); some are humorous (Oakley 1981:336–37), and differences exist within any one feminist perspective (see, e.g., Eisenstein 1983 on radical feminism; Sargeant 1981 on socialist feminism). Because the dominant voice of American feminism is white, middle-class, first-world, and heterosexual, modified feminisms (such as black, Chicana, Asian-American, Jewish, lesbian, and others) reflect racial, ethnic, cultural, and sexual specificities (Cole 1986; Darty and Potter 1984; hooks 1981, 1984; Joseph and Lewis 1981; Moraga and Anzaldúa 1983; Smith 1983). In short, the ferment and debate among feminist scholars and activists today can no longer be contained within or characterized accurately as one perspective.

In assessing these myths about feminist thought, we offer a partial view of feminism and feminist inquiry by describing what they are not. Feminist investigations are not limited to women, nor are feminist analyses any less objective than nonfeminist. Different views of gender arrangements and the specific ways in which class, race and ethnicity, religion, sexuality, and so forth intersect in women's lives yield multiple analyses and visions for social change. Is there any common ground, then, to feminist thought? What distinguishes a feminist from a nonfeminist analysis?

Defining Feminism

What is Feminism?

In their introduction to *What is Feminism?* Mitchell and Oakley (1986:3) suggest that it is "easier to define feminism in its absence rather than its presence." Delmar (1986) offers a "baseline definition" on which feminists and nonfeminists might agree: a feminist holds that women suffer discrimination because of their sex, that they have needs which are negated and unsatisfied, and that the satisfaction of these needs requires a radical change. "But beyond that," Delmar says, "things immediately become more complicated" (1986:8).

This complication arises because feminism is a set of theories about women's oppression *and* a set of strategies for social change. Cott (1987) identifies the paradoxes of first-wave feminism (the "woman movement" in the nineteenth and early twentieth centuries), which reflect the merging of these theoretical and political impulses. These paradoxes include acknowledging diversity among women but claiming women's unity, requiring gender consciousness but calling for an eradication of gender-based distinctions and divisions, and aiming for individual freedom and autonomy by mobilizing a mass-based movement. The same paradoxical elements are seen in second-wave feminism (the contemporary women's movement beginning in the 1960s). Unfriendly interpretations of these contrary tendencies include, "These women don't know what they want" or "They want it both ways." Yet as Harding (1986:244) suggests, "The problem is that we [feminists] do not know and should not know just what we want to say about a number of conceptual choices with which we are presented—except that the choices themselves create no-win dilemmas for our feminisms." The task of describing *and* changing a spectrum of women's experiences, which have been formed by particular and often competing allegiances to class, race, and other social groups, is not straightforward but a blurred and contingent enterprise.

Distinguishing Feminist from Nonfeminist Analyses

It is not easy to know when a work or action is feminist. Delmar asks, for example, "Are all actions and campaigns prompted or led by women, feminist?" (1986:11). "Can an action be 'feminist' even if those who perform it are not?" (1986:12). She contrasts several views of feminism. It may be diffuse activity, any action motivated out of concern for women's interests, whether or not actors or groups acknowledge them as feminist. This view empties feminism of any meaning because all actions or analyses having women as their object fall into the same category. Delmar opts instead for another approach, which is to "separate feminism and feminists from the multiplicity of those concerned with women's issues." Feminism can be defined as a field—even though diverse—but feminists can "make no claim to an exclusive interest in or copyright over problems affecting women" (1986:13).

Neither a scholar's gender nor the focus of scholarship—whether women, gender difference, or anything else—can be used to distinguish feminist, nonfeminist, or even antifeminist works. Scholars' theoretical and methodological points of view are defined by the way in which they frame questions and interpret results, not by the social phenomenon alone. Thus to Morris's (1987:15) question—"Does feminist criminology include criminologists who are feminist, female criminologists, or criminologists who study women"—we reply that research on women or on gender difference, whether conducted by a male or a female criminologist, does not in itself qualify it as feminist. Conversely, feminist inquiry is not limited to topics on or about women; it focuses on men as well. For criminology, because most offenders and criminal justice officials are men, this point is especially relevant; allied social institutions such as the military have not escaped feminist scrutiny (Enloe 1983, 1987). When feminist, nonfeminist, or not-really-feminist distinctions are drawn, the main source of variation is how inclusively scholars (or activists) define a continuum of feminist thought.

Pateman (1986), for example, compares theories addressing "women's issues" with those that are "distinctly feminist." She terms the former "domesticated feminism" and sees it in liberal and socialist thought when scholars try to fit women or gender relations into existing theories, making "feminism . . . safe for academic theory" (1986:4). Such efforts deny that "sexual domination is at issue, or that feminism raises a problem [patriarchy], which is repressed in other theories" (1986:5). A more distinctive feminist approach assumes that individuals are gendered, and that "individuality is not a unitary abstraction but an embodied and sexually differentiated expression of the unity of humankind" (1986:9).

The implications of a distinctive feminist approach are profound—in Pateman's and others' words, "subversive"—for social, political, criminological, and other theories. It is one thing to say that women have been excluded from general theories of social phenomenon. It is another matter to wonder how theories would appear if they were fashioned from women's experiences and if women had a central place in them. In addition, it is equally important to query the gender-specific character of existing theories fashioned from men's experiences.

Although some scholars (typically, liberal and Marxist feminists who do not accord primacy to gender or to patriarchal relations) assume that previous theory can be corrected by including women, others reject this view, arguing that a reconceptualization of analytic categories is necessary. Working toward a reinvention of theory is a major task for feminists today. Although tutored in "male-stream" theory and methods,[5] they work within and against these structures of knowledge to ask new questions, to put old problems in a fresh light, and to challenge the cherished wisdom of their disciplines. Such rethinking comes in many varieties, but these five elements of feminist thought distinguish it from other types of social and political thought:

- Gender is not a natural fact but a complex social, historical, and cultural product; it is related to, but not simply derived from, biological sex difference and reproductive capacities.
- Gender and gender relations order social life and social institutions in fundamental ways.
- Gender relations and constructs of masculinity and femininity are not symmetrical but are based on an organizing principle of men's superiority and social and political-economic dominance over women.
- Systems of knowledge reflect men's views of the natural and social world; the production of knowledge is gendered.
- Women should be at the center of intellectual inquiry, not peripheral, invisible, or appendages to men.

These elements take different spins, depending on how a scholar conceptualizes gender, the causes of gender inequality, and the means of social change. Generally, however, a feminist analysis draws from feminist theories or research, problematizes gender, and considers the implications of findings for empowering women or for change in gender relations. Finally, we note that scholars may think of themselves as feminists in their personal lives, but they may not draw on feminist theory or regard themselves as feminist scholars. For personal or professional reasons (or both), they may shy away from being marked as a particular kind of scholar.

The Relevance of Feminist Thought to Criminology

What can feminist thought bring to studies of crime and justice? Sophistication in thinking about gender relations is one obvious contribution. Unfortunately, most criminologists draw on unexplicated folk models of gender and gender difference, or do not even consider the impact of gender relations on men's behavior. It is common to hear, for example, that because theories of crime exclude women, we can rectify the problem by adding women. It is even more common to find that theories are developed and tested using male-only samples without any reflection on whether concepts or results may be gender-specific. We suggest first that efforts to overcome these persistent problems must start with a conceptual framework for gender and gender relations. The four feminist perspectives (in addition to the traditional perspective) offer a comparative foothold. Each makes different assumptions about men's and women's relations to each other and to the social order; therefore each may pose different questions, use different methods, and offer distinctive interpretations. These perspectives have been applied in other areas of sociological, economic, psychological, and political philosophical inquiry (Andersen 1983; Jaggar 1983; Kahn and Jean 1981; Sokoloff 1980; Tong 1984); thus why not in criminology, which borrows from these disciplines in varying degrees and combinations? In fact, we would put the case more strongly: we see no other means of comparing and evaluating efforts to include gender in theories of crime, to explain men's or women's crime, or to assess criminal justice policy and practices, among other foci of criminological inquiry, without explicit reference to these perspectives. We will give examples to illustrate our point throughout this essay.

Second, criminologists need not engage in surmise or guesswork about women's experiences. Again, it has become common to take the field to task for its distorted representations of women (this situation also holds true for men, but perhaps to a lesser extent). One obvious remedy is to read feminist journals[6] and books that offer studies of women's and men's lives and provide the structural and social contexts for their behavior. Criminologists must depart from the narrow confines of their discipline and its journals; otherwise we will continue to suffer from commonsense and *ad hoc* interpretations of data, as well as poorly informed research questions.

Third, criminologists should begin to appreciate that their discipline and its questions are a product of white, economically privileged men's experiences. We are not suggesting some simpleminded conspiracy theory; conscious intent would be hard to prove, and ultimately it is beside the point. Rather, we note simply who the scholars and practitioners have been over the last few centuries. Turning to the future, we wonder what will happen as increasing numbers of white women, as well as men and women of color, enter the discipline and try to find their place in it. One cannot expect that the first generation of new scholars will be confident or sure-footed after centuries of exclusion from the academy. One might expect, however, that we will ask different questions or pursue problems that our discipline has ignored. These differences must be heard and nurtured, not suppressed. To be sure, the generational relations of elder and younger white men are also fraught with conflict, but that conflict occurs on a common ground of shared experiences and understandings. It is familiar terrain; the older men see bits of themselves in their younger male colleagues. By contrast, our differences with the mainstream of the discipline are likely to break new ground.

Finally, points of congruence exist between feminist perspectives and other social and political theories, and consequently between feminist perspectives and theoretical trajectories in criminology. Much of what is termed mainstream criminology easily embraces a liberal feminist perspective. The critical and Marxist criminologies have affinities with radical, Marxist, and socialist feminist perspectives. More can be done to exploit and contrast these points of affinity. Not surprisingly, the sharpest feminist critique today is leveled at the varieties of leftist criminology precisely because they hold the greatest promise for incorporating class, race, and gender relations in theories of crime and justice. This feminist critique has been aired mostly, but not exclusively, in British criminology (see Gelsthorpe and Morris 1988; Heidensohn 1985, 1987; Messerschmidt 1986; Morris 1987); it may foster a larger coalition of men and women seeking a transformation, not simply a correction, of criminology.

Can There Be a Feminist Criminology?

Morris (1987:17) asserts that "*a* feminist criminology cannot exist" because neither feminism nor criminology is a "unified set of principles and practices." We agree. Feminists engaged in theory and research in criminology may work within one of the feminist perspectives; thus, like feminist thought generally, feminist criminology cannot be a monolithic enterprise. We also agree with Morris's observation that "the writings of Adler and Simon do not constitute a feminist criminology" (p. 16). Yet we think it important to identify Simon's and Adler's arguments as liberal feminist, to assess them on those terms, and to compare them with analyses adopting other feminist perspectives. Similarly, in the debates between radical and socialist feminists about controlling men's violence toward women, one can evaluate their different assumptions of gender and sexuality. A single feminist analysis across many crime and justice issues is not possible, but that fact does not preclude a criminologist who uses feminist theory or research from calling herself (or himself) a feminist criminologist. It's a convenient rubric, but only as long as criminologists appreciate its multiple meanings.

Feminist theories and research should be part of any criminologist's approach to the problems of crime and justice. They demonstrate that a focus on gender can be far more than a focus on women or sexism in extant theories. They offer an opportunity to study still-unexplored features of men's crime and forms of justice, as well as modes of theory construction and verification. In tracing the impact of feminist thought on studies of crime and justice, we find that the promise of feminist inquiry barely has been realized.

Tracing Developments: The Awakening to the 1980s

The Awakening

In the late 1960s, Bertrand (1969) and Heidensohn (1968), respectively a Canadian and a British female criminologist, drew attention to the omission of women from general theories of crime. Although they were not the first to do so, their work signaled an awakening of criminology from its androcentric slumber. Several years earlier Walter Reckless had observed in the third edition of *The Crime Problem* (1961:78):

> If the criminologist, before propounding or accepting any theory of crime or delinquency, would pause to ask whether that theory applied to women, he would probably discard it because of its inapplicability to women.

Then, as today, the problem identified by Bertrand, Heidensohn, and Reckless has two dimensions. First, it is uncertain whether general theories of crime can be applied to women's (or girls') wrongdoing. Second, the class-, race-, and age-based structure of crime forms the core of criminological theory, but the gender-based structure is ignored. Although related, these dimensions pose different questions for criminology. The first is whether theories generated to describe men's (or boys') offending can apply to women or girls (the *generalizability problem*). The second is why females commit less crime than males (the *gender ratio problem*). Both questions now occupy a central role in research on gender and crime, which we shall address below. The early feminist critiques of criminology, however, centered on a third and more obvious problem: intellectual sexism in theories of female crime and institutional sexism in the juvenile and criminal justice systems.

Early Feminist Critiques

In the now-classic reviews of the literature on female crime, Klein (1973) and Smart (1976) analyzed how such crime had been described and explained. Millman (1975) offered a related analysis for the literature on women's deviance. These reviews and recent summaries in Carlen and Worrall (1987:1–14), Heidensohn (1985:110–62), and Morris (1987:1–18, 41–78) identified the following problems: women's and girls' crime and deviance were explained more often by biological factors than by social or economic forces; representations of their motives or of the circumstances leading to crime were wrong or distorted; and sexual deviance (which could range from broken hymens to "immorality" or prostitution) was merged with criminal deviance. These critiques focused on the sexist assumptions of predominantly, but not exclusively, male criminologists who aimed to describe women's or girls' crime, but who seemingly had little understanding of their social worlds.

At about the same time, several papers appeared that examined the assumptions and practices then operating in the juvenile and criminal justice systems in the response to delinquency and crime. Chesney-Lind (1973) pointed out that girls' wrongdoing was "sexualized" and that noncriminal status offenses such as running away or curfew violations formed a larger portion of girls' than of boys' delinquency subject to juvenile justice control and intervention. Temin (1973) analyzed current gender-based differences in sentencing statutes, which allowed for indeterminate sentences for women but not for men. Others focused on the unequal treatment of girls and women in training schools and prisons (Burkhart 1976; Rodgers 1972; Singer 1973).

In this early phase, scholars challenged the "separate spheres" assumptions then operating explicitly in law, criminological theory and research, and justice practices. Separate spheres is a set of ideas about the place of men and of women in the social order that emerged in the first quarter of the nineteenth century in the United States, as well as in other countries undergoing capitalist industrialization. This ideology placed men in the public sphere (paid workplace, politics, law) and women in the private sphere (household, family life); it characterized gender relations for white, middle-class, married heterosexual couples. Woman's place as mother and wife conferred her status (albeit limited) as the moral guardian of the home and the culture, but man's place as father, husband, and paid worker conferred his status as creator and formal arbiter of morality and culture.

First- and second-wave feminists challenged the separate spheres ideology in different ways, reflecting their historical circumstances. At the risk of oversimplifying, we may say that first-wave feminists embraced women's capacities as mothers and moral guardians of the home to make the public sphere more accountable to women's interests. In the process, however, those feminists became involved in crusades for moral and social purity that resulted in unprecedented state involvement in the lives of young women. In efforts to raise the age of consent and to limit or eliminate prostitution, for example, reform-minded women unwittingly assisted the state in incarcerating large numbers of girls and young women for "immoral behavior" in the years just before and during World War I (Bland 1985; Musheno and Seeley 1986; Rosen 1982; Schlossman and Wallach 1978).

Second-wave feminists, especially during the 1960s and early 1970s, denounced the domestic or private sphere as oppressive to women and sought to achieve equality with men in the public sphere. In this intellectual context, feminists challenged gender-based laws and legal practices formulated from separate spheres thinking. Early feminist critiques of criminology and criminal law were similarly motivated, but as we shall see, such analyses and strategies for change omitted more subtle questions of equality and difference now being raised by feminists.

The problematic and limiting aspects of an essentially liberal feminist response to the separate spheres ideology became clear with the appearance of two books analyzing women's arrest trends in the 1960s and early 1970s. Adler's (1975) *Sisters in Crime* and Simon's (1975) *Women and Crime* proposed ideas about women's criminality that were troubling to feminists because they were largely an outgrowth of the unexamined assumption that the emancipation of women resided solely in achieving legal and social equality with men in the public sphere. Although the books differed in tone and reached somewhat different conclusions, they touched a raw nerve by linking women's crime to the women's movement and to the goal of equality with men in the public sphere.

Women's Emancipation and Crime

The merits and flaws of Simon's, but more especially Adler's, analyses of women and crime have been discussed extensively. We shall not catalog the critiques and empirical tests of their ideas because others have done so (see, e.g., Chapman 1980; Datesman and Scarpitti 1980b; Giordano, Kerbel, and Dudley 1981; Gora 1982; Heidensohn 1985; Miller 1986; Smart 1979; Steffensmeier 1978, 1980). Our interest is in Adler's and Simon's conception of the role of gender in crime causation. In the process we will demonstrate why the issues they raised continue to be discussed by criminologists today.

Both Adler's and Simon's analyses assumed that female criminality had been kept in check by women's limited aspirations and opportunities. They argued that social circumstances, not biology, explained gender differences in crime. For Adler, the lifting of restrictions on women's behavior gave women the opportunity to act like men—that is, to be as violent, greedy, and crime-prone as men. Simon took a more qualified view because she read the statistical evidence more accurately. Having found no changes in women's share of arrests for violent crime, she reasoned that their increasing share of arrests for property crime (especially larceny, fraud, and embezzlement) might be explained by their increasing opportunities in the workplace (or public sphere) to commit crime. Moreover, she wondered whether the ideology of equality for men and for women might make police and court officials more interested in treating men and women the same.

Adler has been faulted extensively for claiming a link between feminist goals of emancipation for women and increases in female crime. In characterizing female crime as the "darker side" (1975:3) of women's liberation, reflecting feminist attitudes of female offenders, Adler assumed that low-income women somehow were seeking equality with their male counterparts, as though crime in some sense was a desirable occupation. Simon has been criticized for assuming that increases in female crime were due to new workplace opportunities for some women, not to increasing economic immizeration for other women. Critics took Adler and Simon to task by pointing out that occupational structures had changed little, that arrested or imprisoned women held traditional (not feminist) views of work and family life, and that careful analyses of arrest data failed to support their claims.

On a broader scale, the challenges to Adler and Simon have been limited to questions of whether the trends they described were actually occurring. Little has been said about the limitations of the liberal feminist perspective on gender that informed their work. This perspective typically ignores class and race differences among women, and defines gender either as the possession of masculine or feminine attitudes or as role differences between men and women. Such a view assumes that when women become less feminine in outlook or enter roles occupied previously by men, they will begin to think and act like men. This line of thinking continues to dominate research on gender differences in crime and delinquency.

By contrast, a radical or socialist feminist views gender as constructed by power relations, not simply by roles (see Lopata and Thorne 1978 for a critique of applying role theory to gender). These feminist perspectives consider the impact of patriarchy (a social structure of men's control over women's labor and sexuality), and they assume that both roles and attitudes are embedded in this larger structure. Although radical and socialist feminists differ in regard to the role played by class and race, both call for placing men's and women's criminality in its patriarchal social context, just as Marxist criminologies seek to place criminal behavior in its class context.

Debate over women's emancipation and crime has not been fruitful, but important questions for criminology are latent in this and related debates. What is the relationship between crime and women's changing social and economic situation? What happens when some women enter positions, circumstances, or social arenas previously occupied only by men? How do gender relations shape the patterns of men's and women's crime? Adler and Simon, their critics, and others have presupposed the answers to these questions in the absence of appropriate empirical inquiry or an understanding that different feminist perspectives on gender will yield different interpretations.

During this period, however, second-wave feminist scholarship was just gaining momentum, and criminologists were only dimly aware of the dimensions of the problem they had encountered. Lacking theoretical guidance, they focused on a compelling empirical deficit: little was known about women's crime or gender differences in crime. For that matter, little was known about girls' or women's experience in any facet of the juvenile or criminal justice systems—whether as offenders, victims, or workers. Therefore filling these empirical gaps was a major task.

Portraits of Crime and Justice

Offenders. The next decade (1975–85) witnessed a proliferation of important but largely atheoretical studies of the character of girls' and women's crime, and of their treatment in the juvenile and criminal justice systems (e.g., Bowker 1978, 1981; Chapman 1980; Crites 1976; Datesman and Scarpitti 1980a; Feinman 1980; Hepperle and Crites 1978; Mann 1984; Mukherjee and Scutt 1981; Price and Sokoloff 1982; Rafter and Stanko 1982; Weisberg 1982). (Another focus of study was female workers in the criminal justice system, an area we do not address in this essay.) Many of these studies were collections of emerging work, although a few were book-length efforts to pull together what was known about women and crime. Of necessity, efforts to describe women's crime or gender differences in crime tended to focus on descriptive detail from statistical sources of information such as self-reports of delinquent behavior, analyses of national arrest data, and information on the numbers of girls and women incarcerated in training schools, jails, and prisons. The authors raised many questions from a position sympathetic to feminism, but few tied their thinking explicitly to feminist theory or to feminist perspectives on gender (some exceptions are Price and Sokoloff 1982:485–90; Rafter and Natalizia 1982).

Why was this the case? One reason was that neither feminist analyses nor theories of crime using a power relations framework offered an immediate analytical grasp on the gender ratio problem. Although offenses such as prostitution or sexual violence were amenable to such inquiry, aggregate arrest patterns were not. To put it simply, if men had more power than women, why were so many more men arrested? Why were incarcerated populations composed almost exclusively of men? Because the dynamics of gender relations are distinctive from those of class, race, or age, scholars were uncertain how these relationships could be linked in explaining crime.

Women's Victimization. During the same decade, even greater attention was given to female victims and survivors of men's sexual and physical violence (for bibliographies and reviews see Breines and Gordon 1983; SchWeber and Feinman 1984:121–29; Weisheit and Mahan 1988:112–35). The women's movement, in combination with important early works (Brownmiller 1975; Griffin 1971; Martin 1976; Pizzey 1974), awakened feminist and public consciousness to the dimensions of rape and intimate violence. Victimization of women and girls has been (and is) more likely anchored in one of several feminist perspectives, whether Marxist (Schwendinger and Schwendinger 1983), socialist feminist (Klein 1982; Schechter 1982), or radical feminist (Dobash and Dobash 1979; MacKinnon 1982, 1983; Stanko 1985); the last is the most prevalent. There are several reasons why feminist approaches are more likely to be taken in analyzing women's victimization than women's offending. First, men's violence against women is linked more easily to patriarchal power; it defines and reflects such power. This link, identified early in second-wave feminism, moved large numbers of grass-roots feminists and some academic feminists to document the then-hidden forms of violence suffered almost exclusively by women.[7] Second, criminology was affected by this larger feminist milieu. Men's violence against women was a new and untheorized terrain in criminology, and even some nonfeminist criminologists had to digest and deal with feminist scholarship. Finally, these developments were taking place as more women (and more feminists) moved into criminology and related academic disciplines. It is likely that they felt a greater sense of urgency about controlling men's violence against women, as well as a greater sense of affinity toward female victims than female offenders.

Reflections

We used broad brush strokes in describing the emergence and consolidation of "the woman question" in criminology, the vitality of feminist thought in explaining some crimes, and its virtual absence in explaining the pattern and structure of other crimes. In proceeding to consider current issues and debates, we offer some historical context.

A set of "new" criminals, victims, and crimes became the object of criminological scrutiny beginning in the mid-1970s: female victims and offenders, men's rape and battery of wives and intimates, other forms of sexual and familial violence, and corporate and occupational crime. Such "new" crimes and offenders have disrupted the field's traditional focus on low-income boys' delinquency and men's street crime, and have upset criminological paradigms. At the same time, two other changes occurred: a "get-tough" stance on crime control and the introduction of methods to reduce sentencing disparity. We turn to a discussion of three significant areas for feminism and criminology that are tied to this changing climate: theory development, controlling men's violence toward women, and gender equality in the criminal justice system.

Approaches to Building Theories of Gender and Crime

Theories of gender and crime can be built in several ways, and we see criminologists taking three tacks. Some are focusing on what we have called the generalizability problem, while others are interested in what we have termed the gender ratio problem. Still others want to bracket both problems, regarding each as premature for an accurate understanding of gender and crime.

The Generalizability Problem

Do theories of men's crime apply to women? Can the logic of such theories be modified to include women? In addressing the generalizability problem, scholars have tested theories derived from all-male samples to see if they apply to girls or women (e.g., Cernkovich and Giordano 1979; Datesman and Scarpitti 1975; Figueira-McDonough and Selo 1980; Giordano 1978; Warren 1982; Zietz 1981). Others have borrowed elements from existing theories (e.g., Moyer 1985 on conflict theory) or have recast the logic of a theory altogether (e.g., Schur 1984 on labeling). According to Smith and Paternoster's (1987) review of the large body of studies taking this approach, the available evidence is limited, mixed, and inconclusive. More studies likely will confirm a consistent, logical answer to the question "Do theories of men's crime apply to women?" The answer is "yes and no": the truth lies in this equivocation.

The Gender Ratio Problem

The gender ratio problem poses the following questions: Why are women less likely than men to be involved in crime? Conversely, why are men more crime-prone than women? What explains gender differences in rates of arrest and in variable types of criminal activity? In contrast to the gender composition of generalizability scholars, almost all gender ratio scholars seem to be men. Their approach is to develop new theoretical formulations by drawing primarily from statistical evidence, secondary sources, elements of existing theory (e.g., social control, conflict, Marxist), and at times from feminist theory. Box (1983), Gove (1985), Hagan, Simpson, and Gillis (1987), Harris (1977), Messerschmidt (1986), Steffensmeier (1983), and Wilson and Herrnstein (1985) have offered ideas on this issue. Heidensohn (1985) is one of few female criminologists to take this route.

Juxtaposing the Generalizability and Gender Ratio Problems

Much of the confusion and debate that surround the building of theories of gender and crime can be resolved when scholars realize that they are on different tracks in addressing the generalizability and gender ratio problems. Members of each camp seem to be unaware of the other's aims or assumptions; but when the two are juxtaposed, their logic and their limitations are revealed. Analogous developments have taken place in building theories of gender and the labor market; thus we sketch some of that literature to clarify problems in developing theories of gender and crime.

A model of occupational status attainment, outlined by Blau and Duncan (1967) and using an all-male sample, was applied subsequently to samples of women. This research suggested that the same variables predicted occupational status for men and for women (see Sokoloff's 1980 review); the implication was that the processes of intergenerational occupational mobility were the same for men and women. Those taking a more structural approach to the labor market soon raised this question, however: how was it that the "same" processes produced such distinctive distributions of men and women in the paid occupational structure (job segregation) and caused such marked differences in men's and women's wages? That query inspired a rethinking of the structural and organizational contexts of men's and women's work (paid and unpaid), which now commands the attention of many sociologists and economists.

The gender and labor market literature today is several steps ahead of that for gender and crime, but similarities at different stages are clear. Generalizability scholars are not concerned with gender differences in rates of arrest or in arrests for particular crimes (or in rates and types of delinquent acts). Instead they want to know whether the same processes (or variables) describe intragender variability in crime and delinquency.

Setting aside the mixed research findings, they (like status attainment theorists) confront a vexing question. Even if (for the sake of argument) the same processes or variables explain intragender variability in crime and delinquency or in its detection, why do such similar processes produce a distinctive gender-based structure to crime or delinquency? Moreover, what does it mean to develop a gender-neutral theory of crime, as some scholars now advocate, when neither the social order nor the structure of crime is gender-neutral?[8]

Smith and Paternoster (1987) propose developing a gender-neutral theory of crime because gender-specific theories of the past (meaning theories of *female* criminality) held sexist and stereotypic assumptions of female behavior. (Note that theories of male crime are assumed to be universal and are not construed as gender-specific.) When Smith and Paternoster then consider the gender ratio problem, they suggest that the volume of criminal deviance may reflect "*differential exposure* to factors that precipitate deviant behavior among both males and females" (1987:156). Their surmise begs the question of *how* gender relations structure "differential exposure" and "factors," and seemingly denies the existence of gender relations.

Like structural analysts of gender and the labor market, gender ratio criminologists take the position that patterns of men's and women's crime are sufficiently different to warrant new theoretical formulations. Focusing on intergender variability in rates of arrest or in arrests for particular crimes, several theorists offer these starting points: the power relations both between and among men and women, the control and commodification of female sexuality, sources of informal social control, and the greater enforcement of conformity in girls' and women's lives. In contrast to generalizability scholars, gender ratio scholars assume that different (or gender-specific) variables predict intergender variability in crime or delinquency.

In the wake of arguments developed by gender ratio scholars, those who pursue the generalizability problem may begin to rethink concepts or variables, or they may abandon their enterprise as too limiting. That change may require some time, however, because the contributions of the gender ratio scholars to date are also limited or provisional. Although they acknowledge that crime (like the occupational order) is gendered, many display only a primitive understanding of what this fact means, and all face problems of slim evidence (save statistical distributions) from which to develop sound propositions about female crime or gender differences in crime.

Bracketing the Two Problems

Many feminist criminologists tend for the present to bracket the generalizability and the gender ratio problems. They are skeptical of previous representations of girls' or women's lives and want a better understanding of their social worlds. Moreover, they are unimpressed with theoretical arguments derived from questionable evidence and having little sensitivity to women's (or men's) realities. Like criminologists of the past (from the 1930s to the 1960s), they seek to understand crime at close range, whether through biographical case studies, autobiographical accounts, participant observation, or interviews (e.g., Alder 1986; Bell 1987; Campbell 1984; Carlen 1983, 1985; Carlen and Worrall 1987; Chesney-Lind and Rodriguez 1983; Délacoste and Alexander 1987; Miller 1986; Rosenbaum 1981). For this group of scholars, the quality and the depth of evidence are insufficient to address the generalizability or gender ratio problems. Perhaps more important, the ways in which questions are framed and results are interpreted by many (though not all) of those pursuing the generalizability or gender ratio problems remain tied to masculinist perspectives, ignoring the insights from feminist scholarship.

Observations

Because the building of theories of gender and crime is recent, and because a focus on women or on gender difference is viewed as a marginal problem for the field, we think it imprudent to judge some efforts more harshly than others. We may find, for example, that different explanations for intra- and intergender variability are necessary, or that a more careful examination of patterns of girls' or women's crime may improve our understanding of boys' or men's criminal deviance, among other possibilities. At this stage of theory building, all approaches must be explored fully. In advocating this position we are aware that some varieties of theory building and some methodological approaches are thought to be more elegant (or, as our male colleagues like to say, more powerful). Specifically, global or grand theoretical arguments and high-tech statistical analyses are valued more highly by the profession. Thus we examine the approaches taken by criminologists in this intellectual context. Our concern is that scholars begin to see that the dimensions of a major criminological problem—the place of men and of women in theories of crime—cannot be separated from a problem for the sociology of knowledge—the place of men and of women in constructing theory and conducting research. Harris (1977:15) alluded to this problem when he said:

> Dominant typifications about what kinds of actors "do" criminal behavior—typifications which have served dominant male interests and have been held by both sexes—have played a crucial dual role in . . . keeping sociologists from seeing the sex variable in criminal deviance and . . . keeping men in crime and women out of it.

If the words "criminal behavior," "criminal deviance," and "crime" are replaced with "criminology" in this statement, we can extend Harris's insight with the following observations.

Preferable modes of theory building are gender-linked. Male scholars, for example, have moved rather boldly into theoretical work on the gender ratio problem in both juvenile (e.g., Hagan et al. 1987) and adult arenas (e.g., Messerschmidt 1986). Meanwhile female scholars have displayed more tentativeness and a discomfort with making global claims. In a related vein, it is clear that preferred modes of data collection are also gender-linked. Although both male and female criminologists are required to display their statistical talents, the women's empirical approaches in understanding crime today are more likely than the men's to involve observations and interviews. They are more interested in providing texture, social context, and case histories; in short, in presenting accurate portraits of how adolescent and adult women become involved in crime. This gender difference is not related to "math anxiety" but rather to a felt need to comprehend women's crime on its own terms, just as criminologists of the past did for men's crime.

As increasing numbers of women (and feminists) enter criminology, they face dilemmas if they wish to understand men's, women's, or gender differences in crime or delinquency. A safe course of action—intellectually and professionally—is to focus on the generalizability problem and to use a domesticated feminism to modify previous theory. Something may be learned by taking this tack (i.e., intragender variability), but there remains an issue, not yet pursued vigorously: whether theoretical concepts are inscribed so deeply by masculinist experiences that this approach will prove too restrictive, or at least misleading.

Our final observation is more speculative. It is inspired by Heidensohn's (1985) remarks on studies of adolescent boys' gangs, both the classics and more recent efforts. She suggests that the men conducting these studies were "college boys . . . fascinated with the corner boys" (1985:141). These researchers "vicariously identified" with the boys, romanticizing their delinquency in heroic terms. We think that this sense of affinity has eluded female criminologists thus far in their analyses of girls' or women's crime. An example will illustrate this point.

Miller (1986:189) reports at the close of her book on street hustlers that "the details of these women's lives would run together in my mind and make me angry, generally upset, and depressed." Angered at the lives these women had led as children and at the daily brutality in their current lives, she saw little hope for the women's or their children's futures. As empathetic as Miller was in describing women's illicit work, her story contains few heroines; the initial excitement of criminal activity turns into self-destruction and pain. How strongly her impressions differ from men's ethnographies of juvenile males, who are described as "cool cats" or as "rogue males [engaging in] untrammelled masculinity" (Heidensohn 1985:125–44). Heidensohn terms this genre the "delinquent machismo tradition in criminology" (1985:141), in which the boys' deviance, and to some degree their violence, are viewed as normal and admirable. By contrast, it is far more difficult for female criminologists to find much to celebrate in girls' or women's crime.

As suggested earlier, all three approaches to reformulating theories of gender and crime have merit. Nevertheless we think that the most pressing need today is to bracket the generalizability and the gender ratio problems, to get our hands dirty, and to plunge more deeply into the social worlds of girls and women. The same holds true for boys and men, whose patterns of crime have changed since the 1950s and 1960s, when ethnographies of delinquency flourished in criminology. Recent changes in youth gangs highlight the need for this work (Hagedorn 1988; Huff 1988; Moore 1978). Our concern is that explicitly feminist approaches to women's crime or to the gender patterns of crime will not be noticed, will be trivialized merely as case studies, or will be written off as not theoretical enough. That sort of dismissal would be unfortunate but perhaps not surprising, in view of the professional norms governing the discipline and their masculinist bias.

Controlling Men's Violence toward Women

The victimization (and survivorship) of women is a large and growing part of criminology and is of central interest to feminists in and outside criminology. The relatively high feminist visibility in this area may lead criminologists to regard it as the only relevant site for feminist inquiry in criminology. Not so; the more one reads the literature on victimization—the physical and sexual abuse of children, women, and men—the more difficult it becomes to separate victimization from offending, especially in the case of women (Browne 1987; Chesney-Lind forthcoming; Chesney-Lind and Rodriguez 1983; McCormack, Janus, and Burgess 1986; Silbert and Pines 1981).

In research on physical abuse and sexual violence by men against women, these major themes and findings are seen:

- Rape and violence—especially between intimates—are far more prevalent than imagined previously.
- Police, court officials, juries, and members of the general public do not take victims of rape or violence seriously, especially when victim-offender relations involve intimates or acquaintances.
- Myths about rape and intimate violence are prevalent. They appear in the work of criminologists, in criminal justice practices, and in the minds of members of the general public.
- Whereas female victims feel stigma and shame, male offenders often do not view their behavior as wrong.
- Strategies for change include empowering women via speakouts, marches, shelters and centers, and legal advocacy; and changing men's behavior via counseling, presumptive arrest for domestic violence, and more active prosecution and tougher sanctions for rape.

Although feminists of all types agree that men's rape and battery of women require urgent attention, scholars and activists have different views on the causes and the malleability of men's sexual and physical aggression. Pornography (and its links to men's sexual violence) and prostitution (and its links to pornography) are prominent in the dissensus. We turn to these debates and their implications for criminal justice policy.

Causes of Men's Violence toward Women

Radical feminists tend to construct men's nature as rapacious, violent, and oriented toward the control of women (see, e.g., Brownmiller 1975; Dworkin 1987; MacKinnon 1982, 1983, 1987; Rich 1980). Both rape and intimate violence are the result and the linchpin of patriarchal systems, in which women's bodies and minds are subject to men's dominion. Marxist and socialist feminists (e.g., hooks 1984; Klein 1982; Messerschmidt 1986; Schwendinger and Schwendinger 1983) differ from radical feminists on one key point: they believe that men's nature cannot be described in universalistic (or biologically based) terms but is a product of history and culture, and is related to other systems of domination such as classism, racism, and imperialism. In contrast, liberal feminists offer no theory of causes, but like Marxist and socialist feminists they envision the possibility that men's socially structured violent nature can change. What role, then, should the state play in controlling men's violence and protecting women from such violence? Feminist responses are contradictory and the dilemmas are profound.

Questioning the Role of the State

Pornography. Differences among feminists over the causes of men's violence and the state's role in controlling it are nowhere so clear as in the pornography issue. Part of the debate concerns the effect of pornography on increasing or causing men's sexual violence toward women. Research ethics preclude an answer, but clinical evidence to date shows that pornography with violent content increases aggression, whereas pornography without violent content diminishes aggression (see Baron and Straus 1987:468). Such evidence hardly settles the matter either for antipornography or for anticensorship feminists. At issue are different views of men's sexuality and the causes of men's violence, with radical feminists initiating the antipornography movement. Also at issue is whether state officials can be trusted to render the judgments that antipornography activists seek via the proposed civil remedy (Waring 1986). Finally, anticensorship feminists see greater harm for women and sexual minorities in efforts to suppress the many forms of commercialized pornography.

Prostitution. Debates among and between feminists and sex-trade workers (Bell 1987; Délacoste and Alexander 1987) reveal differences in how women view sexuality and sexual power, as well as problems in relying on a male-dominated state to protect women. These differences are often submerged in a coalition of civil liberties groups, women's groups, and sex-trade workers' organizations who reject state regulation *or* criminalization of prostitution. In advocating the decriminalization of prostitution and a range of issues associated with prostitutes' right to work, the concerned groups achieve a short-term solution: women can make a living and are not singled out as criminals in a commercial activity that men control, use, and profit from. Nevertheless, the institution of prostitution remains intact, and with it this feminist dilemma: will support for some women's right to work perpetuate an institution that ultimately objectifies women and exploits them sexually, may foster violence against women, and may harm female prostitutes? Today, however, as in the past, the state's stance on vigorous enforcement of prostitution and other related ordinances depends on how prostitution harms men via sexually transmitted diseases, rather than on the institution's impact on women (Alexander 1987; Bland 1985; Daly 1988; Walkowitz 1980).

In juxtaposing prostitution and pornography, one sees the contradictions and dilemmas for feminists who campaign for redress against men's violence toward women (often by seeking an expanded role for the state in protecting women) while simultaneously advocating women's economic and sexual freedom. Similar dilemmas arise in controlling intimate violence.

Intimate Violence and Rape. State criminal laws for the arrest and prosecution of spouse (or intimate) abuse and rape have changed significantly in a short period of time (see reviews by Bienen 1980; Lerman 1980). Civil remedies such as the temporary restraining order to protect battered women are more readily available than in the past. These legal changes are a symbolic victory for many feminists, who see in them the state's accommodation to their demands for protection against men's violence. Yet the effect of new laws and programs on changing police and court practices seems far less impressive. Officials' resistance and organizational inertia are common themes; program success can be short-lived (Berk, Loseke, Berk, and Rauma 1980; Berk, Rauma, Loseke, and Berk 1982; Crites 1987; Grau, Fagan, and Wexler 1984; Quarm and Schwartz 1984; Spencer 1987). Some scholars think legal reforms may serve a deterrent and educative function over the long term, and thus that it may be unreasonable to expect immediate change in men's violence or in the state's response (Osborne 1984).

A thread of hope hangs on the promise of presumptive arrest as a method of reducing intimate (or spouse) violence. Sherman and Berk's (1984) study in Minneapolis found that arrest may deter men from future assaults on their mates, more so than the police actions of ordering the suspect to leave the premises or giving the suspect advice. This study's findings were diffused quickly and were embraced by many feminists as evidence that intimate abuse would be reduced by a tougher state stance. A program of field experiments in six other American cities is currently under way; it may tell us more about the wisdom and the special deterrent effect of presumptive arrest for intimate violence.[9]

We wear our criminologist hats in questioning feminist (or nonfeminist) optimism in a presumptive arrest policy. Certainly, a get-tough, "lock-'em-up" response offers women short-term protection and retributive justice, but it is part of a more general incarceral "solution" to crime that has arisen in the last decade. Apart from short-term incapacitation, however, it is difficult to see how this or any other reactive policy can be effective in reducing violent crime. Other methods, aimed at the structural sources of men's violence toward women, must be pursued more strenuously. These include empowering women to leave destructive relationships, to be freed from continued predation by their mates, and to impugn the normative supports for men's sexual and physical violence.

Many people might argue that in the absence of presumptive arrest, men's violence toward women is condoned; thus some state intervention is better than none. At the margins, a more active state role in controlling intimate violence may alleviate women's suffering and reduce spousal (or intimate) homicide, but there are disadvantages to state intervention. For example, will presumptive arrest of male suspects also lead to the arrest of women because the police are uncertain which is the batterer and which is the victim? Will a battered woman's ambivalence about arresting a mate be ignored? Will women be jailed for failing to testify against an abusive mate? We await studies of the implementation and effect of these policies over the next decade; perhaps our skepticism will prove unfounded. Like a handful of others (e.g., Carlen and Worrall 1987:13), however, we suspect that such policies are short-sighted. Harris (1987:34) poses this issue as a dilemma of safety and protection for women, but it can be applied more broadly: "How can we respond effectively to people who inflict injury and hardship on others without employing the same script and the same means that they do?" That dilemma should be explored fully by the entire criminological community in contemplating the role of the state and its citizens in reducing crime.

Gender Equality in the Criminal Justice System

In the early days of second-wave feminism, calls for legal equality with men were apparent everywhere, and the early feminist critics of criminal law and justice practices reflected this ethos. Today feminist legal scholars are more skeptical of a legal equality model because the very structure of law continues to assume that men's lives are the norm, such that women's legal claims are construed as "special treatment." Alternatives to thinking about equality and difference have been proposed in view of women's social and economic subordinate status and gender differences in paid employment, sexuality, and parenthood; see, e.g., *International Journal of the Sociology of Law* 1986; MacKinnon 1987; Rhode 1987; Vogel forthcoming; *Wisconsin Women's Law Journal* 1987. Feminist dissensus over what should be done partly reflects different perspectives on gender, but increasingly one finds that strategies for change reflect lessons learned from engaging in the legal process. As feminists have moved to change the law, so too has the law changed feminism.[10]

Questioning Equality Doctrine and the Equal Treatment Model

Feminist analyses of criminal justice practices reflect a similar shift by moving away from a liberal feminist conceptualization of gender discrimination as a problem of equal treatment. This recent change is more pronounced in British than in American criminology (related, no doubt, to the preponderance of statistical approaches in the United States). It is seen in studies and literature reviews by Allen (1987), Chesney-Lind (1986, 1987), Daly (1987a, 1987b, forthcoming), Eaton (1983, 1985, 1986, 1987), Heidensohn (1986, 1987), Smart (1985), and Worrall (1987). Unlike previous statistical studies of gender-based disparities in court outcomes (for reviews see Nagel and Hagan 1983; Parisi 1982), more recent qualitative studies of legal processes analyze the interplay of gender, sexual and familial ideology, and social control in courtroom discourse and decisionmaking at both the juvenile and the adult levels. This work addresses how gender relations structure decisions in the legal process, rather than whether men and women are treated "the same" in a statistical sense. Eaton (1986:15) sums up the limitations of analyzing sentencing as an equal treatment problem in this way: "The [discrimination] debate is conducted within the terms of legal rhetoric—'justice' and 'equality' mean 'equal treatment,' existing inequalities are to be ignored or discounted." Thus, just as feminist legal scholars are critiquing equality doctrine, feminist criminologists now are questioning how research on discrimination in the courts is conducted.

While feminist scholars are identifying the limitations of an equal treatment model in law or in research on legal practices, that model, and the statistical evidence on which it is based, are the centerpiece of sentencing reforms in the United States. Although these reforms are taking shape in different ways (Blumstein, Cohen, Martin, and Tonry 1983; Shane-DuBow, Brown, and Olsen 1985; Tonry 1987), they aim to reduce sentencing disparity by punishing "like crimes" in the same way. A major problem is that sentencing reforms are designed to reduce race- and class-based disparities in sentencing men. Their application to female offenders may yield equality with a vengeance: a higher rate of incarceration and for longer periods of time than in the past.[11] Like reforms in divorce (Weitzman 1985) and in child custody (Fineman 1988), devised with liberal feminist definitions of equality, sentencing reform also may prove unjust and may work ultimately against women.

The limitations of current equality doctrine are also apparent for changing the prison (or jail) conditions of incarcerated women. Litigation based on equal protection arguments can improve conditions for women to some degree (e.g., training, educational, or work release programs), but such legal arguments are poorly suited to the specific health needs of women and to their relationships with children (Leonard 1983; Resnik and Shaw 1980). Indirectly they may also make it easier to build new facilities for female offenders than to consider alternatives to incarceration. Historical studies of the emergence of women's prisons in the United States suggest that separate spheres notions, which were applied to penal philosophy, may have offered somewhat better conditions of confinement for women (notably white, not black women; see Rafter 1985) than an equality-with-men model (Freedman 1981; SchWeber 1982). Therefore equality defined as equal treatment of men and women, especially when men's experiences and behavior are taken as the norm, forestalls more fundamental change and in some instances may worsen women's circumstances.

Reflections

We are in a time of transition in which gender equality (or equality for other social groups), founded on legal principles of equal access to and due process in social institutions, offers a limited prospect for changing the panoply of inequalities in daily life. In the case of gender relations we cannot retreat to separate spheres, nor can we embrace equality doctrine uncritically. Criminologists, especially those involved in the formation of policy, should be aware that equal treatment is only one of several ways of redressing discrimination and of moving toward a more humane justice system.

Conclusion

In this essay we attempted to make feminist thought accessible to criminologists and to show its significance for criminology. We also pointed out that the problems confronting criminology and the manner in which they are addressed cannot be separated from the social standpoints of those producing knowledge. The field would do well to nourish rather than belittle alternative visions. Even though a male-dominated academy tends to reward competition and even demolition of the work of others, it is our view that intellectual life is lonely enough; we need not estrange ourselves further.

We are encouraged by the burst of research attention that has been given to women and to gender differences in crime, to the response to delinquency and crime in the juvenile and criminal justice systems, and to women's victimization. Yet with the possible exception of women's victimization, criminology has not felt the full impact of feminism except in its most rudimentary liberal feminist form. In this vein we underscore a point made several times in the essay: feminist inquiry is relevant and should be applied to *all* facets of crime, deviance, and social control. A focus on gender and gender difference is not simply a focus on women or on what some scholars term "women's issues" in a narrow sense. It is and should be a far more encompassing enterprise, raising questions about how gender organizes the discipline of criminology, the social institutions that fall within its scope, and the behavior of men and women.

We are surprised by those who continue to say that a focus on gender is unimportant for theories of crime because there are "so few women criminals." We have also been told that discussions of women's crime are "entertaining," meaning that they are a trivial footnote to more general and important problems. Still the fact remains: of whatever age, race, or class and of whatever nation, men are more likely to be involved in crime, and in its most serious forms. Without resorting to essentialist arguments about women's nature, we see in this pattern some cause for hope. A large price is paid for structures of male domination and for the very qualities that drive men to be successful, to control others, and to wield uncompromising power. Most theories of crime suggest the "normalcy" of crime in the light of social processes and structures, but have barely examined the significance of patriarchal structures for relations among men and for the forms and expressions of masculinity. Gender differences in crime suggest that crime may not be so normal after all. Such differences challenge us to see that in the lives of women, men have a great deal more to learn.

Appendix
Five Perspectives on Gender: A Schematic

These perspectives are sketched only in very brief terms. In view of historical and contemporary debates in feminism, they are crude and oversimplified, but they offer a starting point for different ways of conceptualizing gender in social and political theory. Women of different racial and ethnic groups, sexualities, or religions can be liberal, radical, Marxist, or socialist feminist, although they will modify the terms of a feminist perspective accordingly. See Jaggar (1983) and Jaggar and Rothenberg (1984) for the political philosophies and conceptions of human nature, which ground these perspectives, and Carrigan, Connell, and Lee (1985) for discussion of these perspectives in the literature about men's lives and masculinity.

This schematic combines two ways of conceptualizing gender and gender relations in the social sciences. "Causes of gender inequality" refers to the structural basis for men's social dominance and women's oppression. "Process of gender formation" refers to how individuals become gendered, namely the social-psychological processes by which an individual becomes a girl/woman or boy/man. Structural approaches focus on inequality and often do not explicate the processes of gender formation, which are either assumed or implicit. Those who attend to how gender is learned, imposed, or internalized often ignore the structural and historical contexts of inequality. These different foci recapitulate the "level problem" in sociology and criminology: how to link macro and micro social processes. Moreover, some domains (like sexuality) are likely not "knowable" through standard methodological approaches.

Traditional (or Conservative)

Causes of gender inequality: Biological sex differences, including hormonal differences (greater testosterone production in males) or reproductive capacities (female child bearing and lactation). "Social inequality frequently denied."

Process of gender formation: Social behavior derived from or an amplification of biological sex difference: greater strength and innate aggression among males, and innate nurturing and care-giving among females.

Strategies for social change: None offered because men's and women's behaviors reflect bio-evolutionary adaptations of sex differences from an earlier time in human history.

Key concepts: Biological imperatives; natural differences between men and women.

Liberal Feminist

Causes of gender inequality: Not stated explicitly, but assumed to stem from societal inhibitions on women's full exposure to and participation in intellectual inquiry (reading and writing), physical education (competitive sports and physical fitness), and other activities in the public sphere.

Process of gender formation: Socialization into gender roles; psychological theories such as social learning, cognitive development, or schema used.

Strategies for social change: Removal of all obstacles to women's access to education, paid employment, political activity, and other public social institutions; enabling women to participate equally with men in the public sphere; emphasis on legal change.

Key concepts: Socialization, sex (or gender) roles, equal opportunity, equal treatment of men and women, equal rights.

Marxist Feminist

Causes of gender inequality: Derived from hierarchical relations of control with the rise of private property and its inheritance by men. Class relations are primary; gender relations, secondary.

Process of gender formation: Not stated explicitly in early works, but implicitly a master-slave relationship applied to husband and wife. Some twentieth-century arguments draw from psychoanalytic theories.

Strategies for social change: In the transformation from a capitalist to a democratic socialist society, bringing women fully into economic production, socializing housework and child care, abolition of marriage and sexual relations founded on notions of private property, eradication of working-class economic subordination.

Key concepts: Capitalist oppression and working-class resistance, women as a "sex class" or a reserve army of labor for capital, husbands' exploitation of wives' labor.

Radical Feminist

Causes of gender inequality: Needs or desires of men to control women's sexuality and reproductive potential. Patriarchy—a set of social relations in which individual men and men as a group control—predating the rise of private property; "ownership" of women the precursor to ownership of territory. Some arguments assume a biological basis for men's needs or desires to control women.

Process of gender formation: Power relations between men and women structure socialization processes in which boys and men view themselves as superior to and as having a right to control girls and women. Gender power relations amplified and reinforced by heterosexual sexuality (male-defined). Psychological and psychoanalytic theories used.

Strategies for social change: Overthrowing patriarchal relations, devising methods of biological reproduction to permit women's sexual autonomy, creating women-centered social institutions (and women-only organizations). In strategies for change, dealing explicitly with the oppressive nature of sexual and familial relations for women and with their link to relations in the public sphere. Eradication of women's social subordination without obliterating gender difference. A new offshoot of radical feminism (or perhaps an amalgam of liberal and radical feminism)—cultural feminism—celebrates gender differences, especially women's special capacities or talents, but does not situate gender differences in the framework of power relations.

Key concepts: Patriarchy, women's oppression, men's control of women's bodies and minds, heterosexism.

Socialist Feminist

Causes of gender inequality: Flexible combination of radical and Marxist feminist categories, i.e., universal male domination and historically specific political-economic relations, respectively. Focus on gender, class, and racial relations of domination, in which sexuality (including reproduction) and labor (paid and unpaid) are linked. Differs from Marxist feminism in that both class and gender relations are viewed as primary.

Process of gender formation: Similar to radical feminism, but with greater emphasis on making psychological or psychoanalytical arguments historically and culturally specific and on analyzing women's agency and resistance.

Strategies for social change: Amalgam of Marxist and radical feminist strategies; simultaneous focus on transforming patriarchal and capitalist class relations (includes similar relations in self-defined socialist or communist societies).

Key concepts: Capitalist patriarchy, women's subordination and resistance to men; men's exploitation and control of women's labor and sexuality.

Notes

1 First-wave feminism (termed "the woman movement") arose in the United States and in some European countries in conjunction with the movement to abolish slavery. Its beginning in the United States is typically marked by the Seneca Falls, New York, convention (1848), and its ending by the passage of the 19th Amendment to the United States Constitution (granting women's suffrage), coupled with the falling-out among women activists over the Equal Rights Amendment proposed in the early 1920s. See DuBois (1981) for the nineteenth-century context, Cott (1987) for the early twentieth-century context when the term "feminist" was first used, Giddings (1984) for black women's social movement activity, Kelly-Gadol (1982) for "pro-woman" writers in the four centuries before the nineteenth century, and Kimmell (1987) for men's responses to feminism. Second-wave American feminism emerged in the mid-1960s in conjunction with the civil rights movement, the new left, and a critical mass of professional women (see Evans 1979; hooks 1981, 1984). It has not ended (but see Stacey 1987 for an analysis of "postfeminist" consciousness). Note that the conventional dating of the first- and second-wave is rightly challenged by several scholars who find greater continuity in feminist consciousness and action (Cott 1987; Delmar 1986; Kelly-Gadol 1982).

2 As we make clear later, the kind of feminist perspective we take is socialist feminist, which colors our commentary throughout this essay.

3 We focus primarily on criminology in the United States, although we include the work of feminist criminologists in other countries, especially Great Britain. See Gelsthorpe and Morris (1988) for an analysis of feminism and criminology in Britain.

4 There are different explanations for the emergence of patriarchy, as well as disputes over the definition of the term and over the degree of women's agency in and resistance to gender oppression; almost all are Eurocentric. We think it unlikely that any one set of "causes" can be identified through many cultures and nation states, and across millennia. See Lerner (1986) for a recent bold effort and a discussion of central concepts in feminist thought.

5 We are uncertain who introduced the concept "male-stream" because citations vary. *The Feminist Dictionary* (Kramarae and Treichler 1985:244) says "coined by Mary Daly," but does not say where.

6 Some American feminist journals are *Signs: Journal of Women in Culture and Society, Feminist Studies, Gender and Society,* and *Women and Politics;* others, such as the *International*

Journal of Women's Studies and *Women's Studies International Forum*, take a more international focus; a journal for "pro-feminist" men is *Changing Men*. A new journal with an international and feminist focus on crime and justice, *Women and Criminal Justice*, will appear in 1989.

[7] Men's violence against women was also an issue for first-wave feminists. See DuBois and Gordon (1984), Gordon (1988), Pleck (1979, 1987), and Walkowitz (1980).

[8] The same question could be raised for other theories of crime, which take this position although they do not purport to be "class-neutral" or "race-neutral." They include varieties of social learning, social control, and rational choice theories. The generalizability problem is not confined to theories of gender and crime; it is also seen in efforts to apply theories of male juvenile offending to white-collar crime (e.g., Hirschi and Gottfredson 1987).

[9] For a conceptualization of the project and a sketch of start-up designs, see National Institute of Justice (1985 and 1988 respectively). In addition to Minneapolis, field experiments are being conducted in Omaha, Colorado Springs, Dade County (Florida), Atlanta, Charlotte, and Milwaukee. Cohn and Sherman (1987:1) report the following policy changes from surveys taken in 1984, 1985, and 1986 of all police departments in American cities with a population of greater than 100,000. Of the 146 departments surveyed each year, the proportion saying that their preferred policy was arrest for minor domestic assault cases increased from 10 percent in 1984 to 31 percent in 1985 and to 46 percent in 1986.

[10] This observation paraphrases a remark made by Martha Fineman at the Feminism and Legal Theory Conference, University of Wisconsin Law School, July 1988. Feminist analyses of law and strategies for change are prodigious; see Graycar (1987) for a summary of some themes. Majury (1987), Rights of Women, Family Law Subgroup (1985), and Schneider (1986) illustrate dilemmas in legal strategy.

[11] For example, California's determinate sentencing law may have had an impact on increasing the length of prison sentences for women (Blumstein et al. 1983, volume 1:114, 213–14). To our knowledge, evidence on the impact of sentencing reform in changing the rates of incarceration for women is not yet available. We note, however, that the female share of the jail and prison population has increased in the last decade. Of those in jail, women were 6 percent in 1978 and 8 percent in 1986 (Bureau of Justice Statistics 1987:5); of those in state and federal prisons, women were 4 percent in 1978 (Flanagan and McCleod 1983:545) and 5 percent in 1987 (Bureau of Justice Statistics 1988:3).

References

Abel, Elizabeth and Emily K. Abel, eds. (1983) *The Signs Reader: Women, Gender, and Scholarship.* Chicago: University of Chicago Press.

Ackoff, Linda (1988) "Cultural Feminism versus Post-Structuralism." *Signs: Journal of Women in Culture and Society* 13(3):406–36.

Adler, Freda (1975) *Sisters in Crime: The Rise of the New Female Criminal.* New York: McGraw-Hill.

Alder, Christine (1986) "'Unemployed Women Have Got It Heaps Worse': Exploring the Implications of Female Youth Unemployment." *Australian and New Zealand Journal of Criminology* 19:210–25.

Alexander, Priscilla (1987) "Prostitutes Are Being Scapegoated for Heterosexual AIDS." In Frederique Delacoste and Priscilla Alexander (eds.), *Sex Work: Writings by Women in the Sex Industry.* San Francisco: Cleis, pp. 248–63.

Allen, Hilary (1987) "Rendering Them Harmless: The Professional Portrayal of Women Charged with Serious Violent Crimes." In Pat Carlen and Anne Worrall (eds.), *Gender, Crime and Justice.* Philadelphia: Open University Press, pp. 81–94.

Andersen, Margaret L. (1983) *Thinking About Women: Sociological and Feminist Perspectives.* New York: Macmillan.

Banks, Olive (1981) *Faces of Feminism.* Oxford, UK: Martin Robertson.

Baron, Larry and Murray A. Straus (1987) "Four Theories of Rape: A Macrosociological Analysis." *Social Forces* 34(5):467–88.

Beauvoir, Simone de (1949) *The Second Sex.* Translated and edited by H. M. Parshley, 1952 (Knopf). Page reference to 1961 Bantam edition. New York: Bantam.

Bell, Laurie, ed. (1987) *Good Girls/Bad Girls: Feminists and Sex Trade Workers Face to Face.* Seattle: Seal.

Berk, Richard A., Donileen R. Loseke, Sarah Fenstermaker Berk, and David Rauma (1980) "Bringing the Cops Back In: A Study of Efforts to Make the Criminal Justice System More Responsive to Incidents of Family Violence." *Social Science Research* 9:193–215.

Berk, Richard A., David Rauma, Donileen R. Loseke, and Sarah Fenstermaker Berk (1982) "Throwing the Cops Back Out: The Decline of a Local Program to Make the Criminal Justice System More Responsive to Incidents of Family Violence." *Social Science Research* 11:145–79.

Bertrand, Marie Andree (1969) "Self-Image and Delinquency: A Contribution to the Study of Female Criminality and Women's Image." *Acta Criminologia: Etudes sur la Conduite Antisociale* 2 (January):71–144.

Bienen, Leigh (1980) "Rape III—Rape Reform Legislation." *Women's Rights Law Reporter* 6(3):170–213.

Bland, Lucy (1985) "In the Name of Protection: The Policing of Women in the First World War." In Julia Brophy and Carol Smart (eds.), *Women in Law: Explorations in Law, Family, and Sexuality.* Boston: Routledge and Kegan Paul, pp. 23–49.

Blau, Peter and Otis Dudley Duncan (1967) *The American Occupational Structure.* New York: Wiley.

Bleier, Ruth (1984) *Science and Gender: A Critique of Biology and Its Theories on Women.* New York: Pergamon.

Blumstein, Alfred, Jacqueline Cohen, Susan E. Martin, and Michael H. Tonry, eds. (1983) *Research on Sentencing: The Search for Reform.* Vols 1 and 2. Washington, DC: National Academy Press.

Bowker, Lee H., ed. (1978) *Women, Crime, and the Criminal Justice System.* Lexington, MA: Lexington Books.

———, ed. (1981) *Women and Crime in America.* New York: Macmillan.

Bowles, Gloria and Renate D. Klein, eds. (1983) *Theories of Women's Studies.* Boston: Routledge and Kegan Paul.

Box, Steven (1983) *Power, Crime, and Mystification.* New York: Tavistock.

Breines, Wini and Linda Gordon (1983) "The New Scholarship on Family Violence." *Signs: Journal of Women in Culture and Society* 8(3):490–531.

Browne, Angela (1987) *When Battered Women Kill.* New York: Free Press.

Brownmiller, Susan (1975) *Against Our Will: Men, Women, and Rape.* New York: Simon and Schuster.

Bureau of Justice Statistics, U.S. Department of Justice (1987) "Jail Inmates 1986," NCJ-107123. Washington, DC: U.S. Government Printing Office.

——— (1988) "Prisoners in 1987," NCJ-110331. Washington, DC: U.S. Government Printing Office.

Burkhart, Kathryn W. (1976) *Women in Prison.* New York: Popular Library.

Campbell, Anne (1984) *The Girls in the Gang: A Report from New York City.* New York: Blackwell.

Carlen, Pat (1983) *Women's Imprisonment. A Study in Social Control.* Boston: Routledge and Kegan Paul.

———, ed. (1985) *Criminal Women: Autobiographical Accounts.* Cambridge, UK: Polity.

Carlen, Pat and Anne Worrall, eds. (1987) *Gender, Crime and Justice.* Philadelphia: Open University Press.

Carrigan, Tim, Bob Connell, and John Lee (1985) "Toward a New Sociology of Masculinity." *Theory and Society* 14:551–604.

Cernkovich, Stephen A. and Peggy C. Giordano (1979) "Delinquency, Opportunity and Gender." *Journal of Criminal Law and Criminology* 70 (Summer):145–51.

Chapman, Jane Roberts (1980) *Economic Realities and the Female Offender.* Lexington, MA: Lexington Books.

Chesney-Lind, Meda (1973) "Judicial Enforcement of the Female Sex Role: The Family Court and the Female Delinquent." *Issues in Criminology* 8(2):51–69.

——— (1986) "Women and Crime: The Female Offender." *Signs: Journal of Women in Culture and Society* 12(1):78–96.

——— (1987) "Female Offenders: Paternalism Reexamined." In Laura L. Crites and Winifred L. Hepperle (eds.), *Women, the Courts, and Equality.* Newbury Park, CA: Sage, pp. 114–39.

——— (forthcoming) "Girls' Crime and Women's Place: Towards a Feminist Model of Female Delinquency." *Crime and Delinquency.*

Chesney-Lind, Meda and Noelie Rodriguez (1983) "Women under Lock and Key." *The Prison Journal* 63:47–65.

Cohn, Ellen G. and Lawrence W. Sherman (1987) *Police Policy on Domestic Violence, 1986: A National Survey.* Washington, DC: Crime Control Institute.

Cole, Johnnetta B., ed. (1986) *All American Women: Lines That Divide, Ties That Bind.* New York: Free Press.

Collins, Patricia Hill (1986) "Learning from the Outsider Within: The Sociological Significance of Black Feminist Thought." *Social Problems* 33(6):14–32.

Cott, Nancy (1987) *The Grounding of Modern Feminism.* New Haven: Yale University Press.

Crites, Laura L., ed. (1976) *The Female Offender.* Lexington, MA: Lexington Books.

——— (1987) "Wife Abuse: The Judicial Record." In Laura L. Crites and Winifred L. Hepperle (eds.), *Women, the Courts, and Equality.* Newbury Park, CA: Sage, pp. 38–53.

Culley, Margo and Catherine Portuges, eds. (1985) *Gendered Subjects: The Dynamics of Feminist Teaching.* Boston: Routledge and Kegan Paul.

Daly, Kathleen (1987a) "Structure and Practice of Familial-Based Justice in a Criminal Court." *Law and Society Review* 21(2):267–90.

——— (1987b) "Discrimination in the Criminal Courts: Family, Gender, and the Problem of Equal Treatment." *Social Forces* 66(1):152–75.

——— (1988) "The Social Control of Sexuality: A Case Study of the Criminalization of Prostitution in the Progressive Era." In Steven Spitzer and Andrew T. Scull (eds.), *Research in Law, Deviance, and Social Control.* Volume 9. Greenwich, CT: JAI, pp. 171–206.

——— (forthcoming) "Paternalism Re-Examined: Gender, Work-Family Relations, and Sentencing." *Gender and Society.*

Darty, Trude and Sandee Potter, eds. (1984) *Women-Identified Women.* Palo Alto: Mayfield.

Datesman, Susan K. and Frank R. Scarpitti (1975) "Female Delinquency and Broken Homes: A Reassessment." *Criminology* 13 (May):33–55.

———, eds. (1980a) *Women, Crime, and Justice.* New York: Oxford University Press.

——— (1980b) "Women's Crime and Women's Emancipation." In Susan K. Datesman and Frank R. Scarpitti (eds.) *Women, Crime, and Justice.* New York: Oxford University Press, pp. 355–76.

Délacoste, Frédérique and Priscilla Alexander, eds. (1987) *Sex Work: Writings by Women in the Sex Industry.* San Francisco: Cleis.

Delmar, Rosalind (1986) "What Is Feminism?" In Juliet Mitchell and Ann Oakley (eds.), *What is Feminism?* New York: Pantheon, pp. 8–33.

Dobash, R. Emerson and Russell P. Dobash (1979) *Violence against Wives: The Case against Patriarchy.* New York: Free Press.

Donovan, Josephine (1985) *Feminist Theory: The Intellectual Traditions of American Feminism.* New York: Ungar.

DuBois, Ellen Carol (1981) *Elizabeth Cady Stanton/Susan B. Anthony: Correspondence, Writings, and Speeches.* New York: Schocken.

DuBois, Ellen Carol and Linda Gordon (1984) "Seeking Ecstasy on the Battlefield: Danger and Pleasure in Nineteenth-Century Feminist Sexual Thought." In Carole S. Vance (ed.), *Pleasure and Danger. Exploring Female Sexuality.* Boston: Routledge and Kegan Paul, pp. 31–49.

DuBois, Ellen Carol, Gail Paradise Kelly, Elizabeth Lapovsky Kennedy, Carolyn W. Korsmeyer, and Lillian S. Robinson (1985) *Feminist Scholarship: Kindling in the Groves of Academe.* Urbana: University of Illinois Press.

Dworkin, Andrea (1987) *Intercourse.* New York: Free Press.

Eaton, Mary (1983) "Mitigating Circumstances: Familiar Rhetoric." *International Journal of the Sociology of Law* 11:385–400.

——— (1985) "Documenting the Defendant: Placing Women in Social Inquiry Reports." In Julia Brophy and Carol Smart (eds.), *Women in Law: Explorations in Law, Family, and Sexuality.* Boston: Routledge and Kegan Paul, pp. 117–38.

——— (1986) *Justice for Women? Family, Court and Social Control.* Philadelphia: Open University Press.

——— (1987) "The Question of Bail: Magistrates' Responses to Applications for Bail on Behalf of Men and Women Defendants." In Pat Carlen and Anne Worrall (eds.), *Gender, Crime and Justice.* Philadelphia: Open University Press, pp. 95–107.

Eisenstein, Hester (1983) *Contemporary Feminist Thought.* Boston: G.K. Hall.

Enloe, Cynthia H. (1983) *Does Khaki Become You? The Militarization of Women's Lives.* Boston: South End.

——— (1987) "Feminists Thinking about War, Militarism, and Peace." In Beth B. Hess and Myra Marx Feree (eds.), *Analyzing Gender.* Newbury Park, CA: Sage, pp. 526–47.

Evans, Sarah (1979) Personal Politics. *The Roots of Women's Liberation in the Civil Rights Movement and the New Left.* New York: Knopf.

Fee, Elizabeth (1981) "Is Feminism a Threat to Scientific Objectivity?" *International Journal of Women's Studies* 4(4):378–92.

Feinman, Clarice (1980) *Women in the Criminal Justice System.* New York: Praeger.

Figueira-McDonough, Josefina and Elaine Selo (1980) "A Reformulation of the 'Equal Opportunity' Explanation of Female Delinquency." *Crime and Delinquency* 26:333–43.

Fineman, Martha (1988) "Dominant Discourse, Professional Language, and Legal Change in Child Custody Decisionmaking." *Harvard Law Review* 10(4):727–74.

Flanagan, Timothy J. and Maureen McLeod, eds. (1983) *Sourcebook of Criminal Justice Statistics—1982*. Bureau of Justice Statistics, U.S. Department of Justice. Washington, DC: U.S. Government Printing Office.

Flax, Jane (1987) "Postmodernism and Gender Relations in Feminist Theory." *Signs: Journal of Women in Culture and Society* 12(4):621–43.

Freedman, Estelle B. (1981) *Their Sisters' Keepers: Women's Prison Reform in America, 1830–1930*. Ann Arbor: University of Michigan Press.

Gelsthorpe, Loraine and Allison Morris (1988) "Feminism and Criminology in Britain." *British Journal of Criminology* 28(2):223–40.

Giddings, Paula (1984) *When and Where I Enter: The Impact of Black Women on Race and Sex in America*. New York: Morrow.

Giordano, Peggy C. (1978) "Girls, Guys and Gangs: The Changing Social Context of Female Delinquency." *Journal of Criminal Law and Criminology* 69 (Spring):126–32.

Giordano, Peggy C., Sandra Kerbel, and Sandra Dudley (1981) "The Economics of Female Criminality: An Analysis of Police Blotters, 1890–1975." In Lee H. Bowker (ed.), *Women and Crime in America*. New York: Macmillan, pp. 65–82.

Gora, JoAnn (1982) *The New Female Criminal: Empirical Reality or Social Myth*. New York: Praeger.

Gordon, Linda (1988) *Heroes of Their Own Lives: The Politics and History of Family Violence*. New York: Viking.

Gove, Walter R. (1985) "The Effect of Age and Gender on Deviant Behavior: A Biopsychosocial Perspective." In Alice S. Rossi (ed.), *Gender and the Life Course*. New York: Aldine, pp. 115–44.

Grau, Janice, Jeffrey Fagan, and Sandra Wexler (1984) "Restraining Orders for Battered Women: Issues of Access and Efficacy." *Women and Politics* 4(3):13–28.

Graycar, Regina (1986) "Yes, Virginia, There is a Feminist Legal Literature: A Survey of Some Recent Publications." *Australian Journal of Law and Society* 3:105–35.

Griffin, Jean Thomas, and Nancy Hoffman, eds. (1986) "Teaching About Women, Race, and Culture." *Women's Studies Quarterly* 14(1–2).

Griffin, Susan (1971) "Rape: The All-American Crime." *Ramparts* 10(3):26–35.

Gross, Elizabeth (1986) "What Is Feminist Theory?" In Carole Pateman and Elizabeth Gross (eds.), *Feminist Challenges: Social and Political Theory*. Boston: Northeastern University Press, pp. 190–204.

Hagan, John, John Simpson, and A.R. Gillis (1987) "Class in the Household: A Power-Control Theory of Gender and Delinquency." *American Journal of Sociology* 92(4):788–816.

Hagedorn, John (1988) *People and Folks: Youth Gangs, Crime, and the Underclass in a Rustbelt City*. Chicago: Lake View.

Harding, Sandra (1986) *The Science Question in Feminism*. Ithaca: Cornell University Press.

Harding, Sandra and Merrill Hintikka, eds. (1983) *Discovering Reality: Feminist Perspectives on Epistemology, Metaphysics, Methodology and Philosophy of Science*. Boston: Reidel.

Harris, Anthony R. (1977) "Sex and Theories of Deviance: Toward a Functional Theory of Deviant Type-Scripts." *American Sociological Review* 42(1):3–16.

Harris, M. Kay (1987) "Moving into the New Millennium: Toward a Feminist Vision of Justice." *The Prison Journal* 67(2):27–38.

Heidensohn, Frances M. (1968) "The Deviance of Women: A Critique and an Enquiry." *British Journal of Sociology* 19(2):160–76.

——— (1985) *Women and Crime: The Life of the Female Offender.* New York: New York University Press.

——— (1986) "Models of Justice: Portia or Persephone? Some Thoughts on Equality, Fairness and Gender in the Field of Criminal Justice." *International Journal of the Sociology of Law* 14:287–98.

——— (1987) "Women and Crime: Questions for Criminology." In Pat Carlen and Anne Worrall (eds.), *Gender, Crime and Justice.* Philadelphia: Open University Press, pp. 16–27.

Hepperle, Winifred L. and Laura L. Crites, eds. (1978) *Women in the Courts.* Williamsburg, VA: National Center for State Courts.

Hirschi, Travis and Michael Gottfredson (1987) "Causes of White Collar Crime." *Criminology* 25(4):949–74.

hooks, bell (1981) *Ain't I a Woman?* Boston: South End.

——— (1984) *Feminist Theory: From Margin to Center.* Boston: South End.

Hubbard, Ruth (1982) "Have Only Men Evolved?" In Ruth Hubbard, M.S. Henifin, and Barbara Fried (eds.), *Biological Woman—The Convenient Myth.* Cambridge, MA: Schenkman, pp. 17–46.

Huff, C. Ronald (1988) "Youth Gangs and Public Policy in Ohio: Findings and Recommendations." Paper presented at the Ohio Conference on Youth Gangs and the Urban Underclass. Ohio State University, Columbus.

International Journal of the Sociology of Law (1986), vol. 14. Special Edition of Selected Papers, Feminist Perspectives on Law. European Critical Legal Studies Conference, London.

Jaggar, Alison M. (1983) *Feminist Politics and Human Nature.* Totowa, NJ: Rowman and Allenheld.

Jaggar, Alison M. and Paula S. Rothenberg, eds. (1984) *Feminist Frameworks: Alternative Theoretical Accounts of the Relations between Men and Women.* 2nd edition. New York: McGraw-Hill.

Joseph, Gloria I. and Jill Lewis (1981) *Common Differences: Conflicts in Black and White Feminist Perspectives.* Boston: South End.

Kahn, Arnold S. and Paula J. Jean (1983) "Integration and Elimination or Separation and Redefinition: The Future of the Psychology of Women." *Signs: Journal of Women in Culture and Society* 8(4):659–71.

Keller, Evelyn Fox (1984) *Reflections on Gender and Science.* New Haven: Yale University Press.

Kelly-Gadol, Joan (1977) "Did Women Have a Renaissance?" Reprinted 1987 in Renate Bridenthal, Claudia Koonz, and Susan Stuard, eds., *Becoming Visible: Women in European History.* 2nd edition. Boston: Houghton Mifflin, pp. 175–201.

——— (1982) "Early Feminist Theory and the *Querelle des Femmes,* 1400–1789." *Signs: Journal of Women in Culture and Society* 8(1):4–28.

Kimmel, Michael S. (1987) "Men's Responses to Feminism at the Turn of the Century." *Gender and Society* 1(3):261–83.

Klein, Dorie (1973) "The Etiology of Female Crime: A Review of the Literature." *Issues in Criminology* 8:3–30.

——— (1982) "The Dark Side of Marriage: Battered Wives and the Domination of Women." In Nicole Hahn Rafter and Elizabeth A. Stanko (eds.), *Judge, Lawyer, Victim, Thief.* Boston: Northeastern University Press, pp. 83–107.

Klein, Renate D. (1987) "The Dynamics of the Women's Studies Classroom: A Review Essay of the Teaching Practice of Women's Studies in Higher Education." *Women's Studies International Forum* 10(2):187–206.

Kramarae, Cheris and Paula A. Treichler (1985) *A Feminist Dictionary.* Boston: Pandora/Routledge and Kegan Paul.

Leonard, Eileen B. (1983) "Judicial Decisions and Prison Reform: The Impact of Litigation on Women Prisoners." *Social Problems* 31(1):45–58.

Lerman, Lisa G. (1980) "Protection of Battered Women: A Survey of State Legislation." *Women's Rights Law Reporter* 6(4):271–84.

Lerner, Gerda (1986) *The Creation of Patriarchy.* New York: Oxford University Press.

Lopata, Helena Z. and Barrie Thorne (1978) "On the Term 'Sex Roles.'" *Signs: Journal of Women in Culture and Society* 3(3):718–21.

MacKinnon, Catharine A. (1982) "Feminism, Marxism, Method, and the State: An Agenda for Theory." *Signs: Journal of Women in Culture and Society* 7(3):515–44.

——— (1983) "Feminism, Marxism, Method, and the State: Toward Feminist Jurisprudence." *Signs: Journal of Women in Culture and Society* 8(4):635–58.

——— (1987) *Feminism Unmodified: Discourses on Life and Law.* Cambridge, MA: Harvard University Press.

Majury, Diana (1987) "Strategizing in Equality." *Wisconsin Women's Law Journal* 3:169–87.

Mann, Coramae Richey (1984) *Female Crime and Delinquency.* Tuscaloosa, AL: University of Alabama Press.

Martin, Del (1976) *Battered Wives.* New York: Pocket Books.

McCormick, Arlene, Mark-David Janus, and Ann Wolbert Burgess (1986) "Runaway Youths and Sexual Victimization: Gender Differences in an Adolescent Runaway Population." *Child Abuse and Neglect* 10:387–95.

Messerschmidt, James W. (1986) *Capitalism, Patriarchy, and Crime: Toward a Socialist Feminist Criminology.* Totowa, NJ: Rowman and Littlefield.

Miller, Eleanor M. (1986) *Street Woman.* Philadelphia: Temple University Press.

Millman, Marcia (1975) "She Did It All for Love: A Feminist View of the Sociology of Deviance." In Marcia Millman and Rosabeth Moss Kanter (eds.), *Another Voice: Feminist Perspectives on Social Life and Social Science.* Garden City, NY: Anchor/Doubleday, pp. 251–79.

Mitchell, Juliet and Ann Oakley, eds. (1986) *What is Feminism?* New York: Pantheon.

Moore, Joan W. (1978) *Homeboys: Gangs, Drugs, and Prison in the Barrios of Los Angeles.* Philadelphia: Temple University Press.

Moraga, Cherrie and Gloria Anzaldúa, eds. (1983) *This Bridge Called My Back: Writings by Radical Women of Color.* 2nd edition. New York: Kitchen Table/Women of Color.

Morris, Allison (1987) *Women, Crime and Criminal Justice.* New York: Blackwell.

Moyer, Imogene L. (1985) "Crime, Conflict Theory, and the Patriarchal Society." In Imogene L. Moyer (ed.), *The Changing Roles of Women in the Criminal Justice System.* Prospect Heights, IL: Waveland, pp. 1–29.

Mukherjee, Satyanshu and Jocelynne A. Scutt, eds. (1981) *Women and Crime.* Sydney: Australian Institute of Criminology.

Musheno, Michael and Kathryn Seeley (1986) "Prostitution Policy and the Women's Movement." *Contemporary Crises* 10:237–55.

Nagel, Ilene H. and John Hagan (1983) "Gender and Crime: Offense Patterns and Criminal Court Sanctions." In Michael H. Tonry and Norval Morris (eds.),

Crime and Justice: An Annual Review of Research. Volume 4. Chicago: University of Chicago Press, pp. 91–144.

National Institute of Justice, U.S. Department of Justice (1985) "Replicating an Experiment in Special Deterrence: Alternative Police Responses to Spouse Assault," Research solicitation.

——— (1988) "Spouse Assault Replication Program, Start-up Designs." Unpublished mimeo.

Oakley, Ann (1981) *Subject Women.* New York: Pantheon.

Osborne, Judith A. (1984) "Rape Law Reform: A New Cosmetic for Canadian Women." *Women and Politics* 4(3):49–64.

Parisi, Nicolette (1982) "Are Females Treated Differently? A Review of the Theories and Evidence on Sentencing and Parole Decisions." In Nicole Hahn Rafter and Elizabeth A. Stanko (eds.), *Judge, Lawyer, Victim, Thief.* Boston: Northeastern University Press, pp. 205–20.

Pateman, Carole (1986) "The Theoretical Subversiveness of Feminism." In Carole Pateman and Elizabeth Gross (eds.), *Feminist Challenges: Social and Political Theory.* Boston: Northeastern University Press, pp. 1–10.

Pizzey, Erin (1974) *Scream Quietly or the Neighbors Will Hear.* Middlesex, UK: Penguin.

Pleck, Elizabeth (1979) "Wife Beating in Nineteenth-Century America." *Victimology* 4(1):62–74.

——— (1987) *Domestic Tyranny: The Making of American Social Policy Against Family Violence from Colonial Times to the Present.* New York: Oxford University Press.

Price, Barbara Raffel and Natalie J. Sokoloff, eds. (1982) *The Criminal Justice System and Women.* New York: Clark Boardman.

Quarm, Daisy and Martin D. Schwartz (1984) "Domestic Violence in Criminal Court: An Examination of New Legislation in Ohio." *Women and Politics* 4(3):29–46.

Rafter, Nicole Hahn (1985) *Partial Justice: Women in State Prisons, 1800–1935.* Boston: Northeastern University Press.

Rafter, Nicole Hahn and Elena M. Natalizia (1982) "Marxist Feminism: Implications for Criminal Justice." In Barbara Raffel Price and Natalie J. Sokoloff (eds.), *The Criminal Justice System and Women.* New York: Clark Boardman, pp. 465–83.

Rafter, Nicole Hahn and Elizabeth A. Stanko, eds. (1982) *Judge, Lawyer, Victim, Thief.* Boston: Northeastern University Press.

Reckless, Walter C. (1961) *The Crime Problem.* 3rd edition. New York: Appleton-Century-Crofts.

Resnik, Judith and Nancy Shaw (1980) "Prisoners of Their Sex: Health Problems of Incarcerated Women." In Ira Robbins (ed.), *Prisoners' Rights Sourcebook: Theory, Litigation and Practice.* Volume 2. New York: Clark Boardman, pp. 319–413.

Rhode, Deborah (1987) "Justice, Gender, and the Justices." In Laura L. Crites and Winifred L. Hepperle (eds.), *Women, the Courts, and Equality.* Newbury Park, CA: Sage, pp. 13–34.

Rich, Adrienne (1980) "Compulsory Heterosexuality and Lesbian Existence." *Signs: Journal of Women in Culture and Society* 5(4):631–60.

Rights of Women, Family Law Subgroup (1985) "Campaigning around Family Law: Politics and Practice." In Julia Brophy and Carol Smart (eds.), *Women in Law: Explorations in Law, Family, and Sexuality.* Boston: Routledge and Kegan Paul, pp. 188–206.

Rodgers, Kristin O. (1972) "For Her Own Protection . . . Conditions of Incarceration for Female Juvenile Offenders in the State of Connecticut." *Law and Society Review* 7(2):223–46.

Rohrlich-Leavitt, Ruby, Barbara Sykes, and Elizabeth Weatherford (1975) "Aboriginal Woman: Male and Female Anthropological Perspectives." In Rayna R. Reiter (ed.), *Toward an Anthropology of Women.* New York: Monthly Review Press, pp. 110–26.

Rosen, Ruth (1982) *The Lost Sisterhood: Prostitution in America, 1900–1918.* Baltimore: Johns Hopkins University Press.

Rosenbaum, Marsha (1981) *Women on Heroin.* New Brunswick, NJ: Rutgers University Press.

Sargeant, Lydia, ed. (1981) *Women and Revolution: A Discussion of the Unhappy Marriage of Marxism and Feminism.* Boston: South End

Schechter, Susan (1982) *Women and Male Violence: The Vision and Struggle of the Battered Women's Movement.* Boston: South End.

Schlossman, Steven and Stephanie Wallach (1978) "The Crime of Precocious Sexuality: Female Juvenile Delinquency and the Progressive Era." *Harvard Educational Review* 48(1):65–94.

Schneider, Elizabeth M. (1986) "Describing and Changing: Women's Self-Defense Work and the Problem of Expert Testimony on Battering." *Women's Rights Law Reporter* 9(3–4):195–225.

Schur, Edwin M. (1984) *Labeling Women Deviant: Gender, Stigma, and Social Control.* New York: Random House.

SchWeber, Claudine (1982) "'The Government's Unique Experiment in Salvaging Women Criminals': Cooperation and Conflict in the Administration of a Women's Prison—The Case of the Federal Industrial Institution for Women at Alderson." In Nicole Hahn Rafter and Elizabeth A. Stanko (eds.), *Judge, Lawyer, Victim, Thief.* Boston: Northeastern University Press, pp. 277–303.

SchWeber, Claudine and Clarice Feinman, eds. (1984) "Criminal Justice Politics and Women: The Aftermath of Legally Mandated Change." *Women and Politics* 4(3). Reprint, Haworth (1985).

Schwendinger, Julia R. and Herman Schwendinger (1983) *Rape and Inequality.* Newbury Park, CA: Sage.

Shane-DuBow, Sandra, Alice P. Brown, and Erik Olsen (1985) *Sentencing Reform in the United States: History, Content, and Effect.* National Institute of Justice, U.S. Department of Justice. Washington, DC: U.S. Government Printing Office.

Sherman, Julia A. and Evelyn Torton Beck, eds. (1979) *The Prism of Sex: Essays in the Sociology of Knowledge.* Madison: University of Wisconsin Press.

Sherman, Lawrence A. and Richard A. Berk (1984) "The Specific Deterrent Effects of Arrest for Domestic Violence." *American Sociological Review* 49(2):261–92.

Silbert, Mimi and Ayala M. Pines (1981) "Sexual Child Abuse as an Antecedent to Prostitution." *Child Abuse and Neglect* 5:407–11.

Simon, Rita J. (1975) *Women and Crime.* Lexington, MA: Lexington Books.

Singer, Linda (1973) "Women and the Correctional Process." *American Criminal Law Review* 11(2):295–308.

Slocum, Sally (1975) "Woman the Gatherer: Male Bias in Anthropology." In Rayna R. Reiter (ed.), *Toward an Anthropology of Women.* New York: Monthly Review Press, pp. 36–50.

Smart, Carol (1976) *Women, Crime and Criminology: A Feminist Critique.* Boston: Routledge and Kegan Paul.

——— (1979) "The New Female Criminal: Reality or Myth?" *British Journal of Criminology* 19(1):50–59.

——— (1985) "Legal Subjects and Sexual Objects: Ideology, Law and Female Sexuality." In Julia Brophy and Carol Smart (eds.), *Women in Law: Explorations in Law, Family and Sexuality.* Boston: Routledge and Kegan Paul, pp. 50–70.

Smith, Barbara, ed. (1983) *Home Girls: A Black Feminist Anthology.* New York: Kitchen Table/Women of Color.

Smith, Dorothy E. (1979) "A Sociology for Women." In Julia A. Sherman and Evelyn Torton Beck (eds.), *The Prism of Sex: Essays in the Sociology of Knowledge.* Madison: University of Wisconsin Press, pp. 135–87.

Smith, Douglas A. and Raymond Paternoster (1987) "The Gender Gap in Theories of Deviance: Issues and Evidence." *Journal of Research in Crime and Delinquency* 24(2):140–72.

Sokoloff, Natalie J. (1980) *Between Money and Love: The Dialectics of Women's Home and Market Work.* New York: Praeger.

Spencer, Cassie C. (1987) "Sexual Assault: The Second Victimization." In Laura L. Crites and Winifred L. Hepperle (eds.), *Women, the Courts, and Equality.* Newbury Park, CA: Sage, pp. 54–73.

Spender, Dale, ed. (1981) *Men's Studies Modified: The Impact of Feminism on the Academic Disciplines.* New York: Pergamon.

Stacey, Judith (1987) "Sexism by a Subtler Name? Postindustrial Conditions and Postfeminist Consciousness in the Silicon Valley." *Socialist Review* 17(96):7–28.

Stacey, Judith and Barrie Thorne (1985) "The Missing Feminist Revolution in Sociology." *Social Problems* 32(4):301–16.

Stanko, Elizabeth Anne (1985) *Intimate Intrusions: Women's Experiences of Male Violence.* Boston: Routledge and Kegan Paul.

Stanley, Liz and Sue Wise (1983) *Breaking Out: Feminist Consciousness and Feminist Research.* Boston: Routledge and Kegan Paul.

Steffensmeier, Darrell J. (1978) "Crime and the Contemporary Woman: An Analysis of Changing Levels of Female Property Crime, 1960–75." *Social Forces* 57(2):566–84.

——— (1980) "Sex Differences in Patterns of Adult Crime, 1965–77." *Social Forces* 58(4):1080–1109.

——— (1983) "Organizational Properties and Sex-Segregation in the Underworld: Building a Sociological Theory of Sex Differences in Crime." *Social Forces* 61(4):1010–32.

Temin, Carolyn Engel (1973) "Discriminatory Sentencing of Women Offenders." *American Criminal Law Review* 11(2):355–72.

Tong, Rosemary (1984) *Women, Sex, and the Law.* Totowa, NJ: Rowman and Allanheld.

Tonry, Michael H. (1987) *Sentencing Reform Impacts.* National Institute of Justice, U.S. Department of Justice. Washington, DC: U.S. Government Printing Office.

Vogel, Lise (forthcoming) "Debating Difference: The Problem of Special Treatment of Pregnancy in the Workplace." *Feminist Studies.*

Walkowitz, Judith R. (1980) *Prostitution and Victorian Society: Women, Class and the State.* New York: Cambridge University Press.

Waring, Nancy W. (1986) "Coming to Terms with Pornography: Towards a Feminist Perspective on Sex, Censorship, and Hysteria." In Steven Spitzer and Andrew

T. Scull (eds.), *Research in Law, Deviance and Social Control.* Volume 8. Greenwich, CT: JAI, pp. 85–112.

Warren, Marguerite Q. (1982) "Delinquency Causation in Female Offenders." In Nicole Hahn Rafter and Elizabeth A. Stanko (eds.), *Judge, Lawyer, Victim, Thief.* Boston: Northeastern University Press, pp. 181–202.

Weisberg, D. Kelly, ed. (1982) *Women and the Law.* Volumes 1 and 2. Cambridge, MA: Schenkman.

Weisheit, Ralph and Sue Mahan (1988) *Women, Crime, and Criminal Justice.* Cincinnati: Anderson.

Weitzman, Lenore J. (1985) *The Divorce Revolution: The Unexpected Social and Economic Consequences for Women and Children in America.* New York: Free Press.

Wilson, James Q. and Richard J. Herrnstein (1985) *Crime and Human Nature.* New York: Simon and Schuster.

Wisconsin Women's Law Journal (1987), Volume 3. Papers from the 1986 Feminism and Legal Theory Conference, University of Wisconsin Law School, Madison.

Worrall, Anne (1987) "Sisters in Law? Women Defendants and Women Magistrates." In Pat Carlen and Anne Worrall (eds.), *Gender, Crime and Justice.* Philadelphia: Open University Press, pp. 108–24.

Zietz, Dorothy (1981) *Women Who Embezzle or Defraud: A Study of Convicted Felons.* New York: Praeger.

2

Feminism in Criminology
Engendering the Outlaw

Dana M. Britton

Criminology remains one of the most thoroughly masculinized of all social science fields; certainly, it is one of the last academic bastions in which scholars regularly restrict their studies to the activities and habits of men without feeling compelled to account for this (Rafter and Heidensohn 1995). The reason lies, at least in part, in the fact that criminology is in possession of one of the most consistently demonstrated findings in all of the social sciences: as long as statistics have been collected, they have revealed that men are considerably more likely than women to engage in activities defined as criminal. Students are thus attracted to criminology courses by the promise of studying dangerous men; so, too, have scholars been fascinated for decades by the allure of the male outlaw, "hoping perhaps that some of the romance and fascination of this role will rub off" (Chesney-Lind 1995, xii).

In this context, the phrase "feminist criminology" may well seem something of an oxymoron. However, while the vast overrepresentation of men as criminals has served some as a rationale for ignoring women, for others, it has been a point of departure for considering them. The founding of feminist criminology can be somewhat arbitrarily fixed at 1976, with the publication of Carol Smart's *Women, Crime and Criminology: A Feminist Critique*. Though a handful of earlier works had addressed some of the general themes she raised, Smart's book brought them together in a systematic critique of the treatment (or lack thereof) of women offenders in mainstream criminology and the neglect of women's experiences as victims in an attempt to set out some directions for the new field of feminist inquiry.

Britton, Dana. "Feminism in Criminology: Engendering the Outlaw." *Annals, AAPSS*, 571, pp. 57–76.

Almost 25 years later, a substantial body of research has accumulated in the areas specified in Smart's pioneering work, and the field has moved considerably beyond these boundaries. As has been the case for many disciplines, however, the feminist revolution in criminology is still incomplete. Some universities do now routinely offer courses like "Women and Crime," and the Division on Women and Crime has taken its place among other specialty sections in the American Society of Criminology. Even so, these labels bespeak the marginalization of feminist criminology, which is still regarded, by and large, as something outside the mainstream. Feminist criminologists have made great strides in terms of adding women in at the margins of the discipline, but they have, as yet, been less successful in deconstructing its central frames of reference and theoretical and methodological assumptions (Morris and Gelsthorpe 1991).

As is the case in most areas of academic feminism, there is ongoing debate over what the aims of feminist inquiry in criminology should be and over what counts as work that can carry the name. I will not attempt to resolve this debate here. The emerging subject divisions in the field are easier to discern. Feminist criminology may be divided into work that focuses on women as criminal offenders, women as victims of crime, and women as workers in the criminal justice system. Reviews of the field generally do not include the third category, which is something of a hybrid, attracting scholars from both criminology and the sociology of work. I will focus here, however, on all three areas, attempting to give readers a very brief sense of what we know, a review of some key work and important debates, and a sense of the directions in which the field seems to be moving. I will conclude with a discussion of some of the central challenges that remain for feminist criminology.

Before moving on, a caveat is necessary. Although I have referred to the discipline thus far as if it existed as a unified set of frameworks and assumptions, this is not really the case. There are a wide variety of theoretical and methodological perspectives in criminology, and some (for example, critical, interactionist, and Marxist approaches) have been more receptive to feminism than others. My focus here, however, will be on the mainstream in criminology, which I take to be a set of theoretical and methodological frameworks and empirical studies aimed at understanding the etiology of crime (a category taken to be a given) and proposing, implementing, and evaluating methods of crime control. This kind of criminology has historically been very closely allied with state mechanisms of social control, and it is the state that provides the lion's share of research funding in these areas. Therefore, while one might accurately say that there are a variety of criminologies currently extant, mainstream criminology is clearly hegemonic and has most thoroughly marginalized feminist research and theory. It will be my focus in the analysis to follow.

Women as Offenders

Women are vastly underrepresented as criminal offenders. Of course, any data claiming to represent the facts about crime are always the end product of an interaction between the responses of social control authorities and the behaviors of the individuals involved. Even so, there is no serious dispute among criminologists that the extant data substantially misrepresent the actual sex ratio of criminal offending. The primary source of such data, the Uniform Crime Reports (UCR) program of the Federal Bureau of Investigation (FBI), reports detailed information on eight index crimes (these are homicide, forcible rape, robbery, aggravated assault, burglary, larceny-theft, motor vehicle theft, and arson). Women composed 26 percent of those arrested for these offenses in 1997. The UCR also reports statistics for less serious offenses, which constitute the bulk of all arrests. For men and women, these offenses are consistently similar, with larceny-theft (a category largely of petty theft, including shoplifting), simple (non-aggravated) assault, drug offenses, and driving under the influence of alcohol (DUI) topping the list for women in 1997, accounting for 45 percent of women's arrests. For men, the top four offenses were drug crimes, DUI, simple assault, and larceny-theft, composing 38 percent of men's arrests (Maguire and Pastore 1999).

These data indicate that men and women are actually quite similar in terms of the offenses for which they are most often arrested and that the majority are crimes that most would view as petty, for example, larceny-theft. The most striking difference is the absolute level of men's and women's offending. Although larceny-theft accounts for 16 percent of arrests of women, men's arrest rate for this crime is almost 2.5 times higher. Data for violent offenses illustrate this pattern in much clearer detail. In 1997, women were only 16 percent of those arrested for the index offenses of homicide, forcible rape, robbery, and aggravated assault (known collectively as the index of violent crime). Men's arrest rate for homicide was 9 times higher than women's; for rape, 83 times higher; for robbery (defined as the taking or attempted taking of property by force or fear), 10 times higher; and for aggravated assault, 5 times higher. The only offenses for which women's arrests exceed men's are prostitution, for which women are 60 percent of those arrested, and running away from home (a juvenile offense), for which girls were 58 percent of those arrested in 1997.

Arrest rates vary by race as well. In 1997, whites were 63 percent of those arrested for all index offenses; African Americans were 35 percent. For violent index offenses, whites accounted for 57 percent of arrests, versus 41 percent for African Americans. The FBI does not publish arrest statistics by sex and race. We do know, however, that African American men and women are overrepresented among those arrested.

Studies of unpublished UCR data and self-reports show that African American women have higher rates of arrest and participation in homicide, aggravated assault, and other index offenses than white women (Simpson and Elis 1995). For some offenses, such as larceny-theft, arrest rates for African American women most closely match those for white men (Chilton and Datesman 1987); black men's arrest rates are the highest; white women generally rank at the bottom, regardless of the offense.

This statistical picture illustrates some of the challenges facing feminist criminology. The sex ratio of offending is remarkably constant, which seems to indicate the need for theory that would account for why it is that women are so much less likely than men to offend. Indeed, this was the place that criminology, when it considered women at all, often began. Paradoxically, however, rather than being viewed as successes, women have been seen by mainstream theorists as aberrant because they do not commit crime. Newer feminist work in this vein has viewed women's conformity in a somewhat more positive light, relying, for example, on Carol Gilligan's theories of moral development to suggest that women's "ethic of care" makes them less likely to offend (Steffensmeier and Allan 1996). Even a cursory examination of the statistics on sex and race, however, reveals the dangers that can come from viewing women as a unitary category. Differences in arrest rates between African American and white women are often dramatic, and feminist criminology has only just begun to grapple with the implications of these differences (Daly and Maher 1998). Even more problematic is the almost complete lack of data about criminal offending among other racial groups, such as Asian or Hispanic women.

The first studies of women and offending that fell, at least putatively, in the realm of feminist criminology appeared in 1975, with the publication of Freda Adler's *Sisters in Crime* and Rita James Simon's *Women and Crime*. Though these books differ slightly in focus, both make the same general theoretical argument, which has come to be known as emancipation theory. Adler and Simon both contended that women's lower rates of participation in criminal activity could be explained by their confinement to domestic roles and by discrimination that limited their aspirations and opportunities (Daly and Chesney-Lind 1988). With the advent of the women's movement, the situation could be expected to change, however. Adler saw increasing participation in violent crime as inevitable as women became more like men as a result of their social and political emancipation. Simon believed that opportunities created by women's higher levels of formal labor market activity would lead to higher arrest rates for property and occupational crimes, such as fraud, larceny, and embezzlement. Adler did consider race, arguing that black women's higher rates of participation in crime could be explained by their more liberated status: "If one looks at where Black women are as criminals today, one can appreciate where white women are headed as liberated criminals in the coming years" (154).

This argument has obvious appeal for opponents of the feminist movement; but empirically, the theory has received very little support. While women's rates of violent crime have increased, in absolute terms, their rates relative to men's have not changed substantially since 1960 (Steffensmeier 1995). Contrary to popular mythology, there is simply no evidence of the large-scale existence of a new, more violent female offender (Maher 1997). Women's rates of property offending relative to men's have increased since the 1960s, but almost all of the increase has come from higher rates of arrest for larceny-theft, mostly shoplifting (Chilton and Datesman 1987). Rather than reflecting expanding opportunities, however, this increase is more likely due to women's increasing economic marginalization and changing views of women by social control authorities (Morris 1987). There is also no evidence that women with more feminist attitudes are more likely to be criminal; in fact, the opposite is true (Simpson 1989). Although there is now fairly broad consensus that Adler's and Simon's work would not fall within the purview of feminist criminology (Morris and Gelsthorpe 1991; cf. Brown 1986), these books did put women's crime on the empirical agenda for the discipline, and they were groundbreaking in their attempts to build a theory that would explain men's as well as women's crime.

In addition to documenting the levels of women's criminal offending, feminist criminologists have drawn attention to women's (and men's) treatment by police, the courts, and the prison system. Contradicting popular stereotype, studies of women's experiences with the criminal justice system have revealed that women do not benefit, at least not uniformly, from chivalry at the hands of police, prosecutors, and judges. In some instances, such as juvenile status offenses, girls are subject to much harsher treatment than boys (Chesney-Lind 1989). Some research reveals that African American women receive more negative treatment by police, are more likely to be sentenced to prison, and receive longer sentences than white women (Mann 1995), although there is still considerable debate around this issue. A series of studies (for example, Daly 1987) has shown that women who are married and have children do sometimes receive more leniency than other defendants. This effect is double edged, however; women who do not conform to traditional stereotypes of wives and mothers or who are perceived to shirk their responsibilities may be dealt with especially severely (Morris and Wilczynski 1994).

The kinds of quantitative studies reviewed here have provided some answers to the question of how women's rates of offending and treatment by the system compare to men's and, as such, are a crucial first step. This equity approach (Cain 1990) has been guided largely by liberal feminist precepts, conceptualizing gender as an independent variable and seeing men and women as essentially equal and therefore deserving of equal treatment (Daly and Maher 1998). The fundamental limitation of such a strategy is put best by Cain (1990):

> Equity studies do not enable us to pose the question whether or not even absolutely equal sentences might be unjust . . . too high or too low in themselves, or [whether] behaviour . . . should not, from some

> standpoints at least, be subject to penalty. A concern with equity leaves the substance of what is being equalised unanalysed. (2–3)

This kind of liberal feminist approach poses men as the criminal yardstick and equates justice with equality. Larger questions about the processes of criminalization of some acts, rather than others, and the inherent justice or injustice of the system are left unanswered. Such studies also fail to question the meanings and active construction of the categories of sex, race, and class, taking them simply as givens.

More recently, a substantial body of ethnographic and interview research has appeared that takes as its central focus the construction and meaning of such categories. This work has substantially deepened our understanding of the lives of women involved in crime. Mirroring overall trends in feminist theory, the best of this work is moving toward a nuanced and contingent conception of women's agency, one that sees women neither exclusively as victims nor as unfettered actors. Lisa Maher's richly textured ethnographic study of women involved in street-level sex and drug markets (1997) is a particularly good example. Maher convincingly demonstrates that the women she studies are not liberated drug kingpins, nor are they mindless slaves, willing to sink to any depth of depravity to serve their addictions. Rather, they actively work within the constraints of the male-dominated informal economy, rarely controlling significant resources; they perform a range of gender-typed tasks, such as "copping" (buying) drugs for customers fearful of being arrested. While women do sometimes initiate violence, they are more likely to be the targets of victimization by police, male partners, and "tricks."

Feminist research and theorizing on women's offending have also been closely connected with activism. This has been the case on a number of fronts but has perhaps been most visible in the area of women's imprisonment. America is in the throes of an imprisonment binge—since 1990, our prison population has grown by about 6.5 percent per year. Women constitute only about 7 percent of those incarcerated, but their rates of imprisonment have been rising much faster than men's. Between 1988 and 1997, arrests for men increased by only 11 percent, and the number of men incarcerated increased by 96 percent. For women, the situation was much starker: arrests increased by 40 percent, and women's prison population increased 146 percent. This increase fell particularly heavily on Hispanic and African American women, whose rates of incarceration, respectively, are 3.5 and 8.0 times those of white women (Maguire and Pastore 1999).

Advocates for women in prison have been instrumental in bringing these facts to light and in generating public concern over women's rising rates of imprisonment. They have also brought about practical changes that have improved the lives of women inmates, including the elimination of some laws that imposed harsher (indeterminate) sentences on women, the expansion of medical services, improvements in job training and educational opportunities, and even some in-prison nurseries, such as the pioneering program at New York's Bedford Hills (Price and Sokoloff 1995). This work has also generated serious policy alternatives that take into account men's and women's different life histories (for example, women in prison are six times more likely to report prior sexual abuse than their male counterparts), the context of their offending (women are much more likely than men to be first-time offenders or to have committed only nonviolent offenses previously), and women's much lower rates of recidivism compared to men (Chesney-Lind 1996; Davis 1997).

Women as Victims

As in the case of offending, women are underrepresented as victims of crime, at least as victimization is measured by the statistics most widely used by criminologists. The primary source of data derives from the National Crime Victimization Survey (NCVS), conducted annually since 1973 by Census Bureau personnel for the Bureau of Justice Statistics. The NCVS is administered to approximately 101,000 individuals, who are asked questions about their crime victimization. NCVS data consistently show that men are more likely to be victimized by all kinds of violent crime than are women, except rape and sexual assault. Men's overall rate of violent crime victimization in 1997 was 45.8 (per 1,000 population aged 12 years or older); women's was 33.0. Data on homicide, collected by the FBI, show that men are three times as likely to be victims.

NCVS data also indicate that African Americans and Hispanics are more likely to be victims of violent crime than whites and that the young and those with lower incomes also have higher rates of victimization. Unlike the UCR, the NCVS does publish victimization statistics that are disaggregated by sex and race combined, and the dramatic differences they reveal again demonstrate the danger of treating women (or men) as a unitary category. For homicide, white women have the lowest rates of victimization; African American women's rates are about four times higher, and African American women are more likely even than white men to be victims. African American men's rates of homicide victimization—eight times higher than those of white men—starkly testify to an epidemic level of violence, as does the persistent finding that for violent crimes other than homicide, African American men are about one and a half times as likely to be victims as white men. Among women, African Americans are generally much more likely than whites to be victims of all kinds of violent crime; generally, their rates of victimization most closely match white men's rather than white women's.

Feminist criminology has perhaps made its greatest impact on mainstream criminology in the area of women's victimization. The realm in which this has happened, however, has been somewhat limited, as the literature has generally focused on the kinds of offenses of which women are most likely to be victims. As the foregoing data suggest, rape has been a central concern and so, too, has intimate violence. NCVS data indicate that, although women's levels of violent victimization are lower than men's overall, their victimization is much more likely to be personal; from 1992 to 1996, women were five to eight times more likely than men to be victimized by intimates (Maguire and Pastore 1999). Though there is little question that women face specifically gendered violence of this kind, concentrating only on these offenses has had the effect of highlighting the differences between men and women as victims and excludes an analysis of the ways in which other kinds of victimization (which account for far more incidents overall) may be gendered (Chesney-Lind 1995). Even so, feminist research in these areas has clearly been influential; mainstream criminology texts now invariably include sections on rape and intimate violence, and many discuss feminist empirical work and theory.

Unlike studies of female offenders, which did exist before feminist criminology drew attention to them in the 1970s, there simply was no comparable research in mainstream criminology on women's experiences of victimization or on the crimes that disproportionately affect women. A rare exception is Menachem Amir's *Patterns in Forcible Rape* (1971). Although this was one of the first attempts to untangle the dimensions along which rape offending varies (for example, sex, race, class, circumstances), the study paid no attention to the experiences of the victims themselves. The effect of this omission becomes particularly clear in Amir's introduction (or perhaps official legitimation) of the concept of "victim-precipitated" rape, which he claimed accounted for about 19 percent of the cases in his study:

> [Victim-precipitated rape occurs in] those rape situations in which the victim actually, or so it was deemed, agreed to sexual relations but retracted before the actual act or did not react strongly enough when the suggestion was made by the offender(s). The term applies also to cases in risky situations marred with sexuality, especially when she uses what could be interpreted as indecency of language and gestures, or constitutes what could be taken as an invitation to sexual relations. (266)

Feminist critics, both within and outside criminology, quickly charged that this notion clearly placed criminology in collusion with the rapist, who can apparently claim sexual access whenever he deems that his victim has aroused him (Schwendinger and Schwendinger 1983).

The first influential feminist studies of women's victimization appeared during the 1970s and focused on wife battering and rape. Susan Brownmiller's work (1975), in particular, is a deft synthesis of mainstream criminological research on rape offenders (including Amir's study) with a radical feminist perspective that views rape as the sine qua non of men's control of women under patriarchy. Both in content and in timing, these early feminist accounts posed a powerful challenge even to radical criminology, which was rising to prominence during the 1970s. At the heart of the radical perspective was a view of crime as resistance to class and race domination (Taylor, Walton, and Young 1973) and a conceptualization of the offender as the "rogue male" using the only resources available to him in fighting an unjust system. Radical criminologists were caught off guard by the rising tide of radical feminist research on the experiences of women who disproportionately suffered at the hands of such outlaws (Gelsthorpe and Morns 1988). Roger Matthews and Jock Young, two leading British radical criminologists, have admitted that feminist research convinced them of "the limits of the romantic conception of crime and the criminal" (Matthews and Young 1986, 2). Subsequently, radical criminology has taken a more "realist" turn, attempting to come to terms with women's victimization as well as the fact that the poor and working classes are disproportionately the victims of crime (DeKeseredy 1996).

Unlike research on women's offending, which has been guided largely by liberal feminist ideas and methodologies, women's victimization has been a central issue for radical feminists. The relationship with mainstream criminology has been an awkward one, complicated both by radical feminism's antipositivist assumptions and by its advocacy of social change. Modern mainstream criminology, born at the turn of the twentieth century, is also called the positivist school. To oversimplify, this means that most traditional criminologists have used the tools of the scientific method, such as the social survey and statistical methodology, to document what has been conceptualized as a universe of pre-existing social categories. Such inquiry has been framed as value neutral, and it posits the discovery of facts about the social world as an eventual goal. In criminology, scholars have gone about measuring crime and victimization as if these behaviors were readily apparent, uncontested, and invariant in their meaning across social groups. The equity studies discussed previously are examples of this approach, and some of its limitations have already been noted.

Radical feminists take this critique one step further. Radical feminist accounts, like Brownmiller's, have argued that violence against women cannot simply be equated with the victimization of men but, rather, that it takes on a different meaning in the context of a social system in which men are dominant over women. Thus women's violence against men is not the same as men's violence against women. Radical feminists have also pointed to the role of social institutions (such as the criminal justice system and the family) and social norms around sexuality and violence in working together to erase and normalize women's victimization. As a result, victims of rape and battery are often persuaded that such things are either normal or justified, and their victimization may not be apparent, even to themselves. This stance clearly renders any mere quantification of experiences of victimization necessarily incomplete. In addition, radical feminists have argued for the use of research as a tool for social change, a position also at odds with mainstream criminology.

Fault lines have formed around a number of issues, but the ongoing debate over statistics on women's victimization is a particularly apposite case. As noted earlier, the NCVS serves as the primary source of victimization data used by criminologists. Yet before 1992, this instrument did not query sample respondents specifically about rape or sexual assault, asking instead only whether they had been "beaten up" or attacked in other ways. Nor did the survey specifically attempt to measure victimization in the home, inquiring only whether "anyone" had committed violence against the respondent. An extensive redesign process, prompted in part by criticisms from feminist advocacy groups (although general methodological criticisms had also been raised by others), led to the inclusion of questions specifically about rape as well as an item addressing victimization in the home. After the redesign, overall estimates of personal victimization increased by 44 percent, but rape and sexual assault victimization rates increased by 157 percent. The new instrument also produced a 72 percent increase in women's reporting that they had been victimized by intimates, and a 155 percent increase in reports of victimization by other relatives (Bachman and Saltzman 1995). There is little doubt that the statistical picture has become a more accurate one.

Even so, criminology has remained resistant to the implications of radical feminism's assumption that women may not see violence against them in terms of standard legal categories, such as those used in the NCVS. Much feminist empirical work on women's victimization has employed substantive definitions of these acts, asking respondents in general terms if they, for example, have had sex against their will due to force, threat of force, or incapacity to consent. Such studies typically yield higher prevalence estimates than those reflected in official statistics. For example, while 14.0 percent of the ever-married women in Russell's sample (1982) reported incidents of victimization by their husbands that fit the legal definition of rape, only 0.9 percent of these women mentioned these experiences when asked directly if they had ever been the victim of a rape or an attempted rape. Such research has been the subject of a considerable backlash from critics, however, who typically rely on official statistics, such as the UCR and NCVS, to assert that feminists have vastly inflated the extent of women's victimization.

A second area of dispute has arisen around the radical feminist assumption that any analysis of victimization is incomplete without an understanding of the patriarchal context that shapes the meaning of these acts (Hanmer and Maynard 1987). The implication of this critique is that any simple count of events, no matter how accurate, will necessarily fail to tell the whole story. Perhaps the best example of this controversy is the debate over statistics on rates of partner or spousal violence, which has crystallized recently around the mutual combat hypothesis. Briefly, this notion arose from research employing an instrument (the Conflict Tactics Scale) that directs respondents to count instances of their own use of a wide spectrum of physically aggressive techniques against their partners during marital or relationship conflicts (Straus, Gelles, and Steinmetz 1980). Surprisingly, studies using this instrument indicate that women are just as likely to use physical violence as men. This result has been offered as a fundamental challenge to feminist constructions of marital violence as a problem experienced primarily by women in the patriarchal context of marriage. Calls for attention to the problem of battered husbands have followed, and the mutual combat hypothesis has achieved wide cultural and disciplinary currency. Criminology texts now largely refer to "partner" or "spousal" violence; I recently reviewed a criminology textbook-in-development that began the section on violence in marriage by framing the problem as one of mutual combat.

Feminist critics have responded that the context in which violence is experienced is crucial. Women are much more likely than men to use violence in self-defense, more likely to be injured by acts of intimate violence directed against them, more likely to feel seriously threatened by it, less likely to be able to effectively defend themselves, and less likely to have the resources to leave violent relationships (Nazroo 1995; for a review, see Gelles and Loeske 1993). Again, this controversy illustrates the uneasy relationship between criminology's positivist tradition and the antipositivist implications of the assumptions that undergird radical feminist research and theorizing on women's experiences of violence. A similar controversy exists in research on fear of crime, an area in which women's much higher rates of expressed fear are seemingly unaccounted for by their lower rates of victimization. Pioneering work by Elizabeth Stanko (1990) and others, however, has revealed that much of women's victimization is hidden (that is, not accounted for by official statistics), routine, and socially legitimated (Madriz 1997) and that women have ample reason to express high levels of fear.

As in the case of women offenders, activism both within and outside the discipline has been instrumental in framing women's victimization as a legitimate social problem and in making concrete changes in the criminal justice system. Presumptive arrest policies regarding domestic violence incidents, now in place in the majority of U.S. jurisdictions, were prompted in large part by empirical research conducted by criminologists (Sherman and Berk 1984). While such a strategy represents an important symbolic step, indicating that such violence is finally being taken more seriously by the system, subsequent research (Sherman 1992) indicates that such policies are not working as well as their proponents had hoped, and in some cases, they appear to increase the chances of repeat violence. Debate and research within criminology continue to be influential in shaping policy in this area. Other significant legal and political changes include revisions in laws defining rape or sexual assault; the passage of "rape shield" laws, which do not allow the discussion of victims' sexual histories in court; and the recent passage of the Violence Against Women Act, which defines gender-based victimization as a hate crime and allocates increased funds for battered women's shelters, rape crisis centers, and policing and research efforts directed to reducing the number of crimes against women.

Women as Workers

During the last 25 years, increasing numbers of women have entered criminal justice occupations. Most research to date has addressed women's experiences in policing, prison work, and law, and these will be my focus here. Before the 1970s, few women were employed in any of these jobs. A variety of factors eased women's entry. As has been the case with most male-dominated occupations, legislative change and legal pressure have been most influential; Title VII and the Equal Employment Opportunity Act formally opened all of these occupations to women. Title IX was also important for women in law, as it struck down policies that had either barred them from law schools entirely or kept their numbers to a minimum. Even so, administrators, coworkers, and clients did not immediately welcome women. Lawsuits challenging recruitment and promotion practices, among other things, were necessary to fully open the doors for women's entry (Martin and Jurik 1996).

Women have also benefited from demographic changes. The sheer number of people employed in all of these jobs has increased dramatically over the last two decades, and women have filled the gap as the supply of male workers has not been adequate to meet the rising demand. This effect has been particularly dramatic in prison work. Between 1983 and 1995, the number of staff in prisons and jails increased 187 percent, but the number of female staff almost quadrupled, increasing by 372 percent (American Correctional Association 1984; Maguire and Pastore 1999). Additional factors, specific to law, policing, and prison work, have also contributed to women's increasing representation in these fields. By 1998, women constituted 12 percent of all police officers, 24 percent of all prison officers, and 34 percent of all attorneys (Bureau of Labor Statistics 1999).

Increasing access has not necessarily meant equal rewards. There is a considerable wage gap in each occupation; women's incomes in policing are only 86 percent of those of their male counterparts; in prison work, 89 percent; and in law, 70 percent. The relatively smaller gaps in policing and prison work are undoubtedly due to the fact that the employer in these cases is the government, a labor market sector in which recruiting and promotion practices are at least somewhat formalized. Law, on the other hand, is practiced in highly diverse settings, each with its own set of employment practices and its own reward structure. Regardless, women in all three occupations are likely to be found at the lowest rungs of their respective occupational ladders. In policing, for example, women are 16 percent of municipal officers but only 7 percent of state police (National Center for Women in Policing 1999). Women in prison work continue to face blocked access to supervisory positions (Britton 1997), and women in law are concentrated in the least prestigious specialties (for example, family law and public defense) and work in the lowest-paid settings (Pierce 1995).

While there have always been women criminals and women victims, until a quarter-century ago, there was a paucity of women working in criminal justice occupations. What this means is that, although mainstream criminological research existed on police, prison workers, and attorneys prior to 1975, these studies essentially focused on "the men and their work" and lacked an analysis of gender. Subsequently, a considerable volume of literature on women in criminal justice occupations has appeared. I will not attempt to cover the literature on each occupation here (for a review, see Martin and Jurik 1996). Two clear, though sometimes overlapping, areas of research have emerged in studies of women's experiences in all three occupations, however. The first has involved a focus on difference, asking questions about how or whether women perform their jobs differently from men and about the unique gendered characteristics women bring to their work. The second line of research has contended that these jobs and the organizations in which they are performed are themselves gendered and has looked at the ways in which gendered organizational structures, ideologies, policies and practices, interactions, and worker identities assume and reinforce inequality.

Theoretical and empirical work in the first vein is in some ways a response to critics who have long argued that women, on account of their gender, do not possess the characteristics necessary for success in these heavily masculinized and male-dominated occupations. As a male attorney interviewed by Pierce (1995) put it, "I think Clarence Darrow once said women are too nice to be lawyers. I think he was right. It's not that I don't think women are bright or competent—they just don't have that *killer* instinct" (26). Similar, and usually less charitable, sentiments can be found in both popular and academic discussions of the role of women in prison work and in policing. Research from the difference perspective has attempted to turn this critique on its head, arguing that women are not the same as their male counterparts but that the gendered qualities that they bring with them are actually assets.

In some ways, this line of argument represents a return to the discourse employed by women criminal justice system reformers of the nineteenth century. Claims that women were simply inherently better able to deal with women victims, suspects, clients, and prisoners were largely successful in persuading state and local governments to hire policewomen, whose main responsibility was to deal with delinquent women and girls and to build reformatories, staffed exclusively by women, to hold women inmates (Appier 1998; Freedman 1981). The principal change is that such rhetoric is now being used to argue for the integration of women into male-dominated occupations, rather than the establishment of separate, sex-segregated jobs and institutions. Menkel-Meadow (1987), for example, argues that women bring a "different voice" to the practice of law and that women, by virtue of their socialization and experiences, will be less adversarial, more interested in substantive justice (rather than strict procedural fairness), and will ultimately seek to empower their clients, rather than themselves. Advocates for women in policing have long contended that women's supposedly superior communication skills will make them better at resolving conflicts through dialogue, rather than force, and that they will be more empathetic and effective in working with victims and suspects (Appier 1998; Martin 1997). A similar argument has been made for increasing the number of women officers in men's prisons, where their presence is held to "normalize" and "soften" the work environment (Britton 1997).

On balance, however, empirical research and experience have not been supportive of these kinds of claims. Neither policing, nor prison work, nor law have been radically transformed or even become much kinder and gentler as women have increasingly moved into these occupations. The reason lies, in part, in a factor left out of the difference equation, the gendered structure of occupations and organizations themselves. This has been the focus of the second line of research. Pierce (1995), for example, finds that the adversarial structure of the legal profession, and litigation work in particular, leaves women few options; to succeed, they must adopt the tactics of their successful male peers, developing qualities such as aggression, intimidation, and impersonality. This creates a double bind for women, as those who take on this role are usually perceived more negatively than their male counterparts. Some women do resist, but most do so at the cost of success, at least as it has been defined by others. The gendered structure of the practice of litigation leaves little room for the meaningful assertion of difference, even if women lawyers were so inclined. Further, the masculinization of these occupations and of the organizations in which they are performed means that the rewards that accrue to difference vary dramatically by sex. Britton (1997) finds that male officers in men's and women's prisons benefit from asserting their unique abilities to use physical force. Women's purportedly unique gendered abilities, such as higher levels of empathy, emotionality, and communication skills, are often seen by administrators and coworkers, particularly in men's prisons, as either dangerous or extraneous.

These kinds of findings should not be taken to mean, however, that difference is immaterial. Women in these occupations do often differ from their male counterparts, particularly in relationship to issues like balancing work and family. Research also demonstrates that many do see themselves as different, both in terms of work styles and personality. It is also clear that we can meaningfully speak of characteristics that have been more or less associated with masculinity and femininity. Whether they display these characteristics or not, research and experience tell us that individual workers will be held accountable for them. An emerging trend in research on women in criminal justice occupations (and research on women and work more generally) recognizes this but at the same time argues that organizational and occupational structures are also important. This approach is in some ways a synthesis of the two perspectives outlined earlier and contends that the crucial issue is context; some work settings are more amenable to, or at least less penalizing of, gendered characteristics associated with women workers (Britton 2000). Miller (1999), for example, finds that community policing draws on traits like empathy, a service orientation, and communication skills and that women are often drawn to the work for this reason. Ely (1995) finds that women in law firms with a higher proportion of women in positions of power are less likely to see feminine-stereotyped characteristics as impediments to success and are more flexible in their ideas about gender overall. Anleu's research (1992) indicates that women have greater career opportunities in corporate legal departments than in private law firms, at least partly because occupational demands and domestic responsibilities are not as incompatible. Taken together, these findings suggest that while increasing the number of women in these occupations is an important step, structural changes in policing, prison, and legal organizations are also necessary to produce significant change in the direction of equality for women.

Emerging Issues

Kathleen Daly and Lisa Maher (1998) divide feminist criminology into two periods. The first phase, into which much of the work previously described falls, has focused on the tasks of filling in gaps, comparison, and critique. With little knowledge about women offenders, victims, and workers in the criminal justice system available, the first chore of feminist criminology was to provide this information. Though a substantial beginning has been made, it is likely that research in these areas will continue.

The second phase is characterized by work that disrupts the existing frameworks of criminology in more fundamental ways, resulting in the growth of a body of research and theory that Maureen Cain (1990) has called "transgressive criminology." For example, some feminist criminologists have crossed the traditional division between offending and victimization. As research on women offenders accumulated, it became clear that they were usually also victims, having experienced substantial physical and verbal abuse at the hands of intimates. The "blurred boundaries" thesis argues that women's offending is intimately linked to their previous victimization; a central task for feminist criminology in the years to come will be filling in the black box (Daly 1992) that connects the two. Undoubtedly, this will require a new, more nuanced conception of women offenders that disrupts the dichotomy in which they have been seen only either as innocent victims or as hardened criminals. Some work in this vein has already appeared; Lisa Maher's research (1997), described earlier, is but one example.

This dichotomy is deeply racialized, and this presents yet another challenge for feminist criminology. There is little doubt that the face of the much-mythologized new, more dangerous, female offender is that of a woman of color and that the most innocent victims have always been white. Feminist criminology is just beginning to come to terms with this. Whatever the difficulties posed by official statistics, research and theorizing must continue to reject the essentialism inherent in treating women as a unitary category (Simpson 1989). We already know much about the ways in which race, class, and sexual inequality interweave with women's experiences as victims, offenders, and workers. The challenge for feminist criminology in the years to come will lie in formulating theory and carrying out empirical studies that prioritize all of these dimensions, rather than relegating one or more of them to the background for the sake of methodological convenience.

Given men's overrepresentation as offenders and victims, the screaming silence in criminology around the connection between masculinity and crime has always been something of a paradox. Feminist criminology has recently begun to draw attention to this issue. Messerschmidt's (1993) was one of the first significant theoretical contributions in this area; it argues that, for men who lack access to other resources, crime can serve as an alternate means of doing masculinity. More recent accounts (see Newburn and Stanko 1994 for a review) have begun to untangle the contexts in which this use of crime is more or less likely and to explore the kinds of masculinities that result. A similar line of research has very recently begun to inquire into the social construction and reproduction of gendered identities among women involved in crime. On a parallel track, studies of work in criminal justice occupations are drawing attention to the individual and organizational construction of gender among both men and women workers (Britton 1997; Miller 1999; Pierce 1995). This research represents a promising direction for the field, both because it finally acknowledges men as men and because it moves us beyond dichotomized, static, individualistic notions about gender.

Finally, one of the most important issues facing activists in the discipline during the coming years will undoubtedly lie in rethinking feminist criminology's relationship with the state. Those working on issues connected to women offenders have already recognized the perils of the liberal strategy of strict legal equality. Such policies, when imposed in an already unequal and gendered context, have almost invariably disadvantaged women. Victimization activists have been more enthusiastic about the criminal justice system as a force for change but find that even well-intentioned policies, such as presumptive arrest for domestic violence offenders, have had unanticipated negative consequences. Women in policing, prison work, and law have also found that obtaining the legal right of access to these jobs is not enough to ensure equality.

Simply creating new laws to enforce, providing more offenders to incarcerate, and allowing women to work in the system have done little to disrupt its underlying structure, which is deeply gendered and racialized. As Carol Smart (1998) notes, the turning point for feminist criminology will come in realizing that "law is not simply. . . a set of tools or rules that we can bend into a more favourable shape" (31). Smart herself, arguably one of the founding mothers of feminist criminology, has recently disavowed the project entirely, arguing instead for a deconstructionist approach that disrupts and subverts criminology's traditional categories and frames of reference (Smart 1995). Rethinking feminist criminology's relationship to the state and to the criminal justice system does not necessarily mean that feminists in the discipline (or elsewhere) should reject efforts directed toward legal change. What this critique does suggest is that in feminism's continuing encounter with criminology, conceptions of justice, rather than law, should occupy a much more central place in our thinking (Klein 1995).

References

Adler, Freda. 1975. *Sisters in Crime: The Rise of the New Female Criminal.* New York: McGraw-Hill.

American Correctional Association. 1984. *Juvenile and Adult Correctional Departments, Institutions, Agencies and Paroling Authorities, United States and Canada.* College Park, MD: American Correctional Association.

Amir, Menachem. 1971. *Patterns in Forcible Rape.* Chicago: University of Chicago Press.

Anleu, Sharon Roach. 1992. Women in Law: Theory, Research and Practice. *Australian and New Zealand Journal of Sociology* 28(3):391–410.

Appier, Janis. 1998. *Policing Women: The Sexual Politics of Law Enforcement and the LAPD.* Philadelphia: Temple University Press.

Bachman, Ronet and Linda E. Saltzman. 1995. *Violence Against Women.* Washington, DC: Bureau of Justice Statistics.

Britton, Dana M. 1997. Gendered Organizational Logic: Policy and Practice in Men's and Women's Prisons. *Gender & Society* 11:796–818.

———. 2000. The Epistemology of the Gendered Organization. *Gender & Society* 14(3):418–435.

Brown, Beverley. 1986. Women and Crime: The Dark Figures of Criminology. *Economy and Society* 15(3):355–402.

Brownmiller, Susan. 1975. *Against Our Will: Men, Women, and Rape.* New York: Simon & Schuster.

Bureau of Labor Statistics. 1999. *Highlights of Women's Earnings in 1998.* Washington, DC: Government Printing Office.

Cain, Maureen. 1990. Towards Transgression: New Directions in Feminist Criminology. *International Journal of the Sociology of Law* 18:1–18.

Chesney-Lind, Meda. 1989. Girls' Crime and Women's Place: Toward a Feminist Model of Female Delinquency. *Crime and Delinquency* 35(1):5–29.

———. 1995. Preface. In *International Feminist Perspectives in Criminology: Engendering a Discipline,* ed. Nicole Hahn Rafter and Frances Heidensohn. Philadelphia: Open University Press.

———. 1996. Sentencing Women to Prison: Equality Without Justice. In *Race, Gender, and Class in Criminology: The Intersection,* ed. M. D. Schwartz and D. Milovanovic. New York: Garland.

Chilton, Roland and Susan K. Datesman. 1987. Gender, Race, and Crime: An Analysis of Urban Arrest Trends, 1960–1980. *Gender & Society* 1(2):152–71.

Daly, Kathleen. 1987. Discrimination in the Criminal Courts: Family, Gender, and the Problem of Equal Treatment. *Social Forces* 66(1):152–75.

———. 1992. Women's Pathways to Felony Court: Feminist Theories of Law-breaking and Problems of Representation. *Southern California Review of Law and Women's Studies* 2:11–52.

Daly, Kathleen and Meda Chesney-Lind. 1988. Feminism and Criminology. *Justice Quarterly* 5:497–538.

Daly, Kathleen and Lisa Maher. 1998. Crossroads and Intersections: Building from Feminist Critique. In *Criminology at the Crossroads*, ed. Kathleen Daly and Lisa Maher. New York: Oxford University Press.

Davis, Angela Y. 1997. Race and Criminalization: Black Americans and the Punishment Industry. In *The House That Race Built*, ed. Wahneema Lubiano. New York: Pantheon.

DeKeseredy, Walter S. 1996. The Left-Realist Perspective on Race, Class, and Gender. In *Race, Gender, and Class in Criminology*, ed. M. D. Schwartz and D. Milovanovic. New York: Garland.

Ely, Robin J. 1995. The Power in Demography: Women's Social Constructions of Gender Identity at Work. *Academy of Management Journal* 38(3):589–634.

Freedman, Estelle. 1981. *Their Sister's Keepers: Women's Prison Reform in America, 1830–1930.* Ann Arbor: University of Michigan Press.

Gelles, Richard and Donileen Loeske, eds. 1993. *Current Controversies on Family Violence.* London: Sage.

Gelsthorpe, Loraine and Allison Morris. 1988. Feminism and Criminology in Britain. *British Journal of Criminology* 28(2):93–110.

Hanmer, J. and M. Maynard. 1987. *Women, Violence, and Social Control.* London: Macmillan.

Klein, Dorie. 1995. Crime Through Gender's Prism: Feminist Criminology in the United States. In *International Feminist Perspectives in Criminology: Engendering a Discipline*, ed. Nicole Hahn Rafter and Frances Heidensohn. Philadelphia: Open University Press.

Madriz, Esther. 1997. *Nothing Bad Happens to Good Girls: Fear of Crime in Women's Lives.* Berkeley: University of California Press.

Maguire, Kathleen and Ann L. Pastore. 1999. *Sourcebook of Criminal Justice Statistics.* Washington, DC: Government Printing Office. Available at http:/ www.albany.edu/sourcebook.

Maher, Lisa. 1997. *Sexed Work: Gender, Race, and Resistance in a Brooklyn Drug Market.* New York: Oxford University Press.

Mann, Coramae Richey. 1995. Women of Color and the Criminal Justice System. In *The Criminal Justice System and Women: Offenders, Victims, and Workers*, ed. Barbara Raffel Price and Natalie J. Sokoloff. New York: McGraw-Hill.

Martin, Patricia Y. 1997. Gender, Accounts, and Rape Processing Work. *Social Problems* 44(4):464–82.

Martin, Susan E. and Nancy C. Jurik. 1996. *Doing Justice, Doing Gender: Women in Law and Criminal Justice Occupations.* Thousand Oaks, CA: Sage.

Matthews, Roger and Jock Young. 1986. *Confronting Crime.* London: Sage.

Menkel-Meadow, Carrie, 1987. Portia in a Different Voice: Speculating on a Women's Lawyering Process. *Berkeley Women's Law Journal* 1(1):39–63.

Messerschmidt, James W. 1993. *Masculinities and Crime.* Boston: Rowman & Littlefield.

Miller, Susan L. 1999. *Gender and Community Policing.* Boston: Northeastern University Press.

Moms, Allison. 1987. *Women, Crime, and Criminal Justice.* New York: Basil Blackwell.

Morris, Allison and Loraine Gelsthorpe. 1991. Feminist Perspectives in Criminology: Transforming and Transgressing. *Women & Criminal Justice* 2(2):3–26.

Morris, Allison and Ania Wilczynski. 1994. Rocking the Cradle: Mothers Who Kill Their Children. In *Moving Targets: Women, Murder, and Representation*, ed. Helen Birch. Berkeley: University of California Press.

National Center for Women in Policing. 1999. *Equality Denied: The Status of Women in Policing, 1998.* Arlington, VA: Feminist Majority Foundation.

Nazroo, James. 1995. Uncovering Gender Differences in the Use of Marital Violence: The Effect of Methodology. *Sociology* 29(3):475–94.

Newburn, Tim and Elizabeth A. Stanko, eds. 1994. *Just Boys Doing Business? Men, Masculinities and Crime.* New York: Routledge.

Pierce, Jennifer. 1995. *Gender Trials: Emotional Lives in Contemporary Law Firms.* Berkeley: University of California Press.

Price, Barbara Raffel and Natalie J. Sokoloff, eds. 1995. *The Criminal Justice System and Women: Offenders, Victims, and Workers.* New York: McGraw-Hill.

Rafter, Nicole Hahn and Frances Heidensohn. 1995. Introduction: The Development of Feminist Perspectives on Crime. In *International Feminist Perspectives in Criminology: Engendering a Discipline*, ed. Nicole Hahn Rafter and Frances Heidensohn. Philadelphia: Open University Press.

Russell, Diana E. H. 1982. *Rape in Marriage.* New York: Macmillan.

Schwendinger, Julia R. and Herman Schwendinger. 1983. *Rape and Inequality.* Newbury Park, CA: Sage.

Sherman, Lawrence A. 1992. *Policing Domestic Violence.* New York: Free Press.

Sherman, Lawrence A. and Richard A. Berk. 1984. The Specific Deterrent Effects of Arrest for Domestic Violence. *American Sociological Review* 49(2):261–92.

Simon, Rita James. 1975. *Women and Crime.* Lexington, MA: Lexington Books.

Simpson, Sally S. 1989. Feminist Theory, Crime, and Justice. *Criminology* 27:605–31.

Simpson, Sally S. and Lori Elis. 1995. Doing Gender: Sorting out the Caste and Crime Conundrum. *Criminology* 33(1):47–81.

Smart, Carol. 1976. *Women, Crime and Criminology: A Feminist Critique.* Boston: Routledge & Kegan Paul.

———. 1995. *Law, Crime and Sexuality: Essays in Feminism.* London: Sage.

———. 1998. The Woman of Legal Discourse. In *Criminology at the Crossroads*, ed. Kathleen Daly and Lisa Maher. New York: Oxford University Press.

Stanko, Elizabeth. 1990. *Everyday Violence.* London: Pandora.

Steffensmeier, Darrell. 1995. Trends in Female Crime: It's Still a Man's World. In *The Criminal Justice System and Women*, ed. Barbara R. Price and Natalie J. Sokoloff. New York: McGraw-Hill.

Steffensmeier, Darrell and Emilie Allan. 1996. Gender and Crime: Toward a Gendered Theory of Female Offending. *Annual Review of Sociology* 22:459–88.

Straus, Murray A., Richard J. Gelles, and Suzanne Steinmetz. 1980. *Behind Closed Doors.* New York: Doubleday.

Taylor, Ian, Paul Walton, and Jock Young. 1973. *The New Criminology.* London: Routledge & Kegan Paul.

3

Feminism for the Mainstream Criminologist
An Invitation

Jeanne Flavin

Introduction

It seems pro forma to begin an article on feminism deploring the fact that mainstream criminologists do not "get it." This work, however, is authored by someone who herself did not always "get" feminism and only in recent years has come to recognize feminist insights as not just helpful to understanding the relationship between gender and crime, but essential. This article assumes that many criminologists' dismissal of feminism stems as much from ignorance and misinformation as deliberate, ideological resistance. The purpose here is neither to attack mainstream approaches nor to unequivocally defend feminist ones. Rather, this article represents an invitation to academicians and practitioners from all intellectual and professional backgrounds to consider the contributions of feminist thought in theory, methods, policy, and practice.[1]

The rapidly expanding body of literature on women and gender suggests that the days when a criminologist could pass off a study of men as being a general and generalizable study of crime are numbered.[2] Accompanying the increased attention to gender has been increased opportunities for funding for research on women, gender, and crime. For instance, the 1994 Violence Against Women Act not only provided additional rights to victims of stalking, domestic violence, and sexual assault, but also

Reprinted from *Journal of Criminal Justice* vol. 29, Jeanne Flavin, "Feminism for the Mainstream Criminologist: An Invitation," pp. 271–285.

marked $1.6 billion for programs providing services to women victims of domestic violence. To take full advantage of the opportunities available to integrate gender into this research, teaching, and practice, however, requires an understanding of the myriad ways in which gender shapes both men's and women's experiences in the criminal justice system.

Feminist criminologists have been at the forefront in pointing out that when women and other marginalized groups are ignored, devalued, or misrepresented, society in general and the understanding of crime and justice in particular suffer as a result. "Feminism" and "feminist criminology" refer not to one perspective but a diverse set of perspectives that, generally speaking, focus on women's interests, are overtly political, and strive to present a new vision of equality and social justice (Rafter & Heidensohn, 1995). Feminists generally share a view that gender inequalities exist in society and that these inequalities should be addressed, though they may differ in their location of the source of the problem and the measures to be pursued.[3] As will be described in greater detail below, feminist contributions to the understanding of crime and justice cannot be underestimated: Arguably "no other perspective has done as much to raise societal consciousness about the oppression of women and gender inequality" (Wonders, 1999, p. 113).

Despite feminism's impact on the study and practice of criminal justice, many scholars and practitioners lack an understanding of even the most rudimentary aspects of feminist criminological thought, much less feminism's relevance to criminal justice. Part of the problem is that much feminist scholarship is still published in specialized journals (e.g., *Women and Criminal Justice, Gender and Society, Violence Against Women, Feminist Theory*), included in "special issues" focusing on some aspect of women and crime [cf. *Journal of Contemporary Criminal Justice, 14* (2) (1998); *American Psychologist, 54* (1) (1999); *Homicide Studies, 2* (4) (1998); *Corrections Today, 60* (7) (1998); *International Journal of Comparative and Applied Criminal Justice, 21* (2) (1997); *Crime and Delinquency, 41* (4) (1995); *Journal of Criminal Justice Education, 3* (2) (1992); *Southern California Review of Law and Women's Studies, 2* (1) (1992); *Social Pathology, 3* (2) (1997); *Law and Social Inquiry, 19* (4) (1995); *Justice Quarterly, 12* (1) (1995); *Crime and Delinquency, 35* (1) (1989)] or receives book-length treatments that require more of a commitment than many nonfeminist criminologists are willing to invest.[4] This literature frequently assumes a baseline level of knowledge that nonfeminists or scholars new to the study of gender and crime may not possess. As with other approaches, feminist scholarship often relies on terminology (e.g., "androcentricism," "intersectionality," "standpoint epistemology," "gender essentialism," "reflexivity," "doing gender," "hegemonic masculinity") that—while widely recognized by many feminist-oriented criminologists—alienates rather than informs practitioners or scholars from more mainstream orientations.[5]

Feminism and mainstream criminology seem trapped in, if not a vicious cycle, at least an unproductive one. Historically, feminism has had a peripheral relationship to the discipline on the whole and mainstream criminologists have not been widely exposed to feminist perspectives. Many men and women continue to assume (falsely) that "feminism is about women, while criminology is about men" (Naffine, 1996: pp. 1–2), which, in turn, keeps feminist perspectives marginal to the discipline.[6] The result is that many academicians, practitioners, and policymakers have yet to understand, much less appreciate, the importance of gender and feminism's contribution to criminology.

To address this problem, the present work dedicates itself to explaining some of the major feminist insights in the interrelated areas of theory (including theories of knowledge), methodology, and policy to criminologists unfamiliar with feminism. Following an overview of how gender was addressed in the study and practice of criminal justice, examples are presented that illustrate feminist concerns as well as the diversity of feminist scholarship.[7]

Women and Gender in Criminology

When the question arises as to why many standard criminal justice texts dedicate relatively little attention to women, one of the most oft-cited responses is that women comprise a small percentage of those involved in the criminal justice system. For example, according to official crime statistics, women comprise only around 7 percent of prison inmates and 11 percent of jail inmates, 21 percent of those arrested, and 14 percent of all sworn officers in large police departments (Federal Bureau of Investigations [FBI], 1998; Gilliard, 1999; National Center for Women and Policing, 1999).

As a justification for neglect, many people recognize that this explanation falls short on a number of fronts. First, while women are underrepresented as victims, offenders, and workers, the *number* of women involved in the criminal processing system is large and growing. Currently, women account for nearly 2.3 million of those arrested, including half a million arrests for index crimes and 83,000 arrests for violent crimes (FBI, 1998). Nearly 64,000 adult women were being held in local jails at midyear 1998 and almost 83,000 women were imprisoned under the jurisdiction of state and federal authorities (Gillard, 1999). Over 32,000 women are employed in large law enforcement agencies and another 42,000 are custody/security staff employed in state and federal correctional facilities (Bureau of Justice Statistics [BJS], 1997; National Center for Women and Policing, 1999).

Secondly, policies and practices that disproportionately affect men have an impact on women as well. For instance, it is women who shoulder the economic and emotional responsibility for childcare when a male parent is incarcerated. Also, as corrections budgets have been increased, state funds to support low-income women and their children have been cut along with social service jobs that are disproportionately staffed by women (Danner, 1998).

Moreover, while the criminal justice system is overwhelmingly male, gender is relevant when we are discussing men's involvement in the system as well as women's. Gender is the strongest predictor of criminal involvement: boys and men perpetrate more, and more serious, crimes than do girls and women. There is a benefit from asking, "Why are women so underrepresented in crime?" as well as examining why men are overrepresented. Also, both men and women "do gender," that is, handle situations in such a way that the outcome is considered gender-appropriate. Studying how men and women accomplish masculinity and femininity prompts one to consider how social structures constrain and channel behavior that, in turn, may influence a person's criminal or law-abiding behavior or their actions in the workplace (Martin & Jurik, 1996; Messerschmidt, 1997; West & Zimmerman, 1987).

Discussing gender and crime is definitely an easier exercise now than it would have been thirty years ago. Since the 1970s, hundreds of books and articles have appeared that reflect the in-roads feminism has made into criminology and related fields. Feminism's influence, though, has been far from uniform. Most criminal justice scholarship, practice, and policymaking that consider women and gender adopt one of three general approaches (Daly, 1995; Goodstein, 1992).

In the main, most criminological scholarship focuses on men or extends theorizing based on men's experiences to women without offering any reconceptualization (Daly, 1995). In contrast, some scholars recognize that women's criminal justice experiences are often ignored or distorted when one simply "adds women and stirs." A second approach, then, includes feminist research that focuses attention on crimes that adversely affect women more than they affect men, such as domestic violence. This approach also pays attention to the ways in which women's experiences differ not just from men's, but from each other based on characteristics such as race, ethnicity, class, age, and sexual orientation. While addressing women's "invisibility" is an improvement over simply adding women and stirring, scholarship in this category still evinces a tendency to treat men as the norm and women as the anomalies. Such an approach precludes efforts to achieve fairer treatment of men and women throughout the criminal justice system. If an entire field has been shaped by a male norm, then one must seriously question whether the issues deemed important to the understanding of victims, offenders, and workers include those that are important for women.

Recognizing the importance of studying women on their own terms, some scholars have adopted a more advanced feminist approach. For example, Beth E. Richie's (1996) interviews with women inmates led her to develop the idea of "gender entrapment" as a means of understanding the criminal behavior of battered African American women. For many of these women, Richie (p. 4) concluded criminal behavior is a logical extension of "their racialized gender identities, their culturally expected gender roles, and the violence in their intimate relationships." Richie found that nearly all of the battered Black women in her study occupied a privileged status in their families growing up, receiving extra attention, opportunities, and material possessions. These women, however, also felt burdened by a responsibility to "make good" on their families' investments in their futures. As a result, their identities were closely aligned with meeting the needs of others, an identity that made them vulnerable to abuse as adults (Richie, 1996).

Feminist criminologists hope that, in the future, approaches such as Richie's, which recognize a multiplicity of factors and offer a richer contextual analysis, will be the rule rather than the exception. Theories and research will "reach beyond the current stereotypes of women, and beyond the current real lives of women, to think of women differently" (Naffine, 1996, p. 143). The knowledge base will be transformed to include a theoretical and analytical focus on the interacting relations of class, race, and gender, as well as sexual orientation, age, and ethnicity. Admittedly, to date, feminist approaches have worked better to criticize than to construct core theoretical frameworks as Richie did. Although critiques are valuable in that they call attention to women's invisibility or misrepresentation in criminology, feminists and nonfeminists alike generally recognize that feminist perspectives must move beyond criticizing from the sidelines if the criminal justice system's approach to gender is to be reconstructed. This poses a major challenge given that one's inherited ways of thinking obstruct one's ability to imagine or comprehend new ways of viewing crime and criminal justice (Collins, 1998; Daly, 1995; Eichler, 1988). By acknowledging some of the limitations of mainstream approaches and considering feminist perspectives as one possible means of advancing the understanding of gender and crime, feminist and nonfeminist scholars hopefully can work together to address the criminal justice ground remaining not only to be covered, but plowed and replanted.

Feminist Epistemologies

Epistemology refers to "theories of what knowledge is, what makes it possible, and how to get it" (Harding, 1991, p. 308). Feminist perspectives have made more progress in fields that have stronger traditions of interpretive understanding such as literature and history. By contrast, the criminological tradition continues to be deeply embedded in the scientific method (Naffine, 1996). Much of mainstream criminology is rooted in claims that "science is value neutral" and "scientific methods protect against our scholarship being contaminated by subjectivity." Studies can be replicated, positivism assumes, because researchers produce knowledge in similar ways, rendering individual criminologists interchangeable with others.

Are some beliefs better supported by empirical evidence than others? Yes. Are there advantages to using traditional (e.g., quantitative) research methods? Absolutely. Does the use of certain research procedural safeguards mitigate against biased results? Of course. These points are not disputed here. What is challenged is the assumption that one can and should strive to achieve "absolute objectivity" and universally valid knowledge.

Recently, in a special issue of *The New York Times Magazine*, Richard Powers heralded the "vesting of authority in experiment" as the best idea of the millennium. Powers (1999, p. 83) acknowledged, however, that thinkers "from Ludwig Wittgenstein to Thomas Kuhn and beyond" have expressed concern

> that fact and artifact may be closer than most empiricists are comfortable accepting . . . That great empiricists have rejected initial data on hunches, until their observations produced more acceptable numbers. That scientists need pre-existing theory and supposition even to ask the questions that will lead to data. That the shape of a question produces the data that answer it.

These concerns and others lie at the heart of feminist epistemology.[8] The most conservative feminist epistemological program, feminist empiricism, basically accepts the value of the scientific method, but points out that ignoring women or misrepresenting their experiences is methodologically unsound. Feminist empiricism tries to correct "bad science" through stricter adherence to existing norms of scientific inquiry. This approach has filled in gaps in the knowledge of women victims of crime (particularly violence in the home and between intimates), the judicial treatment of offending women and girls, and the experiences of women criminal justice workers (Martin & Jurik, 1996; Naffine, 1996; Smart, 1995).

By contrast, other feminist epistemologies—feminist standpoint theories, for example—go beyond critiquing empirical practice to challenging mainstream criminology's empirical assumptions. Many feminists consider science and knowledge (as well as our definitions of crimes, masculinity, and femininity) to be socially situated and question how disinterested knowledge or "objectivity" is possible in a society that is deeply stratified by gender, race, and class. As philosopher Sandra Harding (1991, p. 59) observes, ". . . [T]he subject of belief and of knowledge is never simply an individual, let alone an abstract one capable of transcending its own historical location. It is always an individual in a particular social situation."

Feminist standpoint theories assume that the perspective of the researcher influences what is known. Standpoint feminists try to construct knowledge from the perspective of the persons being studied on the grounds that the perspective of the oppressed or marginalized tends to be less distorted. The powerful have more interest in obscuring the conditions that produce their privileges and authority than the dominated groups have in hiding the conditions that produce their situation (Harding, 1991).

A third feminist epistemological approach, feminist postmodernism, criticizes standpoint feminists for assuming that women are a "clearly defined and uncontroversially given interest group"' (Smart, 1995, p. 10). While positivists and other "modernists" (including many feminists) claim that the truth can be determined provided all agree on responsible ways of going about it, postmodern critics argue for multiple truths that take context into account (Collins, 1998, pp. 196–197; Wonders, 1999). Many criminologists recognize that "knowledge" or "truth" often reflects the perspective of those with more power (e.g., definitions of what actions are considered illegal, what constitutes a fair punishment). Postmodernists take this further, questioning whether any knowledge is knowable and rejecting the ideas that there is a universal definition of justice, i.e., one that would be true for all people, all of the time (DeKeseredy & Schwartz, 1996; Wonders, 1999). Toward this end, postmodernism emphasizes the importance of alternative discourses and accounts and frequently takes the form of examining the effects of language and symbolic representation, e.g., how legal discourse constructs different "types of woman" such as "prostitute" or "bad mother" (Smart, 1998, pp. 28–30).

Some charge that postmodernism basically amounts to a "call to inaction" (Tong, 1989, p. 232). If justice is different for everyone depending on one's perspective, then what is the point of trying to pursue it? If one cannot be certain that the good quality knowledge produced will provide useful insight (or a fair outcome) then, as one student asked, "Why not just sit by the pool?" (Smart, 1995, p. 212). Such criticism, however, paints an overly dismal view of the postmodern perspective. Postmodern and feminist scholars recognize a responsibility to build bridges across diverse groups in order to work collectively—not to arrive at a universal understanding of justice, but "to do our best to make judgments that make the world a good place to be" for everyone (Wonders, 1999, p. 122).

Regardless of where one falls on the "knowledge is scientifically derived" to "knowledge is socially produced" to "knowledge is power/power is knowledge" continuum, it is hard to imagine a criminal justice enterprise where epistemology is irrelevant. Yet rarely does it receive even passing mention. Given that one routinely encounters "totalitarianism," "bureaucratization," "psychopharmacology," and "heteroskedasticity" in academic publications, it is more than a matter of "epistemology" being a word that does not roll easily off the tongue.

The nature of the concept itself may contribute to the reluctance to address it. It is far easier to open a discussion by stating "The following are some of the major theories of crime causation . . ." than challenging whether one can ever claim to "know" why people commit crimes or any other class of "truths." Questioning how knowledge has been or ought to be produced can be unsettling, and the process of inquiry—almost by definition—does not lead to straightforward, universally accepted answers. Even among feminists, this process has been described as painful, if inevitable and productive (Smart, 1995, p. 11). At the root of the problem, no doubt, is that most people were not intellectually reared to appreciate the importance of epistemology, much less articulate it. Yet recognition of the importance of epistemology and the biases of the scientific method lies at the core of transforming the discipline. Gaining a better understanding of gender and crime requires not only filling in gaps in knowledge but also challenging the assumptions upon which existing "knowledge" is based.

Theoretical Contributions

Charges that criminology is "male-centered" (or "androcentric") raise hackles among students, practitioners, and scholars alike who incorrectly reduce the criticism to an attack on the sex of the researchers. The reality is that women are vulnerable to androcentric bias just as men are capable of overcoming it. Male dominance of the discipline contributes to androcentricity, but is by no means the only source.

Ideally, theoretical development is grounded in a larger literature, building upon the insights and strengths of past scholarship. Past theorizing regarding the relationship between gender and crime has been seriously hampered by the fact that historically, most of it has focused on explaining men's experiences of crime and justice and assuming these explanations also apply to women. By contrast, feminist scholarship has strengthened criminological theory in two major ways: by pointing out the limitations of applying theories of male criminality to women and by developing theories of men's and women's criminality.

Scholars such as Dorie Klein (1973/1995) and Eileen Leonard (1973/1995) have made systematic attempts to apply traditional theories of crime (i.e., anomie theory, labeling theory, differential association, subcultural theory, and Marxism) to women, and concluded that these theories are unsuited for explaining female patterns of crime. For example, Robert Merton (1938) also neglected to apply his anomie theory to women. His theory holds that when people lack legitimate means (e.g., a job, a savings account) to achieve socially accepted goals (e.g., material and monetary success), they innovate (e.g., steal, write bad checks). His theory also assumes that financial success is as important a goal for women as it is for men and fails to address why women—who are overrepresented among the poor and thus arguably subjected to more strain than men—are less likely to deviate.

Feminists have also taken issue with more recent theorizing that, while showing signs of trying to be more sensitive to issues of women and gender, also has shortcomings. One pitfall occurs when scholars strive to create a "gender-neutral" theory that makes no differentiation regarding the theory's applicability to men and women. For example, Michael R. Gottfredson and Travis Hirschi's (1990) *A General Theory of Crime* (1990) attempts to be linguistically gender-neutral in discussing victimization and parenting. In doing so, Gottfredson and Hirschi overlook the reality that violent victimization is not gender-neutral (nor race- or class-neutral, for that matter); nearly two-thirds of men's nonfatal violent victimizations are committed by a stranger, while nearly two-thirds of women's nonfatal violent victimizations are committed by someone she knows (Craven, 1997). Elsewhere, Gottfredson and Hirschi assert that mothers and fathers are interchangeable in their influence in the socialization process, apparently denying the gendered character of parenting. Gottfredson and Hirschi's inattention to gendered inequalities is illustrated by "both their gender-neutral stance when inappropriate and by lack of gender specificity when appropriate" (Miller & Burack, 1993, p. 116).

Feminist scholarship has been invaluable in calling attention to the "generalizability problem" of many traditional theoretical approaches (Daly & Chesney-Lind, 1988), but feminist contributions to theory have not been confined to the level of critique. Increasingly, feminist perspectives are serving as the basis for theories of crime and crime control. For example, Julia and Herman Schwendinger's (1983) Marxist feminist analysis, *Rape and Inequality,* links the nature and extent of rape to the unequal gender relations and class struggles that capitalism produces. James Messerschmidt's (1986) socialist feminist work, *Capitalism, Patriarchy, and Crime*, sees both class and patriarchy as contributing to the type and seriousness of crime. Radical feminist approaches, which emphasize the role of patriarchy and masculine control of women's labor and sexuality, arguably have had more impact on woman abuse research than any other theoretical perspective (Simpson, 1989).

Another feminist theoretical contribution has been to point out the absence of research on masculinity. Men have been treated as the norm in the criminal justice system to such a degree that their gender has been ignored. The failure of criminological theories to address gender has led not only to the neglect of women in theory and research, but also to the delay in recognizing that gender shapes men's experiences as well as women's. Naffine (1996, p. 6) observes that "crime, men and masculinity have an intimate relationship, so intimate that we often fail to see it, and so intimate that it can seem natural."

In recent years, the attention to women and gender prompted the reconsideration of what is "known" about men's experiences and led to studies of masculinities and crime. Much of this research relies on Robert W. Connell's (1987, 1995) conceptualizations of "hegemonic masculinity" and "emphasized femininity" that is, the "dominant forms of gender to which other types of masculinity and femininity are subordinated or opposed" (Messerschmidt, 1997, p. 10). In the United States, the dominant, culturally supported form of masculinity is based on White, middle-class, heterosexual men and emphasizes characteristics such as paid employment, subordination of women and girls, authority, control, and rationality (Pyke, 1996).

This scholarship emphasizes that race, gender, and class are not only social constructs, but also processes involving creative human actors, rather than static, categorical variables. As such, gender, race, and class are not equally significant in every social setting, but vary in importance depending upon the context (Messerschmidt, 1997; West & Zimmerman, 1987). Crime provides one structurally permitted means of establishing a man's masculinity when other channels for doing so are blocked due to one's race, ethnicity, class, or age.

For example, Jana Bufkin (1999) relies on James Messerschmidt's structured action theory to illustrate how bias crimes are a means of "doing" gender. These overwhelmingly male bias crime offenders situationally achieve masculinity by attacking members of groups (i.e., women, homeless people, people with disabilities, religious, racial, and ethnic minorities, and homosexuals/bisexuals) who undermine the hegemonic masculine ideal. Several characteristics of known bias crimes (i.e., age, sex, number, and alcohol consumption of the perpetrators, the language used during and after the attacks, the seriousness of the injuries) suggest that the prime motivation for bias crimes is to accomplish masculinity.

Similarly, Jody Miller (1998) reports that while the women and men in her study reported similar motivations to commit robbery, the ways in which they commit robbery highlight the clear gender hierarchy that exists on the streets. Men tend to use physical violence and/or a gun to confront the victim, and typically target other men. Miller (1998, pp. 50–51) concludes that "male robbers . . . clearly view the act of robbery as a masculine accomplishment in which men compete with other men for money and status . . . The routine use of guns, physical contact, and violence in male-on-male robberies is a reflection of the masculine ideologies shaping men's robberies." By contrast, women robbers take into account the gendered nature of their environment by robbing other females who are less likely than males to be armed and are perceived as weak and easily intimidated. When women do rob men, they use perceptions of women as weak and sexually available to their advantage to manipulate men into situations where they become vulnerable to being robbed.

The growing body of scholarship that considers the situational constructions of gender, race, and class also helps to address concerns that much feminist criminology (as with mainstream criminology) tends to be gender essentialist; implying that there is a universal "women's experience" or "men's experience" that can be described independently of other facets of experience such as race, ethnicity, and class (Rice, 1990). The effect of essentialist perspectives has been to "reduce the lives of people who experience multiple forms of oppression to addition problems: 'racism + sexism = straight Black women's experience'" (Harris, 1997, p. 11). Racial and ethnic minority women victims, offenders, and workers are not simply subjected to "more" disadvantage than White women; their oppression is often of a qualitatively different kind. Theories of crime and justice need to acknowledge, for example, that "Black women experience sexual and patriarchal oppression by Black men but at the same time struggle alongside them against racial oppression" (Rice, 1990, p. 63).

In sum, overcoming androcentric theorizing involves more than simply extending theories designed to explain male criminality to women or presenting theories in gender-neutral terms. It requires recognizing gender as a social process relevant to the actions of men as well as women. It demands that we overcome essentialist tendencies in order to consider the complex ways in which gender interacts with other social characteristics. Compared to thirty years ago, more research and policymaking efforts consider feminist theoretical contributions. By and large, however, feminist theories have not been fully integrated into the study and practice of criminal justice and consequently have not received the same attention as varieties of strain theories, social control theories, or individualist theories. As a result, the richness and insights of feminist perspectives have yet to be widely appreciated.[9] At minimum, evaluations of a theory's merits should be broadened to include feminist critiques and to consider how a given theory might be revised to recognize gender as a central organizing factor in social life (Renzetti, 1993). Ideally, to ensure that successive generations of practitioners and scholars will not replicate existing androcentric and essentialist biases, efforts to fully integrate feminist theoretical critiques and feminist theorizing into undergraduate and graduate curricula should be expanded (see Goodstein, 1992; Wilson, 1991; Wonders & Caulfield, 1993, for specific strategies for doing so).

Research Methodology and Methods

Just as feminists vary in their theoretical orientation and their views of how knowledge should be acquired, "there is not a distinctive feminist methodology but rather a feminist perspective on the research process" (Taylor & Rupp, 1991, p. 127). With this in mind, the following sections discuss major feminist methodological themes as they are manifested in criminological research. These themes relate to the choice of topic, choice of research methods, the subjective experiences of doing research (or "reflexivity"), and the relationship between the researcher and the research subjects (Gelsthorpe, 1990). Another area of feminist concern—the relationship between policy/action and research—is discussed in the next section. Admittedly, many of the methodological issues presented below are not unique to feminism but are shared by scholars of other orientations, particularly other critical ones, but their close identification with feminism warrants their inclusion here.

Choice of Research Topic

As the work cited throughout this article illustrates, feminist criminological scholarship comprises a substantial and mature body of literature that poses "some of the more difficult and interesting questions about the nature of (criminological) knowledge" (Naffine, 1996, p. 4). For example,

> [t]here are feminists who have carried out the more conventional (but necessary) empirical work of documenting sex bias within the criminal justice system. Feminists have questioned the scientific methods deployed by criminologists, as well as their highly orthodox approach to the nature of knowledge. Feminists have engaged with criminological theory, across the range, questioning its ability to provide general explanations of human behaviour. Feminists have provided an abundance of data about crime from the viewpoint of women (to counter the more usual viewpoint of men), and feminists have also helped to develop new epistemologies that question the very sense of writing from the perspective of a woman (or, for that matter, from the perspective of a man). (Naffine, 1996, p. 4)

While sharing a view that gender is central to the understanding of crime and justice, feminist criminological scholarship reflects considerable diversity and originality in the choice of topic. As the above quotation suggests, feminists have addressed time-honored criminological questions. More recently, feminists have applied themselves to newer lines of criminological inquiry such as the impact of sentencing policies on women (cf., Raeder, 1993), the blurred boundaries between victimization and criminalization (cf. Daly & Maher, 1998), and the media's role in shaping perceptions of crime and justice (cf. Chancer, 1998; Danner & Carmody, 1999), to name but a few.

M. Joan McDermott (1992) observes that feminist research has evolved such that it is no longer just scholarship that is "on, by, and for women" but encompasses a larger sphere of inquiry. Feminist scholarship includes research "on" gender that includes men and masculinity; it recognizes that research conducted "by" a woman is not representative of all women's experiences nor does being biologically male disqualify one from working from a feminist perspective. And, though remaining committed to positions "for" women, feminism ultimately aims to benefit both men and women.

Choice of Research Methods and Methodologies

One of the thorniest points of contention is the discussion surrounding the use of qualitative and quantitative research methodologies; a debate that has been described as "sterile and based on false polarization" (Jayartne & Stewart, 1991, p. 85). Despite a perception that feminist scholarship is primarily qualitative, "feminist researchers use just about any and all of the methods . . . that traditional androcentric researchers have used. Of course, precisely how they carry out these methods of evidence gathering is often strikingly different . . . it is not by looking at research methods that one will be able to identify the distinctive features of the best of feminist research" (Herding, 1987, pp. 2–3). Not all feminist research is qualitative and not all studies that rely on qualitative methods are conducted from a feminist orientation.

Quantitative approaches obviously offer a number of advantages to the study of gender and crime, e.g., findings from representative samples may be more generalizable, statistical techniques can handle more contextual variables and permit simultaneous evaluation of complex theoretical models and interaction terms. Quantitative methods have come under fire, though, for obscuring the experience of women. Surveys frequently require coding individuals' responses into categories predefined by researchers, but the reality is that "experiences don't come in little boxes that are ready to be labeled and counted" (McDermott, 1992, p. 247). Also, when using existing data, it is hard to avoid adopting a "dataset mentality" and limit research questions to those that can be answered by available variables. These problems present a Catch-22 of sorts: one only collects and records information thought to be important, but characteristics cannot be established as important until the data are possessed. For example, because most large databases were originally designed to capture information salient to the processing and treatment of men offenders, characteristics that were particularly salient to women might not be recorded (e.g., extent of caretaking responsibilities for children and the elderly, childhood victimization experiences, obstetric/gynecological history).[10]

By contrast, qualitative approaches such as interviews, ethnographies, and life histories permit women and men to articulate or conceptualize their experiences more completely and in their own terms, potentially providing more accurate and valid information. This is particularly important given many feminists' interest in examining the situation-at-hand, "taking real life as the starting point, its subjective concreteness as well as its societal entanglements" (Mies, 1991, p. 66). This view that subjective experience is part of science should not be misconstrued as a belief that simply describing an individual's experiences or feelings in itself comprises a scientific treatment of a problem. Feminists in the main recognize the problem of viewing "the personal as inherently paradigmatic, the individual life story as coherent, unified, morally inspiring" (Kauffman, 1992/1993, pp. 262–263). Instead, many feminist scholars use narrative statements to identify important themes while at the same time giving their findings a human face. For example, one can report that many incarcerated girls are concerned about leaving the institutional setting, but the point is better illustrated by quoting girls' statements such as, "I've been here so long, I don't want to just be thrown out. I'm anxious" and "I was scared to help an old lady [cross the street] when I was on [a day] leave once. I felt like I had institution written all over me" (Belknap, Holsinger, & Dunn, 1997, p. 396).

Despite their advantages and roots in the Chicago School in the work of scholars such as W. I. Thomas and Robert Park, qualitative research methods have had to fight off a reputation as an oxymoron in mainstream criminal justice circles.[11] Qualitative methods are sometimes stereotyped as unsystematic and politically motivated and therefore unscientific and overtly biased (Jayartne & Stewart, 1991, p. 93). Also, because qualitative research may be very time-consuming since it tends to involve more and more intensive contact with the research subjects, the samples in a qualitative study tend to be relatively small and homogenous (Cannon, Higginbotham, & Leung, 1988/1991). In view of the limitations of both methodologies, many feminists join mainstream methodologists in employing a combination of quantitative and qualitative methods in order to compensate for the weaknesses in one method by incorporating the strengths of another. For example, Barbara Owen's (1998) study of women prisoners, *In the Mix*, includes a quasi-ethnographic study of a women's prison as well as a systematic survey of female prisoners and parolees. Kathleen Daly's (1994) *Gender, Crime and Punishment* uses both a statistical analysis of sentencing disparity for a wide sample of cases, as well as qualitative analysis of a "deep sample" of forty matched pairs of women and men convicted of similar offenses.

Reflexivity

While most scholars support acknowledging the limitations of a particular methodological technique employed (be it quantitative or qualitative), feminist scholarship also emphasizes the importance of critically examining the nature of the research process itself. "Reflexivity" refers to identifying the assumptions underlying the research endeavor and often includes the investigator's reaction to doing the research.

> For the most part, criminology is unreflective. While conscious that researchers should not bring their prejudices to the research table, many criminologists, in their search for neutrality, fail to consider their own identity in their investigative enterprises. Perhaps this is the aftershock of attempting to impose the strictures and methods of the physical sciences on criminology in our effort to make it more "scientific." (Pettiway, 1997, pp. xv–xvi)

Reflecting on the research process calls attention to possible sources of bias introduced as well as provides guidance to future researchers. Reflexivity also prompts examination of whether research can ever truly be said to be "objective." The identity of a researcher shapes even a deliberately noninterpretive research endeavor such as presenting transcripts of taped interviews with women involved in drugs and crime given that the researcher frames the questions, focuses the interviews, and edits the transcripts for publication (Pettiway, 1997). Not only do many feminists consider subjectivity as unavoidable, but some argue it may be a strength of a study. Barbara Owen (1998) reported that the relationships she formed with several prisoners led her to better appreciate the women's experiences from their own point of view. The result, she suggested, is a study that not only contributed to a "scientific" understanding of women prisoners, but to a political awareness of their marginalized status.

In other words, it cannot simply be assumed that one's choice of methods guarantees objective research. Reflexivity strengthens the research process by promoting greater honesty and awareness of the limitations and biases inherent in the research. It also provides a valuable guide to other researchers who may be considering undertaking similar research projects. Further, as will be discussed next, reflexivity encourages one to think about the relationship between themselves as researchers and the people who comprise the research subjects.

Relationship between Researcher and Subjects

Feminists have criticized researchers' objectification and exploitation of their subjects, particularly when information is gained through interviews or surveys. Objectification occurs when it is assumed that a radical difference exists between the roles of scientist and subject. In the most extreme positivist forms, studying human beings is treated, in principle, as no different from studying things (Gorelick, 1996, p. 24). While conventional criminology assumes that scientific detachment requires emotional detachment, the quest for neutrality and objectivity can be a disadvantage when so much emphasis is placed on "maintaining distance" that context and recognition of the individual humanity of the subjects are stripped away.

Part of the problem is that traditional guidelines for interviewing (i.e., advise interviewers to adopt an objective, noninvolved stance; view interviews as noninteractive) assume the situation is a one-way hierarchical process. When one assumes that the interviewer's role is to collect but never to provide information, the interviewee is reduced to mere data (Carty, 1996). By contrast, many feminists propose treating interviewees as informants or experts, and using an open-ended format in order to permit new questions to emerge during the course of the interview (Taylor & Rupp, 1991). A feminist methodological approach tries to minimize hierarchical relationships within the research process. Ideally, the research enterprise will strive for a collaborative and reciprocal association between the researcher and the subject consistent with Ann Oakley's maxim: "No intimacy without reciprocity" (quoted in May, 1993, p. 90).

Admittedly, there are difficulties and some drawbacks in minimizing the distance between interviewer and subject. Researchers responsible to funding agencies may not have total control of how their studies are conducted. The subjects themselves may not embrace the idea of collaboration. Particularly in criminal justice, it seems unlikely that offenders, victims, and even many criminal justice workers will see themselves on equal footing with the academic researchers. Language, dress, age, and other cues may serve as constant reminders of the differences in roles and status between the researcher and the subjects. For instance, Belknap et al. (1997) noticed that while juvenile justice professionals seemed to forget the presence of researcher-onlookers while participating in a focus group, many of the incarcerated girls in the same study tended to check how the researchers responded to their own and their peers' comments (Belknap et al., 1997).

Confidentiality and privacy issues—always a concern when a study involves human subjects—become even more important when researchers form rapport, ties, even friendships with the study participants. Women respondents may find it easier to reveal intimate details of their victimization or offending experiences when the interviewer is a woman. All researchers "must take extra precautions not to betray the trust so freely given" (Fonow & Cook, 1991, p. 8), since researchers may not have complete control of how information will be used once it is gathered from respondents. In spite of these obstacles, a number of specific actions may be undertaken to reduce the distance between researchers and subjects, e.g., sharing drafts of the report with the subjects and soliciting their feedback, encouraging subjects to ask questions and responding with reasonable answers, and reciprocating subjects for the help they provide.

As noted earlier, "feminist research methods" is something of a misnomer. Many of the measures championed by feminist criminologists can be and have been adopted by researchers from mainstream orientations. There remains a need, though, for criminologists to give more thought to the approach to research. This not only means giving qualitative methods their due but also considering reflexivity and the relationship between researcher and subject. For example, research proposals routinely justify their choice of a mail survey versus face-to-face interviews on the grounds of time and money. It should also be considered how the subject's race, gender, and class might influence the choice of research methods. Proposals should be critiqued not only on the basis of sample selection and measurements, but also whether subjects were reciprocated for their participation in the study and what steps were taken to reduce the distance between researcher and subject. Attending to these aspects of the research process does not constitute subscribing to a "feminist methodology" per se. Rather, it indicates a commitment to good research practices designed to give greater visibility to the experiences of women (and other historically marginalized groups) and to increase the subject's involvement in the research process.

Policy and Action

In reviewing the presidential addresses to the American Society of Criminology, Ngaire Naffine (1996) observes that increasingly mainstream criminologists are encouraged to be applied and practical, to inform policymakers, and contribute to the public debate about crime. Here again is an area where feminist criminology has proven valuable to the larger criminal justice arena. Feminists have always placed a premium on policy and action; one of feminism's defining components is a standing and overt commitment to identifying "a set of strategies for change" (Daly & Chesney-Lind, 1988, p. 502).

Feminists are perhaps best known for raising awareness of violence against women and the need for laws and policies regarding marital rape, acquaintance rape, stalking, and other crimes that disproportionately involve women victims. Feminists have also called for responses to women victims of crime that reflect an appreciation for the differences that exist among women. For example, a shortage of bilingual and bicultural criminal justice workers creates a system ill prepared to address many battered Latinas' claims. Latinas and other racial and ethnic minority women must decide whether to seek assistance from an outsider who "may not look like her, sound like her, speak her language, or share any of her cultural values" (Rivera, 1994/1997, p. 261). Minority women may fear that the police will not do enough (ignoring their complaints) and/or that the police will do too much (being overly zealous toward the minority men they arrest). Some women also may encounter a failure on the part of their racial, ethnic, religious, and community leaders to recognize "a sexist problem within the community. . . as important as a racist problem outside of it" (Rasche, 1988/1995, p. 257).

Feminism's impact in the arena of domestic violence and other forms of violence against women has been substantial, but to confine feminism's contribution to these issues is to sell feminism short. Feminists also engage in policy evaluation, asking "What is this policy supposed to accomplish?," "How will it actually be implemented?," "Who wins and who loses if this policy is adopted?," "What can we do to improve on this?" (Miller, 1998a, 1998b; Renzetti, 1998).

Women's stake in the "war on crime" is important, though often unrecognized. While the public construction of the criminal is male, "the hidden victims of many of the get-tough policies have been women, particularly women of color" (Chesney-Lind, 1998, p. xi). Feminists have played an important role in calling attention to the unintended or unforeseen consequences of purportedly "gender-neutral" policies. New sentencing policies have been implemented with the goal of treating women and men the same. With regard to the Federal Sentencing Guidelines, Myrna Raeder (1993) suggests considering sentencing fewer men to prison on the grounds that it would be more humane for men, women, and their children. Instead, women have been increasingly incarcerated; a shift that has been described as "equality with a vengeance." There are other, less well-known examples to consider too, such as Massey, Miller, and Wilhelmi's (1998) finding that in civil forfeiture cases (involving the confiscation of assets from suspected drug offenders), judges falsely assume that social and economic power are equally distributed in a marriage or intimate relationship. Moreover, judges blame wives for their failure or inability to control their husband. Judicial interpretations thus "often ignore not only the gendered power dynamics within intimate relationships but also the structural limits to women's efficacy in disentangling themselves from such relationships that are present in these situations" (p. 29).[12]

In addition to women being banned by purportedly "gender-neutral" policies or policies aimed primarily at men, some policies have been targeted specifically at women and therefore are cause for concern. For instance, according to a 1996 report prepared by the Center for Reproductive Law and Policy, at least 200 women in more than thirty states have been arrested for their alleged drug use or other actions during pregnancy. Feminist perspectives encourage us to recognize the harmful consequences of criminalizing pregnant women's behavior rather than expanding the availability of treatment for pregnant women (including those who have small children, are infected with HIV, and/or on Medicaid). One major concern is that criminalizing maternal conduct discourages drug-using women from seeking prenatal care and drug treatment out of fear that they will be subjected to prosecution (Humphries, 1999).

Feminists have not limited their interests to policies aimed at or affecting women, but have also challenged the masculine basis of many programs and policies. Feminists have been critical of correctional officer and police training programs for their overemphasis on physical strength, intimidation, and aggressiveness as a means for resolving disputes while devaluing interpersonal skills. Similarly, feminist criminologists are among those critical of boot camps for being unnecessarily demeaning and abusive to inmates. The boot camp model embodies a distorted image of masculinity, one that emphasizes aggressiveness, unquestioned authority, and insensitivity to others' pain while deemphasizing "feminine" characteristics such as group cooperation and empathy. "Why," Merry Morash and Lila Rucker (1990/1998, pp. 35 and 38) ask, "would a method that has been developed to prepare people to go into war, and as a tool to manage legal violence, be considered as having such potential in deterring or rehabilitating offenders? . . . [T]he program elements of militarism, hard labor, and fear engendered by severe conditions do not hold much promise, and they appear to set the stage for abuse of authority."

The aforementioned examples are just a few of the myriad ways in which feminists have contributed to criminal justice policymaking and evaluation. Feminist scholarship has called attention to previously ignored policy issues, evaluated the impact of purportedly "gender-neutral" policies on women, examined the effects of policies targeted specifically at women, and challenged the value of criminal justice policies and practices based on stereotypical ideas of masculinity and femininity. By definition, feminism gives great weight to identifying strategies for social change and ending domination in all its forms. Feminist perspectives remind one—not only of one's professional responsibilities—but also one's social responsibility to consider the implications of our research and policy for women.

Conclusions

"If I can't dance, it's not my revolution." Emma Goldman's statement may make a great T-shirt, but her view is hardly universal among feminists. While feminist criminologists generally agree that a transformation of criminal justice discipline is desirable, there is less consensus regarding how to go about actually carrying it out. Do feminists wait for mainstream criminology to invite them to the dance? If invited, do feminists attend even if it means being reduced to standing against the walls waiting to be asked to dance, or dancing by themselves as a token feminist or woman on the faculty or editorial board? Do feminists hold their own dance, that is, continue to publish articles in specialized journals and books, teach specialized classes on "gender and crime," and sit on panels comprised almost entirely of like-minded scholars? While this approach offers the benefit of facilitating the exchange of ideas and support, it also risks making feminism even more peripheral to the discipline. As the scholarship cited throughout this article illustrates, feminists engage in a variety of strategies, working as both insiders and outsiders to the criminal justice enterprise. By attempting to meet mainstream criminologists midway by explaining the strength and diversity of feminist perspectives, this article presents another strategy.

Regardless of one's political or theoretical orientation, feminism challenges criminology to reject androcentric thinking. More generally, it challenges all people working in the discipline to be thoughtful and relevant: thoughtful in the theoretical assumptions upon which the research is based, the methods used, the conclusions drawn, and the policies recommended. Thoughtful in developing the content of the classes taught. Thoughtful in acknowledging the limitations of criminological scholarship, in considering the complexities and diversity of the people's lives and experiences upon which scholarship is based, and in communicating with research participants, students, and colleagues.

Given the overt emphasis placed upon policy and action, feminism also challenges one to be relevant. A colleague once observed that best-selling detective fiction writer Walter Mosley had more of an impact on what the public thought of crime and justice than academics did if for no other reason than millions of people read Mosley's novels while most criminological research was not considered outside of academic circles. Part of being relevant means making scholarship accessible in how and where it is presented. Prioritizing relevance also encourages collaboration—not only among academics at other universities, and of other ranks and disciplinary backgrounds—but also with people outside the university setting, including policymakers, practitioners, lawmakers, journalists, victims, offenders, and advocates. It means treating the implications of research for policy and practice as being at least as important as individual careers and egos.

Although feminist perspectives pose a demanding set of standards, the pursuit of these standards can be very rewarding. Feminism presents an invitation to criminologists, practitioners, and policymakers to recognize the existence of sexism, to try to understand its causes, and to work toward identifying and overcoming all forms of discrimination that operate throughout the justice system. Fellow criminologists, consider yourselves invited.

Notes

[1] As used here, the terms "mainstream criminology" and "conventional criminology" do not refer to a theory but to an amalgam of dominant sociological approaches to crime, such as strain, social control, interactionist, and ecological theories (DeKeseredy & Schwartz, 1996; Thomas & O'Maolchatha, 1989).

[2] While in the 1970s, the typical article published in one of four major criminology journals used an all-male sample, by the 1990s, most articles published in these same journals included a sample of both men and women (Hannon & Dufour, 1998).

[3] Readers interested in a discussion of the various feminist theories are urged to consult Daly and Chesney-Lind (1988), Martin and Jurik (1996), and Tong (1989).

[4] Readers interested in learning more about feminist approaches to criminology are urged to consult any number of the excellent texts on the subject (cf. Belknap, 1996; Daly & Maher, 1998; Gelsthorpe & Morris, 1990; Heidensohn, 1995; Naffine, 1996; Price & Sokoloff, 1995; Smart, 1976, 1995).

[5] Obviously, other factors serve to marginalize feminism from criminology. For instance, Comack (1999, p. 165) posits that "the essentialist and dualistic thinking that has pervaded our approaches to understanding issues like violence against women [i.e., 'women as victims/men as offenders'] . . . has had significant implications for the placement of feminism within the criminological enterprise. So long as women are recognized only as victims and not as active agents, there is little need to embrace or integrate feminist analyses into the criminological agenda." Others (including one of the reviewers of this article) point to "a refusal to engage in the ideas . . . [It is] too hard and ultimately scary for those scholars or practitioners who have devoted their lives to either ignoring gender or to developing 'gender-neutral' theories to change."

[6] The peripheral position of feminism is not unique to criminology but is a problem of larger sociology as well. In the classic essay, *The Missing Feminist Revolution in Sociology,* Judith Stacey and Barrie Thorne (1985/1993, p. 177) observe that feminist perspectives have made more progress in fields which have stronger traditions of interpretive understanding. Scholars in anthropology, literature, and history are more open to questions such as "What are the effects of the social and political circumstances in which knowledge is created and received? . . . What are the effects of the gender of the researcher, the audience, or those studied or written about?"

[7] Before proceeding, three caveats are in order. First, this article is a primer rather than a comprehensive treatment of feminist criminology. In the interests of clarity and conciseness, some concepts have been omitted from discussion and some important distinctions have been glossed over. While feminists tend to share a general notion of what is meant by a particular concept, the reality is that a given term encompasses a range of perspectives and understandings. In some respects, the concepts presented in this article and any categories discussed in connection with them are "ideal types." Relatedly, issues of epistemology, theory, methods and methodology, and policy are presented in separate sections here, even though they are intertwined. Every attempt has been made to make the overlap and interconnections apparent without being overly repetitious. Lastly, the near-exclusive focus on feminist perspectives is not meant to suggest that only feminism has "the answers" or asks the right questions. Many concerns presented in this article are shared by

other criminological approaches, particularly critical ones. For example, feminism generally shares a view with other critical approaches that the major sources of crime are the class, ethnic, and patriarchal relations that control society, and regards structural and cultural change as essential to reducing criminality (DeKeseredy & Schwartz, 1996; Thomas & O'Maolchatha, 1989).

8 The present discussion of epistemology is grossly simplified in the interest of clarity and brevity. For excellent treatments of epistemology, empiricism, and criminology, readers are encouraged to consult Carol Smart's (1995) *Law, Crime and Sexuality: Essays in Feminism* or Ngaire Naffine's (1996) *Feminism and Criminology.*

9 This deficiency is also found in standard textbooks. Earlier studies of introductory criminal justice and criminology textbooks conclude that women are typically ignored or depicted in stereotypical ways (Baro & Eigenberg, 1993; Wright, 1992). A nonrandom sampling of the texts on my shelves suggests the problem persists and the short shrift extends to feminist perspectives as well. For example, in discussing "other branches of conflict theory," Senna and Siegel (1998) cite only one feminist perspective—radical feminism—ignoring other major critical feminist perspectives such as Marxist feminism, socialist feminism, and postmodern feminism.

10 As Jayartne and Stewart (1991) point out, quantitative procedures that are inconsistent with feminist values can be adapted without abandoning those strategies that can be beneficial to the research enterprise.

11 Thomas's own work on female crime showed an appreciation for the interaction between society and the individual. He, however, saw women's physiology and biology as being at the root of their inferior position in society (see Klein 1973/1995).

12 For example, in one case a woman claimed she lived in fear of bodily harm from her husband—a man who had threatened her in the past and had beaten to death his previous wife. The appellate court, however, rejected her claim of lack of consent under duress because the threat was not "immediate."

References

Baro, A., & Eigenberg, H. (1993). Images of gender: a content analysis of photographs in introductory criminology and criminal justice textbooks. *Women and Criminal Justice, 5,* 3–36.

Belknap, J. (1996). *The invisible woman: gender, crime, and justice.* Belmont, CA: Wadsworth Publishing.

Belknap, J., Holsinger, K., & Dunn, M. (1997). Understanding incarcerated girls: the results of a focus group study. *Prison Journal, 77,* 381–404.

Bufkin, J. L. (1999). Bias crime as gendered behavior. *Social Justice, 26,* 155–176.

Bureau of Justice Statistics. (1997). *Correctional populations in the United States, 1995.* Washington, DC: US Department of Justice.

Cannon, L. W. W., Higginbotham, E., & Leung, M. L. A. (1991). Race and class bias in qualitative research on women. In: M. M. Fonow & J. A. Cook (Eds.), *Beyond methodology: feminist scholarship as lived research* (pp. 107–118). Bloomington: Indiana University Press.

Carty, L. (1996). Seeing through the eye of difference: a reflection on three research journeys. In: H. Gottfried (Ed.), *Feminism and social change: bridging theory and practice* (pp. 123–142). Champaign: University of Illinois Press.

Chancer, L. S. (1998). Playing gender against race through high-profile crime cases. *Violence Against Women, 4,* 100–113.

Chesney-Lind, M. (1998). Foreword. In: S. L. Miller (Ed.), *Crime control and women* (pp. ix–xii). Thousand Oaks, CA: Sage Publications.

Collins, P. H. (1998). *Fighting words: black women and the search for justice.* Minneapolis: University of Minnesota Press.

Comack, E. (1999). New possibilities for a feminism in criminology? From dualism to diversity. *Canadian Journal of Criminology, 41,* 161–170.

Connell, R. W. (1987). *Gender and power: society, the person, and sexual politics.* Stanford, CA: Stanford University Press.

Connell, R. W. (1995). *Masculinities.* Los Angeles: University of California Press.

Craven, D. (1997). *Sex differences in violent victimization, 1994.* Washington, DC: US Department of Justice.

Daly, K. (1994). *Gender, crime and punishment.* New Haven, CT: Yale University Press.

Daly, K. (1995). Looking back, looking forward: the promise of feminist transformation. In: B. R. Price & N. J. Sokoloff (Eds.), *The criminal justice system and women* (2nd ed.) (pp. 443–457). New York: McGraw-Hill.

Daly, K., & Chesney-Lind, M. (1988). Feminism and criminology. *Justice Quarterly, 5,* 497–538.

Daly, K., & Maher, L. (1998). *Criminology at the crossroads: feminist readings in crime and justice.* Oxford: Oxford University Press.

Danner, M. J. E. (1998). Three strikes and it's women who are out: the hidden consequences for women of criminal justice police reforms. In: S. L. Miller (Ed.), *Crime control and women* (pp. 1–14). Thousand Oaks, CA: Sage Publications.

Danner, M. J. E., & Carmody, D. C. (1999). *Missing gender in cases of infamous school violence: investigating research and media explanations.* Unpublished manuscript.

DeKeseredy, W. S., & Schwartz, M. D. (1996). *Contemporary criminology.* Belmont, CA: Wadsworth Publishing.

Eichler, M. (1988). *Nonsexist research methods: a practical guide.* Winchester, MA: Allen & Unwin.

Federal Bureau of Investigations. (1998). *Crime in the United States, 1997.* Washington, DC: United States Government Printing Office.

Fonow, M. M., & Cook, J. A. (1991). Back to the future: a look at the second wave of feminist epistemology and methodology. In: M. M. Fonow & J. A. Cook (Eds.), *Beyond methodology* (pp. 1–15). Bloomington: Indiana University Press.

Gelsthorpe, L. (1990). Feminist methodologies in criminology: a new approach or old wine in new bottles. In: L. Gelsthorpe & A. Morris (Eds.), *Feminist perspectives in criminology* (pp. 89–106). Buckingham, UK: Open University Press.

Gelsthorpe, L., & Moms, A. (1990). *Feminist perspectives in criminology.* Buckingham, UK: Open University Press.

Gilliard, D. K. (1999). *Prison and jail inmates at midyear 1998.* Washington, DC: US Department of Justice.

Goodstein, L. (1992). Feminist perspectives and the criminal justice curriculum. *Journal of Criminal Justice Education, 3,* 165–181.

Gorelick, S. (1996). Contradictions of feminist methodology. In: H. Gottfried (Ed.), *Feminism and social change: bridging theory and practice* (pp. 23–45). Champaign: University of Illinois Press.

Gottfredson, M. R., & Hirschi, T. (1990). *A general theory of crime.* Stanford, CA: Stanford University Press.

Hannon, L., & Dufour, L. R. (1998). Still just the study of men and crime? A content analysis. *Sex Roles, 38,* 63–71.

Harding, S. (Ed.) (1987). *Feminism and methodology: social science issues.* Bloomington: Indiana University Press.

Harding, S. (1991). *Whose science? Whose knowledge?* Ithaca, NY: Cornell University Press.

Harris, A. P. (1997). Race and essentialism in feminist legal theory. In: A. K. Wing (Ed.), *Critical race feminism: a reader* (pp. 11–18). New York: New York University Press.

Heidensohn, F. M. (1995). *Women and crime* (2nd ed.). New York: New York University Press.

Humphries, D. (1999). *Crack mothers: pregnancy, drugs, and the media.* Columbus: Ohio State University Press.

Jayartne, T. E., & Stewart, A. J. (1991). Quantitative and qualitative methods in the social sciences: current feminist issues and practical strategies. In: M. M. Fonow & J. A. Cook (Eds.), *Beyond methodology: feminist scholarship as lived research* (pp. 85–106). Bloomington: Indiana University Press.

Kauffman, L. S. (1993). The long goodbye: against personal testimony, or an infant grifter grows up. In: L. S. Kauffman (Ed.), *American feminist thought at century's end: a reader* (pp. 258–280). Cambridge, MA: Blackwell.

Klein, D. (1995). The etiology of female crime: a review of the literature. In: B. R. Price & N. J. Sokoloff (Eds.), *The criminal justice system and women* (2nd ed.) (pp. 30–53). New York: McGraw-Hill.

Leonard, E. (1995). Theoretical criminology and gender. In: B. R. Price & N. J. Sokoloff (Eds.), *The criminal justice system and women* (2nd ed.) (pp. 54–70). New York: McGraw-Hill.

Martin, S. E., & Jurik, N. C. (1996). *Doing justice, doing gender: women in law and criminal justice occupations.* Thousand Oaks, CA: Sage Publications.

Massey, J., Miller, S. L., Wilhelmi, A. (1998). Civil forfeiture of property: the victimization of women as innocent owners and third parties. In: S. L. Miller (Ed.), *Crime control and women* (pp. 15–31). Thousand Oaks, CA: Sage Publications.

May, T. (1993). Feelings matter: inverting the hidden equation. In: D. Hobbs & T. May (Eds.), *Interpreting the field: accounts of ethnography* (pp. 69–97). Oxford: Oxford University University Press.

McDermott, M. J. (1992). The personal is empirical: feminism, research methods, and criminal justice education. *Journal of Criminal Justice Education, 3,* 237–249.

Merton, R. K. (1938). Social structure and anomie. *American Sociological Review, 3,* 672–683.

Messerschmidt, J. W. (1986). *Capitalism, patriarchy, and crime.* Totowa, NJ: Rowman & Littlefield.

Messerschmidt, J. W. (1997). *Crime as structured action: gender, race, class, and crime in the making.* Thousand Oaks, CA: Sage Publications.

Mies, M. (1991). Women's research or feminist research? The debate surrounding feminist science and methodology. In: M. M. Fonow & J. A. Cook (Eds.), *Beyond methodology* (pp. 60–84). Bloomington: Indiana University Press.

Miller, J. (1998). Up it up: gender and the accomplishment of street robbery. *Criminology, 36,* 37–65.

Miller, S., & Burack, C. (1993). A critique of Gottfredson and Hirschi's general theory of crime: selective (in)attention to gender and power positions. *Women and Criminal Justice, 4,* 115–134.

Miller, S. L. (1998). Introduction. In: S. L. Miller (Ed.), *Crime control and women* (pp. xv–xxiv). Thousand Oaks, CA: Sage Publications.

Morash, M., & Rucker, L. (1998). A critical look at the idea of boot camp as a correctional reform. In: S. L. Miller (Ed.), *Crime control and women* (pp. 32–51). Thousand Oaks, CA: Sage Publications.

Naffine, N. (1996). *Feminism and criminology.* Philadelphia, PA: Temple University Press.

National Center for Women and Policing. (1999). *Equality denied, the status of women and policing: 1998.* Los Angeles: National Center for Women and Policing.

Owen, B. (1998). *In the mix: struggle and survival in a woman's prison.* Albany: State University of New York Press.

Pettiway, L. E. (1997). *Workin' it: women living through drugs and crime.* Philadelphia, PA: Temple University Press.

Powers, R. (1999). Eyes wide open. *New York Times Magazine* (April 18, special issue), *6,* 80–83.

Price, B. R., & Sokoloff, N. J. (1995). *The criminal justice system and women: offenders, victims, and workers* (2nd ed.). New York: McGraw-Hill.

Pyke, K. D. (1996). Class-based masculinities: the interdependence of gender, class, and interpersonal power. *Gender and Society, 10,* 527–549.

Raeder, M. S. (1993). Gender and sentencing: single moms, battered women, and other sex-based anomalies in the gender-free world of the federal sentencing guidelines. *Pepperdine Law Review, 20,* 905–920.

Rafter, N. H., & Heidensohn, F. (1995). *International feminist perspectives in criminology: engendering a discipline.* Buckingham, UK: Open University Press.

Rasche, C. E. (1995). Minority women and domestic violence. In: B. R. Price & N. J. Sokoloff (Eds.), *The criminal justice system and women* (2nd ed.) (pp. 246–261). New York: McGraw-Hill.

Renzetti, C. M. (1993). On the margins of the malestream (or, they still don't get it, do they?): feminist analyses in criminal justice education. *Journal of Criminal Justice Education, 4,* 219–234.

Renzetti, C. M. (1998). Connecting the dots: women, public policy, and social control. In: S. L. Miller (Ed.), *Crime control and women* (pp. 181–189). Thousand Oaks, CA: Sage Publications.

Rice, M. (1990). Challenging orthodoxies in feminist theory: a black feminist critique. In: L. Gelsthorpe & A. Morris (Eds.), *Feminist perspectives in criminology* (pp. 57–69). Buckingham, UK: Open University Press.

Richie, B. E. (1996). *Compelled to crime: the gender entrapment of battered black women.* New York: Routledge.

Rivera, J. (1997). Domestic violence against Latinas by Latino males: an analysis of race, national origin, and gender differentials. In: A. K. Wing (Ed.), *Critical race feminism: a reader* (pp. 259–266). New York: New York University Press.

Schwendinger, J. R., & Schwendinger, H. (1983). *Rape and inequality.* Newbury Park, CA: Sage Publications.

Senna, J. J., & Siegel, L. J. (1998). *Essentials of criminal justice* (2nd ed.). Belmont, CA: Wadsworth Publishing.

Simpson, S. S. (1989). Feminist theory, crime, and justice. *Criminology, 27,* 605–631.

Smart, C. (1976). *Women, crime and criminology: A feminist critique.* Boston: Routledge and Kegan Paul.

Smart, C. (1995). *Law, crime and sexuality: Essays in feminism.* London: Sage Publications.

Smart, C. (1998). The woman of legal discourse. In: K. Daly & L. Maher (Eds.), *Criminology at the crossroads* (pp. 21–36). New York: Oxford University Press.

Stacey, J., & Thorne, B. (1993). The missing feminist revolution in sociology. In: L. S. Kauffman (Ed.), *American feminist thought at century's end: a reader* (pp. 167–188). Cambridge, MA: Blackwell.

Taylor, V., & Rupp, L. J. (1991). Researching the women's movement: we make our own history, but not just as we please. In: M. M. Fonow & J. A. Cook (Eds.), *Beyond methodology: Feminist scholarship as lived research* (pp. 119–132). Bloomington: Indiana University Press.

Thomas, J., & O'Maolchatha, A. (1989). Reassessing the critical metaphor: an optimistic revisionist view. *Justice Quarterly, 6,* 143–172.

Tong, R. (1989). *Feminist thought: a comprehensive introduction.* Boulder, CO: Westview Press.

West, C., & Zimmerman, D. H. (1987). Doing gender. *Gender and Society, 1,* 125–151.

Wilson, N. K. (1991). Feminist pedagogy in criminology. *Journal of Criminal Justice Education, 2,* 81–93.

Wonders, N. (1999). Postmodern feminist criminology and social justice. In: B. A. Arrigo (Ed.), *Social justice/criminal justice* (pp. 111–128). Belmont, CA: West/Wadsworth.

Wonders, N. A., & Caulfield, S. L. (1993). Women's work?: the contradictory implications of courses on women and the criminal justice system. *Journal of Criminal Justice Education, 4,* 79–100.

Wright, R. (1992). From vamps and tramps to teases and flirts: stereotypes of women in criminology textbooks, 1956 to 1965 and 1981 to 1990. *Journal of Criminal Justice Education, 3,* 223–236.

SECTION II

Understanding Women and the Crimes They Commit

Traditionally, female offenders have been essentially ignored or overlooked when studying crime; those few studies that have focused on women, however, have usually been grounded in sexist and stereotypic assumptions. Over the last thirty years, there has been a growing body of research in the area of women offenders. In this section, four articles were selected that illustrate the continuing efforts among scholars to further our understanding of female criminality. The first two articles emphasize the importance of "gendering" research on women offenders; these criminologists demonstrate that it is essential to move beyond studying gender as just a demographic variable. Rather, these scholars stress that research needs to focus on how gender organizes criminal activity. In this vein, most research on female offenders has examined women involved in such offenses as shoplifting, fraud, and prostitution. The remaining two articles examine an often neglected focus of study—the violent female offender.

In their article, "Gender and Crime: Toward a Gendered Theory of Female Offending," Darrell Steffensmeier and Emilie Allan attempt to explain gender differences in offending. Specifically, they develop a paradigm that explains why women are less likely to be involved in criminal activity compared to men. These scholars argue that traditional criminological theories have not been recognized sufficiently for providing any insight in explaining *both* female and male criminality trends. Steffensmeier and Allan maintain that, in fact, these sociological theories can provide criminologists with an enhanced understanding of how various social forces interact with gender to explain differences between women and men involved in minor acts of crime and delinquency. These traditional frameworks, however, are problematic when explaining serious crimes. Thus, Steffensmeier and Allan's proposed gendered paradigm recognizes the explanatory value of both traditional theories while also realizing the need to understand how gender organizes behavior.

Lisa Maher and Kathleen Daly's article, "Women in the Street-Level Drug Economy: Continuity or Change?" focuses on disentangling mixed images of women's roles in the contemporary drug economy and comparing these to women's roles in the U.S. drug markets during the 1960–1985 period. These mixed images include *change, continuity,* or *both change and continuity.* Their research is based on an ethnographic study of 45 women from New York City. The results reveal that the "new opportunities" in the crack cocaine drug economy were not necessarily equal opportunities for women. Rather, these "new opportunities" were realized by men; thus, Maher and Daly's study demonstrates how the underworld has maintained a form of "institutionalized sexism" that limits women's roles and participation in this type of criminal activity.

In her article, "Up It Up: Gender and the Accomplishment of Street Robbery," Jody Miller examines the experiences of female and male street robbers in an urban setting. She addresses two questions: 1) *Why* women and men engage in robbery, or motivations; and 2) *How* gender organizes the commission, or enactment, of robbery. Based on in-depth interviews, both women and men reveal more similarities than dissimilarities for motivations to commit robberies. Essentially, these motivations are economic (e.g., to get money or jewelry). There are gender dissimilarities, however, when examining how female and male offenders committed street robberies. Miller notes that the women considered the gendered aspects of their environment. These women recognize that street robbery is essentially a male-dominated type of crime. When committing these robberies, their choices and actions reflect this understanding.

Using National Incident-Based Reporting System (NIBRS) data, Barbara Koons-Witt and Pamela Schram explore women who have been considered "nontypical" female offenders—women who have committed violent offenses including murder, nonnegligent manslaughter, robbery, and aggravated assault. Among their findings in article 8, women were more likely to be involved in aggravated assaults rather than robberies and murder or nonnegligent manslaughter, especially if they committed these offenses alone. When women co-offended with other women or men, however, they were more likely to commit robberies. If weapons were involved in these offenses, women are more likely to use either personal weapons (e.g., hands, feet, or teeth) or knives/cutting instruments. Women co-offending with males, however, were more likely to use guns. Koons-Witt and Schram conclude that further inquiry needs to explore the contextual aspects of violent offending among females such as the relation between the victim and the perpetrator.

4

Gender and Crime
Toward a Gendered Theory of Female Offending

Darrell Steffensmeier
Emilie Allan

Introduction

The principal goal of this article is to advance theory and research by reviewing selected issues in the gender and crime literature; by advancing a gendered paradigm of female offending which builds on existing theory and on the growing body of work on gender; and by proposing a series of recommendations for further research.

No single article can do justice to the vast literature on gender and crime, to both the old and especially the new writings. If criminologists were ever indifferent to female crime, it is certainly the case no longer. Although profound questions remain, more is known about gender and crime than is known about age and crime or about race and crime.

Sociologists may also welcome the solid evidence that confirms the utility of traditional sociological theories of crime in explaining crime by women as well as by men, and in explaining gender differences in crime—at least for the minor crimes that dominate both official and unofficial data on crime. Much of what we still need to learn has to do with the profound gender differences in patterns of serious offending, rather than the less consequential differences in patterns of minor crime.

We first assess similarities and differences between female and male patterns of offending. Next we briefly review explanations of those patterns and of the gender gap, particularly the so-called "gender equality" hypothesis that gender differences in crime converge as male and female roles become more similar. We then seek to advance theory and research in the field by expanding on a "gendered" paradigm begun elsewhere (Steffensmeier & Allan 1995) that can illuminate the critical relationship between gender and crime and by setting forth a number of recommendations for future work.

Female and Male Patterns of Offending

Patterns of offending by men and by women are notable both for their similarities and for their differences. Both men and women are more heavily involved in minor property and substance abuse offenses than in serious crimes like robbery or murder. However, men offend at much higher rates than women for all crime categories except prostitution. This gender gap in crime is greatest for serious crime and least for mild forms of lawbreaking such as minor property crimes.

Many sources provide data that permit comparison of male and female offending. We review FBI arrest statistics (US Department of Justice 1990) for men and women, and we draw also upon offender information from the National Crime Victimization Survey, and on findings from surveys on self-reported crime, from studies of criminal careers and delinquent gangs, and from case studies that provide a wealth of qualitative data on the differing contexts of male and female offending.

Table 1 summarizes a variety of information drawn from male and female arrest data for all FBI offense categories except rape (a male crime) and runaway and curfew (juvenile offenses): trends in male and female arrests rates per 100,000 population (columns 1–6), trends in the female percent of arrests (columns 7–9), and the offending profile of males and females (columns 10–13). All calculations in table 1 adjust for the sex composition in the population as a whole and are based on ages 10–64 (i.e. the population most at risk for criminal behavior).

Arrest Rates, 1960, 1975, 1990

For both males and females, arrest rates are higher for less serious offenses, and both male and female rates trended upward during both periods (1960–1975, 1975–1990) for many offense categories. Large increases are found mainly for petty property crimes like larceny and fraud, for substance abuse (DUI, drugs, and liquor law violations), and for assault. A number of the public order offense categories trended downward, especially public drunkenness, gambling, and many of the sex-related offenses. The similarity in male and female trends suggests that the rates of both sexes are influenced by similar social and legal forces, independent of any condition unique to women or men.

Arrest Profiles

The similarities are even more evident in the profiles of male and female arrest patterns displayed in columns 10–13. These profiles reflect the percentage of total male and total female arrests represented by each crime category for 1960 and 1990. The homicide figures of 0.2 for men in 1990 and 0.1 for women mean, respectively, that only two tenths of 1% of all male arrests were for homicide, and only one tenth of 1% of all female arrests were for homicide.

For both men and women, the three most common arrest categories in 1990 are DUI, larceny-theft, and "other except traffic"—a residual category that includes mostly criminal mischief, public disorder, local ordinance violations, and assorted minor crimes. Together, these three offense categories account for 48% of all male arrests and 49% of all female arrests. Note, however, that larceny arrests are the most numerous category (20% in 1990) for females; but that for males, DUI arrests are more important (15%). Arrests for murder, arson, and embezzlement are relatively rare for men and women alike, while arrests for offenses such as liquor law violations (mostly underage drinking), simple assault, and disorderly conduct represent "middling ranks" for both sexes.

The most important gender differences in arrest profiles involve the proportionately greater female involvement in minor property crimes (collectively, about 28% of female arrests in 1990, compared to 13% of male arrests), and the relatively greater involvement of males in crimes against persons and major property crimes (17% of male arrests, but only 11% of female arrests). Ironically, men and women were slightly closer in their profiles in these more "masculine" categories in 1960, when they represented 11.4% of male arrests and 8.4% of female arrests.

Female Percentage of Arrests

Although some authors profess to see major changes over time in the female percentage of arrests (e.g. Adler 1975, Simon 1975), the numbers for 1960, 1975, and 1990 are perhaps more remarkable for their similarity than for their differences. For all three periods, the female share of arrests for most categories was 15% or less and was typically smallest for the most serious offenses. Major change is found principally for the female share of arrests for minor property crimes such as larceny and fraud, which averaged between 15% and 17% in 1960, but jumped to between 30% and 43% by 1990.

National Crime Victimization Survey (NCVS)

The relatively low female participation in serious offending is corroborated by data from the NCVS (Bureau of Justice Statistics 1992). In NCVS interviews, victims are asked the sex of offender, and totals turn out to be

Table 1
Male and Female Arrest Rates/100,000, Male and Female Arrest Profiles, and Female Percentage of Arrests (1960–1990, Uniform Crime Reports)

Offenses	Male Rates			Female Rates		
	1960 (1)	1975 (2)	1990 (3)	1960 (4)	1975 (5)	1990 (6)
Against Persons						
Homicide	9	16	16	2	3	2
Aggravated assault	101	200	317	16	28	50
Weapons	69	137	165	4	11	14
Simple assault	265	354	662	29	54	129
Major Property						
Robbery	65	131	124	4	10	12
Burglary	274	477	319	9	27	32
Stolen property	21	103	121	2	12	17
Minor Property						
Larceny-Theft	391	749	859	74	321	402
Fraud	70	114	157	12	59	133
Forgery	44	46	51	8	18	28
Embezzlement	—	7	8	—	3	5
Melicious Mischief						
Auto theft	121	128	158	5	9	18
Vandalism	—	187	224	—	16	28
Arson	—	15	13	—	2	2
Drinking/Drugs						
Public drunkeness	2573	1201	624	212	87	71
DUI	344	971	1193	21	81	176
Liquor laws	183	276	428	28	43	102
Drug abuse	49	523	815	8	79	166
Sex/Sex Related						
Prostitution	15	18	30	37	45	62
Sex offenses	81	55	78	17	5	7
Disorderly conduct	749	597	499	115	116	119
Vagrancy	265	45	26	23	7	4
Suspicion	222	31	13	28	5	3
Miscellaneous						
Against family	90	57	51	8	7	12
Gambling	202	60	14	19	6	2
Other Exc. traffic	871	1139	2109	150	197	430
Total	7070	7850	9211	831	1383	2122

Offender-Profile Percentage				Female Percentage (of arrests)		
Males		Females				
1960 (7)	1990 (8)	1960 (9)	1990 (10)	1960 (11)	1975 (12)	1990 (13)
.1	.2	.2	.1	17	14	11
1	3	2	2	14	13	13
1	2	.5	.7	4	8	7
4	6	4	5	10	13	15
1	1	.5	.5	5	7	8
4	3	1	1	3	5	8
.3	1	.2	.5	8	10	11
6	10	9	20	17	30	30
1	2	2	7	15	34	43
.5	.5	1	1	16	28	34
—	.2	—	.1	—	28	37
2	1	1	1	4	7	9
—	2	—	1	—	8	10
—	.3	—	.1	—	11	14
36	8	25	4	8	7	9
5	15	3	9	6	5	11
3	5	4	5	13	14	17
1	7	1	6	15	13	14
.2	.4	4	3	73	73	65
1	1	2	.3	17	8	8
11	5	14	6	13	17	18
4	.3	3	.2	8	14	12
3	.1	3	.1	11	13	15
1	.5	1	.5	8	10	16
3	.2	2	.2	8	9	15
13	23	19	20	15	15	15
				11	15	19

quite close to those found in UCR data. In 1990, for example, women are reported to be responsible for about 7% of robberies, 12% of aggravated assaults, 15% of simple assaults, 5% of burglaries, and 5% of motor vehicle thefts reported by victims. These percentages have held unchanged since the NCVS began in the mid-1970s.

Self-Report Studies

The pattern of a higher female share of offending for mild forms of lawbreaking and a much lower share for serious offenses is confirmed by the numerous surveys in which persons (generally juveniles) have been asked to report on their own offenses (Canter 1982). This holds both for prevalence of offending (the percent of the male and female samples that report any offending) and especially for the frequency of offending (the number of crimes an active offender commits in a given period). However, gender differences are less for self-report data than for official data (Jensen & Eve 1976, Smith & Visher 1980), and gender differences are smaller still for self-report prevalence data on minor offenses such as shoplifting and minor drug use (Canter 1982).

Gang Participation

Girls have long been members of gangs (Thrasher 1927), and some girls today continue to solve their problems of gender, race, and class through gang membership. At issue is not their presence but the extent and form of their participation. Early studies, based on information from male gang informants, depicted female gang members as playing secondary roles as cheerleaders or camp followers, and ignored girls' occasionally violent behavior.

Recent studies, which rely more on female gang informants, indicate that girls' roles in gangs have been considerably more varied than early stereotypes would have it. Although female gang members continue to be dependent on male gangs, the girls' status is determined as much or even more so by her female peers (Campbell 1984). Also, relative to the past, girls in gangs appear to be fighting in more arenas and even using many of the same weapons as males (Quicker 1974), and the gang context may be an important source of initiating females into patterns of violent offending (Fagan 1990). The aggressive rhetoric of some female gang members notwithstanding, their actual behavior continues to display considerable deference to male gang members, avoidance of excessive violence, and adherence to traditional gender-scripted behaviors (Campbell 1990, Chesney-Lind & Shelden 1992, Swart 1991). Ganging is still a predominantly male phenomenon (roughly 90%). The most common form of female gang involvement has remained as auxiliaries or branches of male gangs (Miller 1980, Swart 1991), and girls are excluded from most of the economic criminal activity (Bowker et al 1980).

Criminal Careers

The study of individual careers in crime—the longitudinal sequence of crimes committed by an individual offender—has become an increasing focus of criminology. The research comparing male and female criminal careers is limited to violent career offenders and has found substantial gender variation: (i) Although violent offenses comprise only a small percentage of all the offenses committed by offenders in any population, females participate in substantially less violent crime than males during the course of their criminal careers; (ii) the careers of violent females both begin and peak a little earlier than those of males; (iii) females are far less likely than males to repeat their violent offenses; and (iv) females are far more likely to desist from further violence (see reviews in Denno 1994, Kruttschnitt 1994, Weiner 1989).

Case studies and interviews, even with serious female offenders, indicate no strong commitment to criminal behavior (Arnold 1989, Bottcher 1986, Miller 1986). This finding stands in sharp contrast to the commitment and self-identification with crime and the criminal lifestyle that is often found among male offenders (Sutherland 1937, Prus & Sharper 1977, Steffensmeier 1986, Commonwealth of Pennsylvania 1991).

Applying Traditional Theory to the Explanation of Gendered Crime Patterns

A long-standing issue concerns whether female crime can be explained by theories developed mainly by male criminologists to explain male crime. Do the macro social conditions producing male crime also produce female crime? Are the pathways or processes leading to crime similar or distinct across the sexes? A variety of evidence suggests that there is considerable overlap in the "causes" of male and female crime, and that both traditional and more recent theoretical perspectives can help explain both female offending patterns and gender differences for less serious crime. The explanation of serious female crime and of gender differences in serious crime is more problematic.

Similarity in Social Backgrounds

The social backgrounds of female offenders tend to be quite similar to those of male offenders (see reviews in Chesney-Lind & Shelden 1994, Denno 1994, Steffensmeier & Allan 1995). Like male offenders, female offenders (especially the more serious ones) are typically of low socioeconomic status, poorly educated, under- or unemployed, and disproportionately from minority groups. The main difference in their social profile is the greater presence of dependent children among female offenders.

Regression of Female Rates on Male Rates

The extent to which male rates can predict female rates provides indirect evidence of similarity in the etiology of female and male crime (Steffensmeier & Allan 1988, Steffensmeier et al 1989). Groups or societies that have high male rates of crime also have high female rates, whereas groups or societies that have low male rates also have low female rates. Over time, when the male rate rises, declines, or holds steady across a specific historical period, the female rate behaves in a similar fashion. Statistically, when the female rates for a given group are regressed on the male rates for the same group, across time or across crime categories, the results for most comparisons do not differ significantly from a prediction of no difference (Steffensmeier & Allan 1988, Steffensmeier & Streifel 1992). Such findings suggest that female rates respond to the same social and legal forces as male rates, independent of any condition unique to women or to men (Bortitch & Hagan 1990, Steffensmeier 1980, Steffensmeier & Streifel 1992).

Aggregate Analysis

In an aggregate study of structural correlates of female crime rates, Steffensmeier and Streifel (1993) report findings similar to those for comparable aggregate studies of male rates. For example, rates of female crime tend to be higher in cities with high levels of economic inequality and poverty. There is a major need for further macro-aggregate studies of female offending.

Theory Testing with Self-Report Data

Theory testing with individual-level self-report data has identified causal factors for female offending that are quite consistent with those suggested by traditional theories of crime such as anomie, social control, and differential association (Akers et al 1979, Giordano et al 1986, Hagan 1989, Jensen & Eve 1976, Paternoster & Triplett 1988, Rankin 1980, Smith 1979, Smith & Paternoster 1987, Tittle 1980). Measures of bonds, associations, learning, parental controls, perceptions of risk, and so forth have comparable effects across the genders.

However, such findings apply mainly to minor offending; available self-report data sets do not lend themselves to the study of serious offending—either male or female—due to limited sample size, question content and format, and other problems. Aggregate methodology is perhaps even less adapted to the study of gender differences in criminal career paths and in the context of offending.

Shortcomings of Traditional Theories. The traditional theories are helpful in explaining overall patterns of female and male offending, and they shed some light on why female levels of offending are lower than for males. These approaches are less enlightening when seeking answers for a variety of both subtle and profound differences in female and male offending patterns.

For example:

Why are serious crimes against property and against persons so much less a feature of female offending? Male criminal participation in serious crime greatly exceeds female involvement, regardless of data source, crime type, level of involvement, or measure of participation (Kruttschnitt 1994, Steffensmeier 1983, Steffensmeier & Allan 1995). Women are far less likely to be involved in serious offenses, and the monetary value of female thefts, property damage, drugs, and injuries is typically smaller than that for similar offenses committed by men.

Why are female offenders less likely to participate in or lead criminal groups? Females are also more likely than males to be solo perpetrators, or to be part of small, relatively nonpermanent crime groups. When female offenders are involved with others, particularly in more lucrative thefts or other criminal enterprises, they typically act as accomplices to males who both organize and lead the execution of the crime (see Steffensmeier 1983, for a review). Perhaps the most significant gender difference is the overwhelming dominance of males in more organized and highly lucrative crimes, whether based in the underworld or the "upperworld" (Steffensmeier 1983, Daly 1989, Commonwealth of Pennsylvania 1991).

Why do women seem to need a higher level of provocation before turning to crime, especially serious crime? For example, in comparison to male offenders, female offenders are more likely to also be victims as children or adults (Chesney-Lind & Shelden 1992, Daly 1994, Gilfus 1992, Widom 1989). In her analysis of the Philadelphia cohort data, Denno (1994) reports that, although many factors are as predictive of female as male criminality, female offenders are more likely to have had records of neurological and other biological or psychological abnormalities. Likewise, Daly (1994) reports that female offenders (in comparison to male offenders) in a New Haven felony court had greater childhood and adult exposure to abuse, but that the female felons were nevertheless more conventional than the males in having greater responsibilities for children, commitment to education, and legitimate sources of income.

Why does female offending often involve relational concerns? Situational pressures such as threatened loss of valued relationships may play a greater role in female offending. Although the saying, "She did it all for love" is sometimes overplayed in reference to female criminality, the role of men in initiating women into crime—especially serious crime—is a consistent finding across research (Gilfus 1992, Miller 1986, Pettiway 1987, Steffensmeier 1983, Steffensmeier & Terry 1986). Such findings also suggest that women are not uniformly less amenable to risk, but rather that their risk-taking is less violative of the law and more protective of relationships and emotional commitments.

These and other questions often involve subtle issues of context that are not addressed by most traditional and contemporary theories, and which tend to be invisible (or nearly so) to quantitative analyses. Fortunately, as we discuss later, contextual issues are illuminated by a wealth of qualitative information to be found both in the traditional criminological literature (Elliott 1952, Reitman 1937) and in the profusion of qualitative research produced by feminist criminologists in recent years.

The Gender Gap and Crime

The gender gap in crime—the low level of female offending in relation to that of males—is universally recognized by criminologists. Almost as universal is the assumption that the gender gap varies significantly by age, race, geographic area, and time. In fact, Sutherland and other early criminologists cited variations in the ratio of female to male arrests to demonstrate the superiority of sociological explanations of crime over biological explanations (see the review in Steffensmeier & Clark 1980): If the gender gap had a biological basis, it would not vary, as it does, across time and space.

The Gender Equality Hypothesis

It also was assumed that variations could be best explained by differences in gender equality over time and among social groups (Sutherland 1924, see review in Steffensmeier & Clark 1980b). This interpretation is depicted in figure 1.

Figure I Gender Equality and Crime

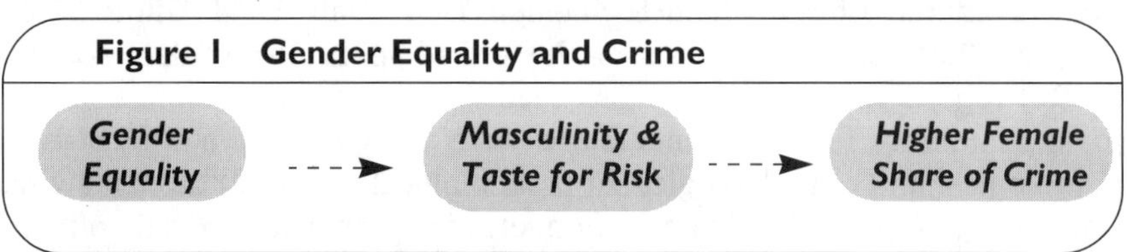

Specifically, the assertion was that the gender gap in crime is less in social settings where female roles and statuses presumably differ less from those of men: that is, in developed nations, compared to developing countries; in urban, compared to rural settings; among blacks, compared to whites; among people of older ages, compared to younger; and in time of war, compared to peacetime.

This early explication of the gender equality and crime hypothesis became the standard sociological explanation for the gender gap in crime, but it never attracted widespread public attention until the 1970s when several feminist criminologists suggested that increases in the female share of arrests could be attributed to gains in gender equality as a result of the women's movement (Adler 1975, Simon 1975). The media enthusiastically embraced this interpretation of the "dark side" of female liberation.

The gender equality hypothesis continues to influence theories of gender and crime, as exemplified in the power-control approach developed by Hagan and his colleagues (1993). According to power-control theory, the gender gap in "common delinquency" is minimized for girls raised in "egalitarian" families (families headed by women and families in which the mother works in a position of authority equal to or greater than that of the father). As with the earliest statements of the gender-equality hypothesis, greater gender equality is assumed to lead to higher rates of female crime (although the precise mechanisms are more complex).

Recent challenges to the assumptions of the gender equality hypothesis have questioned (i) whether the gender gap in crime varies as much as previously believed; (ii) whether women in fact have experienced greater social equality in the specified groups and times; (iii) whether the gender gap in crime is in fact less in the specified groups and times; and (iv) whether the gender equality approach fares better than alternative hypotheses for explaining whatever time-space variations in the gender gap do in fact exist.

The evidence for time-space variations is meager and often statistically flawed. Variation in the gender gap is sometimes found for this or that offense, mainly for less serious forms of lawbreaking. But across most offenses, the more systematic analyses of self-report data and official arrest statistics reveal that the gender effect is far more stable than variant across race, age, social class, rural-urban comparisons, and in comparisons of less-developed and developed nations (Cantor 1982, Steffensmeier & Allan 1988, Tittle 1980, Steffensmeier et al 1989). Even the apparent narrowing of the gender gap during war largely disappears when controls are included for the wartime absence of young men most at risk for crime (Steffensmeier et al 1980). Further, structural factors other than gender equality appear to better explain those instances where the gender gap is not stable across societies or population subgroups.

Recent Trends in Female Crime and the Women's Movement

It also is questionable whether the women's movement has led to a significant narrowing of the gender gap in crime over recent decades. Looking again at UCR data on the female percentage of arrests for the periods 1960, 1975, and 1990 (columns 7–9 in table 1), significant increases across both periods are found mainly for minor property crimes (larceny, fraud, forgery, and embezzlement); women averaged around 15% in 1960 and between 30% to 40% of arrestees for these crimes in 1990. The largest increases (12% to 19%) in the female share of arrests for these categories occurred between 1960 and 1975, before the women's movement had gained much momentum. Consistent but small increases (1% to 3% for each period) are found for major property crimes and malicious mischief offenses. However, no clear trends are found for the categories of crimes against persons, drinking and drugs, and the sex-related crimes. For all three periods, the female share of arrests for most offense categories was 15% or less, and was typically smallest for the most serious offenses.

It is plausible to argue that greater freedom has increased female participation in the public sphere (work, shopping, banking, driving, and the like), and this could help account for some of the increases in the female share of arrests for petty property offenses like larceny (shoplifting, employee theft), fraud (misuse of credit cards), or forgery (writing bad checks). But do such behaviors as shopping, banking, or working in shops really reflect female emancipation? Such offense categories do not reflect white-collar crimes, as Simon argued, but petty offenses committed by economically marginal women (Chesney-Lind 1986, Daly 1989, Steffensmeier 1980, 1993).

Alternative Explanations for Gender Gap Differences and Trends

Of course, for many offense categories, trends in the female share of offending are inconsistent with the gender equality hypothesis. However, a variety of alternative explanations provide more plausible and more parsimonious accounts for those increases in the female percent of arrests that did occur.

Gender Inequality. Some feminists (and others) espouse a position diametrically opposed to that of Adler and Simon (Chesney-Lind 1989, Daly 1989, Miller 1986, Richie 1995). They point to the peculiarity of considering "a hypothesis that assumed improving girls' and women's economic conditions would lead to an increase in female crime when almost all the existing criminological literature stresses the role played by discrimination and poverty (and unemployment or underemployment) in the creation of crime" (Chesney-Lind & Shelden 1992:77; see also Steffensmeier 1980).

Patriarchal power relations shape gender differences in crime, pushing women into crime through victimization, role entrapment, economic marginality, and survival needs. Nowhere is the gender ratio more skewed than in the great disparity of males as offenders and females as victims of sexual and domestic abuse. The logic of the gender inequality (or marginality) approach, depicted in figure 2, suggests that greater gender equality would lead to a lower female share of crime.

The role of inequality may be seen in career paths of female teens who drift into criminality as a consequence of running away from sexual and physical abuse at home. The struggle to survive on the streets may then lead to other status offenses and crimes (Gilfus 1992, Chesney-Lind 1989), including prostitution and drug dealing (English 1993). Especially when drug abuse is involved, other criminal involvements are likely to escalate (Anglin & Hser 1987, Inciardi et al 1993). Other feminist researchers have chronicled how female vulnerability to male violence may drive women into illegal activities (Miller 1986, Richie 1995). Despite histories of victimization or economic hardship, many of these women display considerable innovation and independence in their "survival strategies" (Mann 1984).

The gender inequality argument is also supported by Steffensmeier (1993), who points out that increases in petty property crimes are less likely to result from workforce gains than from the economic pressures on women that have been aggravated by heightened rates of divorce, illegitimacy, and female-headed households, coupled with greater responsibility for children. In addition to increased economic pressures, Steffensmeier (1993) goes on to enumerate several other factors that can help explain increases in the female percentage of arrests for property offenses, including the increased formalization of law enforcement, increased opportunities for "female" types of crime, and trends in female drug dependency.

Increased Formalization of Law Enforcement. Steffensmeier (1993) enumerates a number of other alternative explanations for increases in the female percent of arrest for some categories. For example, some increases in female arrests may have been an artifact of improved records processing that provided more complete tabulation of female arrests for some categories of arrest, particularly during the 1960s.

Figure 2 Gender Inequality and Crime

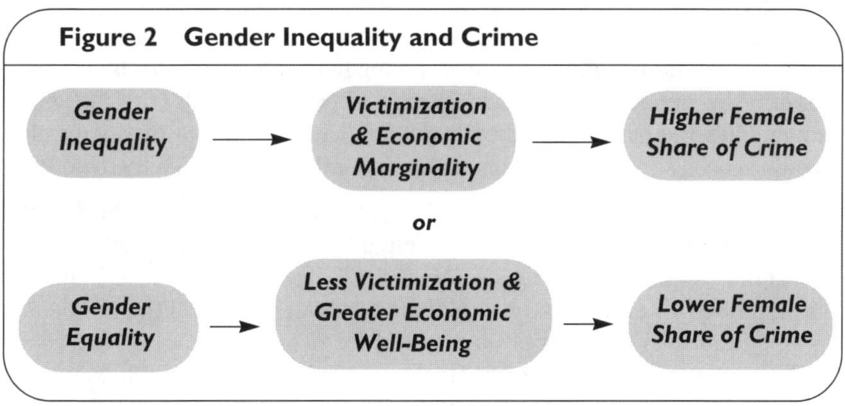

Increased Opportunities for "Female" Types of Crime. The increased percentage of arrests of women for petty property crimes reflects not only economic marginalization, but also an increase in opportunities for these crime categories (Steffensmeier 1993). Largely excluded from lucrative forms of crime (Steffensmeier 1983), women have increased their share of arrests for economically motivated crimes largely in those categories that (i) require little or no criminal "skill"; (ii) have expanded due to changes in merchandising and credit; (iii) are easily accessible to women in their roles as consumers and heads of families. Together, growing economic adversity among large subgroups of women has increased the pressure to commit consumer-based crimes, which are likewise expanding, such as shoplifting, check fraud, theft of services, and welfare fraud.

Trends in Female Drug Dependency. Rising levels of illicit drug use by women appear to have had a major impact on female crime trends, even though female drug arrests have not outpaced male arrests since 1960. Drug dependency amplifies income-generating crimes of both sexes, but more so for women because they face greater constraints against crime and need a greater motivational push to deviate (Anglin et al 1987, Inciardi et al 1993). Female involvement in burglary and robbery, in particular, typically occurs after addiction and is likely to be abandoned when drug use ceases (Anglin et al 1987).

Drug use is also more likely to initiate females into the underworld and criminal subcultures and to connect them to drug-dependent males who use them as crime accomplices or exploit them as "old ladies" to support their addiction (Miller 1986, Pettiway 1987, Steffensmeier & Terry 1986). The drug trends also help explain the small rise in the female percentage of incarcerated felons, from about 3% in the 1960s to 6% in the 1990s (but compare to 6% in the 1920s).

Other Criticisms of the Gender Equality Hypothesis

Several criticisms of the gender equality hypothesis have focused on power-control theory, on contradictory evidence such as the traditional gender-role definitions commonly found among female offenders, or on the manner in which gender gap trends in specific crimes are at odds with the gender equality hypothesis. Perhaps the most telling criticism is that theory development has been suppressed by the popularity of the gender equality hypothesis.

Criticisms of Power Control. The power-control version of the gender equality approach has been challenged for its uncritical acceptance of the gender equality hypothesis (Morash & Chesney-Lind 1991) and for adding little or nothing to the explanatory power of control theory (Jensen 1993). Empirical challenges have come from several studies that report findings at odds with power-control assertions (Jensen 1993, Morash & Chesney-Lind 1991, Singer & Levine 1988, but see Grasmick, Bursik & Sims 1993). However, these studies employed somewhat different operationalizations of the independent variables.

Traditional Gender-Role Definitions of Female Offenders. The gender equality hypothesis is further undermined by the prevalence of traditional gender-role definitions assumed by most male and female offenders (Bottcher 1995). A few studies report a relationship between nontraditional or masculine gender role attitudes and female delinquency on a given item but not on other items (Heimer 1995, Shover et al 1979, Simpson & Ellis 1995). The bulk of studies, however, report that traditional rather than nontraditional views are associated with greater delinquency (see reviews in Chesney-Lind & Shelden 1992, Pollock-Byrne 1990, Steffensmeier & Allan 1995).

Homicide and Burglary Trends. The basic irrelevance of the gender equality hypothesis to trends in the female share of arrests can be seen by looking in greater depth at the patterns for homicide (for which the female percent of arrests declined) and burglary (for which the female percent of arrests increased). In the case of murder, the decline in the female share of arrests (from 17% in 1960 to 10% in 1990) is accounted for not by any sharp drop in female arrests for murder, but by the great increases in male arrests for felony murders connected with the drug trade and the increased availability of guns.

Similarly, much of the increase (from 5% to 8%) in the female share of arrests for burglary between 1975 and 1990 resulted from drops in recorded male arrests, partly because of a shift from burglary to drug dealing on the part of male offenders, and partly because of increased police compliance with UCR reporting recommendations that theft from cars be reported as larceny rather than burglary (Steffensmeier 1993).

Suppression of Theory Development. Over-reliance on the gender equality hypothesis has retarded sociological efforts to develop a multivariate framework to explain gender differences in crime. In a sense, reliance on the gender equality hypothesis can be seen as another example of seeking unique explanations where female crime is at issue.

Application of Traditional Theory to Explanation of the Gender Gap

It is perhaps premature to abandon traditional criminological theories without fully exploiting their insights, which would suggest that females offend less than males: because they are less subject than males to the cultural emphasis on material success (anomie); because they are less exposed to influence from delinquent peers (differential association and/or social learning); because they have stronger social bonds and are subjected to greater supervision (social control); and because they are less likely to become involved in gangs (cultural transmission).

Findings from a number of self-report studies support the ability of traditional criminological theories to partially account for the gender gap in crime. These studies show that the relationship between gender and delinquency is significantly reduced when controls are included for friends who support delinquency (Simons et al 1980), parental controls (Hagan 1989), and social bonds (Jensen & Eve 1976). However, as with power-control theory (but framed explicitly in terms of "common delinquency"), the significance of the traditional theories for explaining the gender gap is limited by the fact that these studies have been confined to minor (mainly male) delinquencies. As already noted, they also lack sensitivity to the manner in which the criminal behavior of women differs from that of men in terms of paths to crime (e.g. prior experience as victims) and in terms of context.

The critical need is for an approach that can explain not just minor but serious female offending, and one that can explain the gender gap not just where it is least, but where it is greatest. Gender differences are most robust in both the prevalence and incidence of serious offending, yet robust theoretical tests for these differences are notable for their absence. Until such tests can be carried out, the relevance of traditional theories will remain unknown with regard to that domain of criminality where gender differences are greatest and where statistical variation is sufficient for theory testing.

Toward a Gendered Theory

No satisfactorily unified theoretical framework has yet been developed for explaining female criminality and gender differences in crime. Criminologists disagree as to whether gender-neutral (i.e. traditional theories derived from male samples) or gender-specific theories (i.e. recent approaches derived from female samples and positing unique causal paths for female as compared to male criminality) are better suited to these tasks. We take the position that the traditional gender-neutral theories provide reasonable explanations of less serious forms of female and male criminality, and for gender differences in such crime categories. Their principal shortcoming is that they are not very informative about the specific ways in which differences in the lives of men and women contribute to gender differences in type, frequency, and context of criminal behavior. Gender-specific theories are likely to be even less adequate if they require separate explanations for female crime and male crime.

Here we build on a framework for a "gendered" approach begun elsewhere (Steffensmeier & Allan 1995). This approach is compatible with the traditional, gender-neutral theories. The broad social forces suggested by traditional theories exert general causal influences on both male and female crime. But it is gender that mediates the manner in which those forces play out into sex differences in types, frequency, and contexts of crime involvements.

Key Elements of a Gendered Approach

A gendered approach should include at least four key elements. First, the perspective should help explain not only female criminality but male criminality as well, by revealing how the organization of gender deters or shapes delinquency by females but encourages it by males. We use the term "organization of gender" to refer broadly to things gendered—norms, identities, arrangements, institutions, and relations by which human sexual dichotomy is transformed into something physically and socially different.

Second, a gendered perspective should account not only for gender differences in type and frequency of crime, but also for differences in the context of offending. Even when men and women commit the same statutory offense, the "gestalt" of their offending is frequently quite different.

Because the gender differences in context are small for trivial or mild forms of lawbreaking, but large for violent and other serious forms of crime, contextual analysis can shed light on the gender differences for serious offenses—hitherto the most difficult to explain.

Third, compared to theories based on male crime, we need to consider several key ways in which women's routes to crime (especially serious crime) may differ from those of men. Building on the work of Daly (1994) and Steffensmeier (1983, 1993), such differences include: (a) the more blurred boundaries between victim and victimization in women's than men's case histories; (b) women's exclusion from most lucrative crime opportunities; (c) women's ability to exploit sex as an illegal money-making service; (d) consequences (real or anticipated) of motherhood and child care; (e) the centrality of greater relational concerns among women, and the manner in which these both shape and allow women to be pulled into criminal involvements by men in their lives; (f) the greater need of street women for protection from predatory or exploitative males.

Fourth, the perspective should explore the extent to which gender differences in crime derive not only from complex social, historical, and cultural factors, but from biological and reproductive differences as well (Kruttschnitt 1995, Udry 1995).

Figure 3 summarizes a gendered paradigm of offending that takes into account the four criteria enunciated above. We sketch here key features of this paradigm that affect men and women differently in terms of willingness and ability to commit crime.

Figure 3 Gendered Model of Female Offending and Gender Differences in Crime

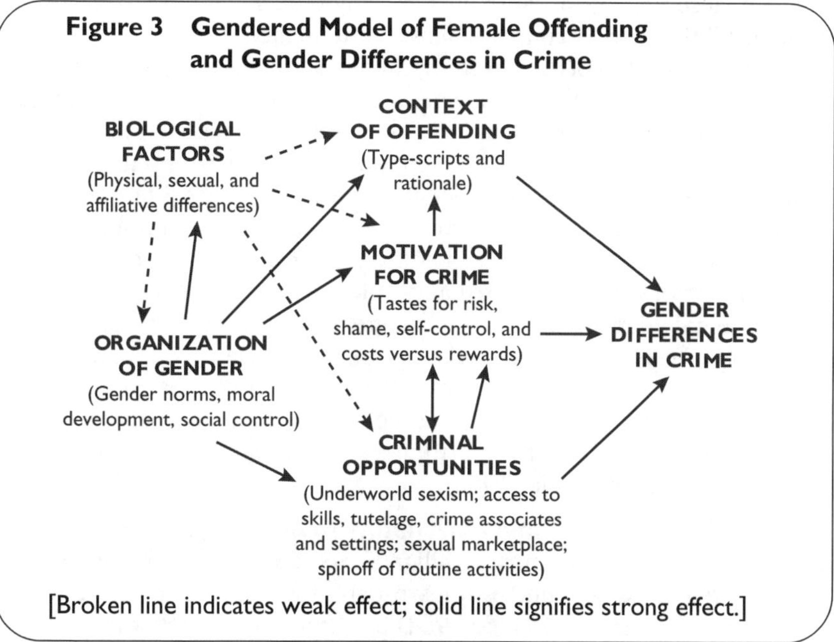

[Broken line indicates weak effect; solid line signifies strong effect.]

The Organization of Gender

The organization of gender together with sex differences in physical/sexual characteristics contributes to male and female differences in several types of relatively enduring characteristics that increase the probability of prosocial and altruistic response on the part of females but antisocial and predatory response on the part of males.

In the discussion that follows we elaborate briefly on five areas of life that inhibit female crime but encourage male crime: gender norms, moral development and affiliative concerns, social control, physical strength and aggression, and sexuality. Gender differences in these areas condition gender differences in patterns of motivation and access to criminal opportunities, as well as gender differences in the type, frequency, and context of offending. These areas are not discrete, but rather they overlap and mutually reinforce one another.

Gender Norms. The greater taboos against female crime stem largely from two powerful focal concerns ascribed to women: (i) nurturant role obligations and (ii) female beauty and sexual virtue. In varied settings or situations, these concerns shape the constraints and opportunities of girls' and women's illicit activities.

Women are rewarded for their ability to establish and maintain relationships and to accept family obligations, and their identity tends to be derived from key males in their lives (e.g. father, husband). Derivative identity constrains deviance on the part of women involved with conventional males but encourages the criminal involvements of those who become accomplices of husbands or boyfriends. Greater child-rearing responsibilities further constrain female criminality.

Femininity stereotypes (e.g. weakness, submission, domestication, nurturance, and "ladylike" behavior) are basically incompatible with qualities valued in the criminal underworld (Steffensmeier 1986). The cleavage between what is considered feminine and what is criminal is sharp, while the dividing line between what is considered masculine and what is criminal is often thin. Crime is almost always stigmatizing for females, and its potential cost to life chances is much greater than for males.

Expectations regarding sexuality and physical appearance reinforce greater female dependency as well as greater surveillance by parents and husbands. These expectations also shape the deviant roles available to women (e.g. sexual media or service roles). Moreover, fear of sexual victimization diverts women from crime-likely locations (bars, nighttime streets) and reduces their opportunities to commit crimes (McCarthy & Hagan 1992, Steffensmeier 1983).

Moral Development and Amenability to Affiliation. Gender differences in moral development (Gilligan 1982) and an apparent greater inherent readiness of women to learn parenting and nurturing (Beutel & Marini 1995, Brody 1985, Rossi 1984) predispose women toward an "ethic of care" that restrains women from violence and other criminal behavior injurious to others. Women are socialized not only to be more responsive to the needs of others but also to fear the threat of separation from loved ones. Such complex concerns inhibit women from undertaking criminal activities that might cause hurt to others and shape the "gestalt" of their criminality when they do offend.

In contrast, men who are conditioned toward status-seeking, yet marginalized from the world of work, may develop an amoral worldview in which the "takers" gain superior status at the expense of the "givers." Such a moral stance obviously increases the likelihood of aggressive criminal behavior on the part of those who become "convinced that people are at each other's throats increasingly in a game of life that has no moral rules" (Messerschmidt 1986, p. 66).

Social Control. Social control powerfully shapes women's relative willingness and ability to commit crime. Female misbehavior is more stringently monitored and corrected through negative stereotypes and sanctions (Simmons & Blyth 1987). The greater supervision and control reduces female risk-taking and increases attachment to parents, teachers, and conventional friends, which in turn reduces influence by delinquent peers (Giordano et al 1986). Encapsulation within the family and the production of "moral culture" restricts the freedom even of adult women to explore the temptations of the world (Collins 1992).

Physical Strength and Aggression. The demands of the crime environment for physical power and violence help account for the less serious nature and less frequent incidence of crimes by women compared to those by men. Women may lack the power, or may be perceived by themselves or by others as lacking the violent potential, for successful completion of certain types of crime or for protection of a major "score." Hustling small amounts of money or property protects female criminals against predators who might be attracted by larger amounts. Real or perceived vulnerability can also help account for female restriction to solo roles, or to roles as subordinate partners or accomplices in crime groups. This can be seen in a variety of female offense patterns, including the exigencies of the dependent prostitute-pimp relationship (James 1977). Together, physical prowess and muscle are useful for committing crimes, for protection, for enforcing contracts, and for recruiting and managing reliable associates.

Sexuality. Reproductive-sexual differences (especially when combined with sexual taboos and titillations of the society as a whole) contribute to the far greater sexual deviance and infidelity among males. Women, on the other hand, have expanded opportunities for financial gain through prostitution and related illicit sexual roles. The possibilities in this arena reduce the need to commit the serious property crimes that so disproportionately involve males.

Although female offenders may use their sexuality to gain entry into male criminal organizations, such exploitation of male stereotypes is likely to limit their criminal opportunities within the group to roles organized around female attributes. The sexual dimension may also heighten the potential for sexual tension which can be resolved only if the female aligns herself with one man sexually, becoming "his woman."

Even prostitution—often considered a female crime—is essentially a male-dominated or male-controlled criminal enterprise. Police, pimps, businessmen who employ prostitutes, and clients—virtually all of whom are male—control, in various ways, the conditions under which the prostitute works.

Access to Criminal Opportunity

The factors above—gender norms, social control, and the like—restrict female access to criminal opportunity, which in turn both limits and shapes female participation in crime. Women are also less likely than men to have access to crime opportunities as a spin-off of legitimate roles and routine activities. Women are less likely to hold jobs as truck driver, dockworker, or carpenter that would provide opportunities for theft, drug dealing, fencing, and other illegitimate activities. In contrast, women have considerable opportunity for commission, and thus for surveillance and arrest for petty forms of fraud and embezzlement.

Females are most restricted in terms of access to underworld crimes that are organized and lucrative. Institutional sexism in the underworld severely limits female involvement in crime groups, ranging from syndicates to loosely structured groups (Steffensmeier 1983, Commonwealth of Pennsylvania 1991). As in the upperworld, females in the underworld are disadvantaged in terms of selection and recruitment, in the range of career paths and access to them, and in opportunities for tutelage, skill development, and rewards.

Motivation

Gender norms, social control, lack of physical strength, and moral and relational concerns also limit female willingness to participate in crime at the subjective level—by contributing to gender differences in tastes for risk, likelihood of shame or embarrassment, self-control, and assessment of costs versus rewards of crime. Motivation is distinct from opportunity, but the two often intertwine, as when opportunity enhances temptation. As in legitimate enterprise, being able tends to make one more willing, just as being willing increases the prospects for being able. Like male offenders, female offenders gravitate to those activities that are easily available, are within their skills, provide a satisfactory return, and carry the fewest risks.

Criminal motivations and involvements are also shaped by gender differences in risk preferences and in styles of risk-taking (Hagan 1989, Steffensmeier 1980, Steffensmeier & Allan 1995). For example, women take greater risks to sustain valued relationships, whereas males take greater risks for reasons of status or competitive advantage. Criminal motivation is suppressed by the female ability to foresee threats to life chances and by the relative unavailability of type scripts that could channel females in unapproved behaviors.

Context of Offending

Many of the most profound differences between the offenses committed by men and women involve the context of offending, a point neglected by quantitative studies based on aggregate and survey data. "Context" refers to the characteristics of a particular offense, including both the circumstances and the nature of the act (Triplett & Myers 1995). Contextual characteristics include, for example, the setting, whether the offense was committed with others, the offender's role in initiating and committing the offense, the type of victim, the victim-offender relationship, whether a weapon was used, the extent of injury, the value or type of property destroyed or stolen, and the purpose of the offense. Even when males and females participate in the same types of crimes, the "gestalt" of their actions may differ markedly (Daly 1994, Steffensmeier 1983, 1993). Moreover, the more serious the offense, the greater the contextual differences by gender.

A powerful example of the importance of contextual considerations is found in the case of spousal murders, for which the female share of offending is quite high—at least one third, and perhaps as much as one half. Starting with Wolfgang's classic study of homicide, a number of writers propose that husbands and wives have equal potential for violence (Steinmetz & Lucca 1988, Straus & Gelles 1990). However, Dobash et al (1992) point out that the context of spousal violence is dramatically different for men and women. Compared to men, women are far more likely to kill only after a prolonged period of abuse, when they are in fear for their lives and have exhausted all alternatives. A number of patterns of wife-killing by husbands are rarely if ever found when wives kill husbands: murder-suicides, family massacres, stalking, and murder in response to spouse infidelity.

In common delinquency, female prevalence approaches that of males in simple forms of delinquency like hitting others or stealing from stores or schools, but girls are far less likely to use a weapon or to intend serious injury to their victims (Kruttschnitt 1994), to steal things they cannot use (Cohen 1966), and to steal from building sites or break into buildings (Mawby 1980).

Similarly, when females commit traditional male crimes like burglary, they are less likely to be solitary (Decker et al 1993), more likely to serve as an accomplice (e.g. drop-off driver), and less likely to receive an equal share of proceeds (Steffensmeier & Terry 1986). Also, female burglaries involve less planning and are more spontaneous, and they are more likely to occur in daytime in residences where no one is at home and with which they have prior familiarity as an acquaintance, maid, or the like (Steffensmeier 1986, 1993).

Application of Gendered Perspective to Patterns of Female Crime

The utility of a gendered perspective can be seen in its ability to explain both female and male patterns of criminal involvement as well as gender differences in crime. The perspective predicts, and finds, that female participation is highest for those crimes most consistent with traditional norms and for which females have the most opportunity, and lowest for those crimes that diverge the most from traditional gender norms and for which females have little opportunity. Let us briefly review some examples of property, violent, and public order offending patterns that can be better understood from a gendered perspective. In the area of property crimes we have already noted that the percentage of female arrests is highest for the minor offenses like small thefts, shoplifting, and passing bad checks—offenses compatible with traditional female roles in making family purchases. The high share of arrests for embezzlement reflects female employment segregation: women constitute about 90% of lower level bookkeepers and bank tellers (those most likely to be arrested for embezzlement), but slightly less than half of all accountants or auditors. Further, women tend to embezzle to protect their families or valued relationships, while men tend to embezzle to protect their status (Zeitz 1981).

Despite Simon's (1975) claim that female involvement in white collar crime was on the increase, in fact it is almost nonexistent in more serious occupational and/or business crimes, like insider trading, price-fixing, restraint of trade, toxic waste dumping, fraudulent product commerce, bribery, and official corruption, as well as large-scale governmental crimes (for example, the Iran-Contra affair and the Greylord scandal). Even when similar on-the-job opportunities for theft exist, women are still less likely to commit crime (Steffensmeier 1980).

The lowest percentage of female involvement is found for serious property crimes whether committed on the "street" such as burglary and robbery or in the "suite" such as insider trading or price-fixing (Steffensmeier & Allan 1995). These sorts of offenses are very much at odds with traditional feminine stereotypes, and ones to which women have very limited access. When women act as solo perpetrators, the typical robbery is a "wallet-sized" theft by a prostitute or addict (James 1977, see also Covington 1985, Pettiway 1987). However, females frequently become involved in such crimes as accomplices to males, particularly in roles that at once exploit women's sexuality and reinforce their traditional subordination to men (American Correctional Association 1983, Miller 1986, Steffensmeier & Terry 1986).

Female violence, although apparently at odds with female gender norms of gentleness and passivity, is also closely tied to the organization of gender. Unlike males, females rarely kill or assault strangers or acquaintances; instead, the female's victim tends to be a male intimate or a child, the offense generally takes place within the home, the victim is frequently drunk, and self-defense or extreme depression is often a motive (Dobash et al 1992). For women to kill, they generally must see their situation as life-threatening, as affecting the physical or emotional well-being of themselves or their children.

The linkage between female crime and the gendered paradigm of figure 3 is perhaps most evident in the case of certain public order offenses with a high percentage of female involvement, particularly the sex-related categories of prostitution and juvenile runaways—the only offense categories where female arrest rates exceed those of males. The high percentage of female arrests in these two categories reflects both gender differences in marketability of sexual services and the continuing patriarchal sexual double standard. Although customers must obviously outnumber prostitutes, they are less likely to be sanctioned. Similarly, although self-report studies show male rates of runaways to be as high as female rates, suspicion of sexual involvement makes female runaways more likely to be arrested (Chesney-Lind & Shelden 1992).

Female substance abuse (as with other patterns of female crime) often stems from relational concerns or involvements, beginning in the context of teenage dating or following introduction to drugs by husbands or boyfriends (Inciardi et al 1993, Pettiway 1987). Women tend to be less involved in heavy drinking or hard drug use—those drugs most intimately tied to drug subcultures and the underworld more generally (Department of Health & Human Services 1984). Female addicts are less likely to have other criminal involvements prior to addiction, so the amplification of income-oriented crime is greater for female drug users. Female addict crimes are mainly prostitution, reselling narcotics or assisting male drug dealers, and property crimes such as shoplifting, forgery, and burglary (Anglin & Hser 1987).

Advantages of Paradigm

A gendered approach helps to clarify the gendered nature of both female and male offending patterns. For women, "doing gender" preempts criminal involvement or directs it into scripted paths. For example, prostitution draws on and affirms femininity, while violence draws on and affirms masculinity.

At present it is unclear whether nontraditional roles for women will contribute to higher or lower rates of female offending. Traditional roles constrain most women from crime but may expose others to greater risks for criminal involvement. Wives playing traditional roles in patriarchal relationships appear to be at greatest risk both for victimization and for committing spousal homicide. Similarly, women emotionally dependent on criminal men are more easily persuaded to "do it all for love." (Note, nevertheless, that men are also more easily persuaded by other men.) Cross-cultural differences complicate the issue further. For example, among gypsies, traditional gender roles prevail and male dominance is absolute. Yet, because gypsy women do practically all the work and earn most of the money, their culture dictates a large female-to-male involvement in thievery (Maas 1973).

A gendered approach can also help explain both stability and variability in the gender effect. A growing body of historical research indicates that the gender differences in quality and quantity of crime described here closely parallel those that have prevailed since at least the thirteenth century (Beattie 1975, Hanawalt 1979). Even where variability does exist across time, the evidence suggests that changes in the female percentage of offending (i) are limited mainly to minor property crimes or mild forms of delinquency (Hagan & Simpson 1993, Steffensmeier 1980) and (ii) are due to structural changes other than more equalitarian gender roles such as shifts in economic marginality of women, expanded availability of female-type crime opportunities, and greater formalization of social control (Beattie 1995, Steffensmeier 1993). The considerable stability in the gender gap for offending can be explained in part by historical durability of the organization of gender (Walby 1990). Certainly for recent decades, research suggests that the core elements of gender roles and relationships have changed little, if at all (for a review, see Steffensmeier & Allan 1995, see also Beutel & Marini 1995). Underlying physical/sexual differences (whether actual or perceived) may also play a part. Human groups, for all their cultural variation, follow basic human forms.

Summary and Recommendations

An examination of gender patterns in crime reveals that there are both similarities and differences in female and male patterns of offending. Traditional criminological theories deserve more credit than they have received in recent writings in terms of their ability to provide general explanations both of female and male offending patterns and of the gender gap in crime. Certainly this is the case with minor acts of crime and delinquency which have been frequent objects of quantitative analysis. Likewise, the manner in which female and male rates of offending parallel one another across differences in time, race, class, and geography suggests that they are responding to similar social forces. Such findings suggest that there is no need for gender-specific theories.

On the other hand, explanation of serious crimes by males and females is more problematic, partly because the lower frequencies of offending complicate the task of quantitative analyses. Qualitative studies reveal major gender differences in the context and nature of offending.

Traditional theories have not adequately explored such gender differences. Our gendered paradigm seeks a middle road that acknowledges both the utility of traditional theory and the need to describe how the organization of gender (and biological/physical differences) specifies the impact of social forces suggested by traditional theory. Space limitations prevent us from broaching some of the most important areas related to female criminality, such as patterns of female victimization (Price & Sokoloff 1995) and gender differences in criminal justice processing (for a review, see Steffensmeier et al 1993). Even our coverage of patterns and etiology of female offending is selective and cursory. Nevertheless, some recommendations emerge from this review that could improve the yield of future theory and research.

We need to examine more closely whether various criminogenic factors (e.g. family, peers, schooling) vary by gender either in the magnitude or the direction of effects. Factors generally seen as uniquely relevant to the explanation of female crime (e.g. childhood abuse, personal maladjustment, victimization) should be explored in relation to male crime (Bjerregaard & Smith 1993).

Conventional theories were never designed to tap the encompassing structure and repetitive process of gender as it affects the criminal involvements of either women or men. Therefore we need to operationalize and test variables drawn from gendered approaches, particularly in relation to the explanation of serious and habitual criminal behavior.

Both theory development and research need to look more closely at the intersection of gender with other dimensions of stratification (Hill & Crawford 1990). Do gender-specific effects of causal variables also vary by race, class, or ethnicity? Care must be taken to avoid confusing gender effects with other subgroup effects, however. Identification of gender effects must entail female-male comparisons within the same population subgroup. For example, the fact that arrest rates for black females exceed arrest rates for white males for some offenses tells us something about race effects but nothing about gender effects (Heimer 1995, Simpson & Ellis 1995, Sommers 1992).

So far, the study of criminal careers has centered almost exclusively on male offenders. As Gilfus (1992:64) notes, "Little attention has been paid to questions such as whether there is such a thing as a female 'criminal career' pattern and, if so, how that career begins and what shapes its contours." In-depth studies of serious female offenders need to focus on career dimensions such as onset, frequency, duration, seriousness, and specialization.

Such studies need to examine both the immediate context of the offense and the larger social setting of serious or habitual offending, following the fine examples set by Miller's (1986) study of street women, Campbell's (1984) research on girls and gangs, Steffensmeier and Terry's (1986) research on institutional sexism in the underworld, and Bottcher's (1995) study of high-risk male and female youths, and their siblings. Such studies reveal the extent to which the lives of delinquent girls and women continue to be powerfully influenced by gender-related conditions of life.

Some of the most profound contributions to our knowledge concerning gender and crime (including the studies cited in the previous paragraph) have come from criminologists who have exploited theory and research from other sociological specialties (e.g. family, organization, network analysis) in the study of female criminality. Also needed is application of a life course perspective to female offending, as Sampson and Laub (1993) have done so effectively in their study of male offending.

We need a clearer understanding of the specific behaviors involved in particular crimes committed by women and men, the nature of their criminal roles, the circumstances leading to criminal involvement, the motivations for committing crimes, and the vocabularies used to justify their crimes. The same statutory charge applied to women and men may reflect very different behaviors and circumstances, as illustrated in the research on spousal homicide described above (reviewed by Dobash et al 1992).

Criminal opportunity has many dimensions that vary dramatically by gender. We need to understand how crime opportunities are shaped by legitimate opportunities, by the structure of the underworld, and by changes in productive and routine activities (Steffensmeier 1983, 1993). As already noted, women have little access to either upperworld or underworld opportunities for lucrative white collar or organized crime. Professional crime, traditionally dominated by white males, is on the decline.

Over the last three decades, the largest gains in female arrests relative to male arrests were for nonviolent economic crimes such as fraud and forgery—crimes now within the reach of virtually every American citizen. Changes in female motivation as well as in the social or economic position of females are likely to be less important than the nature of societal crime opportunities in shaping patterns of female offending and variations in the gender gap. This is a neglected area of research in criminology, and is one where sociologists with their expertise in broad societal trends can make a major contribution to the study not only of female criminality but also to crime more generally.

If significant differences in the gender gap are found, all plausible explanations should be explored. Tests of the gender equality hypothesis should attempt more suitable operationalization than assumed group differences in equality (such as age, race, urban residence). On the other hand, an interesting inquiry into the sociology of knowledge could address the longevity of the gender equality hypothesis in the face of so much contrary evidence.

Our knowledge about fundamental issues in the study of gender and crime has expanded greatly with the proliferation of studies over the past several decades, although significant gaps still exist. Given the relatively low frequency and less serious nature of female crime, expanding research on female offending may seem hard to justify. But research on the gendered nature of crime contributes to the understanding of male as well as female crime. Furthermore, the study of gender and crime is a productive arena for exploring the nature of gender stratification and the organization of gender more generally.

Literature Cited

Adler F. 1975. *Sisters in Crime.* New York: McGraw-Hill.

Akers R., Krohn M., Lanza-Kaduce L., Radosevich M. 1979. Social learning and deviant behavior: a specific test of a general theory. *Am. Sociol. Rev.* 44:298–310.

American Correctional Association. 1983. *Female Inmate Classification: An Examination of the Issues.* Natl. Inst. Correct. Washington, DC: U.S. Government Printing Office.

Anglin D., Hser Y. 1987. Addicted women and crime. *Criminology* 25:359–97.

Arnold R. 1989. Processes of criminalization from girlhood to womanhood. In *Women of Color in American Society,* ed. M. Zinn, B. Dill. Philadelphia: Temple Univ. Press.

Beattie J. 1975. The criminality of women in eighteenth century England. In *Women and the Law: A Social Historical Perspective,* ed. D. K. Weisberg. Cambridge, MA: Schenkman.

Beattie J. 1995. Crime and inequality in 18th-century London. In *Crime and Inequality,* ed. J. Hagan, R. Peterson. Stanford, CA: Stanford Univ. Press.

Berger R. 1990. Female delinquency in the Emancipation era: a review of the literature. *Sex Roles* 21:375–99.

Beutel A., Marini M. 1995. Gender and values. *Am. Sociol. Rev.* 60:436–48.

Bjerregaard B., Smith C. 1993. Gender differences in gang participation, delinquency, and substance use. *J. Quant. Criminol.* 9:329–56.

Boritch H., Hagan J. 1990. A century of crime in Toronto: gender, class and patterns of social control, 1859–1955. *Criminology* 28:601–26.

Bottcher J. 1986. *Risky Lives: Female Versions of Common Delinquent Life Patterns.* Sacramento: Calif. Youth Authority.

Bottcher J. 1995. Gender as social control: a qualitative study of incarcerated youths and their siblings in greater Sacramento. *Justice Q.* 12:33–57.

Bowker L., Gross H., Klein M. 1980. Female participation in delinquent gang activities. In *Women and Crime in America,* ed. L. Bowker, pp. 158–79. New York: Macmillan.

Brody L. R. 1985. Gender differences in emotional development: a review of theories and research. *J. Pers.* 14:102–49.

Bureau of Justice Statistics. 1973–1992. *Criminal Victimization in the United States, 1991.* Washington, DC: Dept. Justice.

Campbell A. 1984. *The Girls in the Gang.* Oxford: Basil Blackwell.

Campbell A. 1990. Female participation in gangs. In *Gangs in America,* ed. C. Huff. Newbury Park, CA: Sage.

Canter R. 1982. Sex differences in delinquency. *Criminology* 20:373–98.

Chesney-Lind M. 1986. Women and crime: the female offender. *Signs* 12:78–96.

Chesney-Lind M. 1989. Girls' crime and woman's place: toward a feminist model of female delinquency. *Crime Delinq.* 35:5–29.

Chesney-Lind M., Shelden R. 1992. *Girls, Delinquency, and Juvenile Justice.* Pacific Grove, CA: Brooks/Cole.

Cohen A. 1966. *Deviance and Control.* Englewood Cliffs, NJ: Prentice-Hall.

Collins R. 1992. Women and the production of status cultures. In *Cultivating Differences*, ed. M. Lamont, M. Fournier. Chicago: Univ. Chicago Press.

Commonwealth of Pennsylvania. 1991. *Organized Crime in Pennsylvania, The 1990 Report.* Conshohocken, PA: Penn. Crime Comm.

Covington J. 1985. Gender differences in criminality among heroin users. *J. Res. Crime Delinq.* 22:329–53.

Daly K. 1989. Gender and varieties of white-collar crime. *Criminology* 27:769–94.

Daly K. 1994. *Gender, Crime and Punishment.* New Haven, CT: Yale Univ. Press.

Daly K., Chesney-Lind M. 1988. Feminism and criminology. *Justice Q.* 5:497–538.

Decker S., Wright R., Refern A., Smith D. 1993. A woman's place is in the home: females and residential burglary. *Justice Q.* 10:1–16.

Deisite A. 1989. Maced greeter gives police key evidence. *The Patriot* p. B1.

Denno D. 1994. Gender, crime, and the criminal law defenses. *J. Crim. Law Criminol.* 85(1):80–180.

Department of Health and Human Services. 1984. *Drug Abuse and Drug Abuse Research.* Rockville, MD: Natl. Inst. Drug Abuse.

Dobash R., Dobash R. E., Wilson M., Daly M. 1992. The myth of sexual symmetry in marital violence. *Soc. Probl.* 39:71–91.

Elliott M. 1952. *Crime in a Modern Society.* New York: Harper & Brothers.

English K. 1993. Self-reported crime rate of women prisoners. *J. Quant. Crimol.* 9:357–82.

Fagan J. 1990. Social processes of delinquency and drug use among urban gangs. In *Gangs in America*, ed. C. Huff. Newbury Park, CA: Sage.

Gilfus M. 1992. From victims to survivors to offenders: women's routes of entry and immersion into street crime. *Women Crim. Justice* 4:63–89.

Gilligan C. 1982. *In a Different Voice: Psychological Theory and Women's Development.* Cambridge, MA: Harvard Univ. Press.

Giordano P., Cernkovich S., Pugh M. 1986. Friendships and delinquency. *Am. J. Sociol.* 91:1170–203.

Grasmick H., Bursik R., Sims B. 1993. Changes in the sex patterning of perceived threats of sanctions. *Law Soc. Rev.* 27:679–705.

Hagan J. 1989. *Structural Criminology.* New Brunswick, NJ: Rutgers Univ. Press.

Hagan J., Gillis A., Simpson J. 1993. The power of control in sociological theories of delinquency. In *Advances in Criminological Theory*, Vol. 4, ed. F. Adler, W. Laufer. New Brunswick, NJ: Transaction.

Hanawalt B. 1979. *Crime and Conflict in English Communities, 1300–1348.* Cambridge: Harvard Univ. Press.

Heimer K. 1995. Gender, race, and the pathways to delinquency: an interactionist explanation. In *Crime and Inequality*, ed. J. Hagan, R. Peterson. Stanford, CA: Stanford Univ. Press.

Hill G., Crawford E. 1990. Women, race, and crime. *Criminology* 28:601–26.

Inciardi J., Lockwood V., Pottieger A. 1993. *Women and Crack-Cocaine.* New York: Macmillan.

James J. 1977. Prostitutes and prostitution. In *Deviants: Voluntary Action in a Hostile World*, ed. E. Sagarin, F. Montanino. New York: Scott Foresman.

Jensen G. 1993. Power-control vs social-control theories of common delinquency: a comparative analysis. In *Advances in Criminlogical Theory*, Vol. 4, ed. F. Adler, W. Laufer. New Brunswick, NJ: Transaction.

Jensen G., Eve R. 1976. Sex differences in delinquency. *Criminology* 13:427–48.

Kruttschnitt C. 1994. Gender and interpersonal violence. In *Understanding and Preventing Violence: Social Influences*, ed. J. Roth, A. Reiss. 3:295–378. Washington, DC: Natl. Acad. Set.

Maas P. 1973. *King of the Gypsies*. New York: Bantam.

Mann C. 1984. *Female Crime and Delinquency*. Birmingham: Univ. Alabama Press.

Mawby R. 1980. Sex and crime: the results of a self-report study. *Br. J. Social.* 31:525–43.

McCarthy B., Hagan J. 1992. Mean streets: the theoretical significance of situational delinquency and homeless youths. *Am. J. Sociol.* 98:597–627.

Messerschmidt J. 1986. *Capitalism, Patriarchy, and Crime: Toward a Socialist Feminist Criminology*. Totowa, NJ: Rowman & Littlefield.

Miller E. 1986. *Street Women*. Philadelphia: Temple Univ. Press.

Miller W. 1980. The molls. In *Women, Crime. and Justice*, ed. S. Datesman, F. Scarpitti. New York: Oxford Univ. Press.

Morash M., Chesney-Lind M. 1991. A reformulation and partial test of the power control theory of delinquency. *Justice Q.* 8:347–76.

Pettiway L. 1987. Participation in crime partnerships by female drug users. *Criminology* 25:741–67.

Pollock-Byrne J. 1990. *Women, Prison, and Crime*. Belmont, CA: Brooks/Cole.

Price B., Sokoloff N. 1995. *The Criminal Justice System and Women*. New York: McGraw-Hill.

Prus R., Sharper CRD. 1977. *Road Hustler*. Lexington, MA: Lexington.

Quicker J. 1983. *Homegirls: Characterizing Chicano Gangs*. San Pedro, CA: Int. Univ. Press.

Reitman B. 1937. *Sister of the Road: The Autobiography of Box-Car Bertha*. New York: Macauley.

Richie B. 1995. *The Gendered Entrapment of Battered, Black Women*. London: Routledge.

Rossi A. 1984. Gender and parenthood. *Am. Sociol. Rev.* 49:1–19.

Sampson R., Laub J. 1993. *Crime in the Making*. Cambridge, MA: Harvard Univ. Press.

Shover N., Norland S., James J., Thorton W. 1979. Gender roles and delinquency. *Soc. Forces* 58:162–75.

Simmons R., Blyth D. 1987. *Moving Into Adolescence*. New York. Aldine.

Simon R. 1975. *The Contemporary Woman and Crime*. Washington, DC: Natl. Inst. Mental Health.

Simons R., Miller M., Aignor S. 1980. Contemporary theories of deviance and female delinqueney. *J. Res. Criminol. Delinq.* 17:42–57.

Simpson S., Ellis L. 1995. Doing gender: sorting out the caste and crime conundrum. *Criminology* 33:47–77.

Singer S., Levine M. 1988. Power-control theory, gender and delinquency. *Criminology* 26:627–48.

Smith D. 1979. Sex and deviance: an assessment of major sociological variables. *Social. Q.* 20:183–95.

Smith D., Paternoster R. 1987. The gender gap in theories of deviance: issues and evidence. *Criminology* 24:140–72.

Smith D., Visher C. 1980. Sex and involvement in deviance/crime: a quantitative review of the empirical literature. *Am. Sociol. Rev.* 65:767–82.

Sommers I., Baskin D. 1992. Sex, race, age, and violent offending. *Violence Vict.* 7:191–201.

Steffensmeier D. 1980. A review and assessment of sex differences in adult crime, 1965–77. *Soc. Forces* 58:1080–1108.

Steffensmeier D. 1983. Sex-segregation in the underworld: building a sociological explanation of sex differences in crime. *Soc. Forces* 61:1010–32.

Steffensmeier D. 1986. *The Fence: In the Shadow of Two Worlds.* Totowa, NJ: Rowman & Littlefield.

Steffensmeier D. 1993. National trends in female arrests, 1960–1990: assessment and recommendations for research. *J. Quant. Criminol.* 9:413–41.

Steffensmeier D., Allan E. 1988. Sex disparities in crime by population subgroup: residence, race, and age. *Justice Q.* 5:53–80.

Steffensmeier D., Allan E. 1995. Gender, age, and crime. In *Handbook of Contemporary Criminology*, ed. J. Sheley. New York: Wadsworth.

Steffensmeier D., Allan E., Streifel C. 1989. Modernization and female crime: a cross-national test of alternative explanations. *Soc. Forces* 68:262–83.

Steffensmeier D., Clark R. 1980. Sociocultural vs. biological/sexist explanations of sex differences in crime: a survey of American criminology textbooks, 1919–1965. *Am. Sociol.* 15:246–55.

Steffensmeier D., Kramer J., Streifel C. 1993. Gender and imprisonment decisions. *Criminology* 31:411–46.

Steffensmeier D., Rosenthal A., Shehan C. 1980. World War II and its effects on the sex differential in arrests: an empirical test of the sex-role equality and crime proposition. *Sociol. Q.* 21:246–55.

Steffensmeier D., Streifel C. 1992. Time-series analysis of female-to-male arrests for property crimes, 1960–1985: a test of alternative explanations. *Justice Q.* 9:78–103.

Steffensmeier D., Streifel C. 1993. *Structural covariates of female as compared to male violence rates.* Presented at Annu. Meet. Am. Sociol. Crim., Phoenix, AZ.

Steffensmeier D., Terry R. 1986. Institutional sexism in the underworld: a view from the inside. *Sociol. Inq.* 56:304–23.

Steinmetz S., Lucca J. 1988. Husband beating. In *Handbook of Family Violence*, ed. R. Hassselt, A. Morrison, S. Bellack, M. Hersen, pp. 233–46. New York: Plenum.

Straus M., Gelles R. 1990. *Physical Violence in American Families.* New Brunswick, NJ: Transaction.

Sutherland E. 1924. *Criminology.* Philadelphia: Lippincott.

Swart W. 1991. Female gang delinquency: a search for "acceptably deviant behavior." *Mid-Am. Rev. Sociol.* 15:43–52.

Thrasher F. 1927. *The Gang.* Chicago: Univ. Chicago Press.

Tittle C. 1980. *Social Sanctions and Social Deviance.* New York: Praeger.

Triplett R., Myers L. 1995. Evaluating contextual patterns of delinquency: gender-based differences. *Justice Q.* 12:59–79.

Udry J. R. 1995. Sociology and biology: what biology do sociologists need to know? *Soc. Forces* 73:1267–78.

US Department of Justice. 1960–1993. *Uniform Crime Reports.* Fed. Bur. Invest. Washington, DC: US Gov. Print. Off.

Walby S. 1990. *Theorizing Patriarchy.* Cambridge, MA: Basil Blackwell.

Weiner N. 1989. Violent criminal careers and "violent career criminals." In *Violent Crime, Violent Criminals*, ed. N. Weiner, M. Wolfgang, pp. 35–138. Newbury Park, CA: Sage.

Widom C. 1989. Child abuse, neglect and violent criminal behavior. *Criminology* 27:251–71.

Zeitz D. 1981. *Women Who Embezzle or Defraud.* New York: Praeger.

5

Women in the Street-Level Drug Economy
Continuity or Change?

Lisa Maher
Kathleen Daly

Images of women in the contemporary drug economy are highly mixed. Most scholars emphasize *change* in women's roles in U.S. drug markets of 1960–1985, organized primarily around heroin, compared to women's roles in more recent drug markets with the advent of crack cocaine (e.g., Baskin et al., 1993; Bourgois, 1989; Dunlap and Johnson, 1992; Inciardi et al., 1993; Mieczkowski, 1994; C. Taylor, 1993). Some emphasize *continuity* from previous decades (Adler, 1985; Koester and Schwartz, 1993; Maher and Curtis, 1992). Others suggest that both change and continuity are evident, with women inhabiting "two social worlds" (Fagan, 1994:212): one of increased participation in, and the other of continued restriction by, male-dominated street and drug networks.

One should expect, on the one hand, to see variation in women's positions in the drug economy. Research on drug markets in New York City (Bourgois, 1995; Curtis and Sviridoff, 1994; Hamid, 1990, 1992; Johnson et al., 1985, 1992; Williams, 1989), Miami (Inciardi et al., 1993), Washington, D.C. (Reuter et al., 1990), Detroit (Mieczkowski, 1986, 1990; C. Taylor, 1990), Chicago (Padilla, 1992), Milwaukee (Hagedorn, 1994), Los Angeles, and the West Coast (Adler, 1985; Morgan and Joe, 1994; Skolnick, 1989; Waldorf et al., 1991) reveals differences in the racial and ethnic composition of participants and who controls markets, the kinds of drugs sold, how

Reprinted with permission of the American Society of Criminology from *Criminology,* vol. 34, no. 4, pp. 465–491.

markets are organized, and participants' responses to law enforcement. Such differences are likely to affect women's positions and specific roles.

At the same time, the varied characterizations of women's roles reflect differences in the theoretical assumptions and methodological approaches taken by scholars. For example, women's increasing presence in the drug economies of the late 1980s and early 1990s is said to reflect (1) emancipation from their traditional household responsibilities (Bourgois, 1989; Bourgois and Dunlap, 1993), (2) an extension of their traditional household responsibilities (Wilson, 1993), and (3) the existence of "new opportunities" in street-level drug markets (Mieczkowski, 1994), especially with increased rates of incarceration of minority group men (Baskin et al., 1993). These explanations reveal different assumptions about changes (or not) in the gendered structure of drug markets and about the links (or not) between women's participation in crime and their domestic responsibilities.

Data sources and methods also affect the quality and content of the inferences drawn. Some have analyzed Uniform Crime Report (UCR) arrest data (e.g., Wilson, 1993), others have interviewed women arrested on drug charges or through snowball samples (e.g., Baskin et al., 1993; Fagan, 1994; Inciardi et al., 1993; C. Taylor, 1993), and a handful have conducted ethnographies of particular neighborhoods (e.g., Bourgois, 1989; Maher and Curtis, 1992). While interview-based studies may offer an empirical advantage over the inferences that can be drawn from UCR arrest data, the one-time interview may not elicit complete or reliable information about the changing contexts of women's income generation in the informal economy.

This article presents the results of an ethnographic study of women drug users conducted during 1989–1992 in a New York City neighborhood. We assess whether women's involvement in U.S. drug markets of the mid-1980s onward reflects change, continuity, or a combination of change and continuity from patterns in previous decades. We find that contrary to the conclusions of Baskin et al. (1993), Fagan (1994), Inciardi et al. (1993), Mieczkowski (1994), and C. Taylor (1993), crack cocaine markets have not necessarily provided "new opportunities" for women, nor should such markets be viewed as "equal opportunity employers" (Bourgois, 1989; Wilson, 1993). Our study suggests that recent drug markets continue to be monopolized by men and to offer few opportunities for stable income generation for women. While women's *presence* on the street and in low-level auxiliary roles may have increased, we find that their *participation* as substantive labor in the drug-selling marketplace has not.

Women in the Drug Economy

Drug Markets of the 1960s to the Mid-1980s

Prior to the advent of crack cocaine in the mid-1980s, research on women in the drug economy used one or more of four elements to explain women's restricted roles in selling and distributing drugs:[1] intimate relationships with men, the availability of alternative options for income generation, restrictions on discretionary time, and institutionalized sexism in the underworld.

Female heroin users were often characterized as needing a man to support their consumption (e.g., File, 1976; File et al., 1974; Hser et al., 1987; Smithberg and Westermeyer, 1985; Sutter, 1966). They were also described as being "led" into crime by individual men (Covington, 1985; Pettiway, 1987), although this may apply more to white than minority group women (Anglin and Hser, 1987; Pettiway, 1987). The typical pattern was of low-status roles in which participation was short-lived, sporadic, and mediated by intimate relationships with men (Adler, 1985; Rosenbaum, 1981). Alternative sources of income generation, such as prostitution and shoplifting, may have been preferable to female drug users, especially heroin users (File, 1976; Goldstein, 1979; Hunt, 1990; Inciardi and Pottieger, 1986; James, 1976; Rosenbaum, 1981). Some suggest, in addition, that women's household and childcare responsibilities may have limited their full participation in the drug economy (e.g., Rosenbaum, 1981; A. Taylor, 1993; see also Wilson, 1993).

Women's peripheral roles in male-dominated drug selling networks (Auld et al., 1986; Goldstein, 1979; Rosenbaum, 1981) can also be explained by "institutionalized sexism" in the "underworld" (Steffensmeier, 1983; Steffensmeier and Terry, 1986; see also Box, 1983). Steffensmeier (1983:1013–1015) argues that male lawbreakers prefer to "work, associate, and do business with other men" (homosocial reproduction); they view women as lacking the physical and mental attributes considered essential to working in an uncertain and violent context (sex-typing and task environment of crime). In the drug economy, in particular, women are thought to be unsuitable for higher-level distribution roles because of an inability to manage male workers through threatened violence (Waterston, 1993:114).

Crack Cocaine Markets of the Mid-1980s Onward

Women have been depicted as more active participants in selling and distributing drugs in the crack cocaine economy of the late 1980s compared to previous drug eras. While some find that women's roles continue to be mediated by relationships with men (Koester and Schwartz, 1993; Murphy et al., 1991) and that women remain at the bottom of the drug market hierarchy (Maher and Curtis, 1992), others suggest that there has been decisive change. Specifically, it is argued that "drug business" crimes (that is, street-level drug sales) generate a higher share of women's income than in the past, with a concomitant decrease in prostitution-generated income (Inciardi et al., 1993). More generally, it is argued that the crack-propelled expansion of drug markets has provided "new opportunities" for women.

The "new opportunities" argument is made by the majority of those in the field (see, e.g., Baskin et al., 1993; Bourgois, 1989; Bourgois and

Dunlap, 1993; Fagan, 1994; Inciardi et al., 1993; Mieczkowski, 1994). It takes two forms: a general claim that women's emancipation in the wider society is evident in "all aspects of inner-city street life" (Bourgois, 1989:643–644) and a more restricted claim that the weakening of male-dominated street networks and market processes has made it possible for women to enter the drug economy. For example, in his study of New York City women, Fagan (1994:210) concludes that

> while women were consigned secondary, gender-specific roles in . . . [drug] businesses in the past, the size and seemingly frantic activity of the current drug markets has made possible for women new ways to participate in street networks. Their involvement in drug selling at high income levels defies the gendered norms and roles of the past, where drug dealing was an incidental income source often mediated by domestic partnerships . . . the expansion of drug markets in the cocaine economy has provided new ways for women to escape their limited roles, statuses and incomes in previous eras.

While two-thirds of the women in Fagan's (1994) sample did not sell drugs and while most who sold drugs acted alone (p. 197), Fagan was struck by "the emergence of women sellers earning high incomes and avoiding prostitution" (p. 211). He concluded that "two social worlds" of continuity and change characterized women's participation in drug markets. One difficulty in assessing this claim is that no estimate is given of the proportion of women who were earning high incomes from drug business, avoiding prostitution, and "def[ying] the gendered norms and roles of the past."

Fagan's research offers a good comparison to our study. He draws from interviews with 311 women, the majority of whom were drug users or sellers, in two New York City neighborhoods (Washington Heights and Central Harlem in northern Manhattan). The interviews were conducted during the late 1980s; the sample included women with police arrest records, in residential treatment programs, and those who had not been arrested. The women in our sample lived just a few miles away in Bushwick, a Brooklyn neighborhood. Very few of the Bushwick women were active dealers, and virtually all supported themselves by prostitution. Whereas Fagan sees two worlds of continuity and change, we see just one of continuity. Before describing that social world, we sketch the study site and the methods used in gathering the data.

Research Site and Methods

Research Site

Bushwick, the principal study site, has been described as hosting "the most notorious drug bazaar in Brooklyn and one of the toughest in

New York City" (*New York Times*, October 1, 1992:A1). Historically home to large numbers of European Jews, by the 1960s Bushwick was dominated by working-class Italians. Since the late 1960s, the area has become the home of low-income Latino populations, predominantly Puerto Ricans, although Dominicans and Colombians have begun to move in. In 1960 the population was 89% white, 6% black, and 5% Hispanic. By 1990 it was 5% white, 25% black, and 65% Hispanic (Bureau of the Census, 1990). In 1990 Bushwick was Brooklyn's poorest neighborhood with a median household income of $16,287; unemployment was twice the citywide rate; and more than half of all families and two-thirds of all children lived under the official poverty line (Bureau of the Census, 1990).

Between 1988 and 1992 drug distribution in Bushwick was intensely competitive; there were constant confrontations over "turf" as organizations strove to establish control over markets. Like many drug markets in New York City (see, e.g., Curtis and Sviridoff, 1994; Waterston, 1993), Bushwick was highly structured and ethnically segmented. The market, largely closed to outsiders, was dominated by Dominicans with networks organized by kin and pseudo-kin relations.[2]

Fieldwork Methods

Preliminary fieldwork began in the fall of 1989 when the senior author established a field presence in several Brooklyn neighborhoods (Williamsburg, East Flatbush, and Bushwick). By fall 1990 observations and interviews were intensified in Bushwick because it hosted the busiest street-level drug market in Brooklyn and had an active prostitution stroll. As fieldwork progressed, it became apparent that the initial plan of conducting interviews with a large number of women crack users was not, by itself, going to yield a complete picture. For example, few women initially admitted that they performed oral sex for less than $20, and none admitted to participating in sex-for-crack trades.

By the end of December 1991, interviews had been conducted with 211 active women crack users in Williamsburg, East Flatbush, and Bushwick. These were tape recorded and ranged from 20 minutes to 3 hours; they took place in a variety of settings, including private or semiprivate locations (e.g., apartments, shooting galleries, abandoned buildings, cars) and public locales (e.g., restaurants, parks, subways, and public toilets).[3] From January to March 1992, a preliminary data sort was made of the interview and observational material. From that process, 45 women were identified for whom there were repeated observations and interview material. Contact with these women was intimate and extensive; the number of tape-recorded interviews for each woman ranged from 3 to 15. Unless otherwise noted, the research findings reported here are based on this smaller group of 45 Bushwick women.

Profile of the Bushwick Women

The Bushwick women consisted of 20 Latinas (18 Puerto Ricans and 2 Dominicans), 16 African-Americans, and 9 European-Americans; their ages ranged from 19 to 41 years, with a mean of 28 years. At the time of the first interview, all the women used smokable cocaine (or crack), although only 31% used it exclusively; most (69%) had used heroin or powder cocaine prior to using crack. The women's average drug use history was 10.5 years (using the mean as the measure); heroin and powder cocaine initiates had a mean of about 12 years and the smokable cocaine initiates, about 6 years.

Most women (84%) were born in the New York City area, and more than half were born in Brooklyn. About one-quarter were raised in households with both parents present, and over one-third (38%) grew up in a household in which they were subjected to physical abuse. Most (84%) had not completed high school, and 55% had no experience of formal-sector work. A high proportion were homeless (91%), alternating between the street and short-term accommodations in shelters, apartments of friends, and homes of elderly men (see also Maher et al., 1996). Most women were mothers (80%); the 36 mothers had given birth to 96 children, whose ages ranged from newborns to 26 years. Few of the mothers (9%) had their children living with them during the study period. Fourteen women (31%) had tested positive for HIV, and an additional five women believed that they were HIV positive; but most women said they did not know their serostatus. By the end of the study period, two women had stopped using illicit drugs, and five had died: two from HIV-related illnesses and three from homicide.

These 45 women represent the range of ages, racial-ethnic backgrounds, life experiences, and histories of crack-using women among the larger group of Brooklyn women interviewed. We are cognizant, however, of the limits of using ethnographic research in one area to generalize to other areas. For example, there is a somewhat higher proportion of Latinas (44%) in our sample than in Fagan's (1994:225) sample in Central Harlem (23%) and Washington Heights (33%). A higher share of the Bushwick women had not completed high school, had no experience in the formal labor force, and were homeless.

Structure of New York City Crack Markets

Street-level crack markets have frequently been characterized as unregulated markets of freelancers engaged in individual entrepreneurial activity (Hunt, 1990; Reuter et al., 1990). Some evidence suggests, however, that once demand has been established, the freelance model may be superseded by a more structured system of distribution. When the crack epidemic was at its peak in New York City during the late 1980s, Bushwick (like other neighborhoods) hosted highly structured street-level drug markets with pooled interdependence, vertical differentiation, and a formal, multi-tiered system of organization and control with defined employer-employee relationships (Curtis and Maher, in press; Johnson et al., 1990, 1992). This model is similar to the "runner system" used in heroin distribution (see Mieczkowski, 1986).

In selling crack cocaine, drug business "owners" employ several "crew bosses," "lieutenants," or "managers," who work shifts to ensure an efficient organization of street-level distribution. Managers (as they were known in Brooklyn) act as conduits between owners and lower-level employees. They are responsible for organizing and delivering supplies and collecting revenues. Managers exercise considerable autonomy in the hiring, firing, and payment of workers; they are responsible for labor force discipline and the resolution of workplace grievances and disputes. Next down the hierarchy are the street-level sellers, who perform retailing tasks having little discretion. Sellers are located in a fixed space or "spot" and are assisted by those below them in the hierarchy: lower-level operatives acting as "runners," "look-outs," "steerers," "touts," "holders," and "enforcers." Runners "continuously supply the sellers," look-outs "warn of impending dangers," steerers and touts "advertise and solicit customers," holders "handle drugs or money but not both," and enforcers "maintain order and intervene in case of trouble" (Johnson et al., 1992:61–64).

In New York City in the early 1990s, it was estimated that 150,000 people were involved in selling or helping to sell crack cocaine on any given day (Williams, 1992:10). Crack sales and distribution became a major source of income for the city's drug users (Hamid, 1990, 1991; Johnson et al., 1994). How, then, did the Bushwick women fit into this drug market structure? We examine women's involvement in a range of drug business activities.

Selling and Distributing Drugs

During the entire three years of fieldwork, including the interviews with the larger group of over 200 women, we did not discover any woman who was a business owner, and just one worked as a manager. The highly structured nature of the market in Bushwick, coupled with its kin-based organization, militated against personal or intimate sexual relationships between female drug users and higher-level male operatives. To the limited extent that they participated in drug selling, women were overwhelmingly concentrated at the lowest levels. They were almost always used as temporary workers when men were arrested or refused to work, or when it was "hot" because of police presence. Table 1 shows how the 45 women were involved in Bushwick's drug economy.

Of the 19 women (42%) who had some involvement, the most common role was that of informal steerer or tout. This meant that they recommended a particular brand of heroin to newcomers to the neighborhood in return for "change," usually a dollar or so. These newcomers were usually white men,

Table 1. Bushwick Women's Roles in the Drug Economy, 1989–92

	N	%
No Role	26	58
Had Some Role	19	42
	45	100

Of the 19 women with roles in the drug economy during the three-year study period, the following shows what they did. Because most women (*N* = 13) had more than one role, the total sums to greater than 19.

Selling and Distributing Roles	
Owner	0
Manager	0
Regular Seller	0
Irregular Seller	7
Runner	0
Look-out	0
Steerer or Tout	9
Holder	0
Enforcer	0
Selling/Renting Paraphernalia	
Works Sellers	4
Stem Renters	6
Running a Gallery	3
Copping Drugs for Others	14
Other Drug Business Hustles	
Street Doc	1

NOTE: While we have tried to be precise, we should note that it can be difficult to characterize women's roles—not only because drug markets are fluid and shifting but also because some women had varied mixes of roles over time.

who may have felt more comfortable approaching women with requests for such information. In turn, the women's perceptions of "white boyz" enabled them to use the situation to their advantage. Although they only used crack, Yolanda, a 38-year-old Latina, and Boy, a 26-year-old African-American woman, engaged in this practice of "tipping" heroin consumers.

> They come up to me. Before they come and buy dope and anything, they ask me what dope is good. I ain't done no dope, but I'm a professional player. . . . They would come to me, they would pay me, they would come "What's good out here?" I would tell them, "Where's a dollar," and that's how I use to make my money. Every-day somebody would come, "Here's a dollar, here's two dollars." (Yolanda) [What other kinds of things?] Bumming up change. [There ain't many people down here with change.] Just the white guys. They give you more faster than your own kind. [You go cop for them?] No, just for change.

> You tell them what's good on [the] dope side. Tell them anything, I don't do dope, but I'll tell them anything. Yeah, it's kicking live man. They buy it. Boom! I got my dollar, bye. (Boy)

Within the local drug economy, the availability of labor strongly determines women's participation in street-level distribution roles. Labor supply fluctuates with extramarket forces, such as product availability and police intervention. One consequence of police activity in Bushwick during the study period was a recurring, if temporary, shortage of male workers. Such labor market gaps promoted instability: The replacement of "trusted" sellers (i.e., Latinos) with "untrustworthy" drug users (i.e., women and non-Latinos) eroded the social and kinship ties that had previously served to reduce violence in drug-related disputes (see also Curtis and Sviridoff, 1994).

Early in the fieldwork period (during 1989 and early 1990), both men and women perceived that more women were being offered opportunities to work as street-level sellers than in the past. Such opportunities, it turned out, were often part of a calculated risk-minimization strategy on the part of owners and managers. As Princess, a 32-year-old African-American woman observed, some owners thought that women were less likely to be noticed, searched, or arrested by police:

> Nine times out of ten when the po-leece roll up it's gonna [be] men. And they're not allowed to search a woman, but they have some that will. But if they don' do it, they'll call for a female officer. By the time she gets there, (laughs) if you know how to move around, you better get it off you, unless you jus' want to go to jail. [So you think it works out better for the owners to have women working for them?] Yeah, to use women all the time.

As the fieldwork progressed and the neighborhood became more intensively policed, this view became less tenable. Latisha, a 32-year-old African-American woman, reported that the police became more aggressive in searching women:

> [You see some women dealing a little bit you know.] Yeah, but they starting to go. Now these cop around here starting to unzip girls' pants and go in their panties. It was, it's not like it was before. You could stick the drugs in your panties 'cause you're a female. Now that's garbage.

Thus, when initially faced with a shortage of regular male labor and large numbers of women seeking low-level selling positions, some managers appear to have adopted the opportunistic use of women to avoid detection and disruption of their businesses. How frequent this practice was is uncertain; we do know that it was short-lived (see also Curtis and Sviridoff, 1994:164).

In previous years (the late 1970s and early 1980s), several Bushwick women had sold drugs in their roles as wives or girlfriends of distributors, but this was no longer the case. During the three-year study period only 12 women (27%) were involved in selling and distributing roles. Of this group of 12, only 7 were able to secure low-level selling positions on an irregular basis. Connie, a 25-year-old Latina, was typical of this small group, and in the following quotation she describes her unstable position within the organization she worked for:

> I'm currently working for White Top [crack]. They have a five bundle limit. It might take me an hour or two to sell that, or sometimes as quick as half an hour. I got to ask if I can work. They say yes or no.

Typically the managers said no to women's requests to work. Unlike many male street-level sellers who worked on a regular basis for this organization and were given "shifts" (generally lasting eight hours), Connie had to work off-hours (during daylight hours), which were often riskier and less financially rewarding. Temporary workers were usually given a "bundle limit" (one bundle contains 24 vials), which ensured that they could work only for short periods of time. As Cherrie, a 22-year-old Latina, said,

> The last time I sold it was Blue Tops [crack]. That was a week ago. [What, they asked you or you asked them to work?] Oh, they ask me, I say I want to work. [How come they asked you?] I don't know. They didn't have nobody to work because it was too hot out there. They was too full of cops.

Similarly, although Princess was well-known to the owners and managers of White Top crack, had worked for them many times in the past year, and had "proved" herself by having never once "stepped off" with either drugs or money, she was only given sporadic employment. She reported,

> Sometime you can't [sell]. Sometime you can. That's why it's good to save money also. So when you don't get work. [How come they wouldn't give you work on some days?] Because of some favor that someone might've done or y'know, jus' . . . [It's not like they're trying to punish you?] No, but they will do that y'know. Somebody go and tell them something, "Oh, this one's doin' this to the bags or this one's doin' this to the bottles." OK, well they check the bags and they don' see nothin' wrong, but they came to look at it so they're pissed off so they'll take it away from you, y'know.

Violence and Relationships. In addition to being vulnerable to arrest and street robbery, street-level sellers who use drugs constantly grapple with the urge to consume the product and to abscond with the drugs and/or the money. Retaliation by employers toward users who "mess up the money" (Johnson et al., 1985:174) was widely perceived to be swift and certain. Rachel, a 35-year-old European-American woman, said,

> Those Dominicans, if you step off with one piece of it, you're gonna get hurt. They don't play. They are sick people.

The prospect of violent retaliation may deter women from selling drugs. Boy, a 26-year-old African-American woman, put it this way:

> I don' like their [the managers'] attitude, like if you come up short, dey take it out on you . . . I don' sell no crack or dope for dese niggers. Because dey is crazy. Say for instance you short ten dollars, niggers come across you wit bats and shit. It's not worth it, you could lose your life. If dey say you are short, you could lose you life. Even if you were not short and dey say you is short, whatever dey say is gonna go, so you are fucked all the way around.

However, considerable uncertainty surrounds the likelihood that physical punishment will be meted out. This uncertainty can be seen in the comments by Princess, who had a long but sporadic history of street-level sales before and after the advent of crack:

> It's not worth it. Number one, it's not enough. Come on, run away, and then *maybe* then these people want to heavily beat the shit out of you. And then they *may* hit you in the wrong place with the bat and *maybe* kill you (emphasis added).

Such disciplinary practices resemble a complex interplay between "patronage" and "mercy," which features in relations of dependence (Hay, 1975). The unpredictability of punishment may work as a more effective form of control than actual punishment itself. In Bushwick, the actuality of violent retaliation for sellers who "messed up" was further mediated by gender and ethnicity. In this Latino- (mainly Dominican) controlled market, the common perception was that men, and black men especially, were more likely than Latinas to be punished for "stepping off." Rachel described what happened after an African-American man had been badly beaten:

> [What happened to him. I mean he stepped off with a package, right?] Yeah, but everybody has at one time or another. But it's also because he's a black and not a Puerto Rican, and he can't, you know, smooze his way back in like, you know, Mildred steps off with every other package, and so does, you know, Yolanda, they all do. But they're Spanish. And they're girls. So, you know, they can smooze their way back in. You know, a guy who's black and ugly, you know, so they don't want to hear about it.

Relationships in the drug economy are fueled by contradictory expectations. On the one hand, attributes such as trust and reliability are frequently espoused as important to drug-selling organizations. On the other hand, ethnographic informants often refer to the lack of trust and solidarity among organization members. This lack of trust is evident in the constant "scams" sellers and managers pull on each other and the ever-present threat of violence in owner-manager-seller relations.

Strategies of Protection and "Being Bad." Women who work the streets to sell or buy drugs are subject to constant harassment and are regularly victimized. The Bushwick women employed several strategies to protect themselves. One of the most important was the adoption of a "badass" (Katz, 1988), "crazy," or "gangsta bitch" stance or attitude, of which having a "bad mouth" was an integral part. As Latisha was fond of saying, "My heart pumps no Kool Aid. I don't even drink the shit." Or as Boy put it,

> Ac' petite, dey treat you petite. I mean you ac' soft, like when you dress dainty and shit to come over here an' sit onna fuckin' corner. Onna corner an' smoke an you dressed to da teeth, you know, you soft. Right then and there you the center of the crowd, y'know what I'm sayin'? Now put a dainty one and put me, she looks soft. Dey look at me like "don't fuck wid dat bitch, she looks hard." Don' mess wit me caus I look hard y'know. . . Dey don't fuck wit me out here. Dey think I'm crazy.

Acting bad and "being bad" are not the same. Although many Bushwick women presented themselves as "bad" or "crazy," this projection was a street persona and a necessary survival strategy (see also Spalter-Roth, 1988). Despite the external manifestation of aggression, a posture and rhetoric of toughness, and the preemptive use of aggression (Campbell, 1993), women were widely perceived (by men and women alike) as less likely to have the attributes associated with successful managers and street-level sellers. These included the requisite "street cred" and a "rep" for having "heart" or "juice"—masculine qualities associated with toughness and the capacity for violence (Bourgois, 1989; Steffensmeier, 1983; Waterston, 1993). Women's abilities to "talk tough" or "act bad" were apparently not enough to inspire employer confidence. Prospective drug business employers wanted those capable of actually "being bad" (Bourgois, 1989:632). Because female drug users were perceived as unreliable, untrustworthy, and unable to deploy violence and terror effectively, would-be female sellers were at a disadvantage.

Selling Drug Paraphernalia

In Bushwick the sale of drug paraphernalia such as crack stems and pipes was controlled by the bodegas, or corner stores, whereas syringes or "works" were the province of the street. Men dominated both markets although women were sometimes employed as part-time "works" sellers. Men who regularly sold "sealed" (i.e., new) works had suppliers (typically men who worked in local hospitals) from whom they purchased units called "ten packs" (10 syringes). The benefits of selling syringes were twofold: The penalties were less severe than those for selling drugs, and the rate of return was higher compared to the street-level sale of heroin or crack.[4]

The women who sold works were less likely than their male counterparts to have procured them "commercially." More often they "happened across" a supply of works through a family member or social contact who was a diabetic. Women were also more likely to sell works for others or to sell "used works." Rosa, a 31-year-old Latina, described in detail the dangerous practice of collecting used works strewn around the neighborhood. While she often stored them and later exchanged them for new works from the volunteer needle exchange (which was illegal at the time), Rosa would sometimes select the works she deemed in good condition, "clean" them with bleach and water, and resell them.

Although crack stems and pipes were available from neighborhood bodegas at minimal cost, some smokers chose not to carry stems. These users, almost exclusively men, were from outside the neighborhood. Their reluctance to carry drug paraphernalia provided the women with an additional source of income, usually in the form of a "hit," in exchange for the use of their stem. Sometimes these men were "dates," but more often they were "men on a mission" in the neighborhood or the "working men" who came to the area on Friday and Saturday nights to get high. As Boy put it,

> I be there on the block an' I got my stem and my lighter. I see them cop and I be askin' "yo, you need a stem, you need a light?" People say "yeah man," so they give me a piece.

An additional benefit for those women who rented their stems was the build up of crack residues in the stems. Many users savored this resin, which they allowed to accumulate before periodically digging it out with "scrapers" fashioned from the metal ribs of discarded umbrellas.

Some women also sold condoms, another form of drug-related paraphernalia in Bushwick. Although condoms were sold at bodegas, usually for $1 each, many of the women obtained free condoms from outreach health workers. Sometimes they sold them at a reduced price (usually 25 cents) to other sex workers, "white boyz," and young men from the neighborhood. Ironically, these same women would then have to purchase condoms at the bodegas when they had "smoked up" all their condoms.

Running Shooting Galleries

A wide range of physical locations were used for drug consumption in Bushwick. Although these sites were referred to generically as "galleries" by drug users and others in the neighborhood, they differed from the traditional heroin shooting gallery in several respects.[5] Bushwick's "galleries" were dominated by men because they had the economic resources or physical prowess to maintain control. Control was also achieved by exploiting women drug users with housing leases. Such women were particularly vulnerable, as the following quotation from Carol, a 40-year-old African-American woman, shows:

> I had my own apartment, myself and my daughter. I started selling crack. From my house. [For who?] Some Jamaican. [How did you get hooked up with that?] Through my boyfriend. They wanted to sell from my apartment. They were supposed to pay me something like $150 a week rent, and then something off the profits. They used to, you know, fuck up the money, like not give me the money. Eventually I went through a whole lot of different dealers. Eventually I stopped payin' my rent because I wanted to get a transfer out of there to get away from

> everything 'cause soon as one group of crack dealers would get out, another group would come along. [So how long did that go on for?] About four years. Then I lost my apartment, and I sat out in the street.

The few women who were able to maintain successful galleries operated with or under the control of a man or group of men. Cherrie's short-lived effort to set up a gallery in an abandoned burned-out building on "Crack Row" is illustrative. Within two weeks of establishing the gallery (the principal patrons of which were women), Cherrie was forced out of business by the police. The two weeks were marked by constant harassment, confiscation of drugs and property, damage to an already fragile physical plant, physical assaults, and the repeated forced dispersal of gallery occupants. Within a month, two men had established a new gallery on the same site, which, more than a year later, was thriving.

Such differential policing toward male- and female-operated galleries is explicable in light of the larger picture of law enforcement in low-income urban communities, where the primary function is not so much to enforce the law but rather to regulate illegal activities (Whyte, 1943:138). Field observations suggest that the reason the police did not interfere as much with activities in the men's gallery was that they assumed that men were better able than women to control the gallery and to minimize problems of violence and disorder.

Other factors contributed to women's disadvantage in operating galleries, crack houses, and other consumption sites. Male drug users were better placed economically than the women in the sample, most of whom were homeless and without a means of legitimate economic support. When women did have an apartment or physical site, this made them a vulnerable target either for exploitation by male users or dealers (as in Carol's case) or for harassment by the police (as in Cherrie's). Even when a woman claimed to be in control of a physical location, field observations confirmed that she was not. Thus, in Bushwick, the presence of a man was a prerequisite to the successful operation of drug-consumption sites. The only choice for those women in a position to operate galleries or crack houses was between the "devils they knew" and those they did not.

Copping Drugs

Many Bushwick women supplemented their income by "copping" drugs for others. They almost always copped for men, typically white men. At times these men were dates, but often they were users who feared being caught and wanted someone else to take that risk. As Rachel explained,

> I charge them, just what they want to buy they have to pay me. If they want twenty dollars they have to give me twenty dollars worth on the top because I'm risking my free time. I could get busted copping. They have to pay me the same way, if not, they can go cop. Most of them can't because they don't know the people.

Those who cop drugs for others perform an important service for the drug market because as Biernacki (1979:539) suggests in connection with heroin, "they help to minimize the possibility of infiltration by undercover agents and decrease the chance of a dealer's arrest." In Bushwick the copping role attracted few men; it was regarded by both men and women as a low-status peripheral hustle. Most women saw the female-dominated nature of the job to be part of the parallel sex market in the neighborhood. Outsiders could readily approach women to buy drugs under the guise of buying sex. As Rosa recounted,

> You would [be] surprise. They'd be ahm, be people very important, white people like lawyer, doctors that comes and get off, you'd be surprised. Iss like I got two lawyer, they give me money to go, to go and cop. And they stay down over there parking. . . . [How do you meet them?] Well down the stroll one time they stop and say you know, "You look like a nice girl though, you know, you wanna make some money fast?" I say, how? So they say you know, "Look out for me." First time they give me like you know, twenty dollars, you know. They see I came back, next time they give me thirty. Like that you know. I have been copping for them like over six months already.

Sometimes this function was performed in conjunction with sex work, as Latisha's comment illustrates,

> He's a cop. He's takin' a chance. He is petrified. Will not get out his car . . . But he never gets less than nine bags [of powder cocaine]. [And he sends you to get it?] And he wants a blow job, right, okay. You know what he's givin' you, a half a bag of blue (blue bag cocaine). That's for you goin' to cop, and for the blow job. That's [worth] two dollars and fifty . . . I can go to jail [for him]. I'm a piece of shit.

Women also felt that, given the reputation of the neighborhood as very "thirsty" (that is, as having a "thirst" or craving for crack), male outsiders were more likely to trust women, especially white women, to purchase drugs on their behalf. Often this trust was misplaced. The combination of naive, inexperienced "white boyz" and experienced "street smart" women produced opportunities for additional income by, for example, simply taking the "cop" money. This was a calculated risk and sometimes things went wrong. A safer practice was to inflate the purchase price of the drugs and to pocket the difference. Rosa explained this particular scam,

> He think it a ten dollar bag, but issa five dollar. But at least I don't be rippin' him off there completely. [But you're taking the risk for him.] Exactly. Sometime he give me a hunert dollars, so I making fifty, right? But sometime he don't get paid, he got no second money, eh. I cop then when I come back the car, he say, "Dear I cannot give you nothin' today," you know. But I still like I say, I gettin' something from him because he think it a ten dollar bag.

Similar scams involved the woman's returning to the client with neither drugs nor money, claiming that she had been ripped off or, less often, shortchanging the client by tapping the vials (removing some crack) or adulterating the drugs (cutting powder cocaine or heroin with other substances). These scams reveal the diversity of women's roles as copping agents and their ingenuity in making the most of limited opportunities.[6]

Other Drug Business Hustles

The practice of injecting intravenous drug users (IDUs) who are unable to inject themselves, because they are inexperienced or have deep or collapsed veins, has been documented by others (e.g., Johnson et al., 1985; Murphy and Waldorf, 1991). Those performing this role are sometimes referred to as "street docs" (Murphy and Waldorf, 1991:16–17). In Bushwick, men typically specialized in this practice. For example, Sam, a Latino injector in his late thirties, lived in one of the makeshift huts or "condos" on a busy street near the main heroin copping area. Those who were in a hurry to consume or who had nowhere else to go would use Sam's place to "get off." Sam had a reputation as a good "hitter" and injected several women in the sample on a regular basis. He provided this service for a few dollars or, more often, a "taste" of whatever substance was being injected.

Only one woman in the sample, Latisha, capitalized on her reputation as a good "hitter" by playing the street doc role. Latisha had a regular arrangement with a young street thug named Crime, notorious for victimizing the women, who had only recently commenced intravenous heroin use and was unable to "hit" himself. While women IDUs were likely to have the requisite level of skill, they were less likely than men to be able to capitalize on it because they did not control an established consumption setting.

Discussion

A major dimension of drug economies, both past and present, is the "human qualities" believed necessary for the performance of various roles. Opportunities for income generation are defined, in part, by who has the necessary qualities or traits and who does not. These traits, whether grounded in cultural perceptions of biology and physiology (e.g., strength and capacity for violence), mental states (e.g., courage and aggressiveness), or kinship (e.g., loyalty and trustworthiness), are primarily differentiated along the lines of gender and race-ethnicity. In this study, we found that women were thought to be not as "strong" as men and that men, particularly black men and Latinos, were thought to be more "bad" and capable of "being bad." The gendered displays of violence that men incorporate into their work routines not only cement their solidarity as men, but also reinscribe these traits as masculine (Messerschmidt, 1993). As a consequence, men are able to justify the exclusion of women from more lucrative "men's work" in the informal economy. All the elements of underworld sexism identified by Steffensmeier (1983)—homosocial reproduction, sex-typing, and the qualities required in a violent task environment—featured prominently in Bushwick's street-level drug economy.

The significance of gender-based capacities and the symbolism used to convey them was evident in the women's use of instrumental aggression. Boy's discussion of how to "dress for success" on the streets reveals that power dressing is "dressing like a man" or "dressing down." It is anything but "dressing dainty." Both on the street and in the boardroom, it appears that a combination of clothing and attitude makes the woman (Kanter, 1981, citing Hennig, 1970). In the drug business, conveying the message "don't mess with me" is integral to maintaining a reputation for "craziness," which the women perceived as affording them some measure of protection.

The Bushwick women's experiences within a highly gender-stratified labor market provide a counter to the romantic notion of the informal drug economy as an "equal opportunity employer" (Bourgois, 1989:630). Their experiences contradict the conventional wisdom, shaped by studies of the labor market experiences of minority group men (e.g., Anderson, 1990; Bourgois, 1989, 1995; Hagedorn, 1994; Padilla, 1992; C. Taylor, 1990; Williams, 1989), that the drug economy acts as a compensatory mechanism, offering paid employment that is not available in the formal labor force. While in theory the built-in supervision and task differentiation of the business model, which characterized drug distribution in Bushwick, should have provided opportunities to both men and women (Johnson et al., 1992), our findings suggest that sellers were overwhelmingly men. Thus, the "new opportunities" said to have emerged with the crack-propelled expansion of drug markets from the mid-1980s onward were not "empty slots" waiting to be filled by those with the requisite skill. Rather, they were slots requiring certain masculine qualities and capacities.

Continuity or Change?

Those scholars who emphasize change in women's roles in the drug economy with the advent of crack cocaine are correct to point out the *possibilities* that an expanded drug economy might have offered women. Where they err, we think, is in claiming that such "new opportunities" were in fact made available to a significant proportion of women. Granted, there were temporary opportunities for women to participate in street-level drug distribution, but they were irregular and short-lived and did not alter male employers' perceptions of women as unreliable, untrustworthy, and incapable of demonstrating an effective capacity for violence.

The only consistently available option for women's income generation was sex work. However, the conditions of street-level sex work have been adversely affected by shifts in social and economic relations produced by widespread crack consumption in low-income neighborhoods like Bushwick.

The market became flooded with novice sex workers, the going rates for sexual transactions decreased, and "deviant" sexual expectations by dates increased, as did the levels of violence and victimization (Maher and Curtis, 1992). Ironically, the sting in the tail of the recent crack-fueled expansion of street-level drug markets has been a substantial reduction in the earning capacities of street-level sex workers.

Of the four elements that have been used to explain women's restricted involvement in drug economies of the past, we see evidence of change in two: a diminishing of women's access to drug-selling roles through boyfriends or husbands, especially when drug markets are highly structured and kin based, and decreased economic returns for street-level sex work. Because few Bushwick women had stable households or cared for children, we cannot comment on changes (if any) in discretionary time. Underworld institutionalized sexism was the most powerful element shaping the Bushwick women's experiences in the drug economy; it inhibited their access to drug business work roles and effectively foreclosed their ability to participate as higher-level distributors. For that most crucial element, we find no change from previous decades.

How can we reconcile our findings with those of researchers who say that the crack cocaine economy has facilitated "new opportunities" for women or "new ways for women to escape their limited roles, statuses, and incomes [compared to] previous eras" (Fagan, 1994:210)? One answer is that study samples differ: Compared to Fagan's sample, for example, our sample of Bushwick women contained a somewhat higher share of Latinas, whose economic circumstances were more marginal than those of the women in Central Harlem and Washington Heights. It is also possible that Latino-controlled drug markets are more restrictive of women's participation than, say, those controlled by African-Americans. Those who have studied drug use and dealing in Puerto Rican (Glick, 1990) and Chicano (Moore, 1990) communities suggest that "deviant women" may be less tolerated and more ostracized than their male counterparts. For Bushwick, it would be difficult to disentangle the joint influences of a male-dominated and Dominican-controlled drug market on women's participation. While seven women (16%) engaged in street-level sales during the study period, all women—whether Latina, African-American, or European-American—were denied access to higher levels of the drug business.

We lack research on how racial-ethnic relations structure women's participation in drug markets. Fagan's (1994:200–202) comparison of Central Harlem and Washington Heights indicates that a lower proportion of women in Central Harlem (28%) than in Washington Heights (44%) reported being involved in drug selling; similar proportions (about 16%) were involved in group selling, however. While Fagan noted that drug markets in Washington Heights were Latino-controlled, he did not discuss the organization or ethnic composition of drug markets in Central Harlem. His study would appear to challenge any clear links between "Latino culture"—

or the Latina share of women studied—and greater restrictions on women's roles compared to other racial-ethnic groups.

While disparate images of women in the drug economy may result from differences in study samples (including racial-ethnic variation in drug market organization, neighborhood-level variation, and when the study was conducted), a researcher's methods and theories are also crucial. For methods, virtually all U.S. studies of women drug users have employed one-time interviews. The ethnographic approach used in this study reveals that in the absence of a temporal frame and observational data, interviews may provide an incomplete and inaccurate picture. For example, in initial interviews with the larger group of Brooklyn women, we found that when women were asked about sources of income, it was more socially desirable for them to say that it came from drug selling or other kinds of crime than from crack-related prostitution (Maher, in press). The one-time interview also misses the changing and fluid nature of relations in the informal economy. For example, for a short period there was a perception in Bushwick that "new opportunities" existed for women to sell crack. That perception faded as it became clear that managers and owners were "using" women to evade the constraints imposed on them by law enforcement and police search practices. Ethnographic approaches can offer a more dynamic contextualized picture of women's lawbreaking. While such approaches are relatively numerous in the study of adolescent and adult men in the United States (e.g., Anderson, 1990; Bourgois, 1989; Sullivan, 1989), they are rarely utilized in the study of women and girls.

For theory, women lawbreakers are rarely studied as members of social networks or as participants in collective or group-based activity (see also Steffensmeier and Terry, 1986). Nor have women been viewed as economic actors in illegal markets governed by occupational norms and workplace cultures (Maher, 1996). Those making a general claim about "women's emancipation" in the current drug economy ignore the obdurateness of a gender-stratified labor market and associated beliefs and practices that maintain it. Those making the more restricted claim that male-dominated street networks and market processes have weakened, thus allowing entry points for women, need to offer proof for that claim. We would expect to see variation in women's roles, and we would not say that Bushwick represents the general case. However, assertions of women's changing and improved position in the drug economy have not been well proved. Nor are they grounded in theories of how work, including illegal work, is conditioned by relations of gender, race-ethnicity, and sexuality (see, e.g., Daly, 1993; Game and Pringle, 1983; Kanter, 1977; Messerschmidt, 1993; Simpson and Elis, 1995).

Our findings suggest that the advent of crack cocaine and the concomitant expansion of the drug economy cannot be viewed as emancipatory for women drug users. To the extent that "new opportunities" in drug distribution and sales were realized in Bushwick and the wider Brooklyn sample, they were realized by men. Women were confined to an increasingly harsh economic periphery. Not only did the promised opportunities fail to materialize, but the expanding crack market served to deteriorate the conditions of street-level sex work, a labor market which has historically provided a relatively stable source of income for women drug users.

Notes

[1] *Selling* refers to the direct exchange of drugs for cash; *distributing* refers to low-level distribution roles that do not involve direct sales but provide assistance to sellers.

[2] At one level, language served as a marker of identity; "outsiders" were those who were not "Spanish," with country of origin often less salient than an ability to speak Spanish or "Spanglish." However, the distribution of opportunities for income generation also involved finely calibrated notions of ethnicity.

[3] Each woman was given $10 or the equivalent (e.g., cash, food, clothing, cigarettes, makeup, subway tokens, or a combination) for the initial tape-recorded interview. However, field observations and many of the repeat interviews were conducted on the basis of relations of reciprocity that did not involve direct or immediate benefit to those interviewed. While this research focused on women's lives, interviews and observations were also undertaken with the women's female kin, male partners, and children.

[4] Street-level drug sellers typically made $1 on a $10 bag of heroin and 50 cents on a $5 vial of crack. Syringe sellers made at least $1.50 per unit, depending on the purchase price and the sale price.

[5] While consumption settings in Bushwick more closely resembled heroin shooting galleries (see, e.g., Des Jarlais et al., 1986; Murphy and Waldorf, 1991) than crack houses (see, e.g., Inciardi et al., 1993; Williams, 1992), many sites combined elements of both and most provided for polydrug (heroin and crack) consumption (for further details see Maher, in press).

[6] By their own accounts, women took greater risks in order to generate income than they had in the past. More generally, the incidence of risky behavior increased as conditions in the neighborhood and the adjacent street-level sex market deteriorated (Maher and Curtis, 1992; see also Curtis et al., 1995).

References

Adler, Patricia A.
1985 Wheeling and Dealing: An Ethnography of an Upper-Level Drug Dealing and Smuggling Community. New York: Columbia University Press.

Anderson, Elijah
1990 Streetwise: Race, Class and Change in an Urban Community. Chicago: University of Chicago Press.

Anglin, M. Douglas and Yih-Ing Hser
1987 Addicted women and crime. Criminology 25:359–397.

Auld, John, Nicholas Dorn, and Nigel South
1986 Irregular work, irregular pleasures: Heroin in the 1980s. In Roger Matthews and Jock Young (eds.), Confronting Crime. London: Sage.

Baskin, Deborah, Ira Sommers, and Jeffrey Fagan
1993 The political economy of violent female street crime. Fordham Urban Law Journal 20:401–407.

Biernacki, Patrick
1979 Junkie work, "hustles," and social status among heroin addicts. Journal of Drug Issues 9:535–549.

Bourgois, Philippe
1989 In search of Horatio Alger: Culture and ideology in the crack economy. Contemporary Drug Problems 16:619–649.
1995 In Search of Respect: Selling Crack in El Barrio. New York: Cambridge University Press.

Bourgois, Philippe and Eloise Dunlap
1993 Exorcising sex-for-crack: An ethnographic perspective from Harlem. In Mitchell S. Ratner (ed.), Crack Pipe as Pimp: An Ethnographic Investigation of Sex-for-Crack Exchanges. New York: Lexington Books.

Box, Steven
1983 Power, Crime and Mystification. London: Tavistock.

Bureau of the Census
1990 Brooklyn in Touch. Washington, D.C.: U.S. Government Printing Office.

Campbell, Anne
1993 Out of Control: Men, Women, and Aggression. London: Pandora.

Covington, Jeanette
1985 Gender differences in criminality among heroin users. Journal of Research in Crime and Delinquency 22:329–354.

Curtis, Richard and Lisa Maher
in press Highly structured crack markets in the southside of Williamsburg, Brooklyn. In Jeffrey Fagan (ed.), The Ecology of Crime and Drug Use in Inner Cities. New York: Social Science Research Council.

Curtis, Richard and Michelle Sviridoff
1994 The social organization of street-level drug markets and its impact on the displacement effect. In Robert P. McNamara (ed.), Crime Displacement: The Other Side of Prevention. East Rockaway, N.Y.: Cummings and Hathaway.

Curtis, Richard, Samuel R. Friedman, Alan Neaigus, Benny Jose, Marjorie Goldstein, and Gilbert Ildefonso
1995 Street-level drug markets: Network structure and HIV risk. Social Networks 17:229–249.

Daly, Kathleen
1993 Class-race-gender: Sloganeering in search of meaning. Social Justice 20:56–71.

Des Jarlais, Don C., Samuel R. Friedman, and David Strug
1986 AIDS and needle sharing within the IV drug use subculture. In Douglas A. Feldman and Thomas M. Johnson (eds.), The Social Dimensions of AIDS: Methods and Theory. New York: Praeger.

Dunlap, Eloise and Bruce D. Johnson
1992 Who they are and what they do: Female crack dealers in New York City. Paper presented at the Annual Meeting of the American Society of Criminology, New Orleans, November.

Fagan, Jeffrey
1994 Women and drugs revisited: Female participation in the cocaine economy. Journal of Drug Issues 24:179–225.

File, Karen N.
1976 Sex roles and street roles. International Journal of the Addictions 11:263–268.

File, Karen N., Thomas W. McCahill, and Leonard D. Savitz
1974 Narcotics involvement and female criminality. Addictive Diseases: An International Journal 1:177–188.
Game, Ann and Rosemary Pringle
1983 Gender at Work. Sydney: George Allen and Unwin.
Goldstein, Paul J.
1979 Prostitution and Drugs. Lexington, Mass.: Lexington Books.
Glick, Ronald
1990 Survival, income, and status: Drug dealing in the Chicago Puerto Rican community. In Ronald Glick and Joan Moore (eds.), Drugs in Hispanic Communities. New Brunswick, N.J.: Rutgers University Press.
Hagedorn, John M.
1994 Homeboys, dope fiends, legits, and new jacks. Criminology 32:197–219.
Hamid, Ansley
1990 The political economy of crack-related violence. Contemporary Drug Problems 17:31–78.
1991 From ganja to crack: Caribbean participation in the underground economy in Brooklyn, 1976–1986. Part 2, Establishment of the cocaine (and crack) economy. International Journal of the Addictions 26:729–738.
1992 The developmental cycle of a drug epidemic: The cocaine smoking epidemic of 1981–1991. Journal of Psychoactive Drugs 24:337–348.
Hay, Douglas
1975 Property, authority, and the criminal law. In Douglas Hay, Peter Linebaugh, John G. Rule, Edward Palmer Thompson, and Cal Winslow (eds.), Albion's Fatal Tree. London: Allen Lane.
Hennig, Margaret
1970 Career Development for Women Executives. Ph.D. dissertation, Harvard University, Cambridge, Mass.
Hser, Yih-Ing, M. Douglas Anglin, and Mary W. Booth
1987 Sex differences in addict careers. Part 3, Addiction. American Journal of Drug and Alcohol Abuse 13:231–251.
Hunt, Dana
1990 Drugs and consensual crimes: Drug dealing and prostitution. In Michael Tonry and James Q. Wilson (eds.), Drugs and Crime. Crime and Justice, Vol. 13. Chicago: University of Chicago Press.
Inciardi, James A. and Anne E. Pottieger
1986 Drug use and crime among two cohorts of women narcotics users: An empirical assessment. Journal of Drug Issues 16:91–106.
Inciardi, James A., Dorothy Lockwood, and Anne E. Pottieger
1993 Women and Crack Cocaine. New York: Macmillan.
James, Jennifer
1976 Prostitution and addiction: An interdisciplinary approach. Addictive Diseases: An International Journal 2:601–618.
Johnson, Bruce D., Paul J. Goldstein, Edward Preble, James Schmeidler, Douglas S. Lipton, Barry Spunt, and Thomas Miller
1985 Taking Care of Business: The Economics of Crime by Heroin Abusers. Lexington, Mass.: Lexington Books.

Johnson, Bruce D., Terry Williams, Kojo Dei, and Harry Sanabria
1990 Drug abuse and the inner city: Impact on hard drug users and the community. In Michael Tonry and James Q. Wilson (eds.), Drugs and Crime. Crime and Justice, Vol. 13. Chicago: University of Chicago Press.
Johnson, Bruce D., Ansley Hamid, and Harry Sanabria
1992 Emerging models of crack distribution. In Thomas M. Mieczkowski (ed.), Drugs and Crime: A Reader. Boston: Allyn & Bacon.
Johnson, Bruce D., Mangai Natarajan, Eloise Dunlap, and Elsayed Elmoghazy
1994 Crack abusers and noncrack abusers: Profiles of drug use, drug sales, and nondrug criminality. Journal of Drug Issues 24:117–141.
Kanter, Rosabeth Moss
1977 Men and Women of the Corporation. New York: Basic Books.
1981 Women and the structure of organizations: Explorations in theory and behavior. In Oscar Grusky and George A. Miller (eds.), The Sociology of Organizations: Basic Studies. 2d ed. New York: The Free Press.
Katz, Jack
1988 Seductions of Crime: Moral and Sensual Attractions of Doing Evil. New York: Basic Books.
Koester, Stephen and Judith Schwartz
1993 Crack, gangs, sex, and powerlessness: A view from Denver. In Mitchell S. Ratner (ed.), Crack Pipe as Pimp: An Ethnographic Investigation of Sex-for-Crack Exchanges. New York: Lexington Books.
Maher, Lisa
in press Making it at the Margins: Gender, Race and Work in a Street-Level Drug Economy. Oxford: Oxford University Press.
1996 Hidden in the light: Discrimination and occupational norms among crack using street-level sexworkers. Journal of Drug Issues 26(1):145–175.
Maher, Lisa and Richard Curtis
1992 Women on the edge of crime: Crack cocaine and the changing contexts of street-level sex work in New York City. Crime, Law, and Social Change 18:221–258.
Maher, Lisa, Eloise Dunlap, Bruce D. Johnson, and Ansley Hamid
1996 Gender, power and alternative living arrangements in the inner-city crack culture. Journal of Research in Crime and Delinquency 33:181–205.
Messerschmidt, James D.
1993 Masculinities and Crime. Lanham, Md.: Rowman and Littlefield.
Mieczkowski, Thomas
1986 Geeking up and throwing down: Heroin street life in Detroit. Criminology 24:645–666.
1990 Crack dealing on the street: An exploration of the YBI hypothesis and the Detroit crack trade. Paper presented at the Annual Meeting of the American Society of Criminology, Baltimore, November.
1994 The experiences of women who sell crack: Some descriptive data from the Detroit crack ethnography project. Journal of Drug Issues 24:227–248.
Moore, Joan W.
1990 Mexican American women addicts: The influence of family background. In Ronald Glick and Joan Moore (eds.), Drugs in Hispanic Communities. New Brunswick, N.J.: Rutgers University Press.

Morgan, Patricia and Karen Joe
1994 Uncharted terrains: Contexts of experience among women in the illicit drug economy. Paper presented at the Women and Drugs National Conference, Sydney, November.

Murphy, Sheigla and Dan Waldorf
1991 Kickin' down to the street doc: Shooting galleries in the San Francisco Bay area. Contemporary Drug Problems 18:9–29.

Murphy, Sheigla, Dan Waldorf, and Craig Reinarman
1991 Drifting into dealing: Becoming a cocaine seller. Qualitative Sociology 13:321–343.

Padilla, Felix M.
1992 The Gang as an American Enterprise. New Brunswick, N.J.: Rutgers University Press.

Pettiway, Leon E.
1987 Participation in crime partnerships by female drug users: The effects of domestic arrangements, drug use, and criminal involvement. Criminology 25:741–766.

Reuter, Peter, Robert MacCoun, and Patrick Murphy
1990 Money from Crime: A Study of the Economics of Drug Dealing in Washington, D.C. Santa Monica, Calif.: Rand Corporation.

Rosenbaum, Marsha
1981 Women on Heroin. New Brunswick, N.J.: Rutgers University Press.

Simpson, Sally S. and Lori Elis
1995 Doing gender: Sorting out the caste and crime conundrum. Criminology 33:47–81.

Skolnick, Jerome H.
1989 The Social Structure of Street Drug Dealing. Report to the State of California Bureau of Criminal Statistics and Special Services. Sacramento: State of California Executive Office.

Smithberg, Nathan and Joseph Westermeyer
1985 White dragon pearl syndrome: A female pattern of drug dependence. American Journal of Drug and Alcohol Abuse 11:199–207.

Spalter-Roth, Roberta M.
1988 The sexual political economy of street vending in Washington, D.C. In Gracia Clark (ed.), Traders Versus the State: Anthropological Approaches to Unofficial Economies. Boulder, Colo.: Westview Press.

Steffensmeier, Darrell
1983 Organization properties and sex-segregation in the underworld: Building a sociological theory of sex differences in crime. Social Forces 61:1010–1032.

Steffensmeier, Darrell J. and Robert M. Terry
1986 Institutional sexism in the underworld: A view from the inside. Sociological Inquiry 56:304–323.

Sullivan, Mercer L.
1989 Getting Paid: Youth Crime and Work in the Inner City. Ithaca, N.Y.: Cornell University Press.

Sutter, A. G.
1966 The world of the righteous dope fiend. Issues in Criminology 2:177–222.

Taylor, Avril
1993 Women Drug Users: An Ethnography of a Female Injecting Community. Oxford: Clarendon Press.

Taylor, Carl S.
1990 Dangerous Society. East Lansing: Michigan State University Press.
1993 Girls, Gangs, Women and Drugs. East Lansing: Michigan State University Press.

Waldorf, Dan, Craig Reinarman, and Sheigla Murphy
1991 Cocaine Changes: The Experience of Using and Quitting. Philadelphia, Pa.: Temple University Press.

Waterston, Alisse
1993 Street Addicts in the Political Economy. Philadelphia, Pa.: Temple University Press.

Whyte, William Foote
1943 Street Corner Society. Chicago: University of Chicago Press.

Williams, Terry
1989 The Cocaine Kids. Reading, Mass.: Addison-Wesley.
1992 Crackhouse: Notes from the End of the Line. New York: Addison-Wesley.

Wilson, Nancy Koser
1993 Stealing and dealing: The drug war and gendered criminal opportunity. In Concetta C. Culliver (ed.), Female Criminality: The State of the Art. New York: Garland Publishing.

6

Up It Up
Gender and the Accomplishment of Street Robbery

Jody Miller

With the exception of forcible rape, robbery is perhaps the most gender differentiated serious crime in the United States. According to the Federal Bureau of Investigation's Uniform Crime Report for 1995, women accounted for 9.3% of robbery arrestees, while they were 9.5%, 17.7%, and 11.1% of arrestees for murder/manslaughter, aggravated assault, and burglary, respectively (Federal Bureau of Investigation, 1996). And while recently there has been considerable attention among feminist scholars to the question of why males are more violent than females, there have been few attempts to examine women's participation in these "male" crimes. Though their numbers are small, women who engage in violent street crime have something significant to teach us about women's place in the landscape of the urban street world.

Simpson (1989:618; see also Kelly, 1991; White and Kowalski, 1994) recently noted that feminist scholars' "reticence [to address issues concerning women's criminality] leaves the interpretive door open to less critical perspectives." Nowhere is this more the case than with the issue of women's participation in violent street crime. Sensational accounts of the "new violent female offender" (e.g., Sikes, 1997; see Chesney-Lind, 1993), which draw heavily on racial imagery of young women of color, must be countered with accurate, nuanced accounts of women's use of violence in the contexts of racial and economic inequalities. This research compares the experiences of male and female robbers active in an urban underclass environment with the goal of expanding understanding of women's use of violence in nondomestic street settings.

Masculinities and Crime: Robbery as Gender Accomplishment

In the late 1980s, feminist sociologists began theorizing about gender as situated accomplishment (West and Fenstermaker, 1995; West and Zimmerman, 1987). According to these authors, gender is "much more than a role or an individual characteristic: it is a mechanism whereby situated social action contributes to the reproduction of social structure" (West and Fenstermaker, 1995:21). Women and men "do gender" in response to normative beliefs about femininity and masculinity. These actions are "the interactional scaffolding of social structure" (West and Zimmerman, 1987:147) such that the performance of gender is both an indication and a reproduction of gendered social hierarchies.

This approach has been incorporated into feminist accounts of crime as a means of explaining differences in women's and men's offending (Messerschmidt, 1993, 1995; Newburn and Stanko, 1994; Simpson and Elis, 1995). Here, violence is described as "a 'resource' for accomplishing gender—for demonstrating masculinity within a given context or situation" (Simpson and Elis, 1995:50). Further, it is suggested that although some women may engage in violent behavior, because their actions transgress normative conceptions of femininity, they will "derive little support for expressions of masculine violence from even the most marginal of subcultures" (Braithwaite and Daly, 1994:190).

Several authors suggest that robbery epitomizes the use of crime to construct masculine identity (Katz, 1988; Messerschmidt, 1993). Messerschmidt argues as follows:

> The robbery setting provides the ideal opportunity to construct an "essential" toughness and "maleness"; it provides a means with which to construct that certain type of masculinity—hardman. Within the social context that ghetto and barrio boys find themselves, then, robbery is a rational practice for "doing gender" and for getting money (Messerschmidt, 1993:107).

Moreover, given the disproportionate use of robbery by African-American versus white men (Federal Bureau of Investigation, 1996), the masculinity that robbery constructs may be one that fits particularly well in urban underclass settings, which are unique from areas in which poor whites live (see Sampson and Wilson, 1995). Katz, in fact, suggests that "for some urban, black ghetto-located young men, the stickup is particularly attractive as a distinctive way of being black" as well as male (1988:239).

Examining violence as masculine accomplishment can help account for women's lack of involvement in these crimes, just as this approach offers explanation for women's involvement in crime in ways scripted by femininity (e.g., prostitution). However, it leaves unexplained women's participation in violent street crime, except as an anomaly. Perhaps this is because femininity in this approach is conceived narrowly—specifically "within the parameters of the white middle class (i.e., domesticity, dependence, selflessness, and motherhood)" (Simpson and Elis, 1995:51). Given urban African-American women's historical patterns of economic self-sufficiency and independence, this passive feminine ideal is unlikely to have considerable influence and is "much more relevant (and restrictive) for white females" (Simpson and Elis, 1995:71).

Messerschmidt himself has recently recognized this oversight. Given that urban African-American females are involved in violent street crime at higher rates than other females, he suggests that "theory must not universalize female crime" (1995:171) and must consider significant women's involvement in presumably "male" crime. Simpson (1991:129; see also White and Kowalski, 1994) concludes: "The simplistic assertion that males are violent and females are not contains a grain of truth, but it misses the complexity and texture of women's lives."

Women's Violence as Resistance to Male Oppression

Feminist scholars who address the use of street violence by women often suggest that women's violence differs from that of men's—women use violence in response to their vulnerability to or actual victimization in the family and/or at the hands of men (Campbell, 1993; Joe and Chesney-Lind, 1995; Maher, 1997; Maher and Curtis, 1992; Maher and Daly, 1996). In her ethnography of a Brooklyn drug market, Maher notes that women adopt violent presentations of self as a strategy of protection. She explains, "'Acting bad' and 'being bad' are not the same. Although many of the women presented themselves as 'bad' or 'crazy,' this projection was a street persona and a necessary survival strategy" (1997:95; see also Maher and Daly, 1996). These women were infrequently involved in violent crime and most often resorted to violence in response to threats or harms against them. She concludes that "unlike their male counterparts, for women, reputation was about 'preventing victimization'" (Maher, 1997:95–96; see also Campbell, 1993). In this account, even when women's aggression is offensive, it can still be understood as a defensive act, because it emerges as resistance to victimization.

Maher's research uncovered a particular form of robbery—"viccing"—in which women involved in the sex trade rob their clients. Although the phenomenon of prostitutes robbing tricks is not new, Maher's work documents the proliferation of viccing as a form of resistance against their greater vulnerability to victimization and against cheapened sex markets within the drug economy. Comparing viccing with traditional forms of robbery, Maher and Curtis conclude, "The fact that the act [of viccing] itself is little different to any other instrumental robbery belies the reality that the motivations undergirding it are more complex and, indeed, are intimately linked with women's collective sense of the devaluation of their bodies and their work" (1992:246). However, it is likely that not all of women's street violence can be viewed as resistance to male oppression; instead, some women may be motivated to commit violent crimes for many of the same reasons some men are. In certain contexts, norms favorable to women's use of violence may exist, and they are not simply about avoiding victimization, but also result in status and recognition.

Race, Class and Gender: Women's Violence as Situated Action

It is necessary to consider that some of women's participation in violent street crime may stem from "the frustration, alienation, and anger that are associated with racial and class oppression" (Simpson, 1989:618). The foregrounding of gender is important; however, there are structural and cultural underpinnings related to racial and economic inequalities that must simultaneously be addressed when one considers women's involvement in violent street crime (Simpson, 1991).

Research suggests that urban African-American females are more likely to engage in serious and violent crime than their counterparts in other racial groups and/or settings (Ageton, 1983; Hill and Crawford, 1990; Laub and McDermott, 1985; Mann, 1993). Ageton's analysis of the National Youth Survey found little difference across race or class in girls' incidence of crimes against persons, but she reports that "lower class females report . . . the greatest involvement in assaultive crime . . . [and] a consistently higher proportion of black females are involved in crimes against persons for all five years surveyed" (1983:565). This is not to suggest that African-American women's participation in these offenses parallel or converge with that of urban African-American males (see Chesney-Lind and Shelden, 1992:21–24; Laub and McDermott, 1985). Rather, my point is to highlight the contexts in which these women negotiate their daily lives. Violence is extensive in the lives and communities of African-American women living in the urban underclass. As a result, some women in these circumstances may be more likely than women who are situated differently to view violence as an appropriate or useful means of dealing with their environment. As Simpson (1991:129) notes,

> Living daily with the fact of violence leads to an incorporation of it into one's experiential self. Men, women, and children have to come to terms with, make sense of, and respond to violence as it penetrates their lives. As violence is added to the realm of appropriate and sanctioned responses to oppressive material conditions, it gains a sort of cultural legitimacy. But not for all.

Evidence of the significance of the link between underclass conditions and African-American women's disproportionate involvement in violence may be found in recent research that examines factors predicting women's criminal involvement. Hill and Crawford (1990) report that structural indicators appear to be most significant in predicting the criminal involvement of African-American women, while social-psychological indicators are more predictive for white women. They conclude that "the unique position of black women in the structure of power relations in society has profound effects not shared by their white counterparts" (Hill and Crawford, 1990:621). In fact, Baskin et al. (1993:413) suggest that "women in inner city neighborhoods are being pulled toward violent street crime by the same forces that have been found to affect their male counterparts. As with males, neighborhood, peer and addiction factors have been found to contribute to female initiation into violence."

This is not to suggest, however, that gender does not matter. Gender remains a salient aspect of women's experiences in the urban street milieu, and must remain—along with race and class—at the forefront of attempts to understand their involvement in violent crime. Some research that stresses race and economic oppression as factors in women's criminality overlooks the significance of gender oppression in these contexts. For instance, Baskin et al. (1993:415) argue that "women's roles and prominence have changed in transformed neighborhoods" such that there exist "new dynamics of crime where gender is a far less salient factor" (p. 417).

However, there is overwhelming evidence that gender inequality remains a salient feature of the urban street scene (Anderson, 1994; Maher, 1997; Maher and Curtis, 1992; Maher and Daly, 1996; Oliver, 1994; Steffensmeier, 1983; Steffensmeier and Terry, 1986; Wilson, 1996). As Maher notes, for scholars who suggest that gender has lost its relevance, women's "activity is confused with [their] equality" (1997:18). Research that examines women's participation in violent street crime without paying sufficient attention to the gendered nature of this participation or the ways in which "gendered status structures this participation" (Maher, 1997:13) cannot adequately describe or explain these phenomena.

The strength of the current study is its comparative analysis of women's *and* men's accounts of the accomplishment of one type of violent crime—street robbery. In comparing both the question of why women and men report engaging in robbery, and *how* gender organizes the commission of robbery, this research provides insight into the ways in which gender shapes women's involvement in what is perhaps the typification of "masculine" street crime. As such, it speaks to broader debates about women's place in the contemporary urban street world.

Methodology

The study is based on semistructured in-depth interviews with 37 active street robbers. The sample includes 14 women and a comparative sample of 23 men, matched approximately by age and age at first robbery.[1]

The respondents range in age from 16 to 46; the majority are in their late teens to mid-twenties.[2] All of the men are African-American; 12 of the women are African-American and 2 are white.[3]

Respondents were recruited on the streets through the use of snowball sampling (Watters and Biernacki, 1989) in impoverished urban neighborhoods in St. Louis, Missouri. An ex-offender was hired to serve as a street ethnographer; he culled from his former criminal associates in order to generate the initial respondents for the study (see also Decker and Van Winkle, 1996; Wright and Decker, 1994). These respondents were then asked to refer other friends or associates who might be willing to be interviewed, and the process continued until an appropriate sample was built. Criteria for inclusion in the sample included the following: the individual had committed a robbery in the recent past, defined him- or herself as currently active, and was regarded as active by other offenders.[4] Though it is not possible to determine the representativeness of this sample of active offenders (see Glassner and Carpenter, 1985), the approach nonetheless overcomes many of the shortcomings associated with interviewing ex-offenders or offenders who are incarcerated (see Agar, 1977). In fact, in the current study snowball sampling allowed for the purposive over-sampling of both female and juvenile robbers.

Perhaps the greatest limitation of the sample is the overrepresentation of African-American robbers and the near absence of white offenders. According to the St. Louis Metropolitan Police Department's (1994) *Annual Report*, whites were 18% of robbery arrestees in that year. As Wright and Decker (1997:11) explain,

> No doubt the racial composition of our sample is a reflection of the social chasm that exists between blacks and whites in the St. Louis underworld. Black and white offenders display a marked tendency to "stick to their own kind" and seldom are members of the same criminal networks. Successfully making contact with active black armed robbers proved to be of almost no help to us in locating white offenders.

This problem was exacerbated because the hired street ethnographer was African-American and was unable to provide any initial contacts with white robbers. In fact, both of the white females interviewed in the study were referred by their African-American boyfriends.

Each respondent was paid $50 for participation in the research and was promised strict confidentiality.[5] Respondents were paid an additional $10 for each successful referral (i.e., a cooperative participant who was currently an active robber). Interviews lasted one to two hours and included a range of questions about the respondents' involvement in robbery, with particular focus on "their thoughts and actions during the commission of their crimes" (Wright and Decker, 1997:8). Respondents were asked to describe their typical approach when committing robbery, as well as to describe in detail their most recent offense; the goal was to gain a thorough understanding of the contexts of these events (see Wright and Decker, 1997, for a full discussion of the research process).

Because this research is concerned with the situational accomplishment of robbery, it does not provide a means to explore fully the contexts of offending as they relate to respondents' life circumstances. Nonetheless, it is worthwhile to situate their discussions with a brief description of the milieu from which they were drawn. As noted above, respondents were recruited from impoverished urban neighborhoods in St. Louis. St. Louis typifies the midwestern city devastated by structural changes brought about by deindustrialization. With tremendous economic and racial segregation, population loss, and resulting social isolation, loss of community resources, and concentrated urban poverty among African-Americans, the neighborhoods the respondents were drawn from are characteristic of "underclass" conditions (Sampson and Wilson, 1995; Wilson, 1996). These conditions no doubt shape respondents' offending through the interactive effects of structural barriers and resulting cultural adaptations (see Sampson and Wilson, 1995). Thus, they should remain in the foreground in examining the accomplishment of robbery.

Motivations to Commit Robbery

In this study, active robbers' articulation of the reasons they commit robbery is more a case of gender similarities than differences. What they get out of robbery, why they choose robbery instead of some other crime, why particular targets are appealing—the themes of these discussions are overlapping in women's and men's accounts. For both, the primary motivation is to get money or material goods. As Libbie Jones notes, "You can get good things from a robbery." For some, the need for money comes with a strong sense of urgency, such as when the individual is robbing to support a drug addiction—a situation more prevalent among older respondents than younger ones. But for the majority of women and men in this sample, robberies are committed to get status-conferring goods such as gold jewelry, spending money, and/or for excitement.[6] For instance, T-Bone says he decides to commit robberies when he's "tired of not having money." When the idea comes about, he is typically with friends from the neighborhood, and he explains, "we all bored, broke, mad." Likewise, CMW says she commits robberies "out of the blue, just something to do. Bored at the time and just want to find some action." She explains, "I be sitting on the porch and we'll get to talking and stuff. See people going around and they be flashing in they fancy cars, walking down the street with that jewelry on, thinking they all bad, and we just go get 'em." For both males and females, robberies are typically a means of achieving conspicuous consumption.

If anything, imperatives to gain money and material goods through robbery appear to be stronger for males than females, so that young men explain that they sometimes commit robberies because they feel some economic pressure, whereas young women typically do not. Masculine street identity is tied to the ability to have and spend money, and included in this is the appearance of economic self-sufficiency. Research has documented women's support networks in urban communities, including among criminally involved women (see Maher, 1997; Stack, 1974). This may help explain why the imperative for young men is stronger than for young women: Community norms may give women wider latitude for obtaining material goods and economic support from a variety of sources, including other females, family members, and boyfriends; whereas the pressure of society's view of men as breadwinners differentially affects men's emotional experience of relying on others economically. This may explain why several young men specifically describe that they do not like relying on their parents in order to meet their consumer needs. As Mike J. notes, "My mother, she gives me money sometimes but I can't get the stuff like I want, clothes and stuff . . . so I try to get it by robbery." Though both males and females articulate economic motives for robbery, young men, more than young women, describe feeling compelled to commit robberies because they feel "broke."

Asked to explain why they commit robberies instead of other crimes with similar economic rewards, both women and men say that they choose robberies, as Cooper explains, because "it's the easiest." Libbie Jones reports that robbery provides her with the things she wants in one quick and easy step:

> I like robbery. I like robbery 'cause I don't have to buy nothing. You have a herringbone, I'm gonna take your herringbone and then I have me a herringbone. I don't have to worry about going to the store, getting me some money. If you got some little earrings on I'm gonna get 'em.

The ease with which respondents view the act of robbery is also reflected in their choice of victims—most frequently other street-involved individuals, who are perceived as unlikely to be able to go to the police, given their own criminal involvement. In addition, these targets are perceived as likely to have a lot of money, as well as jewelry and other desirable items. Less frequently, respondents report targeting individuals who are perceived as particularly easy marks, such as older citizens. However, most robberies, whether committed by females or males, occur in the larger contexts of street life, and their victims reflect this—most are also involved in street contexts, either as adolescents or young adults who hang out on the streets and go to clubs, or as individuals involved (as dealers and/or users) in the street-level drug economy. Because of this, it is not uncommon for robbers to know or at least know of their victims (for more on target selection, see Wright and Decker, 1997:Ch. 3).

In addition to the economic incentives that draw the respondents toward robbery, many also derive a psychological or emotional thrill from committing robberies. Little Bill says, "when my first robbery started, my second, the third one, it got more fun . . . if I keep on doing it I think that I will really get addicted to it." Likewise, Ne-Ne's comment illustrates the complex dynamics shaping many respondents' decisions to commit robberies, particularly the younger ones: "I don't know if it's the money, the power or just the feeling that I know that I can just go up and just take somebody's stuff. It's just a whole bunch of mixture type thing." Others describe a similar mixture of economic and emotional rewards. Buby notes, "you get like a rush, it be fun at the time."

When individuals on the street are perceived as "high-catting" or showing off, they are viewed by both male and female robbers as deserving targets. Ne-Ne describes the following dialogue between herself and a young woman she robbed: "[The girl] said 'if you take my money then I'm gonna get in trouble because this is my man's money.' He told you to keep it, not showboat. You talking 'nigger I got $800 in my pocket,' pulling it out. Yeah, you wanted us to know." Likewise, describing a woman he robbed at a gas station, Treason Taylor says, "really I didn't like the way she came out. She was like pulling out all her money like she think she hot shit." A few respondents even specifically target people they don't like, or people who have insulted or hurt them in the past.

For both women and men, then, motivations to commit robbery are primarily economic—to get money, jewelry, and other status-conferring goods, but they also include elements of thrill seeking, attempting to overcome boredom, and revenge. Most striking is the continuity across women's and men's accounts of their motives for committing robbery, which vary only by the greater pressure reported by some young men to have their own money to obtain material goods. As discussed in the next sections, there are clear differences in the accomplishment of robbery by gender; however, these differences are apparently not driven by differences in motivation.

Men's Enactments of Street Robbery

Men accomplish street robberies in a strikingly uniform manner. Respondents' descriptions of their robberies are variations around one theme—using physical violence and/or a gun placed on or at close proximity to the victim in a confrontational manner. This is reflected in Looney's description of being taught how to commit his first robbery, at the age of 13, by his stepbrother:

> We was up at [a fast food restaurant] one day and a dude was up there tripping. My stepbrother had gave me a .22 automatic. He told me to walk over behind him and put the gun to his head and tell him to give me all his stuff. That's what I did. I walked up to him and said man, this is a jack, man, take off all your jewelry and take you money out of your pockets, throw it on the ground and walk off. So that's what he did. I picked up the money and the jewelry and walked away.

By far the most common form of robbery described by male respondents entails targeting other men involved in street life—drug dealers, drug users, gang members, or other men who look "flashy" because of their clothes, cars, and/or jewelry. Twenty-two respondents (96%) report committing robberies in these contexts, which involve accosting people on the streets or accosting them in their cars. Only Little Bill, who is an addict, does not describe engaging in these types of robberies. Instead, he only targets non-street-involved citizens, whom he feels safer confronting.[7] Seven men (30%) describe robbing women as well as men.

All of the men in this sample report using guns when they rob, though not everyone uses a gun every time.[8] The key is to make sure that the victim knows, as Syco says, "that we ain't playing." This is accomplished either through the positioning of the gun or by physically assaulting the victim. If the victim appears to resist, the physical assault is more severe, a shot is fired in the air or to the side of the victim, or the victim is shot—typically in the foot or the leg. Again, what is striking across men's interviews is the continuity of their approach toward street robberies. Upon spotting a target, they swiftly run up on the victim and physically confront him or her, telling the victim "up it up," "come up off it," or some similar phrase. These robberies frequently are committed with partners, but sometimes are committed alone.

For many male robbers, cooperation is achieved simply by the presence and positioning of the gun. Bob Jones confronts his victims by placing the gun at the back of their head, where "they feel it," and says, "give it up, motherfucker, don't move or I'll blow your brains out." Explaining the positioning of the gun, he says, "when you feel that steel against your head . . . that pistol carries a lot of weight." Describing one of his robberies, Looney says, "I creeped up behind him, this time I had a 12 gauge, I pointed it to the back of his head, told him to drop it." Big Prod notes that he will "have the gun to his head, can't do nothing but respect that." Likewise, Treason Taylor explains that he will "grab [the victim] by the neck and stick the gun to they head. Sometimes I don't even touch them I just point the gun right in front of they face. That really scares people." Prauch says, "I don't even have to say nothing half the time. When they see that pistol, they know what time it is."

A number of respondents report using some measure of physical confrontation, even when using a weapon, in order to ensure the victim's cooperation and/or the robber's getaway. Cooper says, "you always got to either hit 'em, slap 'em or do something to let them know you for real." T-Bone says, "I just hit them with the gun and they give it up quick." Likewise, Mike J. says, "you might shake them a little bit. If there is more than one of you, you can really do that kind of stuff like shake them up a little bit to show them you're not messing around." Sometimes physical confrontation is simply part of the thrill. Damon Jones says that while he typically doesn't physically assault his victims, a friend he often robs with "always do something stupid like he'll smash somebody with the pistol, you know what I'm saying. He'll hit them in the head or something just, I guess, just to do it."

When the victim hesitates or is seen as uncooperative, the respondents describe using a variety of physical measures to ensure the completion of the robbery. The mildest version is described by Carlos Reed: "If I have a revolver, I'll cock it back, that will be the warning right there. If I run up to you like this and then you hesitate I'm gonna cock it back." Others use physical violence to intimidate the victim. Redwood says, "if they think I'm bullshitting I'll smack them up in they motherfucking head." Likewise, Tony Wright notes, "you would be surprised how cooperative a person will be once he been smashed across the face with a .357 Magnum." Other respondents describe shooting the gun, either past the victim or in the leg or foot, in order to ensure cooperation. Prauch says, "one gun shot, they ass in line. If I hit them a couple of times and that don't work, one gun shot by they ear and they in line." And Cooper notes, "If I see he just trying to get tough then sometimes I just straight out have to shoot somebody, just shoot 'em."

Though most robberies involve the use of a weapon, several men also report engaging in strong-arm robberies, sometimes when an opportunity presents itself and there is no time to retrieve a weapon. These robberies involve a great deal of physical violence. Taz says, "if it's a strong-arm, like I'll just get up on them and I'll just hit 'em and [my partner] will grab them or like he will hit them and I'll grab 'em and we keep on hitting them until they fall or something . . . we just go in his pockets, leave him there, we gone." Likewise, Swoop describes a strong-arm robbery he was involved in:

> Me and my two partners saw this dude and he had on a lot of jewelry. I wanted them chains and my partner wanted the rings. We didn't have a weapon. We strong-armed him . . . He was coming from off the lot [at a fast food restaurant], he actually was going to his car so I ran up on him . . . and I hit him in the face. He tried to run. My partner ran and kicked him in the mouth. He just let us, I took the chains off of him, my partner took his rings, my partner took his money, we split the money and that was all it took.

Seven men describe robbing women as well as men. However, male respondents—both those who have robbed women and those who have not—clearly state that robbing women is different from robbing men. Robbing women is seen as less dangerous, and women are believed to be less likely to resist. The following dialogue with Looney is illustrative:

> Interviewer: Do you rob men or women more?
>
> Looney: I rob men.
>
> Interviewer: Why?
>
> Looney: They got money.
>
> Interviewer: Do men behave differently than women?
>
> Looney: Nope. Men gonna try to act like the tough guy, when they see the gun, then they give it up quick. But a lady, I just tell them to give it up and they give me they whole purse or whatever they got.

While physical violence is often used in men's robberies of other men, respondents do not describe assaulting women routinely, typically only if they are seen as resisting. It appears not to be deemed a necessary part of the transaction with female victims. Taz, whose robberies of men typically involve a great deal of physical violence (see above), says, "I did a girl before but I didn't hurt her or nothing, we just robbed her. She was too scared." Having women present is also seen as making male targets more vulnerable. Swoop explains: "If he like by himself or if he with a girl then that's the best time, but if he with two dudes, you know they rolling strapped so you wait." Unlike when a street-involved target is with other males and needs to maintain an air of toughness, Swoop says "you know they ain't gonna try to show off for the little gals, they gonna give it all up."

It is notable that women are widely perceived, as C-Loco says, as "easy to get," and yet as a rule they are not targeted for street robberies. Partly this is because women are perceived as less likely to have a lot of money on them. Moreover, women are not viewed as real players in the action of the streets; they are peripheral, and thus not typically part of the masculine game of street robbery. Antwon Wright sums this up in the following dialogue about the use of physical violence:

> Interviewer: Do you hit everybody?
>
> Antwon Wright: It depends. It depends on who is there and how many. If it's a dude and a gal we might hit the dude and leave the girl.
>
> Interviewer: Why?
>
> Antwon Wright: 'Cause a girl is no threat for real to us. A girl is no threat. We just worry about dudes. Girls is no threat. But if it's about six dudes, man we gonna hit everybody. We gonna get everybody on the ground, bam, bam. Then if they want to get back up we just keep on hitting.

Male robbers, then, clearly view the act of robbery as a masculine accomplishment in which men compete with other men for money and status. While some rob women, those robberies are deviations from the norm of "badass" against "badass" that dominates much of men's discussions of street robbery (see Katz, 1988). The routine use of guns, physical contact, and violence in male-on-male robberies is a reflection of the masculine ideologies shaping men's robberies. Women's enactment of robbery is much more varied than that of men's and provides a telling contrast about the nature of gender on the streets.

Women's Enactments of Street Robbery

The women in the sample describe three predominant ways in which they commit robberies: targeting female victims in physically confrontational robberies, targeting male victims by appearing sexually available, and participating with males during street robberies of men. Ten women (71%) describe targeting female victims, usually on the streets but occasionally at dance clubs or in cars. Seven (50%) describe setting up men through promises of sexual favors, including two women who do so in the context of prostitution. Seven (50%) describe working with male friends, relatives, or boyfriends in street robberies; three (21%) report this as their exclusive form of robbery.

Robbing Females

The most common form of robbery reported by women in the study is robbing other females in a physically confrontational manner. Ten of the 14 female respondents report committing these types of offenses. Of those who do not, three only commit robberies by assisting men, whose targets are other males (see below), and one only robs men in the context of prostitution. Typically, women's robberies of other females occur on the streets, though a few young women also report robbing females in the bathrooms or parking lots of clubs, and one robs women in cars. These robberies are sometimes committed alone, but usually in conjunction with one or several additional women, but not in conjunction with men. In fact, Ne-Ne says even when she's out with male friends and sees a female target, they don't get involved: "They'll say 'well you go on and do her.'"

Most robberies of females either involve no weapon or they involve a knife. Four women report having used a gun to rob women, only one of whom does so on a regular basis.[9] Women are the victims of choice because they are perceived as less likely to be armed themselves and less likely to resist or fight back. CMW explains, "See women, they won't really do nothing. They say, 'oh, oh, ok, here take this.' A dude, he might try to put up a fight." Yolanda Smith reports that she only robs women because "they more easier for me to handle." Likewise, Libbie Jones says, "I wouldn't do no men by myself," but she says women victims "ain't gonna do nothing because they be so scared." The use of weapons in these assaults is often not deemed necessary. Quick explains that she sometimes uses a knife, "but sometimes I don't need anything. Most of the time it be girls, you know, just snatching they chains or jewelry. You don't need nothing for that." Quick has also used a gun to rob another female. She and a friend were driving around when they spotted a young woman walking down the street with an expensive purse they liked. "We jumped out of the car. My friend put a gun up to her head and we just took all of her stuff." However, this approach was atypical.

On occasion, female victims belie the stereotype of them and fight back. Both Janet Outlaw and Ne-Ne describe stabbing young women who resisted them. Janet Outlaw describes one such encounter:

> This was at a little basketball game. Coming from the basketball game. It was over and we were checking her out and everything and she was

> walking to her car. I was, shit fuck that, let's get her motherfucking purse. Said let's get that purse. So I walked up to her and I pulled out the knife. I said "up that purse." And she looked at me. I said "shit, do you think I'm playing? Up that purse." She was like "shit, you ain't getting my purse. Do what you got to do." I was like "shit, you must be thinking I'm playing." So I took the knife, stabbed her a couple of times on the shoulder, stabbed her on the arm and snatched the purse. Cut her arm and snatched the purse. She just ran, "help, help." We were gone.

Ne-Ne describes a similar incident that occurred after an altercation between two groups of young women. When one young woman continued to badmouth her, she followed the girl to her car, pulled out a knife, "headed to her side and showed the bitch [the knife]." The girl responded, "I ain't giving you shit," and Ne-Ne said, "please don't make me stick you." Then, "She went to turn around and I just stuck it in her side . . . She was holding her side, just bleeding. And so when she fell on the ground one of my partners just started taking her stuff off of her. We left her right there."

As with pulling guns on women, stabbing female victims is a rare occurrence. Nonetheless, women's robbery of other women routinely involves physical confrontation such as hitting, shoving, or beating up the victim. Describing a recent robbery, Nicole Simpson says, "I have bricks in my purse and I went up to her and hit her in the head and took her money." Kim Brown says that she will "just whop you and take a purse but not really put a gun to anybody's face." Libbie Jones says she has her victims throw their possessions on the ground, "then you push 'em, kick 'em or whatever, you pick it up and you just burn out." Likewise, CMW describes a recent robbery:

> I was like with three other girls and we was like all walking around . . . walking around the block trying to find something to do on a Saturday night with really nothing to do and so we started coming up the street, we didn't have no weapons on us at the time. All we did was just start jumping on her and beating her up and took her purse.

According to Janet Outlaw, "We push 'em and tell them to up their shit, pushing 'em in the head. Couple of times we had to knock the girls down and took the stuff off of them." She explains the reason this type of physical force is necessary: "It's just a woman-to-woman thing and we just like, just don't, just letting them know like it is, we let them know we ain't playing." As discussed below, this approach is vastly different from women's approaches when they rob men, or when they commit robberies with males. It appears to be, as Janet Outlaw says, "a woman-to-woman thing."

As noted above, sometimes female-on-female robberies occur in or around night clubs, in addition to on the streets. Libbie Jones explains, "you just chill in the club, just dance or whatever, just peep out people that got what you want. And then they come out of the club and you just get them." Likewise, Janet Outlaw says, "we get a couple of drinks, be on the blow, party, come sit down. Then be like, damn, check that bitch out with all this shit on." Libbie Jones came to her interview wearing a ring she had gotten in a robbery at a club the night before, telling the interviewer, "I like this on my hand, it looks lovely." She describes the incident as follows:

> This girl was in the bathroom. I seen the rings on her hands. Everybody was in there talking and putting their makeup on, doing their hair. So I went and got my godsister. She came back with her drink. She spilled it on her and she was like, "oh, my fault, my fault." She was wiping it off her. I pulled out my knife and said "give it up." The girl was taking the rings off her hand so when we got the rings we bounced up out of the club.

Though most of the women who rob females are teenagers or young adults and rob other young women, two women in the sample—Lisa Wood and Kim Brown—also describe targeting middle-aged or older citizens. It is notable that both are older (in their late 30s) and that both describe robbing in order to support drug habits, which make them more desperate.[10] As with the younger women who choose to rob other young women because they believe them unlikely to resist, both of these women choose older targets because they won't fight back. Lisa Wood says sometimes they accomplish these robberies of non-street-involved citizens by getting victims to drop their guard when they are coming out of stores. She describes approaching the person, "say 'hi, how you doing,' or 'do you need any help?' A lot of times they will say yeah. They might have groceries to take to they car and get it like that." She says once they drop their guard she will "snatch they purse and take off running."

To summarize, notable elements of women's robberies of other women are that they most frequently occur within street-oriented settings, do not include male accomplices, and typically involve physical force such as hitting, shoving, and kicking, rather than the use of a weapon. When weapons are used, they are most likely to be knives. In these contexts, women choose to rob other females rather than males because they believe females are less likely to fight back; they typically do not use weapons such as guns because they perceive female targets as unlikely to be armed.

Setting Up Males by Appearing Sexually Available

Women's robberies of men nearly always involve guns.[11] They also do not involve physical contact. Janet Outlaw, who describes a great deal of physical contact in her robberies of other women (see above), describes her robberies of men in much different terms: "If we waste time touching men there is a possibility that they can get the gun off of us, while we wasting time touching them they could do anything. So we just keep the gun straight on them. No touching, no moving, just straight gun at you." The circumstances surrounding the enactment of female-on-male robberies differ as well. The key, in each case, is that women pretend to be sexually interested in their male victims, whose guard drops, providing a safe opportunity for the crime to occur. Two women—Jayzo and Nicole Simpson—rob men in the context of prostitution. The other five typically choose a victim at a club or on the streets, flirt and appear sexually interested, then suggest they go to a hotel, where the robbery takes place. These robberies may involve male or female accomplices, but they are just as likely to be conducted alone.

Nicole Simpson prostitutes to support her drug habit, but sometimes she "just don't be feeling like doing it," and will rob her trick rather than complete the sexual transaction. Sometimes she does this alone, and other times has a female accomplice. She chooses tricks she feels will make safe victims. She explains, "like I meet a lot of white guys and they be so paranoid they just want to get away." When Nicole Simpson is working alone, she waits until the man is in a vulnerable position before pulling out her knife. As she explains, "if you are sucking a man's dick and you pull a knife on them, they not gonna too much argue with you." When she works with a female partner, Nicole Simpson has the woman wait at a designated place, then takes the trick "to the spot where I know she at." She begins to perform oral sex, then her partner jumps in the car and pulls a knife. She explains, "once she get in the car I'll watch her back, they know we together. I don't even let them think that she is by herself. If they know it's two of us maybe they won't try it. Because if they think she by herself they might say fuck this, it ain't nothing but one person." Jayzo's techniques parallel those of Nicole Simpson, though she uses a gun instead of a knife and sometimes takes prospective tricks to hotels in addition to car dating.

Young women who target men outside the context of prostitution play upon the men's beliefs about women in order to accomplish these robberies—including the assumptions that women won't be armed, won't attempt to rob them, and can be taken advantage of sexually. Quick explains, "they don't suspect that a girl gonna try to get 'em. You know what I'm saying? So it's kind of easier 'cause they like, she looks innocent, she ain't gonna do this, but that's how I get 'em. They put they guard down to a woman." She says when she sets up men, she parties with them first, but makes sure she doesn't consume as much as them. "Most of the time, when girls get high they think they can take advantage of us so they always, let's go to a hotel or my crib or something." Janet Outlaw says, "they easy to get, we know what they after—sex." Likewise, CMW and a girlfriend often flirt with their victims: "We get in the car then ride with them. They thinking we little freaks . . . whores or something." These men's assumptions that they can take advantage of women lead them to place themselves at risk for robbery. CMW continues: "So they try to take us to the motel or whatever, we going for it. Then it's like they getting out of the car and then all my friend has to do is just put the gun up to his head, give me your keys. He really can't do nothing, his gun is probably in the car. All you do is drive on with the car."

Several young women report targeting men at clubs, particularly dope dealers or other men who appear to have a lot of money. Describing one such victim, Janet Outlaw says she was drawn to him because of his "jewelry, the way he was dressed, little snakeskin boots and all . . . I was like, yeah, there is some money." She recounts the incident as follows:

> I walked up to him, got to conversating with him. He was like, "what's up with you after the club?" I said "I'm down with you, whatever you want to do." I said "we can go to a hotel or something." He was like "for real?" I was like, "yeah, for real." He was like, "shit, cool then." So after the club we went to the hotel. I had the gun in my purse. I followed him, I was in my own car, he was in his car. So I put the gun in my purse and went up to the hotel, he was all ready. He was posted, he was a lot drunk. He was like, "you smoke weed?" I was like, "yeah shit, what's up." So we got to smoking a little bud, he got to taking off his little shit, laying it on a little table. He was like, "shit, what's up, ain't you gonna get undressed?" I was like "shit, yeah, hold up" and I went in my purse and I pulled out the gun. He was like "damn, what's up with you gal?" I was like, "shit, I want your jewelry and all the money you got." He was like, "shit, bitch you crazy. I ain't giving you my shit." I said, "do you think I'm playing nigger? You don't think I'll shoot your motherfucking ass?" He was like, "shit, you crazy, fuck that, you ain't gonna shoot me." So then I had fired the thing but I didn't fire it at him, shot the gun. He was like "fuck no." I snatched his shit. He didn't have on no clothes. I snatched the shit and ran out the door. Hopped in my car.

Though she did this particular robbery alone, Janet Outlaw says she often has male accomplices, who follow her to the hotel or meet her there. While she's in the room, "my boys be standing out in the hallway," then she lets them in when she's ready to rob the man. Having male backup is useful because men often resist being robbed by females, believing that women don't have the heart to go through with what's necessary if the victim resists. Janet Outlaw describes one such incident. Having flirted with a man and agreed to meet him, she got in his car then pulled her gun on him:

> I said "give me your stuff." He wasn't gonna give it to me. This was at nighttime. My boys was on the other side of the car but he didn't know it. He said "I ain't gonna give you shit." I was like, "you gonna give me your stuff." He was like "I'll take that gun off of your ass." I was like, "shit, you ain't gonna take this gun." My boy just pulled up and said, "give her your shit." I got the shit.

In the majority of these robberies, the victim knows that the woman has set him up—she actively participates in the robbery. Ne-Ne also describes setting up men and then pretending to be a victim herself. Her friends even get physical with her to make it appear that she's not involved. She explains:

> I'll scam you out and get to know you a little bit first, go out and eat and let you tell me where we going, what time and everything. I'll go

> in the restroom and go beep them [accomplices] just to let them know what time we leaving from wherever we at so they can come out and do their little robbery type thing, push me or whatever. I ain't gonna leave with them 'cause then he'll know so I still chill with him for a little while.

Only Ne-Ne reports having ever engaged in a robbery the opposite of this—that is, one in which her male partners flirted with a girl and she came up and robbed her. She explains:

> I got some [male friends] that will instigate it. If I see some girl and I'm in the car with a whole bunch of dudes, they be like "look at that bitch she have on a leather coat." "Yeah, I want that." They'll say "well why don't you go get it?" Then you got somebody in the back seat [saying] "she's scared, she's scared." Then you got somebody just like "she ain't scared, up on the piece" or whatever and then you got some of them that will say well, "we gonna do this together." It could be like two dudes they might get out like "what's up baby," try to holler at her, get a mack on and they don't see the car. We watching and as soon as they pulling out they little pen to write they number, then I'll get out of the car and just up on them and tell them, the dudes be looking like, damn, what's going on? But they ain't gonna help 'cause they my partners or whatever.

Street Robberies with Male Robbers

As the previous two sections illustrate, women's accomplishment of robbery varies according to the gender of their victims. As a rule, women and men do not rob females together, but do sometimes work together to set up and rob males. In addition, half of the women interviewed describe committing street robberies—almost always against males—with male accomplices. In these robberies, women's involvement either involves equal participation in the crime or assisting males but defining their role as secondary. Three women in the sample—Buby, Tish, and Lisa Jones—describe working with males on the streets as their only form of robbery, and each sees her participation as secondary. The rest engage in a combination of robbery types, including those described in the previous two sections, and do not distinguish their roles from the roles of male participants in these street robberies.

Lisa Jones and Tish each assist their boyfriends in the commission of robberies; Buby goes along with her brother and cousins. Lisa Jones says "most of the time we'll just be driving around and he'll say 'let's go to this neighborhood and rob somebody.'" Usually she stays in the car while he approaches the victim, but she is armed and will get out and assist when necessary. Describing one such incident, she says, "One time there was two guys and one guy was in the car and the other guy was out of the car and I seen that one guy getting out of the car I guess to help his friend. That's when I got out and I held the gun and I told him to stay where he was."

Likewise Buby frequently goes on robberies with her brother and cousins but usually chooses to stay in the car "because I be thinking that I'm gonna get caught so I rather stay in the back." She has never done a robbery on her own and explains, "I know what to do but I don't know if I could do it on my own. I don't know if I could because I'm used to doing them with my brother and my cousins." Though her role is not an active one, she gets a cut of the profits from these robberies.

Tish and Lisa Jones are the only white respondents in the study. Each robs with an African-American boyfriend, and—though they commit armed robberies—both reject the view of themselves as criminals. Lisa Jones, for instance, downplays her role in robberies, as the following dialogue illustrates:

> Interviewer: How many armed robberies have you done in your life?
>
> Lisa Jones: I go with my boyfriend and I've held the gun, I've never actually shot it.
>
> Interviewer: But you participate in his robberies?
>
> Lisa Jones: Yeah.
>
> Interviewer: How many would you say in your whole life?
>
> Lisa Jones: About fifteen.
>
> Interviewer: What about in the last month?
>
> Lisa Jones: Maybe five or six.
>
> Interviewer: What other crimes have you done in your life, or participated with others?
>
> Lisa Jones: No, I'm not a criminal.

It is striking that this young woman routinely engages in robberies in which she wields a weapon, yet she defines herself as "not a criminal." Later in the interview, she explains that she would stop participating in armed robberies "if I was to stop seeing him." She and Tish are the only respondents who minimize the implications of their involvement in armed robbery, and it is probably not coincidental that they are young white women—their race and gender allow them to view themselves in this way.

Both also describe their boyfriends as the decision makers in the robberies—deciding when, where, and whom to rob. This is evident in Tish's interview, as her boyfriend, who is present in the room, frequently interjects to answer the interviewer's questions. The following dialogue is revealing:

> Interviewer: How do you approach the person?
>
> Tish: Just go up to them.
>
> Interviewer: You walk up to them, you drive up to them?

> Boyfriend: Most of the time it's me and my partner that do it. Our gals, they got the guns and stuff but we doing most of the evaluating. We might hit somebody in the head with a gun, go up to them and say whatever. Come up off your shit or something to get the money. The girls, they doing the dirty work really, that's the part they like doing, they'll hold the gun and if something goes wrong they'll shoot. We approach them. I ain't gonna send my gal up to no dude to tell him she want to rob him, you know. She might walk up to him with me and she might hit him a couple of times but basically I'm going up to them.

These respondents reveal the far end of the continuum of women's involvement in robbery, clearly taking subordinate roles in the crime and defining themselves as less culpable as a result. Tish's boyfriend also reveals his perception of women as secondary actors in the accomplishment of robbery. For the most part, other women who participate in street robberies with male accomplices describe themselves as equal participants. Older women who rob citizens to support their drug habits at times do so with male accomplices. For instance, Lisa Woods sometimes commits her robberies with a male and female accomplice and targets people "like when they get they checks. Catch them coming out of the store, maybe trip 'em, go in they pocket and take they money and take off running." Among the younger women, robberies with male accomplices involve guns and typically come about when a group of people are driving around and spot a potential victim. Janet Outlaw describes a car jacking that occurred as she and some friends were driving around:

> Stop at a red light, we was looking around, didn't see no police, we was right behind them [the victims] . . . So one of my boys got out and I got out. Then the other boy got up in the driver's seat that was with them. My boy went on one side and I went on the other side and said "nigger get out of the car before we shoot you." Then the dudes got out. It was like, shit, what's up, we down with you all. No you ain't down with us, take they jewelry and shit off. It was like, damn, why you all tripping? Then my boy cocked the little gun and said take it off now or I'm gonna start spraying you all ass. So they took off the little jewelry, I hopped in, put it in drive and pulled on off.

Likewise, Ne-Ne prefers committing street robberies with males rather than females. She explains:

> I can't be bothered with too many girls. That's why I try to be with dudes or whatever. They gonna be down. If you get out of the car and if you rob a dude or jack somebody and you with some dudes then you know if they see he tryin' to resist, they gonna give me some help. Whereas a girl, you might get somebody that's scared and might drive off. That's the way it is.

It is not surprising, then, that Ne-Ne is the only woman interviewed to report having ever committed this type of street robbery of a male victim on her own. Her actions parallel those of male-on-male robbers described above. Ne-Ne explicitly indicates that this robbery was possible because the victim did not know she was a woman. Describing herself physically, she says, "I'm big, you know." In addition, her dress and manner masked her gender. "I had a baseball cap in my car and I seen him . . . I just turned around the corner, came back down the street, he was out by hisself and I got out of the car, had the cap pulled down over my face and I just went to the back and upped him. Put the gun up to his head." Being large, wearing a ballcap, and enacting the robbery in a masculine style (e.g., putting a gun to his head) allowed her to disguise the fact that she was a woman and thus decrease the victim's likelihood of resisting. She says, "He don't know right now to this day if it was a girl or a dude."

Discussion

Feminist scholars have been hesitant to grapple with the issue of women's violence, both because a focus on women's violence draws attention away from the fact that violence is a predominantly male phenomenon and because studying women's violence can play into sensationalized accounts of female offenders. Nonetheless, as this and other studies have shown, "gender alone does not account for variation in criminal violence" (Simpson, 1991:118). A small number of women are involved in violent street crime in ways that go beyond "preventing victimization," and appear to find support among their male and female peers for these activities. To draw this conclusion is not to suggest that women's use of violence is increasing, that women are "equals" on the streets, or that gender does not matter. It does suggest that researchers should continue developing feminist perspectives to address the issue.

What is most notable about the current research is the incongruity between motivations and accomplishment of robbery. While a comparison of women's and men's motivations to commit robbery reveals gender similarities, when women and men actually commit robbery their enactments of the crime are strikingly different. These differences highlight the clear gender hierarchy that exists on the streets. While some women are able to carve out a niche for themselves in this setting, and even establish partnerships with males, they are participating in a male-dominated environment, and their actions reflect an understanding of this.

To accomplish robberies successfully, women must take into account the gendered nature of their environment. One way they do so is by targeting other females. Both male and female robbers hold the view that females are easy to rob, because they are less likely than males to be armed and because they are perceived as weak and easily intimidated. Janet Outlaw describes women's robbery of other women as "just a woman to woman thing." This is supported by Ne-Ne's description that her male friends do not participate with her in robberies of females, and it is supported by men's accounts of robbing women. While women routinely rob other women, men are less likely to do so, perhaps because these robberies do not result in the demonstration of masculinity.

At the same time that women articulate the belief that other women are easy targets, they also draw upon these perceptions of women in order to rob men. Two of the women describe committing robberies much in keeping with Maher's (1997) descriptions of "viccing." In addition, a number of women used men's perceptions of women as weak, sexually available, and easily manipulated to turn the tables and manipulate men into circumstances in which they became vulnerable to robbery—by flirting and appearing sexually interested in them. Unlike women's robberies of other women, these robberies tend not to involve physical contact but do involve the use of guns. Because they recognize men's perceptions of women, they also recognize that men are more likely to resist being robbed by a female, and thus they commit these robberies in ways that minimize their risk of losing control and maximize their ability to show that they're "for real."

West and Zimmerman (1987:139) note that there are circumstances in which "parties reach an accommodation that allow[s] a woman to engage in presumptively masculine behavior." In this study, it is notable that while both women and men recognize the urban street world as a male-dominated one, a few of the women interviewed appear to have gained access to male privilege by adopting male attitudes about females, constructing their own identities as more masculine, and following through by behaving in masculine ways (see also Hunt, 1984). Ne-Ne and Janet Outlaw both come to mind in this regard—as women who completed robberies in equal partnerships with men and identified with men's attitudes about other women. Other women, such as Lisa Jones and Tish, accepted not only women's position as secondary, but their own as well. While Ne-Ne and Janet Outlaw appeared to draw status and identity from their criminality in ways that went beyond their gender identity, Lisa Jones and Tish used their gender identity to construct themselves as noncriminal.

In sum, the women in this sample do not appear to "do robbery" differently than men in order to meet different needs or accomplish different goals. Instead, the differences that emerge reflect practical choices made in the context of a gender-stratified environment—one in which, on the whole, men are perceived as strong and women are perceived as weak. Motivationally, then, it appears that women's participation in street violence can result from the same structural and cultural underpinnings that shape some of men's participation in these crimes, and that they receive rewards beyond protection for doing so. Yet gender remains a salient factor shaping their actions, as well as the actions of men.

Though urban African-American women have higher rates of violence than other women, their participation in violent crime is nonetheless significantly lower than that of their male counterparts in the same communities

(Simpson, 1991). An important line of inquiry for future research is to assess what protective factors keep the majority of women living in underclass settings from adopting violence as a culturally legitimate response. While research shows that racial and economic oppression contribute to African-American women's greater participation in violent crime, they do not ensure its occurrence. Daly and Stephens (1995:208) note: "Racism in criminological theories occurs when racial or cultural differences are overemphasized or mischaracterized *and* when such differences are denied." Future research should strive to strike this balance and attend to the complex issues surrounding women's participation in violence within the urban street world.

Endnotes

[1] The original study (Wright and Decker, 1997) contained 86 interviews, 72 of which were with males. From these, the matched sample of males for the current study was drawn prior to data analysis to avoid sampling biases.

[2] This age distribution differs from that of the larger sample, which included a sizable number of older male robbers. Eighteen of the males in the current sample were under 25 (78%), while only 35 of the 72 males in the larger sample (49%) were under 25.

[3] One white male was interviewed for the original study but was excluded from this analysis because he didn't fit the matching criteria (age, age at first robbery) and had only committed one robbery, which was retaliatory in nature. He was 30 years old and had recently been ripped off by someone, whom he robbed in order to get his money back. Notably though, the physicality of his style in committing the robbery—"I had my left hand on his neck and the gun on his cheekbone"—paralleled the predominant style of the male robbers included.

[4] All but five of the respondents reported that they had committed at least one robbery within the month prior to being interviewed. These five included three men (Woods, C-Loco, and Tony Wright) and two women (Quick and Kim Brown). All nonetheless considered themselves active robbers.

[5] Because the project was partially supported by funds from the National Institute of Justice, respondents' confidentiality was protected by federal law. In addition, completed interviews were kept in a locked file cabinet. For a fuller discussion of human subjects' protections, see Wright and Decker (1997). In regard to confidentiality, one clarification is in order. One of the young women (Tish) was referred by her boyfriend, who had previously been interviewed for the project. They insisted that he be present during her interview, and he occasionally interjected to offer his own clarifications of her responses. Though his presence may have made her more hesitant or self-conscious in answering, his own comments were illuminating regarding the gendered nature of their robberies, as both of them downplayed the seriousness of her involvement.

[6] This pattern is somewhat different from that of the larger sample of 86 active robbers, more of whom described robbing with a greater sense of desperation for money (Wright and Decker, 1997). This difference results from the differences in age structure of the current sample compared to the original sample. Because the majority of female respondents were teenagers or young adults (10 of the 14), the matched sample of males drawn for this study was younger than the larger sample of males (see note 2). Older robbers were more likely to be supporting drug habits and were more likely to have children or family that they made efforts to provide for.

Sommers and Baskin's (1993) study of female robbers offers much the same conclusion regarding motivation. In their study of 44 female robbers, 89% describe committing the crime for money, and 11% for noneconomic reasons such as excitement or vengeance. Of women who committed robbery for money, 81% did so to support drug habits, and only

19% did so to get commodities such as jewelry and clothes. These differences are likely the case because their sample is older than the current sample and because they were incarcerated at the time of the interview, and thus likely represent less successful robbers (perhaps because of their drug habits). In fact, when giving life-history accounts, two-thirds of Sommers and Baskin's sample reported that their initial reasons for committing robbery were less economic and more oriented toward thrill seeking and excitement.

[7] This may be a low estimate. Sometimes it is difficult to discern whether victims are street involved; robbers simply view them as an individual likely to have money because of their physical appearance, dress, and jewelry. In the larger sample, Wright and Decker estimated that 30 of the 86 robbers (35%) targeted citizens.

[8] In the larger sample, approximately 90% of respondents used guns to commit robberies.

[9] This is Yolanda Smith, who robs older women by offering to give them rides in her car. Describing a typical robbery, she says: "I asked her did she need a ride. I said 'if you give me one dollar for gas I'll take you to work.' So she jumped in the car. I took her about three or four blocks and then I said 'do you have any more money?' She had this necklace on so I put a gun up to her head and said 'give it up.'" Her approach was unlike any other woman's in the sample, both in terms of how she approached the victim and in her routine use of a firearm.

[10] These two are also the only women who report having had male accomplices when robbing women in this way.

[11] The only exception to this pattern was Nicole Simpson, who used a knife to rob tricks in the context of prostitution. These findings parallel those of Sommers and Baskin (1993:147), who found that women were not likely to rob men without weapons, but were likely to rob other women without them.

References

Agar, Michael H.

1977 Ethnography in the streets and in the joint: A comparison. In Robert S. Weppner (ed.), Street Ethnography: Selected Studies of Crime and Drug Use in Natural Settings. Beverly Hills, Calif.: Sage.

Ageton, Suzanne S.

1983 The dynamics of female delinquency, 1976–1980. Criminology 21(4):555–584.

Anderson, Elijah

1994 The code of the streets. Atlantic Monthly 273:81–94.

Baskin, Deborah, Ira Sommers, and Jeffrey Fagan

1993 The political economy of violent female street crime. Fordham Urban Law Journal 20:401–417.

Braithwaite, John and Kathleen Daly

1994 Masculinities, violence and communitarian control. In Tim Newburn and Elizabeth A. Stanko (eds.), Just Boys Doing Business? New York: Routledge.

Campbell, Anne

1993 Men, Women and Aggression. New York: Basic Books.

Chesney-Lind, Meda

1993 Girls, gangs and violence: Anatomy of a backlash. Humanity & Society 17(3):321–344.

Chesney-Lind, Meda and Randall G. Shelden

1992 Girls, Delinquency and Juvenile Justice. Pacific Groves, Calif.: Brooks/ Cole.

Daly, Kathleen and Deborah J. Stephens

1995 The "dark figure" of criminology: Towards a black and multi-ethnic feminist agenda for theory and research. In Nicole Hahn Rafter and Frances Heidensohn (eds.), International Feminist Perspectives in Criminology: Engendering a Discipline. Philadelphia: Open University Press.

Decker, Scott and Barrik Van Winkle
1996 Life in the Gang. New York: Cambridge University Press.
Federal Bureau of Investigation.
1996 Crime in the United States, 1995. Washington, D.C.: U. S. Government Printing Office.
Glassner, Barry and Cheryl Carpenter
1985 The feasibility of an ethnographic study of adult property offenders. Unpublished report prepared for the National Institute of Justice, Washington, D.C.
Hill, Gary D. and Elizabeth M. Crawford
1990 Women, race, and crime. Criminology 28(4):601–623.
Hunt, Jennifer
1984 The development of rapport through the negotiation of gender in field work among police. Human Organization 43(4):283–296.
Joe, Karen A. and Meda Chesney-Lind
1995 Just every mother's angel: An analysis of gender and ethnic variations in youth gang membership. Gender & Society 9(4):408–430.
Katz, Jack
1988 Seductions of Crime. New York: Basic Books.
Kelly, Liz
1991 Unspeakable acts. Trouble and Strife 21:13–20.
Laub, John H. and M. Joan McDermott
1985 An analysis of serious crime by young black women. Criminology 23(1):81–98.
Maher, Lisa
1997 Sexed Work: Gender, Race and Resistance in a Brooklyn Drug Market. Oxford: Clarendon Press.
Maher, Lisa and Richard Curtis
1992 Women on the edge of crime: Crack cocaine and the changing contexts of street-level sex work in New York City. Crime, Law and Social Change 18:221–258.
Maher, Lisa and Kathleen Daly
1996 Women in the street-level drug economy: Continuity or change? Criminology 34(4):465–492.
Mann, Coramae Richey
1993 Sister against sister: Female intrasexual homicide. In C.C. Culliver (ed.), Female Criminality: The State of the Art. New York: Garland Publishing.
Messerschmidt, James W.
1993 Masculinities and Crime. Lanham, Md.: Rowman & Littlefield.
1995 From patriarchy to gender: Feminist theory, criminology and the challenge of diversity. In Nicole Hahn Rafter and Frances Heidensohn (eds.), International Feminist Perspectives in Criminology: Engendering a Discipline. Philadelphia: Open University Press.
Newburn, Tim and Elizabeth A. Stanko (eds.)
1994 Just Boys Doing Business? New York: Routledge.
Oliver, William
1994 The Violent Social World of Black Men. New York: Lexington Books.
Sampson, Robert J. and William Julius Wilson
1995 Toward a theory of race, crime, and urban inequality. In John Hagan and Ruth D. Peterson (eds.), Crime and Inequality. Stanford, Calif.: Stanford University Press.

Sikes, Gini
1997 8 Ball Chicks: A Year in the Violent World of Girl Gangsters. New York: Anchor Books.
Simpson, Sally
1989 Feminist theory, crime and justice. Criminology 27(4):605–631.
1991 Caste, class and violent crime: Explaining difference in female offending. Criminology 29(1):115–135.
Simpson, Sally and Lori Elis
1995 Doing gender: Sorting out the caste and crime conundrum. Criminology 33(1):47–81.
Sommers, Ira and Deborah R. Baskin
1993 The situational context of violent female offending. Journal of Research on Crime and Delinquency 30(2):136–162.
St. Louis Metropolitan Police Department
1994 Annual Report—1993/1994.
Stack, Carol B.
1974 All Our Kin: Strategies for Survival in a Black Community. New York: Harper & Row.
Steffensmeier, Darrell J.
1983 Organization properties and sex-segregation in the underworld: Building a sociological theory of sex differences in crime. Social Forces 61:1010–1032.
Steffensmeier, Darrell J. and Robert Terry
1986 Institutional sexism in the underworld: A view from the inside. Sociological Inquiry 56:304–323.
Watters, John and Patrick Biernacki
1989 Targeted sampling: Options for the study of hidden populations. Social Problems 36:416–430.
West, Candace and Sarah Fenstermaker
1995 Doing difference. Gender & Society 9(1):8–37.
West, Candace and Don H. Zimmerman
1987 Doing gender. Gender & Society 1(2):125–151.
White, Jacquelyn W. and Robin M. Kowalski
1994 Deconstructing the myth of the nonaggressive woman: A feminist analysis. Psychology of Women Quarterly 18:487–508.
Wilson, William Julius
1996 When Work Disappears: The World of the New Urban Poor. New York: Alfred A. Knopf.
Wright, Richard T. and Scott Decker
1994 Burglars on the Job: Streetlife and Residential Break-Ins. Boston: Northeastern University Press.
1997 Armed Robbers in Action: Stickups and Street Culture. Boston: Northeastern University Press.

7

The Prevalence and Nature of Violent Offending by Females

Barbara A. Koons-Witt
Pamela J. Schram

Introduction

Female offenders have garnered a growing amount of attention in the criminological literature during the last thirty years. Beginning in the 1970s, scholars such as Adler (1975), Simon (1975), and Smart (1976) introduced female offenders and the fact that much of what was known about those who violated the law was the result of research involving exclusively male populations. These early works set the stage for the abundance of scholarship that would follow and enhance the understanding of the female offender (also victims and workers). The common neglect of violent female offenders is likely the result of several factors, most of which are grounded in gender stereotypes. For example, Goetting (1988) suggests that the inattention to violent female offenders is related to the fact that "traditional female role expectations accommodate the woman as a victim but not as a perpetrator of violence" (p. 3). In committing crime, females violate their gender role expectations. As a result, they have not generated the same responses from scholars, practitioners, and the public as females who have been victimized. This false dichotomy of females as either offenders or victims masks much of what is understood about female criminality. Only recently has this dichotomy been challenged by the "blurring" of these boundaries from those doing research in these respective scholarly areas (Gilfus, 1992; Sanchez, 2001).

These same sexist stereotypes are evident in the early writings of scholars who sought to explain female criminality. More specifically, early scholars such as Lombroso, Thomas, Freud, and Pollak often characterized female offenders as masculine in their orientation and appearance. Masculinity versus femininity and good versus bad images, as defined by appropriate sex roles, shaped much of the early etiology of female criminality (Klein, 1995; Pollock, 1999). Violent female offenders were often portrayed as "monsters" and considered to be much more serious offenders and an affront to the stability of society than their violent male counterparts (Pollock, 1999).

Both Adler (1975) and Simon (1975) maintained that the changing organization of gender in society and varying gender roles would result in an increase in crimes by females. According to Adler, these changes would result in women exhibiting masculine-like behaviors including their involvement in committing violent crimes. This perspective suggests that a gender convergence of crime rates should occur over time and the gap between males' and females' offending would decrease so their patterns would become more similar (Belknap, 2001). Analyses of Uniform Crime Reports (UCR) and National Crime Victimization Surveys (NCVS) failed to provide support for the emancipation or liberation perspective (Belknap, 2001; Kruttschnitt, 2001; Steffensmeier, 2001). Despite several increases and decreases in violent crime rates between the 1960s and the 1990s, violent offending by females has remained, for the most part stable, thereby resulting in an even wider gap between males' and females' violent offending (Kruttschnitt, 2001; Pollock, 1999).[1] Violent female offenders continue to be an anomaly; they commit a very small proportion of all violent crimes.

The profile of the typical female offender reveals her marginalized status: a young, nonviolent offender who is uneducated, a single mother, lacks useful job skills necessary for being the primary caretaker, and a person of color. What is known about female offenders is primarily the result of research examining the typical female offender. The violent female offender is less prominent within the criminal justice system; however, research involving this offender population is necessary and important to understand how gender is linked to the commission of serious crimes. What explains the differences in women who are nonviolent offenders as compared with those who are involved in serious lawbreaking? How does gender influence violent crimes in comparison with nonviolent crimes? Recent work concerning violent female offenders has contributed to the literature in this area by focusing on the situation and context of violent incidents, including explorations of cooffending and crime roles, use of weapons, and differences among women based on race.

Nature and Context of Violent Offending by Females

Scholars generally recognize that the gap in offending patterns between males and females is largest for violent offenses (Pollock, 1999; Kruttschnitt, 2001; Steffensmeier & Broidy, 2001). Despite this significant gap, scholars have a limited understanding and explanation of these offense patterns. The current study examined the relationship between gender, race, cooffending, use of weapons, and type of offense. Specifically, this study analyzed whether gender and race influenced cooffending, the type of weapon used (if any), and the type of offense committed. A particular emphasis was placed on how these factors affected the commission of violent crimes such as murder/negligent manslaughter, robbery, and aggravated assault.

Prior review of the research on trends and patterns of violent offending indicated that men committed the vast majority of homicides. Men kill their current and former wives and girlfriends more often than women kill their current or former husbands or boyfriends. A larger percent of female-perpetrated homicides compared with male-perpetrated homicides involved intimate partners (Belknap, 2001, p. 115; Kruttschnitt, 2001). In 1998, the victims of female-perpetrated homicides included acquaintance (31.9 percent) followed by spouse (28.3 percent), boyfriend/girlfriend (14.0 percent), and child/stepchild (10.4 percent); the victims of male-perpetrated homicides included acquaintance (54.6 percent), stranger (25.1 percent), other family (6.9 percent), and spouse (6.8 percent) (Greenfeld & Snell, 1999, p. 4).

Steffensmeier and Allan's (1998, p. 10) examination of UCR arrest profiles revealed that there was a decline in female arrests for murder (from 17 percent in 1960 to 9 percent in 1995). They argued that the decline may have been due to two main factors: (1) large increases in male arrests for felony murders associated with the drug trade and the increased availability of guns and (2) stable or declining rates of murders committed by women because of the increasing availability of domestic abuse shelters and abuse protection statutes—both of which protect women from abusive males and diminish the opportunity context for victim-precipitated mate slayings involving females as the homicide offender. To gain a better understanding of the general nature and context of violent offending by women, research must explore the importance and relevance of cooffending and crime roles.

Cooffending and Crime Roles

Some prior research on violent female criminality centered around understanding the likelihood of women committing crime alone or with other females or males and their role within these criminal work groups. Between 1993 and 1997, victims of violence attributed the crimes they experienced to approximately 2.1 million female offenders and about 13.1 million male offenders. Of the violent female offenders, 53 percent committed the offense alone, 40 percent committed the offense with at least one other female offender, and approximately 8 percent committed their offense with at least one male offender. Of the male offenders, 47 percent acted alone, 51 percent committed the offense with other male offenders, and another 1 percent committed the offense with at least one female offender (Greenfeld & Snell, 1999, p. 2). This research suggested that female offenders were more likely to commit violent crimes by themselves, without the assistance of other male or female offenders. The general belief was that when women committed crimes with men, they did so with either their boyfriends or husbands or their friends and acquaintances (Alarid, Marquart, Burton, Cullen, & Cuvelier, 1996; Ward, Jackson, & Ward, 1979). Pettiway's (1987) research on women drug users in New York City and Miami supported the notion that when women offended alongside males, it was very likely they had done so with their intimates. Pettiway notes,

> Being married or living with a boyfriend or husband is clearly one of the more important elements in establishing the probability of crime group participation. This measure of domesticity contributes to the likelihood for boyfriend and husband crime groups but reduces the likelihood for mixed-sex crime groups.[2] It is reasonable to assume that women who live with men in intimate arrangements do not find it necessary to enter crime groups with people outside of these primary relationships. (p. 761)

Pettiway (1987) found that women who participated in what would be perceived as "masculine-type" crimes or those of a predatory nature were more likely to occur when women were offending with their intimates (i.e., boyfriend or spouse). On the other hand, he found that women were much more likely to join other women in committing vice crimes.

Prior research involving gender and cooffending appeared to be more developed within the context of the illegal drug trade (Baskin & Sommers, 1993; Pettiway, 1987; Sommers & Baskin, 1997; Steffensmeier, 1983). This, coupled with the fact that there tended to be a strong relationship between use of drugs and involvement with other forms of serious crimes such as robbery, made this a fruitful area for examining the use of violence and the role of women in illegal drug networks (Sommers & Baskin, 1997). Some researchers believed that women's roles within deviant networks, including the illegal drug trade, changed over time and that women assumed more assertive, leadership roles within these deviant networks (Alarid et al., 1996; Bunch, Foley, & Urbina, 1983; Decker, Wright, Redfern, & Smith, 1993; Sommers & Baskin, 1993). Maher and Daly's (1996) work suggested the opposite. They found that women continued to work in marginalized areas of the drug world, either as "coppers" (i.e., buyers for White males who were outsiders) or temporary street-level sellers, and were unlikely to be in positions of power within the organizational hierarchy.

Alarid et al. (1996) attempted to determine the extent to which women served as either leaders or followers during serious offenses (e.g., drug offenses, burglary, and robbery). Results showed that 80 percent of the women in their study were involved with cooffenders when committing drug offenses, robbery, larceny, and burglary. Alarid et al. concluded that "nontraditional criminal behaviors were more likely to be committed with male accomplices who provided women with the opening into deviant networks" (p. 450). When women acted as "sole perpetrators," they did so when committing traditional female offenses such as forgery and theft but also when committing the nontraditional offenses of DWI and assault. This research also uncovered an interesting relationship between race, gender, deviant networks, and crime roles. Alarid et al. found that African-American women committed offenses with other women, while Anglo or Hispanic women were more likely to team with men. The work of Alarid et al. seemed to suggest that the race of the woman and the type of offense were important influences when understanding the inner workings of deviant networks and the crime roles women assumed within them.

Sommers and Baskin (1993) interviewed sixty-five women who were arrested and/or incarcerated for violent street crime. They noted that most literature on female offenders argued that women usually assumed the status of secondary actors in a criminal event. Their research revealed, however, that 63 percent of the robberies were committed with accomplices and 60 percent of these involved female cooffenders. The remaining 37 percent were committed alone. Sommers and Baskin found,

> [f]rom early on in their criminal careers, women in the robbery sample reported that they acted out in self-determination and not in concert with or for boyfriends. Although the women sometimes were involved in criminal activities that involved men or activities that at times were controlled by men, they did so most often as equal partners. (p. 147)

In reference to assaults, many of the respondents reported that these acts were often impulsive and unorganized with many in a state of intoxication and the use of dangerous weapons. Approximately 14 percent of these assaults were related to drug dealing. The interactions between the victim and the offender, and sometimes the interaction (i.e., verbal) of a third party, played an essential role in many of these assaultive incidents.

In conclusion, research on cooffending and crime roles provided mixed results as to whether women were more likely today to be committing violent crimes by themselves, with other women, or with men. It was also unclear whether women were assuming new, more powerful roles when committing violent crimes with members of the opposite sex. Further research is needed to understand whether these arrangements and roles vary by offense type and by the race of the offender or offending group. Information on the use of weapons during the commission of violent crimes is also important to understanding the context and nature of such offenses.

Weapons Use

Prior literature that considered the use of weapons by violent female offenders was scant. The little research that did exist appeared to suggest that the use of weapons by women was conditioned by cooffending, characteristics of the targeted victim, and offense type. For example, Miller's (1998) ethnographic study of gender and street robberies found that women usually committed street robberies with other women. When women attacked other women, they typically did so without a weapon; on those limited occasions when women attacked other women, their choice of weapon was a knife. Both the choice of the victim and whether or not to use a weapon were based on the perception by female perpetrators that female victims were less likely to resist and physically overtake them. Miller (p. 61) reports, "both male and female robbers hold the view that females are easy to rob, because they are less likely to be armed and because they are perceived as weak and easily intimidated." When female targets did behave unexpectedly and resisted or fought back, female street robbers responded aggressively by physically attacking the victim(s) by hitting, punching, or stabbing them (Miller, 1998). When women victimized males, they tended to use this same perceived vulnerability as a member of the weaker sex to commit the crime. Additionally, they avoided the use of physical contact when the victim was male but instead used guns to commit the crime. When women committed street robberies with male accomplices, they were also more likely to carry a gun and the victim was typically male (Miller, 1998).

Pettiway's (1987) work on crime partnerships by female drug users found that females who committed their crimes with other women were not likely to carry or use weapons during their offenses. Pettiway states, "it is not surprising that this factor [weapons] shows a negative effect for female crime groups since most of the females in this sample do not commit offenses that either require weapons or involve the risks associated with most male-type crimes" (p. 762). Carrying and using guns during crimes committed by female drug users was associated with the likelihood of becoming a member of crime groups.

It has been generally thought that when women commit violent offenses they would commit the crime in a way that compensates for their slighter physical stature. For example, they would use a weapon that could offset a physical difference between them and a male victim or they would commit the crime when the victim was in a vulnerable state because of alcohol or sleep (Jurik & Winn, 1990). Jurik and Winn (1990) examined individuals who were charged with nonnegligent manslaughter or homicide and subsequently convicted in Maricopa County, Arizona between 1979 and 1984. Their research revealed that women who cooffended with males were less likely to introduce a weapon into the crime (33 vs. 80 percent) compared with their male counterparts. While previous research suggested that women used weapons such as kitchen knives, this study suggested that women were more inclined to use guns. The researchers discovered that the proportion of both males and females using guns was quite similar. This finding of gun use was related to the other key findings. Jurik and Winn found that women were more likely to kill their victims during a domestic altercation and surprisingly were found to kill a substantially lower proportion of victims who were impaired at the time of the offense.

In conclusion, it appears that the women may be using weapons differently now than they have in the past. Previously, it was thought that women were less inclined to use weapons, or when they did, their weapon of choice was a knife. Other research indicated that women might be more inclined to use guns, particularly in the case of crimes involving homicides. More research is needed to understand when and how women use weapons during a variety of crimes and in a variety of contexts.

Racial Differences Among Women

Previous literature on female criminality suggested that race was an important consideration when developing theory and explaining female criminality (Hill & Crawford, 1990; Simpson, 1991). Research demonstrated that Black female offenders compared with White female offenders were more inclined to commit violent offenses, such as homicides and aggravated assaults (Ageton, 1983: Cernkovich & Giordano, 1979; Laub & McDermott, 1985; Simpson, 1991), and some researchers argued that race might be a better predictor of violent offending than gender (Kruttschnitt, 2001). Black women more often committed violent crimes than White women, and their rates of offending tended to be closer to those of White males as compared with White females. In looking at the intersection of race and gender with regards to violence in other countries, Kruttschnitt (2001) concluded, "It seems likely that Black women's elevated risk of involvement in homicides is directly related to their and their partners' unique, and relatively disadvantageous, position in the U.S. economy and culture" (p. 81).

Hill and Crawford (1990) examined the possibility of varying theoretical perspectives for explaining the criminality of White and Black women. Their results indicated that overall there was no difference in prevalence of crime between Black and White women. When drug crimes were removed from the analysis, however, the authors found that Black women were significantly more likely to be involved in crimes (e.g., major property, minor property, assault, and hustling). Hill and Crawford observed that the criminality of White females was most likely related to sociopsychological factors such as sex role orientation and level of self-esteem, while the criminality of Black females was most likely related to structural and deprivation factors like educational strain and residing in an urban versus rural area. The authors suggested that explanations of differential criminality between White and Black females "may be tied to different experiences and/or to different ways of responding to similar experiences" (p. 622).

In conclusion, much of the literature on women offenders focused on typical female offenders by examining their nonviolent offenses and relating them to their life circumstances. Despite the trend that women had not become more violent in their offending pattern, this study explored the prevalence and context of violent lawbreaking by females. Three research questions were addressed in the current analysis of crime incidents: (1) What is the nature and prevalence of violent offending for females in relation to drug and property offending? (2) How are offending patterns related to whether or not women are cooffenders and use weapons? and (3) How does race influence the nature of violent offending by females?

Data and Methodology

National Incident-Based Reporting System (NIBRS) Data

During the 1980s, efforts were made to replace the UCR with the NIBRS. Since this replacement entailed major changes, however, law enforcement agencies made gradual steps to move to this new system (Maxfield & Babbie, 2001). The essential difference between the UCR and the NIBRS is that the UCR measures the overall number of incidents for an index crime and the NIBRS measures the overall number of incidents as well as the occurrence of each type of crime. NIBRS data provide more detailed information pertaining to the offense or what is referred to as "segments." These segments include administrative, victim, offense, and offender (Rantala & Edwards, 2000).

Data from the 1998 NIBRS[3] were used in order to examine the nature and prevalence of violent offending by women. NIBRS data were organized according to crime incident and permitted researchers to consider different characteristics of incidents, including: offenses, victims, offenders, and arrestees. The 1998 NIBRS data were obtained from the Inter-University Consortium for Political and Social Research (ICPSR) at the University of Michigan. For the current study, the "Offender" segment level and the "Offense" segment level from the overall NIBRS data collection (ICPSR 3031) were used. Each segment was worked with separately to isolate the cases of interest before merging both data files.

Offender Segment Data

The offender segment provided information about any offenders involved in the crime incident. More specifically, NIBRS data contained information on the race, age, and sex of offenders. Specific crime incidents based on offender and offense information were identified and isolated. The main purpose of this study was to examine the offending patterns of women. Therefore, only those incidents that were reported to have involved women were included in the study.[4] This procedure resulted in an initial sample size of 210,016 crime incidents from fifteen states.[5] Another objective of the study was to determine whether or not cooffending was connected to certain types of offenses. Crime incidents were categorized into one of three "offender groups": (1) single female, (2) multiple females, and (3) mixed gender.

Offense Segment Data

The offense segment provided information on all offenses connected to the crime incident (up to ten). This segment detailed information about the incident date, UCR offense codes, whether or not the incident was completed, location of the incident, method of entry, and type of weapon(s) used during the incident. NIBRS comprised data for crime incidents involving twenty-two offense categories grouped together from forty-six distinct crimes. Several violent, property, and drug offenses were selected and included in the analyses and the remaining offenses were dropped (see appendix A for a list of the offenses). A series of dummy variables were created to reflect that the incident involved each type of offense. Once the offenses and offenders were identified and selected, both data files were merged with each other using a unique incident number.

Findings

To explore the relationship between type of offense and type of offender group, a series of cross-tabulations were computed. First, a cross-tabulation was computed for each offender group and each offense category. Next, a cross-tabulation was computed for the type of offender group and the type of violent offense and then the type of weapon used during the course of the incident. Finally, the study examined the relationship between race and offender groups by computing a cross-tabulation for the type of offender group and the racial composition of the offending group.

Offender Groups and Offense Categories

The first step of the analysis consisted of exploring the link between each offender group and the offense categories. Since the NIBRS data were organized so that the incident was the unit of analysis, there existed the possibility that incidents might contain more than one type of offense. For example, an incident could involve both a drug offense and a property offense. When incidents consisting of multiple offense categories were analyzed, it was determined that approximately 17 percent of the incidents had multiple offenses that crossed different offense categories.[6] For the purposes of the present study, those incidents containing more than one offense category were excluded from the current analysis in order to examine the associations between the variables of interest.[7]

The study first considered the relationship between offender group and offense categories. Tests for a measure of association between both variables indicated that there was a significant relationship (Goodman and Kruskal's $\tau = 0.003$, $P < .001$) between whether females offended by themselves, with other females, or with males and the type of offense committed. The results for the first contingency table are presented in table 1 and reflect the percentage of incidents for each offender group (i.e., single female, multiple female, and mixed gender) that pertain to the specific offense category. Overall, when involved in lawbreaking, women tended to commit their crimes by themselves. Just over half of all incidents in this study were committed by females who were acting alone (52.4 percent or n = 68,692), and almost 40 percent (n = 51,552) of all incidents were committed by both male(s) and female(s) perpetrators. For single female offender incidents, the largest number of incidents consisted of property offenses (79.2 percent or n = 54,401) followed by drug offenses (11.9 percent or n = 8,195) and violent offenses (8.9 percent or n = 6,096). In the case of multiple female offender incidents, the largest number of incidents consisted of property offenses (86 percent or n = 9,333) followed by drug offenses (7.4 percent or n = 798) and violent offenses (6.6 percent or n = 719). The results suggested a similar pattern among the mixed-gender incidents. Property offenses accounted for the largest number of incidents (81 percent or n = 41,768) followed by drug offenses (13.5 percent or n = 6,975) and violent offenses (5.4 percent or n = 2,809). The prevalence of incidents for each offense category followed a similar pattern for each of the offender groups.

Table 1
Prevalence and percentage of incidents involving offense category for each offender group (*N* = 131,094)

Offense category	Total *f* (%)	Group 1 (Single female) *f* (%)	Group 2 (Multiple females) *f* (%)	Group 3 (Mixed gender) *f* (%)
Property	105,502 (80.5)	54,401 (79.2)	9,333 (86)	41,768 (81)
Drug	15,968 (12.2)	8,195 (11.9)	798 (7.4)	6,975 (13.5)
Violent	9,624 (7.3)	6,096 (8.9)	719 (6.6)	2,809 (5.4)
Total	131,094	68,692	10,850	51,552

Offender Groups and Violent Offenses

Next, the study considered the relationship between offender group and different violent offenses including murder/nonnegligent manslaughter, robbery, and aggravated assault. As noted previously, violent incidents might involve more than one offense (e.g., aggravated assault and robbery). For incidents where more than one incident was identified, the most serious offense was the one used in the analysis. For example, if a particular incident involved both a robbery and an aggravated assault, then only the robbery would be identified and included in the analysis of association between offender group and offense type. Results from an analysis of the measure of association between these two variables indicated a significant relationship between the type of offender group and the type of violent offense (Goodman and Kruskal's $\tau = 0.020$, $P < .001$). Table 2 presents a summary of the numbers and percentages of these offenses for each offender group. When violent offenses were considered as a whole, the results suggested that women were much more likely to commit these crimes when cooffending with males (64.1 percent or $n = 14{,}997$) rather than with other females (5.3 percent or $n = 1{,}231$) or as sole perpetrators (30.6 percent or $n = 7{,}155$). Violent offenses committed by single females overwhelmingly involved aggravated assaults (91.3 percent or $n = 6{,}530$) followed to a lesser extent by robbery (8 percent or $n = 570$) and murder or nonnegligent manslaughter (0.8 percent or $n = 55$). Although there were changes in distribution, a similar pattern of offending existed for the other offender groups as well. For multiple female incidents, aggravated assaults were the most frequently cited violent offense (85.2 percent or $n = 1{,}049$) followed by robbery (14.4 percent or $n = 177$) and murder/nonnegligent manslaughter (0.4 percent or $n = 5$). Similarly, for incidents involving both male and female perpetrators, aggravated assaults were most prevalent (79.5 percent or $n = 11{,}916$), while robbery (19.4 percent or $n = 2{,}909$) was the second most cited violent offense followed by murder or nonnegligent manslaughter (1.1 percent or $n = 172$).

The findings for each of the offender groups indicated that the largest number of incidents (and proportion) involved aggravated assaults followed by robberies and murder/nonnegligent manslaughter. It did appear, however, that females were more likely to commit aggravated assaults by

Table 2
Prevalence and percentage of incidents involving a violent offense for each offender group ($N = 23{,}383$)

Violent Offense	Total *f* (%)	Group 1 (Single female) *f* (%)	Group 2 (Multiple females) *f* (%)	Group 3 (Mixed gender) *f* (%)
Murder/nonnegligent manslaughter	232 (1)	55 (.8)	5 (.4)	172 (1.1)
Robbery	3,656 (15.6)	570 (8)	177 (14.4)	2,909 (19.4)
Aggravated assault	19,495 (83.4)	6,530 (91.3)	1,049 (85.2)	11,916 (79.5)
Total	23,383	7,155	1,231	14,997

themselves, whereas they were more likely to commit robberies with others including males. To understand more fully the nature of these violent offenses and possible group differences, additional analysis was completed involving the use of weapons.

Offender Groups and Use of Weapons

The study also considered the relationship between the type of offender group and the use of weapons during violent incidents. Table 3 provides descriptive information for each offender group and whether or not a gun[8] was used during a violent incident or a knife/cutting instrument, a blunt object such as a club or hammer, or personal weapons such as one's hands, feet, or teeth. An analysis of association was performed

Table 3
Offender group by type of weapon used during the violent incident (N = 23,383)

Use of weapons	Total *f* (%)	Group 1 (Single female) (n = 7,155) *f* (%)	Group 2 (Multiple females) (n = 1,231) *f* (%)	Group 3 (Mixed gender) (n = 14,997) *f* (%)
Gun				
No	17,920 (76.6)	6,148 (85.9)	1,050 (85.3)	10,722 (71.5)**
Yes	5,463 (23.4)	1,007 (14.1)	181 (14.7)	4,275 (28.5)
Knife/cutting instrument				
No	16,199 (69.3)	4,834 (67.6)	864 (70.2)	10,501 (70)*
Yes	7,184 (30.7)	2,321 (32.4)	367 (29.8)	4,496 (30)
Blunt object				
No	17,497 (74.8)	5,630 (78.7)	938 (76.2)	10,929 (72.9)**
Yes	5,886 (25.2)	1,525 (21.3)	293 (23.8)	4,068 (27.1)
Personal weapons				
No	13,658 (58.4)	4,828 (67.5)	693 (56.3)	8,137 (54.3)**
Yes	9,725 (41.6)	2,327 (32.5)	538 (43.7)	6,860 (45.7)

* $P < .05$.

** $P < .001$.

between the offender group and the type of weapon(s) used during the incident. Each type of weapon was coded as yes or no, with yes indicating that at least one gun, for example, was involved in a particular violent incident. A significant association was found between the type of offender group and whether or not the incident involved any guns (Goodman and Kruskal's $\tau = 0.026$, $P < .001$), knives or cutting instruments (Goodman and Kruskal's $\tau = 0.001$, $P < .05$), blunt instruments (Goodman and Kruskal's $\tau = 0.004$, $P < .001$), and personal weapons (Goodman and Kruskal's $\tau = 0.018$, $P < .001$).

When use of weapons were considered more generally, the results indicated that violent incidents involving female perpetrators were more likely to involve personal weapons such as the use of hands, feet, or teeth (41.6 percent or n = 9,725) followed by knives or cutting instruments (30.7 percent or n = 7,184). Violent crimes committed by females were less likely to involve weapons such as blunt objects (25.2 percent or n = 5,886) or guns (23.4 percent or n = 5,463). When specific offender groups were considered, the findings suggested that females who committed their violent crimes alone more frequently used either personal weapons (32.5 percent or n = 2,327) or knives (32.4 percent or n = 2,321) followed by blunt objects (21.3 percent or n = 1,525) and guns (14.1 percent or n = 1,007). Multiple female offenders committing violent offenses were more likely to use personal weapons such as their hands, feet, or teeth (43.7 percent or n = 538) followed by knives or other cutting instruments (29.8 percent or n = 367) and blunt objects (23.8 percent or n = 293). Like females who violated the laws by themselves, females who committed violent crimes with other females were not as likely to use a gun (14.7 percent or n = 181).

For females who committed violent offenses with males, the results seemed to suggest a different pattern of weapons usage. The results indicated that personal weapons (45.7 percent or n = 6,860) were the most frequently used weapon by this offender group followed by knives or other cutting instruments (30 percent or n = 4,496), guns (28.5 percent or n = 4,275), and blunt objects (27.1 percent or n = 4,068). Although the mixed-gender offender group was less likely to use a gun during the course of their violent crimes when compared with other weapons used by this particular group, offender groups consisting of both males and females were more likely to use guns compared with females who acted alone or with other females (28.5 vs. 14.7 and 14.1 percent). Thus, it appeared that violent incidents that involved both male and female perpetrators were more likely to have at least one gun present during the crime when compared with violent incidents involving just one female or multiple females.

Racial Composition and Offender Groups

The current study was also interested in examining the relationship between the race of the perpetrators and the type of offender group. A test of the measure of association between racial composition of the offenders involved in the violent incident was compared with the type of offender group based on sex. For the purposes of this particular analysis and for the ease of interpretation, only those incidents containing either all White offenders or all Black offenders were considered. Incidents involving both White and Black perpetrators were excluded since observations could not be obtained for incidents involving only single female perpetrators.[9] Table 4 presents cross-tabulation results between the racial composition of perpetrators for each incident and cooffending.

Table 4
Racial composition of perpetrator(s) by offending group for violent offenses (N = 14,433)

Racial composition per group	Total f (%)	Group 1 (Single female) (n = 6,848) f (%)	Group 2 (Multiple females) (n = 960) f (%)	Group 3 (Mixed gender) (n = 6,625) f (%)
All Black offenders	5,333 (37)	3,233 (47.2)	497 (51.8)	1,603 (24.6)
All White offenders	9,100 (63)	3,615 (52.8)	463 (48.2)	5,022 (75.8)

Results from the analysis indicated that there was a significant relationship between the racial composition of the offending group and whether females offended alone, with other females, or with males (Goodman and Kruskal's $\tau = 0.060$, $P < .001$). White females were more likely to commit violent crimes by themselves (52.8 percent or n = 3,615) when compared with Black females (47.2 percent or n = 3,233), whereas Black females were more likely to commit violent offenses with other Black females (51.8 percent or n = 497). Finally, White females were much more likely to commit violent offenses with males (75.8 percent or n = 5,022) than were Black females (24.6 percent or n = 1,603).

Discussion

Violent female offenders had been the focus of an increasing amount of scholarship over the last decade. This was due in part to the belief of some that violent female offenders represented an emerging offender group. While it was true that arrests of women for violent crimes increased during the 1990s, violent offenses for women still represented a small share of their overall offenses. Furthermore, the largest gender gap for offenses occurred with violent crimes because women commit violent crimes much less often when compared with men (Pollock, 1999). Despite the fact that there was little or no evidence to support such an argument, research involving female violent offenders was important in furthering the understanding of why some females became involved in violent offending.

The purpose of this study was to examine the nature and prevalence of violent offending for females in relation to other types of offenses, such as property and drug. The present study also explored the relationship between cooffending and violent offending and uses of weapons. Finally, this study considered the importance of race when looking at the nature of violent offending by females. Each of these issues was addressed using one of the more comprehensive official data sets available for analysis.

Results from the current study suggest that consistent with prior literature, females are more likely to commit property crimes compared with drug crimes and violent crimes. The results presented in table 1 seem to suggest that females are more likely to commit violent offenses by themselves. These results are probably the result of the high number of aggravated assaults committed by single female perpetrators; however, these findings should be interpreted with a certain amount of caution because of the incidents that were excluded from this part of the analysis. Many of the excluded incidents (those incidents involving multiple offense categories) involved both male and female perpetrators, and most of these incidents involved drug and violent offenses. This suggests that females actually had a much higher involvement in drug and violent offenses when they were cooffending with males.

These observations were consistent with the works of Pettiway (1987) and Alarid et al. (1996) who found that women were more likely to commit "masculine-type" crimes or nontraditional crimes with their intimates (male accomplices) but differed from the research of Greenfeld and Snell (1999). They found that the majority of women in their research acted alone when committing violent offenses. In this study, it appeared that women had not necessarily become more active in committing violent crimes but seemed to be more involved in these types of offenses when cooffending with males.

When only violent incidents were considered, females were more likely to be involved in aggravated assaults compared with robberies and murder or nonnegligent manslaughter. This was particularly true for females who committed their violent crimes alone. When females cooffended with other females or males, however, they seemed to be more likely to commit robberies. This finding partially supported Miller's (1998) ethnographic study that found that women usually committed robberies with other women. The findings in the current study also supported the work of Alarid et al. (1996) who looked at differences between Black and White women. As in the case of Alarid et al.'s research, the current study found that Black women were more likely to commit violent offenses with other women, whereas White women were more likely to commit violent offenses with males.

Some prior research questioned whether women were more likely to use guns to commit their offenses. Jurik and Winn's (1990) study, for example, found that women were more inclined to use guns compared with knives when committing murder or nonnegligent manslaughter and that males and females were equally likely to use guns during these violent incidents. The findings from the current study indicated that females overall were more likely to use either personal weapons (e.g., hands, feet, or teeth) or knives/cutting instruments when involved in violent crimes; however, women were more likely to use guns when they were committing violent crimes with males.

The current study had several limitations that were important to note. The first limitation pertained to the generalizability of the findings. The 1998 NIBRS data contained information on crimes for only fifteen states and the findings from this research might not be generalizable to other states that were not included in the data set. Another limitation of the current study involved the examination of whether females committed their crimes alone, with other females, or with males. Researchers were unable to specifically determine the role of women offenders within mixed-gender crime groups. Despite these research limitations and the scant amount of literature on violent women offenders, this study revealed some findings that were informative. This study also provoked questions for further inquiry, including exploring the relationship between the victim and the perpetrator.

Appendix A. Categories and Types of Offenses

Property offenses:

- Arson
- Burglary/breaking and entering
- Shoplifting
- Theft from building
- Theft from motor vehicle
- Theft of motor vehicle parts
- All other larceny
- Motor vehicle theft
- Counterfeiting/forgery
- False pretenses/swindle
- Credit card/automatic teller fraud
- Welfare fraud
- Embezzlement
- Stolen property offenses
- Destruction/damage/vandalism

Drug offenses:

- Drug/narcotics violations
- Drug equipment violations

Violent offenses:
Murder/nonnegligent manslaughter
Robbery
Aggravated assault

Notes

[1] Many scholars maintain that there has been a change for women offenders and that the legal system is much more likely to incarcerate women instead of imposing alternative sanctions (Bloom, Chesney-Lind, & Owen, 1994; Chesney-Lind, 1997; Kruttschnitt, 2001; Nagel & Hagan, 1992). For instance, while arrest rates for women increased 29 percent between 1986 and 1990, during that same time period, incarceration figures increased for women by 73 percent in jails and 77 percent in prisons for women (Chesney-Lind & Pollock, 1995).

[2] Mixed-sex crime groups exclude partnerships between women and their boyfriends or husbands.

[3] U.S. Department of Justice, Federal Bureau of Investigation. National Incident-Based Reporting System, 1998 [Computer file]. Compiled by the U.S. Department of Justice, Federal Bureau of Investigation. ICPSR ed. Ann Arbor, MI: Inter-University Consortium for Political and Social Research [producer and distributor], 2000.

[4] The analysis followed a complicated process in identifying the incidents involving women. First, the gender of each offender was recoded accordingly to "1" for females and "0" for males. Next, the gender variable was aggregated by summing its values according to each incident number. This created a gender score, which ranged "from 0 to 18." For example, if an incident involved two male offenders, then the aggregate score would have been "0," and if an incident involved one male and two females, then the aggregate score would have been "2." Based on the gender score, it could determine those incidents involving only male offenders (score of "0") and those incidents involving at least one female (score of "1" or higher). Lastly, those cases involving only males were filtered out, leaving those incidents involving females.

[5] The 1998 NIBRS data collection contained crime incidents from fifteen states including Colorado, Idaho, Iowa, Kentucky, Massachusetts, Michigan, Nebraska, North Dakota, Ohio, South Carolina, Tennessee, Texas, Utah, Vermont, and Virginia.

[6] Approximately 11.1 percent (n = 21,378) of incidents had offenses from two of the three categories and 2.5 percent (n = 4,816) of incidents had offenses from each of the three categories.

[7] Excluding incidents involving different types of offenses (17 percent) from the current analysis impacted the number of incidents for each offender group, particularly the mixed-gender group. For example, removing these incidents reduced the number of incidents for the mixed-gender group by 31 percent (from 74,492 to 51,552 incidents) compared with a reduction of 9 percent for the multiple female group (from 11,921 to 10,850 incidents) and 3 percent for the single female group (from 70,875 to 68,692 incidents). Specific offense categories involving mixed-gender incidents were also affected. The number of incidents involving violent crimes decreased by approximately 81 percent (from 14,997 to 2,809 incidents) and the number of incidents involving drug offenses decreased 69 percent (from 22,743 to 6,975 incidents). Thus, it appeared that incidents involving both males and females were more likely to involve multiple types of offenses (e.g., drug offense and violent offense).

[8] The gun category includes automatic firearms and handguns, rifles, shotguns, and other types of guns.

[9] Approximately 31 percent of the incidents involved a mixed-race offender group. These were excluded since cells for incidents involving single female offenders would be empty and would influence further analyses. A large amount of the mixed-race offender incidents

were comprised of both Black and White perpetrators (n = 6,588). Ninety-eight percent (n = 6,455) of the incidents involving both Black and White offenders were mixed gender as well, whereas only 2 percent (n = 133) of incidents for the mixed-race offender group consisted of multiple female offenders.

References

Adler, F. (1975). *Sisters in crime: The rise of the new female criminal.* New York: McGraw-Hill.

Ageton, S. S. (1983). The dynamics of female delinquency, 1976–1980. *Criminology, 21,* 555–584.

Alarid, L. F., Marquart, J. W., Burton, V. S., Cullen, F. T., & Cuvelier, S. J. (1996). Women's roles in serious offenses: A study of adult felons. *Justice Quarterly, 13,* 431–454.

Baskin, D. R., & Sommers, I. (1993). Females' initiation into violent street crime. *Justice Quarterly, 10,* 559–583.

Belknap, J. (2001). *The invisible woman: Gender, crime and justice* (2nd ed.). Belmont, CA: Wadsworth.

Bloom, B., Chesney-Lind, M., & Owen, B. (1994). *Women in California prisons: Hidden victims of the war on drugs.* San Francisco: Center on Juvenile and Criminal Justice.

Bunch, B. J., Foley, L. A., & Urbina, S. P. (1983). The psychology of violent female offenders: A sex-role perspective. *Prison Journal, 63,* 66–79.

Cernkovich, S. A., & Giordano, P. C. (1979). A comparative analysis of male and female delinquency. *Sociological Quarterly, 20,* 131–145.

Chesney-Lind, M. (1997). *The female offender: Girls, women and crime.* Thousand Oaks, CA: Sage Publications.

Chesney-Lind, M., & Pollock, J. M. (1995). Women's prisons: Equality with a vengeance. In A. V. Merlo & J. M. Pollock (Eds.), *Women, law, social control* (pp. 155–175). Boston: Allyn and Bacon.

Decker, S., Wright, R., Redfern, A., & Smith, D. (1993). A woman's place is in the home: Females and residential burglary. *Justice Quarterly, 10,* 143–162.

Gilfus, M. (1992). From victims to survivors to offenders: Women's routes to entry and immersion into street crime. *Women and Criminal Justice, 4,* 63–89.

Goetting, A. (1988). Patterns of homicide among women. *Journal of Interpersonal Violence, 3,* 3–20.

Greenfeld, L. A., & Snell, T. L. (1999). *Women offenders.* Washington, DC: U.S. Department of Justice, Office of Justice Programs, Bureau of Justice Statistics.

Hill, G. D., & Crawford, E. M. (1990). Women, race, and crime. *Criminology, 28,* 601–623.

Jurik, N. C., & Winn, R. (1990). Gender and homicide: A comparison of men and women who kill. *Violence and Victims, 5,* 227–242.

Klein, D. (1995). The etiology of female crime: A review of the literature. In B. R. Price & N. J. Sokoloff (Eds.), *The criminal justice system and women: Offenders, victims, and workers* (pp. 30–53). New York: McGraw-Hill.

Kruttschnitt, C. (2001). Gender and violence. In C. M. Renzetti & L. Goodstein (Eds.), *Women, crime, and criminal justice* (pp. 77–92). Los Angeles: Roxbury Publishing.

Laub, J. H., & McDermott, M. J. (1985). An analysis of crime by young Black women. *Criminology, 23,* 81–98.

Maher, L., & Daly, K. (1996). Women in the street-level drug economy: Continuity or change? *Criminology, 34*(4), 465–491.

Maxfield, M. G., & Babbie, E. (2001). *Research methods for criminal justice and criminology* (3rd ed.). Belmont, CA: Wadsworth.

Miller, J. (1998). Up it up: Gender and the accomplishment of street robbery. *Criminology, 36,* 37–66.

Nagel, I. H., & Hagan, J. (1992). Gender and crime: Offense patterns and criminal court sanctions. In N. Morris & M. Tonry (Eds.), *Crime and justice* (vol. 4, pp. 91–144). Chicago: University of Chicago Press.

Pettiway, L. E. (1987). Participation in crime partnerships by female drug users: The effects of domestic arrangements, drug use, and criminal involvement. *Criminology, 23,* 741–766.

Pollock, J. M. (1999). *Criminal women.* Cincinnati, OH: Anderson Publishing.

Rantala, R. R., & Edwards, T. J. (2000). *Effects of NIBRS on crime statistics* [Special Report]. Washington, DC: U.S. Department of Justice.

Sanchez, L. (2001). Gender troubles: The entanglement of agency, violence, and law in the lives of women in prostitution. In C. M. Renzetti & L. Goodstein (Eds.), *Women, crime, and criminal justice* (pp. 60–76). Los Angeles: Roxbury Publishing.

Simon, R. J. (1975). *Women and crime.* Lexington, MA: D.C. Heath.

Simpson, S. S. (1991). Caste, class, and violent crime: Explaining differences in female offending. *Criminology, 29,* 115–135.

Smart, C. (1976). *Women, crime, and criminology: A feminist critique.* Boston: Routledge and K. Paul.

Sommers, I., & Baskin, D. R. (1993). The situational context of violent female offending. *Journal of Research in Crime and Delinquency, 30*(2), 136–162.

Sommers, I., & Baskin, D. R. (1997). Situational or generalized violence in drug dealing networks. *Journal of Drug Issues, 27,* 833–849.

Steffensmeier, D. (1983). Organization properties and sex-segregation in the underworld: Building a sociological theory of sex differences in crime. *Social Forces, 61,* 1010–1032.

Steffensmeier, D. (2001). Female crime trends, 1960–1995. In C. M. Renzetti & L. Goodstein (Eds.), *Women, crime, and criminal justice* (pp. 191–211). Los Angeles: Roxbury Publishing.

Steffensmeier, D., & Allan, E. (1998). The nature of female offending: Patterns and explanation. In R. T. Zaplin (Ed.), *Female offenders: Critical perspectives and effective interventions* (pp. 5–29). Gaithersburg, MD: Aspen Publications.

Steffensmeier, D., & Broidy, L. (2001). Explaining female offending. In C. M. Renzetti & L. Goodstein (Eds.), *Women, crime, and criminal justice* (pp. 111–132). Los Angeles: Roxbury Publishing.

Ward, D. A., Jackson, J., & Ward, R. E. (1979). Crimes of violence by women. In F. Adler & R. J. Simon (Eds.), *Criminology of deviant women* (pp. 116–117). Boston: Houghton Mifflin.

SECTION III

Laws and Policies Affecting Women Offenders

Numerous articles in this text have illustrated the marginalized status of women offenders. These offenders are usually undereducated, under- or unemployed, women of color who are likely to have a history of sexual and physical abuse as well as a drug and/or alcohol problem. Some scholars have argued that due to this marginalized status, these individuals are more vulnerable to agents of social control such as law enforcement, probation, and social services. This section explores how laws and policies have the potential to control, and to negatively affect, the lives of these women. This section begins with an article that provides an overview of issues pertaining to women and the law with a specific focus on sentencing guidelines. The following two articles examine how the recent "war on drugs" policies and laws have affected women offenders with respect to incarceration and prosecution. The last article explores how the war on drugs is interconnected with the war on poor women; specifically this article examines how recent welfare reform efforts affects those women convicted of felony drug offenses.

Ilene Nagel and Barry Johnson's article, "The Role of Gender in a Structured Sentencing System: Equal Treatment, Policy Choices, and the Sentencing of Female Offenders," focuses on how recent sentencing reforms have raised complex and controversial issues pertaining to women offenders. They examine these issues by first providing a brief overview of research exploring differential sentencing of women offenders prior to the "pre-guidelines era" of the 1980s. Some of this research reveals that women received leniency when sentenced. Many scholars maintain that this leniency has been founded on stereotyping women in a paternalistic or chivalrous manner. This pattern of lenient treatment, however, needs to be reconciled with the value of equality stressed by feminists.

Next, Nagel and Johnson focus on the implications of the Sentencing Reform Act of 1984, especially emphasizing gender-neutral sentencing, on women offenders. Using this framework, they argue how sentencing reform policies place feminists in a philosophical dilemma. Specifically, the debate centers on whether to advocate formal, legal equality with men or to advocate special treatment that recognizes relevant gender differences. Some of the issues that are particularly problematic when sentencing women offenders under the federal guidelines include pregnancy, single parenthood, and coercion or abuse by male codefendants. They conclude their article by providing a brief summary of data examining the "real-world" effects of sentencing guidelines on women offenders convicted of drug offenses, embezzlement, and fraud.

In her article, "The War on Drugs and the Incarceration of Mothers," Stephanie Bush-Baskette explores how the passage of the Anti-Drug Abuse Acts of 1986 and 1988 have affected women in the criminal justice system. The objectives of the article are twofold: (1) to provide an overview of the historical and contemporary involvement of women with drugs as well as how the current "war on drugs" has affected women and their children; and (2) to emphasize the need to appreciate the social costs involved when incarcerating mothers for drug offenses. Bush-Baskette concludes by stressing that it is imperative for researchers and policy makers to consider these social costs when assessing the efficacy of such policies and initiatives under the "war on drugs" campaign.

Enid Logan's article, "The Wrong Race, Committing Crime, Doing Drugs, and Maladjusted for Motherhood: The Nation's Fury over 'Crack Babies,'" critically examines recent trends concerning the "crack-baby" phenomenon. She argues that the responses to this phenomenon, in the social, legal, and political realms in the United States, have been greatly shaped by those from racial, gender, and socioeconomic positions of privilege. Logan begins her argument by describing how public opinion has been shaped by the media. She continues by outlining state responses to these women, including: hospital policies requiring the testing of pregnant women suspected of drug abuse; prosecuting pregnant women under such statutes as child abuse, neglect, and drug trafficking; as well as incarcerating these women to protect their fetuses.

According to Logan, this vast amount of attention, by both the media and the legal community, stems from one of three general assumptions: (1) the effects of crack cocaine on fetal and child development, (2) the pregnant addicts themselves, and (3) the efficacy of prosecution and punishment. Rather than further marginalizing these women and their children, Logan maintains that policymakers need to develop programs that empower pregnant addicts; these efforts would provide them with enhanced opportunities to be better mothers to their children.

In her article, "Bringing Back Shame: Women, Welfare Reform, and Criminal Justice," Amy Hirsch maintains that recent welfare reform efforts have strengthened the link between the criminal justice system and the welfare system. The federal Personal Responsibility and Work Opportunity Reconciliation Act of 1996 (PRWORA), as well as state welfare legislation, denies individuals welfare benefits if convicted of certain criminal offenses. The most "draconian" welfare reform, as Hirsch argues, bans individuals convicted of felony drug offenses from receiving any type of assistance during their lifetime. To explore the intersection between the war on drugs and the war on poor women, Hirsch interviewed women convicted of drug offenses in Pennsylvania. These women revealed histories of physical and sexual abuse in which they attempted to "self-medicate" themselves through the use of drugs. When asked about receiving welfare assistance, many of the women noted that such assistance helps them feel connected to society. From their perspective, this type of assistance does not promote *dependence*; rather it promotes *independence* from abusive relationships and deteriorating marriages. Hirsch concludes that public discourse on criminal justice, like public discourse on welfare assistance, has been greatly influenced by punitive rhetoric founded on myths and stereotypes.

8

The Role of Gender in a Structured Sentencing System
Equal Treatment, Policy Choices, and the Sentencing of Female Offenders

Ilene H. Nagel
Barry L. Johnson

Introduction

Historically, female offenders have been at the margins of the criminal justice system. Theories of criminal behavior, as well as studies of arrest, pre-trial, prosecution, and sentencing outcomes, have tended to focus on patterns of criminality derived from studying male offenders.[1] This does not reflect a lack of interest in female offenders, but rather the empirical fact that the vast majority of criminal offenders, especially violent criminal offenders, have been male.[2] In other words, the traditional preoccupation of theorists, researchers, and criminal justice professionals with male offenders derives from the gender-skewed demographics of criminal behavior.

Recently, however, the combination of the women's rights movement, the rise of feminist scholarship, and the noted increase in female criminality,[3] has begun to reverse this long-standing neglect of female criminality and inattention to the outcome of decisions involving females in the criminal justice system. And, "a rich and complex literature . . . devoted to the

Reprinted by special permission of the Northwestern University School of Law, *Journal of Criminal Law and Criminology*, vol. 85, no. 1, pp. 181–221, © 1994.

issues of gender and crime" has emerged.[4] A good deal of this literature examines the treatment of women by key criminal justice decisionmakers, such as police, prosecutors, and judges. One commonly tested hypothesis is that when these decisionmakers are free to exercise discretion, they systematically favor female offenders over similarly situated male offenders.[5] This pattern of gender-based leniency is particularly evident at the sentencing phase. Female offenders tend to benefit at sentencing from what many presume to be a benign form of reverse discrimination.[6]

Despite the recency of the "women and crime" literature, it may describe sentencing patterns that no longer exist. Much of the research contained in these works is based on data collected in the 1960s and 1970s. In the 1980s, however, significant efforts were made to reform sentencing systems at both the state and federal levels. These reforms were designed to substantially reduce judicial sentencing discretion, to reduce unwarranted sentencing disparities, and to reduce race, gender, and class discrimination. Moreover, these reforms, at least at the federal level, shifted the focus of sentencing from "offender" characteristics, such as family and community ties, education, and employment, to "offense" characteristics and the offender's criminal history.[7] If successful, these reforms will reduce the favorable treatment previously afforded female offenders, by increasing both their incarceration rate and the length of their sentences.

One desired effect of these sweeping efforts at sentencing reform was to increase the visibility of policy choices underlying sentencing decisions.[8] As a result, many issues with potentially significant impact on female offenders, previously obscured by a system of unfettered and unreviewed discretionary sentencing, are now ripe for revisitation and debate. These issues include whether a convicted offender's pregnancy or child care responsibilities should affect the type and length of her sentence; whether courts should consider evidence of psychological coercion that does not rise to the level of a complete defense; and whether courts should consider the offender's emotional condition or the offender's role in the offense. While these issues are relevant to all offenders, some authorities believe that they have more, or at least potentially different, relevance for female offenders. These highly complex policy issues raise difficult questions for feminists, who must balance theories of criminal justice against theories of gender equality. Furthermore, people disagree about how to define gender justice and about how to achieve it.

This article explores some of these issues through an analysis of the impact of federal sentencing reform on the sentencing of female offenders. It begins with an examination of the literature analyzing the sentencing of female offenders under the indeterminate, rehabilitative approach which prevailed before the adoption of the Sentencing Reform Act of 1984.[9]

Section I discusses the efforts of Congress and the United States Sentencing Commission, as directed by Congress, to implement facially neutral sentencing guidelines, in order to reduce unwarranted sentencing disparity and eliminate the sentencing impact of extralegal factors such as the offender's race, gender, and socioeconomic status. The implications of the Sentencing Reform Act's goal of gender neutrality are examined in light of the broader debate about "equal treatment" versus "special treatment" that has engaged feminist scholars in other areas of the law.

Section II focuses on several issues in the federal guidelines sentencing scheme that are of special concern to women, because of the potential for a disparate gender-based impact. These issues include pregnancy, single parenthood, coercion, dominance, and the offender's role in the offense.

Finally, Section III contains an empirical review of the sentencing of female offenders under the federal sentencing guidelines. In an effort to assess the impact of guidelines on traditional patterns of lenient treatment of female offenders, this section examines United States Sentencing Commission data on the sentencing patterns for females convicted in any of three offense categories: drug trafficking, embezzlement, and larceny.

I. Differential Sentencing of Women in the Pre-Guidelines Era

Throughout much of the twentieth century, society viewed rehabilitation as the primary purpose of incarceration.[10] The dominance of the rehabilitative ideal is reflected in Justice Black's majority opinion in *Williams v. New York*,[11] in which he explained that "retribution is no longer the dominant objective of the criminal law. Reformation and rehabilitation of offenders have become important goals of criminal jurisprudence."[12] This focus on rehabilitation required a concomitant emphasis on the personal characteristics of the offender: "a prevalent modern philosophy of penology [is] that the punishment should fit the offender and not merely the crime. The belief no longer prevails that every offense in a like legal category calls for an identical punishment without regard to the past life and habits of a particular offender."[13]

Williams reflected the prevailing philosophy not only of the courts, but of criminology experts, and the public as well.[14] The influence of the rehabilitative ideal is evinced by the adoption, throughout this century, of a number of criminal justice reforms designed to replace fixed punishments with more flexible, offender-oriented sentencing.[15]

The focus of rehabilitative sentencing is the offender's need for treatment. Those adhering to this approach view the sentence as the instrument of that treatment. Accordingly, they believe that the sentence should promote the offender's rehabilitation, and not merely reflect the nature of the crime committed.[16] This assessment, often analogized to a doctor's diagnosis and treatment of a patient's disease, requires tremendous flexibility for the sentencer to "individualize" the sentence to best promote the offender's rehabilitation. As Justice Black explained: "highly relevant—if not essential—to [the judge's] selection of an appropriate sentence is the possession of the fullest information possible concerning the defendant's life and characteristics."[17]

The discretionary nature of this sentencing system led to the emergence of unwarranted disparities in the sentencing of offenders convicted of similar offenses, and possessing similar criminal histories. This disparity arose largely because of differences in judicial values, attitudes, and sentencing philosophy. As Willard Gaylin concluded:

> each [judge] has a point of view, a set of standards and values, a bias, if you will, which will color, influence, and direct the nature of his verdicts independently of the specific condition of the criminal being charged. . . .
>
> These sets of values constitute bias in a non-pejorative sense—but bias nonetheless, and a bias that will influence equity and fairness in exactly the same way as naked bigotry does.[18]

Further, the lack of standards governing judges' sentencing decisions created a risk that they would be inappropriately influenced by offender attributes such as race, gender, age, and socioeconomic status.[19] The impact of these extralegal factors on sentencing generated considerable interest in the 1970s and 1980s.[20] While race bias generated the most research, some empirical analyses focused on questions of gender. Research examined whether courts treated female offenders differently than male offenders at the sentencing stage and whether those differences reflected different criminal conduct by males and females, or a preference for leniency toward women which was unrelated to the offense.[21] The results consistently revealed that adult female offenders receive more favorable sentences than similarly situated male offenders.[22]

This preferential treatment is most pronounced with respect to the decision of whether or not to incarcerate the offender. Women are more likely than similarly situated men to receive suspended sentences or probation. However, there is less disparity in the term of incarceration, particularly for serious offenses involving lengthy sentences.[23]

This pattern is subject to some caveats. Commentators have criticized studies reporting a gender impact in sentencing. Some have pointed to the methodological limitations, such as the failure to control adequately for offense seriousness and prior record;[24] others have noted that the small number of cases and offenses analyzed in those studies limit available analytic techniques, as well as the generalizability of the findings.[25] Moreover, studies of gender and sentencing have not been unanimous in finding statistically significant differences between sentences for male and female offenders.[26]

Despite these criticisms, an impressive number of methodologically sound, multivariate studies report that women offenders receive preferential treatment.[27] For example, in a study of sentences meted out to 6,562 offenders convicted in ten federal district courts, Hagan, Nagel, and

Albonetti found that gender affects sentence severity in white collar cases, even after controlling for variables such as the offender's prior record, the number and severity of the charged offenses, the type of offense, and the defendant's age, ethnicity, education, and physical health.[28] In a subsequent study, Hagan, Nagel, and Albonetti analyzed the sentences of 1,239 defendants convicted in the state of New York. They controlled for prior record, offense characteristics, and offender characteristics such as race, age, and employment, and found that females were treated preferentially at sentencing.[29]

These quantitative analyses are consistent with the findings derived from qualitative data collected through interviews with judges, in which many acknowledged treating female offenders preferentially. Simon and Landis cite a 1973 study of twenty-three judges in large midwestern cities, in which more than half said that "they do treat women more leniently and more gently than they do men; that they are more inclined to recommend probation rather than imprisonment; and if they sentence a woman, it is usually for a shorter time than if the crime had been committed by a man."[30] Simon and Landis also cite a 1988 study, in which twelve judges in the Washington D.C. area discussed the sentencing of women. Eleven of them reported that they "tended to treat women more gently than they do men."[31]

In 1983, Professors Ilene Nagel and John Hagan reviewed the existing empirical literature and found that the bulk of research on gender and crime—drawn from a variety of both state and federal courts, and using a variety of methodological techniques—supported the preferential treatment hypothesis.[32] More recent analyses of the literature reach the same conclusion.[33]

Thus, a reading of the extant empirical literature on gender and sentencing compels the conclusion that gender has had a significant impact on sentencing outcomes. While the effect of the gender variable is sometimes small relative to other factors, such as offense severity and the offender's prior criminal record, it is, as Nagel and Hagan noted, "demonstrably present."[34]

The question of why women receive preferential treatment in criminal sentencing is an intriguing one. When the pattern was first recognized, in the late 1970s and early 1980s, much of the sociological literature focused on the chivalry/paternalism thesis.[35] Although chivalry and paternalism are not consistently and precisely defined,[36] these concepts refer generally to a protective attitude toward women, linked to gender stereotypes of women as (1) weaker and more passive than men, and therefore not proper subjects for imprisonment; and (2) more submissive and dependent than men, and therefore less responsible for their crimes.[37] Judges also apparently regarded women as more easily manipulable than men, and hence more amenable to rehabilitative efforts.[38] The chivalry/paternalism thesis is consistent with the Anthony and Musolino judge interview studies, in which many judges voiced chivalrous attitudes toward women. For example, one judge in the Musolino study observed: "I don't think there's any rational or objective thought about it, but there's a feeling that incarceration for a woman is far more degrading than for a man, and you'll never see them (women) back because they'll do everything they can to keep from going back."[39]

Research shows, however, that judges are selectively chivalrous. Empirical evidence indicates that minority women are (or at least have been, in the recent past) treated more harshly by the criminal justice system than white offenders.[40] Further, studies suggest that law enforcement officials reserve chivalrous treatment for middle and upper class women who conform to gender stereotypes.[41] The selective application of chivalrous treatment may exacerbate racial and socioeconomic sentencing disparities.

Although some early researchers did not view the preferential treatment of women as especially troubling,[42] Elizabeth F. Moulds argued convincingly that this benign view of preferential sentencing was misguided.[43] Moulds analyzed the conceptual distinctions between chivalry and paternalism, pointing out that notions of paternalism imply a power relationship analogous to that between parent and child. Paternalism equates women with children, viewing them as incapable of assessing information and making responsible decisions, and thus less culpable for their criminal behavior. The negative social implications of this paternalistic attitude are obvious. Moulds notes that:

> It is important to be wary of a society which permits paternalism to color the perceptions of those who make and enforce the law. Those perceptions profoundly affect behavior of those in power and the behavior of those paternalized in a manner that is inconsistent with the operation of a democratic state. A basic denial of self-determination is what is taking place.[44]

Thus, stereotyping associated with paternalism negatively impacts women and should not be assumed to be benign simply because it results in leniency in a specific context. In fact, such stereotypes can harm female offenders in more direct ways. Nagel and Hagan found empirical support for a corollary to the chivalry/paternalism thesis—the "evil woman" thesis—which hypothesizes that women whose criminal behavior violates sex-stereotypical assumptions about the proper role of women are treated more harshly than their male counterparts.[45] For example, studies have shown that women are sentenced to longer terms than men for such gender role-defying offenses as child abandonment and assault.[46] In other words, not only do certain types of female offenders fail to benefit from paternalistic treatment, they are actually subject to heightened punishment for their choice of an "un-ladylike" offense.

The chivalry thesis is not universally accepted as the explanation for gender differences in sentencing. Some authors attribute these differences to a concern for the parental role of female offenders and the family disruption that judges assume would result from their incarceration.[47] For example, Kathleen Daly's interviews of judges, attorneys, and probation officers revealed that familied defendants of both sexes are treated more leniently than their non-familied counterparts; however, she also reported that familied women are treated more leniently than familied men.[48] Daly attributed this disparity to the fact that judges attach more importance to the predominantly female role of care-giving than to the predominantly male role of bread-winning.[49] She concluded that much of the lenient treatment afforded women is probably related to their role as primary caretakers of children.

Despite the difference in focus, most observers conclude that chivalry or paternalism plays some role in explaining the more lenient treatment of female offenders reported in the empirical literature.[50] The next section attempts to reconcile this pattern of preferential treatment in sentencing with the value feminists attach to equality of treatment in a wide variety of social and legal contexts. As noted, the normative implications of paternalistic, lenient treatment are potentially troubling from a feminist perspective.[51] While paternalism results in some female offenders spending less time in prison, it also reflects damaging stereotypes of female weakness, as well as a fundamental denial of the status of female offenders as responsible moral agents. Moreover, even to the extent that differential treatment reflects perceived differences in parental roles, rather than broader notions of paternalism, such treatment is potentially damaging in that it ratifies traditional gender roles and stereotypes about the child care responsibilities of women.

II. Gender "Neutrality" and Feminist Dilemmas in a Guidelines World

Most of the data discussed in the previous section was collected at a time when rehabilitation was the principal purpose of sentencing, and judges enjoyed substantial latitude in administering their sentences.[52] It is not clear, however, that the patterns reported are replicated in today's criminal justice system. As stated, substantial reforms designed specifically to reduce sentencing discretion, such as the Sentencing Reform Act of 1984 and the ensuing federal Sentencing Guidelines, have restricted judicial discretion and shifted the focus of sentencing away from the personal characteristics of the offender to the circumstances of the offense.[53] This section discusses the Sentencing Reform Act's emphasis on gender neutral sentencing and the implications of this neutrality for the just sentencing of female offenders.

Neutrality and the Guidelines Scheme

The Sentencing Reform Act embodies Congress' rejection of traditional penal rehabilitationism. The Act: (1) abolishes parole and adopts a determinate, "real time" sentencing scheme;[54] and (2) structures and narrows judicial sentencing discretion through the creation of a single administrative agency—the United States Sentencing Commission—empowered to promulgate presumptively binding sentencing guidelines.[55] The Act's legislative history clearly establishes that Congress' "primary goal" in undertaking sentencing reform was the elimination of unwarranted sentencing disparity.[56] Advocates of sentencing reform repeatedly emphasized the unfairness of the fact that offenders convicted of the same crime and possessing similar criminal histories, received vastly different sentences.[57] Moreover, Congress was especially sensitive to the need to reduce disparities associated with such factors as the defendant's race, gender, and socioeconomic status. Thus, Congress instructed the Commission to "assure that the guidelines and policy statements are entirely neutral as to the race, sex, national origin, creed, and socioeconomic status of offenders."[58] Furthermore, Congress instructed the Commission to de-emphasize the traditional "individualizing" factors which predominated in rehabilitative sentencing—e.g., family and community ties, occupation, and education—as part of the overall mandate to shift from a rehabilitative sentencing system focused on the offender to a system emphasizing the seriousness of the offense.[59]

Rather than articulating a single purpose of sentencing, Congress chose an amalgam of goals it wanted the Sentencing Reform Act to meet.[60] It is clear, however, that the dual purposes of "just punishment" for the offense and "crime control," are of primary importance.[61] The principal evil Congress sought to remedy—unwarranted sentencing disparity[2]—implicitly rests on notions of deserved or "just" punishment.[63]

Crime control concerns—deterrence and incapacitation of offenders—were also important to Congress.[64] Indeed, the Sentencing Reform Act is merely one aspect of Congress' rejection of indeterminate, rehabilitation-based sentencing in favor of a sentencing philosophy emphasizing punishment and crime control. Throughout the 1980s Congress increasingly adopted mandatory minimum sentencing schemes, which completely eliminate the consideration of the individual offender characteristics that were the staple of traditional rehabilitative sentencing. Instead, single offense characteristics are the bases for imposing punishment and controlling crime.[65]

Consistent with the statutory mandate, the Commission promulgated guidelines embodying the dual purposes of "just punishment" and "crime control." The guidelines establish sentencing ranges based on the offense, the presence of certain enumerated aggravating and mitigating factors related to the offense, and the offender's criminal history. Other potentially aggravating or mitigating circumstances may allow judges to depart from the guidelines' range, but only if they involve factors "not adequately taken into consideration by the Sentencing Commission in formulating the guidelines" and demand a sentence outside the guidelines' range.[66] Further, these departures are subject to appellate review.[67]

In addition to the sentencing guidelines submitted to Congress, the Commission promulgated a series of policy statements which provide that an offender's age, physical condition, mental or emotional condition, and family and community ties are not ordinarily relevant in decisions to depart from the guidelines.[68] The Commission chose the words "not ordinarily relevant" to make it clear that these factors may be relevant only in extraordinary cases.[69] In marked contrast, gender, like race, national origin, creed, and socioeconomic status, is never relevant.[70] Finally, the guidelines emphasize offense characteristics and culpability factors such as the offender's role in the offense, the level of planning involved in the offense, and whether a weapon was used. This focus is consistent with the goal of "just punishment" for the offense.

The Commission sought to incorporate crime control considerations through provisions requiring sentences at or near the statutory maximum for repeat, violent offenders.[71] The importance of deterrence is evident in the Commission's decision (at Congress' urging) to impose incarcerative sentences for white collar crimes,[72] which many have argued are more easily deterred than typical street crimes.

In short, the 1980s marked a period of increased concern for more equal treatment of similarly situated offenders. Reflecting this concern, the Sentencing Reform Act and the resulting sentencing guidelines embody aspirations of gender-neutral sentencing. One potential consequence of this neutrality, however, is the elimination, or at least reduction, of the traditional leniency afforded female offenders described in section I, above. It is unclear whether Congress specifically intended this result. While Congress was clear in its prescription of gender neutrality, the legislative history contains no discussion of the potential consequences of this neutrality for the overall severity of the sentences of female offenders. As more women are subject to this facially gender-neutral system, the question increasingly asked is whether strict gender neutrality is desirable in the sentencing context.[73] It is here that those favoring leniency come into conflict with those who, for the sake of feminist equality, are willing to forego leniency if it derives from inappropriate values or from gender stereotypes. The next section examines this tension between formal equality and leniency.

Equal Treatment v. Special Treatment of Female Offenders

Feminist legal theorists have vigorously debated whether to advocate formal, legal equality with men, or to support special treatment, recognizing pertinent gender differences. Advocates of an "equal treatment" approach recognize that although men and women differ in many important respects (especially with respect to reproduction), special treatment of women entails significant risks, because the laws meant to protect women have oppressed them.[74] As one commentator noted: "experience with protective-labor legislation, preferential-welfare statutes, child-custody presumptions, and maternity policies makes clear that 'benign discrimination' is a mixed blessing."[75] The early wave of feminist litigators, such as Supreme Court Justice Ruth Bader Ginsburg, successfully emphasized formal, legal, equal treatment in their efforts to break down the gender-based classifications which acted as barriers to women's participation in social and economic institutions.[76]

In contrast to the equal treatment model, special treatment models of gender equality emphasize the cultural and biological differences between men and women and advocate the need for special protection of women's interests based on those differences.[77] Elizabeth Wolgast, one proponent of special rights, contends that women cannot be men's "equals" because equality requires sameness. Instead, she suggests seeking "justice," which in her view requires special treatment of women in light of their special circumstances.[78]

Ultimately, both "equal treatment" and "special treatment" models provide valuable insights into the public policy debate about the role of gender in sentencing. However, a monolithic approach to accounting for gender is insufficiently sensitive to the contexts in which gender equity is evaluated. That is, whether equal treatment or special treatment is appropriate depends largely on the specific legal issues and underlying factual circumstances involved.[79] In addressing the issue of pregnancy in the employment context, Wendy Williams makes a similar point:

> The question is not whether pregnancy is different (it is, of course—it has its own specific physical manifestations, course of development, risks, and a different, usually desirable and certainly life altering outcome), but how it is different. . . . The focus of the pregnancy debate, as with men and women or blacks and whites, should be on whether the differences should be deemed relevant in the context of particular employment rules.[80]

Similarly, broader questions of gender equity turn on whether differences between men and women are pertinent in the context of the particular legal and policy issues addressed. The values underlying criminal sentencing suggest that it is an area in which the need for formal gender neutrality has special resonance.

Divergence from principles of equal treatment is potentially inconsistent with deeply held notions of fairness in a broad range of contexts. As Justice Scalia has remarked:

> As a motivating force of the human spirit, that value [the appearance of equal treatment] cannot be overestimated. Parents know that children will accept quite readily all sorts of arbitrary substantive dispositions—no television in the afternoon, or no television in the evening, or even no television at all. But try to let one brother or sister watch television when the others do not, and you will feel the fury of the fundamental sense of justice unleashed.[81]

This fundamental appeal of equal treatment is heightened by the special characteristics of criminal punishment.

Criminal punishment is distinctive in the law because of its condemnatory character. Unlike other legal sanctions (e.g., for breach of contract), criminal sentencing imparts blame on the offender.[82] The extent of reprobation is represented, in part, by the severity of the punishment imposed. Punishing offenders to a degree inconsistent with the nature of their crimes and the level of their culpability is unjust, because it imparts more or less blame than the offender deserves.[83] And sentencing offenders found guilty of identical crimes to vastly different terms of imprisonment seems inconsistent with common-sense notions of justice.

Moreover, the injustice of unequal treatment in sentencing is highlighted by the stakes involved. Criminal sentencing, which involves drastic deprivations of freedom and associated moral stigma, affects fundamental liberty interests. Congress recognized that the very legitimacy of the criminal justice system is at risk if the appearance of equal treatment is breached.[84]

Special treatment of women in sentencing potentially undermines the strong principles of justice and equity that animate contemporary notions of blameworthiness and proportionality. Moreover, a special treatment approach to criminal sentencing should trouble feminists, because it perpetuates damaging stereotypes of female weakness, implying a moral inferiority that undermines claims to full citizenship and even personhood.[85] The blameworthiness that supports notions of proportional punishment implies a recognition of the full moral agency of the offender.[86] Society believes that it is inappropriate to punish the very young or the insane, because, unlike responsible adults, they cannot be expected to conform their behavior to the norms of the law. Only those fully capable of understanding criminal norms and conforming their behavior to those norms are fit subjects for punishment. Thus, when women are granted special treatment, they are reduced to the moral status of infants.

In short, formal equal treatment under the criminal justice system, and questions of the allocation of criminal sentences, touch on fundamental notions of moral autonomy in a way that questions of formal equal treatment in employment rules or insurance benefits do not. In the context of criminal sentencing, those who advocate special treatment of any particular group, or ostensibly neutral rules designed to benefit a particular group, bear the burden of justifying departure from the traditionally accepted norms governing allocation of criminal sentences. With this general approach in mind, the next section considers some of the particularly difficult issues posed by the sentencing of female offenders under the federal guidelines scheme.

Issues of Special Concern

Pregnancy. One especially difficult sentencing issue posed by female offenders is how pregnancy is to be taken into account at sentencing. The guidelines do not specifically mention pregnancy. In the leading appellate case on the issue, *United States v. Pozzy,*[87] the First Circuit held that pregnancy is not an appropriate basis for downward departure from the applicable guidelines range. In the absence of any specific guidance on the pregnancy issue, the Court looked to 5H1.4 of the guidelines, which provides that a defendant's physical impairment is a basis for departure only in extraordinary cases. The court concluded that the language of this section, in light of the Commission's silence on pregnancy, established that the Commission rejected pregnancy as an independent basis for departure.[88] The court also noted that pregnancy "is neither atypical nor unusual," and hence not extraordinary for purposes of 5H1.4.[89] Finally, the Court expressed concern that a downward departure for pregnancy might encourage female offenders to become pregnant in order to influence sentencing outcomes.[90]

The Commission has taken no steps, since *Pozzy,* to reassess the guidelines' silence on the question of pregnancy. Thus, the guidelines' approach to pregnancy remains one of formal neutrality. The question is, of course, whether such an approach is appropriate in light of the gendered effects of pregnancy.

Equal treatment of men and women in light of the biological and social realities of pregnancy has been a vexing issue for courts, legislatures, and theorists.[91] In *Michael M. v. Superior Court,*[92] the Supreme Court recognized, in the context of statutory rape, the permissibility of treating women and men in a facially unequal manner to account for the possibility of pregnancy. Whether such special treatment of convicted pregnant offenders is good policy in the context of criminal sentencing remains unclear. The Court's ruling in *Michael M.* provides no guidance on this issue.

While a pregnant offender and a non-pregnant offender (male or female) clearly are not similarly situated, it does not necessarily follow that this is a difference relevant for sentencing purposes. Pregnancy does not appear to relate to the sentencing purposes highlighted by the Sentencing Reform Act. It is difficult to imagine a case in which the defendant's status as a mother-to-be is relevant to an objective assessment of the seriousness of her offense or to her culpability for that offense. In this sense, pregnancy has no bearing on the determination of the deserved punishment for the offense. Nor is special, more lenient treatment of pregnant offenders justifiable on the basis of crime control considerations. Unlike certain other physical conditions which may warrant downward departure from the applicable guidelines sentence,[93] pregnancy is not incapacitating in the sense that it does not restrict the individual's ability to commit additional offenses. The pregnant offender is free to engage in criminal activity throughout most of her pregnancy, as well as after completion of her pregnancy. Moreover, downward departures on the basis of pregnancy might have a marginally negative impact on general deterrence.[94]

To the extent that sentence mitigation for pregnancy is justified, it must be justified on the basis of exogenous utilitarian considerations, such as the physical well-being of the offender or her baby. However, barring unusual circumstances, it is difficult to make a penological case for leniency on the basis of pregnancy. From a purely medical standpoint, pregnancy is analogous to a number of physical conditions suffered by inmates, male and female. The Commission has taken the view that such physical impairments can be accommodated by the Bureau of Prisons and should not interfere with the service of an appropriate term of imprisonment.[95] A contrary approach would risk diminishing the import of the criminal sanction and would result in disparate treatment of offenders convicted of similar crimes. Moreover, because pregnancy is a temporary condition, a sentencing judge may delay sentencing in order to permit birth to be completed before the defendant serves her sentence, thereby obviating the need to impose a lesser sentence to account for the offender's pregnancy.[96]

Thus, pregnancy poses no insurmountable obstacle to service of a sentence warranted by traditional penological purposes. Special treatment of pregnant defendants in the sentencing context could be seen as exalting motherhood at the expense of the personal responsibility of female offenders for their criminal conduct. This demeans women as responsible citizens.

Family Ties. Another difficult gender-related issue in guidelines sentencing is the treatment of parenthood, particularly single parenthood. This is clearly a gendered issue; eighty-eight percent of all single parents are female.[97] Although the Commission does not collect data on offenders' single parent status, inmate survey results collected by Myrna Raeder indicate that single parenthood is not uncommon among female inmates and that female inmates are more likely than male inmates to have primary child care responsibilities.[98]

Single parenthood, like pregnancy, is not specifically addressed in the guidelines. However, 5H1.6 of the guidelines provides that a defendant's family ties and circumstances are "not ordinarily relevant" in assessing whether a departure is appropriate.[99] Although there is substantial variation in the case law interpreting this provision,[100] the prevailing view in the appellate courts is that single parenthood is not itself an adequate basis for a downward departure.[101] In other words, the courts generally have held that single parenthood is not sufficiently extraordinary to fall outside the heartland of cases covered by the guidelines.

The Commission's adoption of the 5H1.6 limitations on considering family circumstances at sentencing can be traced directly to the language and legislative history of the Sentencing Reform Act. In 28 U.S.C. 994(e), Congress specified that it is generally inappropriate for judges to consider factors such as employment, family ties, and community ties when they determine a proper sentence. The legislative history indicates that these provisions were motivated by Congress' concern about the biases associated with the traditional practice of lenient sentencing of defendants with good employment prospects, and strong community and family ties. While well-intended, these factors were used to justify light sentences for white, middle class defendants with strong ties to visibly intact families, and lengthy prison terms for unemployed, unmarried minority defendants who had committed offenses of similar seriousness. Reducing reliance on factors such as family ties was designed to redress this disparity.[102]

The Sentencing Reform Act's mandate for a guidelines' structure that de-emphasizes personal offender characteristics, such as family ties, has been criticized extensively, both from traditional and feminist perspectives.[103] For example, some commentators advocate a presumptive downward departure for all offenders with primary parenting responsibility for minor children.[104] However, whether judges should factor parental responsibilities into sentencing, and if so, how, is best approached in a two-pronged fashion: (1) as a descriptive matter, whether recognition of single parenthood as a basis for downward departure is consistent with the guidelines and the goals of the Sentencing Reform Act; and (2) as a normative matter, whether recognition of such a departure would result in a more just and effective sentencing policy.

Family Ties in the Guidelines Scheme. As noted, the Commission specified in 5H1.6 that family ties are "not ordinarily relevant" in assessing the appropriateness of departure. By and large, appellate courts have interpreted 5H1.6 as foreclosing departure solely on the basis of single parenthood, concluding that it is not an "extraordinary" family situation within the meaning of 5H1.6.[105] As the Fourth Circuit explained in *United States v. Brand:*

> A sole, custodial parent is not a rarity in today's society, and imprisoning such a parent will by definition separate the parent from the children. It is apparent that in many cases the other parent may be unable or unwilling to care for the children, and that the children will have to live with relatives, friends, or even in foster homes. . . .
>
> This situation, though unfortunate, is simply not out of the ordinary.[106]

Myrna Raeder argues that this characterization of single parent offenders (particularly females) is inapt:

> The present quandary over the feasibility of granting departures to pregnant women and single mothers ultimately results from the circuits unnecessarily limiting their interpretation of the Section 5H1 factors by defining the opposite of "ordinarily" as "extraordinarily." . . . There are other adjectives which could also be used to describe a case as not ordinary, including uncommon and infrequent. Clearly, single mothers are atypical of the majority of offenders being sentenced.[107]

Raeder correctly notes that single mothers are not typical of the overall offender population. Moreover, judicial efforts to distinguish "ordinary" cases from "extraordinary" cases have been unsatisfactory. Identifying "extraordinary" cases is extremely difficult, given the inherent imprecision of the term. In addition, this focus on whether a particular fact pattern is sufficiently "extraordinary" to justify departure from the guidelines range has tended to distract judges from the more important task of evaluating whether the applicable guidelines in a given case furthers the underlying purposes of guidelines sentencing.[108] Nevertheless, the courts' general conclusion—that single parent status is not an adequate basis for departure—is consonant with the Commission's approach. The Commission is aware of the problems posed in sentencing single parents but has structured the guidelines to permit downward departure for them only if other mitigating factors exist.[109]

Both Congress' guidance in the Sentencing Reform Act and considerations of sentencing policy have influenced the Commission's approach. Specifically, the Commission responded to section 994(e), which requires it to "assure that the guidelines and policy statements, in recommending a term of imprisonment or length of a term of imprisonment, reflect the general inappropriateness of considering the education, vocational skills, employment record, family ties and responsibilities, and community ties of the defendant."[110]

Critics have argued that the Commission has relied too extensively on section 994(e), ignoring other provisions in the statute which emphasize the need to account for offender characteristics in sentencing.[111] These critics correctly assert that the Act has provisions that are inconsistent with the Commission's approach. This is partly the result of the ambiguities in the Act, which arose from compromises among legislators with divergent views on sentencing policy.[112] The Commission might have interpreted its mandate somewhat differently, given the conflicting provisions in the Act. Moreover, in section 994(d), Congress instructed the Commission to consider whether a host of factors, including family ties and responsibilities, "have any relevance" to sentencing and to take them into account "only to the extent that they do have relevance." Thus, even though Congress admonished the Commission regarding the general inappropriateness of including factors such as family ties in the guidelines, it arguably gave the Commission the authority to determine whether the guidelines should account for such factors in some specified contexts.[113] In short, the Commission might have the authority under the Act to permit departures for single parents, if it determines that such departures would be sound sentencing policy.

Should Parental Status be Factored into Guidelines Sentencing? The question of whether courts should factor parental status into their sentences is a difficult one. Those that argue for mitigating sentences on the basis of parental status assert that excessive incarceration of single parents disrupts the parent/child relationship to the detriment of the child. They contend that the social costs of this disruption, both direct and indirect, outweigh the benefits of incarceration and thus warrant mitigation of an otherwise applicable sentence.[114] They also argue that incarcerated single mothers receive a "double punishment." Not only are they incarcerated but they are separated from their children and often lose their parental rights.[115] From this perspective, facially neutral treatment of single mothers is not equal treatment at all, but rather results in disparate gender impact.

Collateral Consequences and Double Punishment. The desire to adjust criminal sentences to reflect collateral consequences of conviction is understandable. Different personal circumstances cause a given term of imprisonment to fall more heavily on some than on others. This is arguably the case for single mothers. According to Eleanor Bush:

> If the "same" sentence has an inconsistent impact on two different defendants, then considering the two sentences as equivalent is unjust. An incarcerative sentence may have a distinctly different impact on a parent than it has on a non-parent. For example, in many states, incarceration constitutes a ground for termination of parental rights. A two-year prison sentence does not equal two years in prison accompanied by a permanent loss of child custody. Justice requires considering the consequences of a sentence for the defendant's children where they lead to such different effective quantities of punishment.[116]

Despite the simple, intuitive appeal of this argument, it leads down a dangerous path. First, it assumes the ability to compare the "effective quantities" of punishment imposed on differently situated defendants as a result of facially equal terms of incarceration. Economists, however, tell us that it is virtually impossible to engage in the kind of intersubjective utility comparisons necessary to evaluate the comparative disutility of imprisonment among different offenders.[117]

Moreover, once people accept the permissibility of adjusting punishment on the basis of such intersubjective comparisons, there is no logical stopping point. A variety of situations create potential reasons for imposing lesser sentences of imprisonment. For instance, offenders often lose their businesses, wind up divorced, or even get deported as a result of their convictions. These serious collateral harms could justify a shorter sentence. Age is another potential consideration. A ten-year sentence arguably is more burdensome for a sixty-year-old male than for a twenty-year-old female, because the elderly offender will spend a greater percentage of his expected life span behind bars. Alternatively, counsel for the twenty-year-old could argue that ten years stolen from her youth is far worse than ten years served by the older man. Permitting these intersubjective comparisons to alter an otherwise applicable sentence leads to a free-for-all of sentence individualization, each defendant arguing that her incarceration would be more painful than that of other defendants. The result would be unfettered judicial discretion and discrimination in application.[118] Recall, it was this very logic which often resulted in the incarceration of minority and disadvantaged offenders, while white offenders were sentenced to probation. Some judges believed that white, middle-class offenders suffered hardship and stigma from incarceration that poor, minority offenders did not. The resulting disparity and discrimination prompted the calls for reform that resulted in the Sentencing Reform Act.[119]

Avoiding Collateral Damage: Children and Incarceration. Another argument in favor of departure for single parents focuses not on the offender, but on her children. As Myrna Raeder argues, incarceration of single parents results in severe disruption of children's lives. They may be placed in foster care, or separated from their siblings.[120] These disruptions, and the ensuing lack of parental guidance, can lead to behavioral problems, and even an increased likelihood of future criminal activity.[121] Raeder makes a plausible utilitarian case for taking these considerations into account:[122]

> Any cost benefit analysis would seem to dictate that children be considered in the sentencing decision, particularly when societal costs regarding any future criminality of the children are weighed. . . . Other societal costs that should be considered might include foster care to replace the incarcerated parent, permanent dissolution of the family when the incarceration provides grounds for terminating parental rights, and the child's dependence upon government aid.[123]

Unquestionably, the imprisonment of single parents has significant social costs. Moreover, no one wants to see innocent children suffer as a result of a parent's incarceration. Yet, a general rule discouraging incarceration of single parents has troubling implications.

Consider, for instance, defendants "A" and "B," two females employed in the personnel section of an agency of the federal government. They are convicted of theft of government funds, arising from a kickback scheme in which each defendant altered other employees' pay documents (effectively creating unauthorized pay raises) in exchange for a percentage of the increased pay. The defendants participated equally in the criminal activity, and each received approximately the same amount of money—neither woman has a prior criminal record.

Based on the nature of the offense, the amount of loss, and the criminal history of the defendants, the applicable guidelines sentencing range for each defendant is forty-six to fifty-seven months imprisonment. Accordingly, the judge sentences defendant "A," who is childless, to forty-six months in prison. Defendant "B," however is a single mother with three minor children. As a result, she receives a substantial downward departure, and the judge sentences her to six months home confinement, to allow her to care for her children.

The sentences imposed in this example do not serve the principal purposes of sentencing articulated in the Sentencing Reform Act. Further, they clearly violate desert principles. Although these defendants do not have the same child care responsibilities, they are equally culpable. Yet one received a lengthy prison sentence while the other did not. As this example illustrates, taking children into account in sentencing shifts the focus from issues of offense seriousness and offender culpability to considerations exogenous to these sentencing purposes. The result is an obvious sentencing disparity. Defendant "A" will have to serve a prison sentence nearly four years longer than that served by "B," her equally culpable codefendant, simply because she does not have children.

Of course, punishment in our society is not totally desert-based. The Sentencing Reform Act mandated that crime control principles—deterrence, incapacitation, and rehabilitation—also play an important sentencing role.[124] However, the disparity in sentencing between defendants "A" and "B" similarly cannot be explained by crime control considerations. Incapacitation and rehabilitation are obviously not served here; defendant "A" is not necessarily more dangerous, or less amenable to rehabilitation than "B." Moreover, these sentences arguably undermine deterrence principles, because they send out the message that potential offenders who have parenting responsibilities can expect to be treated leniently by the courts.[125]

This is not to say that exogenous utilitarian concerns, such as the impact of sentencing on children, should be unimportant in allocating criminal penalties. For example, 5H1.1 of the guidelines permits downward departure for defendants who are "elderly and infirm." This provision reflects an exogenous utilitarian consideration—the judgment that the relative costs of imprisonment of such offenders, including medical expenses, outweighs the benefits of incarceration.[126] However, such exogenous considerations are rarely sufficiently important to outweigh either culpability or crime control considerations in the allocation of sentences. Indeed, 5H1.1 can be explained in terms of incapacitative purposes: the physical limitations of elderly and infirm offenders make them less likely than the typical offender to recidivate.

In sum, those who advocate the consideration of exogenous utilitarian factors in the allocation of criminal penalties bear a heavy burden in justifying a departure from reliance on the sentencing purposes identified by Congress in the Sentencing Reform Act. It is unclear whether the impact of incarceration on children is a sufficient justification. The argument for across-the-board mitigation under these circumstances assumes that maintaining the family unit is necessarily in the best interest of the children. However, this argument may not be true in all cases.[127] A criminal conviction does not necessarily make someone an unfit parent. The unfortunate reality, however, is that many criminal defendants are less than exemplary parents. A large percentage abuse either drugs or alcohol or both,[128] and many have been involved in serious criminal activity that could pose risks to children. Thus, keeping these families together is not necessarily in the best interest of the children. And any net social gain from more lenient sentencing of single parents may not outweigh other sentencing considerations.

Feminists might also consider the gender role implications of taking parental responsibilities into account in sentencing. It is undisputed that the gendered nature of child rearing causes children of some female offenders to be disadvantaged relative to the children of their male counterparts. Therefore, a policy designed to equalize this situation, through mitigation of the sentences of offenders with primary child care responsibilities, may unintentionally reinforce gender stereotypes. Such a policy would effectively use the criminal law to reward women for their status as mothers (or, alternatively, to punish women for not having children). It would say in effect, "you have violated the criminal law, but we'll overlook that so you can do what you are supposed to do—care for your children." This denies single-mother offenders the status of full moral agents and disregards the social contributions of childless women, whose employment and community ties are not given the same consideration in sentencing.

The gendered nature of child care responsibilities and the feminization of poverty are grave public policy concerns that must be addressed in order to achieve a more equitable society. It is not clear, however, that the criminal sentencing system is the appropriate institution to address these pressing problems.

Coercion, Duress, and Abuse. Another issue with gender implications is the extent to which guidelines should account for physical or psychological coercion or abuse by male codefendants.[129] Unlike pregnancy and family ties, the presence of coercion or abuse is part of the traditional assessment of a defendant's culpability under the criminal law, and thus fits more comfortably within the framework of traditional sentencing purposes. There appears to be ample room in the guidelines for judges to use departure to account for the most obvious forms of coercion and abuse.

For example, policy statement 5K2.12 provides that "serious coercion, blackmail or duress, under circumstances not amounting to a complete defense" is a basis for downward departure.[130] Courts have employed this section to justify downward departures for battered female offenders. For example, in *United States v. Johnson,*[131] the court vacated and remanded the sentences of several female participants in a drug trafficking conspiracy headed by a violent, male drug lord. The Ninth Circuit ordered the district court to consider, inter alia, whether downward departures for duress under 5K2.12 should be granted. As the court explained, a defendant need not make a showing of duress equivalent to that required for a complete defense.[132] Further, the fact that the defendant could have escaped does not preclude mitigation:[133]

> Given the court's apparent acceptance of [the defendant's] credibility as to her sad and savage treatment by male abusers and given the court's recognition that [the defendant] had been involved with a manipulative, violent, brutal drug lord, the court did have the discretion to

> depart downward if the court found that [the defendant] had been subject to coercion, even though with effort she could have escaped.[134]

The court in Johnson was sensitive to the gendered nature of duress, expressly noting that "gender is also a factor to be considered" as one of the defendant's personal characteristics in determining whether the defendant's fear is well-grounded, and whether there is a reasonable opportunity to escape.[135] Other courts have also shown a willingness to depart downwardly from the guidelines to account for duress.[136]

Courts may also use 5H1.3 and 5K2.13 to reduce the sentences of battered or coerced female offenders. Section 5H1.3 provides that the defendant's mental or emotional condition is not "ordinarily" relevant in assessing whether departure is appropriate. However, courts have interpreted it to permit departure for "extraordinary" mental or emotional conditions, including those involving abused female offenders. For example, in *United States v. Roe*,[137] the Ninth Circuit held that sentencing judges could consider the long-term abuse the defendant suffered in deciding whether to depart from the guidelines. The court recounted the defendant's horrific history of childhood physical and sexual abuse, as well as later abuse by pimps, customers, and boyfriends. It concluded that such extraordinary abuse might justify a downward departure under the guidelines.

Section 5K2.10, which permits departure if the "victim's wrongful conduct contributed significantly to provoking the offense behavior," may also allow judges to mitigate sentences for battery or coercion. This section encompasses the traditional Battered Woman Syndrome defense—a defendant's violent reprisal against an abuser.[138] Federal courts rarely use it, because it is applicable principally in murder, manslaughter, and assault cases, which are typically tried in state court.[139] Nevertheless, federal courts have applied this provision in cases involving battered female defendants. For example, in *United States v. Whitetail*,[140] the court vacated and remanded for consideration a departure under 5K2.10 a case in which the defendant was convicted of the second-degree murder of her live-in boyfriend.

Moreover, downward departure under 5K2.0 is not limited to cases of severe physical abuse. In *United States v. Yellow Earrings*,[141] the court affirmed a downward departure for assault based on victim misconduct where the defendant knifed a man who had attempted to rape her. The court determined that the victim's verbal abuse of the defendant, combined with his drunkenness and relative size and strength, were sufficient to warrant departure.[142] The court was also influenced by the fact that the defendant had previously been physically abused by a drunken, male relative.[143] Thus, the court in *Yellow Earrings* was sensitive to the gender issues underlying that case.

The principal limitation on these departures is that there must be some nexus between the victimization of the defendant and the commission of the crime. For example, in *United States v. Perkins*,[144] the D.C. Circuit reversed and remanded a downward departure for a female suffering from dependent personality disorder. The court explained that such a departure may be justified only if the sentencing judge finds a causal link between the defendant's condition and the commission of the offense.[145] This nexus requirement follows logically from the culpability-based nature of these departures. If the defendant's victimization did not influence the offense behavior, any departure is merely a "victim" discount, imposed out of pity for the defendant, rather than out of a sense that a lesser sentence is deserved. Such departures would undermine the moral agency of their recipients and would not serve the purposes of sentencing.[146] However, courts should not impose nexus requirements that are too stringent. This could result in unfairly harsh sentences for defendants who deserve mitigation and adversely affect female offenders, who appear to be disproportionately subject to coercion and abuse by co-defendants.

Dominance, Manipulation, and Role in the Offense. The possibility that the criminal behavior of a female offender results from some form of dominance or manipulation, falling short of physical abuse or serious psychological coercion, is a particularly troublesome issue for guidelines sentencing. As Raeder has pointed out, a review of published cases reveals that some female criminals, particularly those involved in drug trafficking offenses, are romantically involved with male co-defendants.[147] Many of these offenders play only a minor role in the illegal activity[48] and might be less culpable than those committing similar offenses on their own, or in concert with co-equals. To the extent that guidelines sentencing fails to permit judges to take this subordination adequately into account,[149] it has a disparate impact on female offenders.

Obviously, these women cannot be absolved completely of criminal liability, yet assessing their culpability is often difficult. The Commission has wrestled with the issue of the non-coercive domination of female offenders by co-defendant males and its role in sentencing. Unfortunately, to this point the Commission has been unable to devise a satisfactory way to take this factor into account in an express fashion, while remaining faithful to the gender neutrality requirement of the statute. Specifically, the Commission has found it difficult to articulate a departure for "bad romantic judgment." The risks involved in devising an express adjustment or departure for this type of situation are highlighted by *United States v. Mast*.[150] In that case, which involved a female bank robber dubbed the "Miss America bandit," the district judge ordered a significant downward departure because of the defendant's domination, even though it did not amount to physical coercion. The judge's comments reveal a paternalistic attitude toward the defendant: "men have exercised traditional control over the activities of women, and I'm not going to ignore that, no matter how much flak I get from women's lib," and "I think it's a fact of life that men can exercise a

Svengali influence over women," and "women are a soft touch, particularly if sex is involved."[151] The judge then concluded that the guidelines "should have taken into consideration the possibility that in some cases, a girl from a good background, from a good family, came [sic] under a malevolent influence and guidance of a bum, then gets caught doing things for him."[152]

This case demonstrates the potential costs involved in countering the gendered effects of sentencing through direct, express mitigation. It perpetuates inappropriate gender stereotypes, denies the defendant's fundamental moral agency, and introduces socioeconomic biases.[153]

The Commission has chosen not to directly address the dominance issue, or the presence of bad romantic judgment in prompting criminal involvement. Instead, most offenders must rely on the more general mitigating role adjustments for individuals playing minor roles,[154] or upon the availability of a downward departure under 5K2.0, the guidelines' general departure provision. But some litigants have been successful. For example, some district courts have recognized female subordination as a basis for departure. In *United States v. Naylor,*[155] the court granted a substantial downward departure to a female whose participation in the offense arose from her romantic relationship with a manipulative, older male co-defendant. Such cases are, however, comparatively rare. The degree of subordination necessary to obtain a departure under the present framework is difficult to establish.

In theory, role adjustments offer a more promising mechanism for achieving proportionality in sentencing this type of defendant. If the offender's involvement in the offense is peripheral, she should get a two to four level reduction in her offense.[156] In practice, however, role adjustments may provide only a relatively limited tool for sentencing mitigation.[157] For example, courts will sometimes find the four level reduction for minimal role inapplicable, if the defendant participates continuously in a conspiracy.[158] Moreover, in drug trafficking cases, which account for a significant percentage of cases in which role adjustments are granted, mandatory minimum sentences often limit the impact of role adjustments on the applicable guidelines sentence.[159]

The Special Problems Posed by Drug Trafficking Cases. Under the current system, drug trafficking cases create distinctive problems in the proper calibration of sentences. As a result, some women are punished more severely than they would have been under a more discretionary regime.[160] The root of these problems is the pervasive effect of mandatory minimum sentences. These mandatories anchor the guidelines sentences, which incorporate the mandatory penalties for given quantities of drugs and extrapolate sentences for additional drug quantities.[161]

The impact of mandatory minimums was exacerbated by Congress' decision in 1988 to extend them to offenders convicted of drug trafficking conspiracies.[162] As a result, courts may determine the sentences of federal drug offenders more by the size of the conspiracy in which they are a participant, rather than by their role in the conspiracy. Female offenders, in particular, may have been adversely affected. Females traditionally have not been the leaders or organizers of drug conspiracies. They are also less likely than male offenders to carry or use firearms or to engage in violent behavior. Indeed, many female drug offenders are involved in drug trafficking conspiracies as a result of their personal relationships with male co-defendants. Under these circumstances, female offenders may be less culpable than the drug amounts for which they are legally held responsible would suggest. This problem is further compounded by the fact that, as noted earlier, some female offenders undoubtedly participate in drug conspiracies as a result of physical or psychological coercion. When the sentence is bounded on the low end by a fixed mandatory minimum, the sentencing judge may not be able to adjust it to fully reflect the lesser culpability of such offenders.

As a result of this combination of developments, female offenders who might otherwise have received more modest sentences of imprisonment, intermediate sentences, or even probation, may have to serve lengthy sentences for their minimal involvement in trafficking large quantities of drugs. The Commission has recognized the potential inequities associated with quantity-driven guidelines and is exploring alternatives which emphasize the presence of weapons and ancillary violence.[163] The pressure to adjust to these inequities has led to the development of means to avoid, for some female offenders, mandatory minimums and the drug guidelines derived from mandatory minimums.[164]

The Unresolved Dilemmas of Guidelines Sentencing of Female Offenders. Replacing a rehabilitation-based sentencing scheme in which female offenders received lenient treatment, with a guidelines sentencing system which includes rules designed to promote race, gender, and socioeconomic neutrality, generates difficult policy choices. Female offenders differ from male offenders in a number of ways: the possibility of pregnancy; the likelihood of sole parenting responsibilities; the possibility that coercion or abuse influenced offense behavior; and the existence of different patterns of co-defendant dominance and role in the offense. The extent to which these differences should be recognized and accommodated in a guidelines sentencing system is debatable. As noted, the sentencing reform movement and the resulting federal sentencing guidelines scheme emphasize considerations of crime control and deserved punishment to a greater degree than was true in the past. From this perspective, courts should limit the accommodation of gender differences to those that bear on the offender's deserved punishment, or on considerations of crime control, such as deterrence or incapacitation. Other policy interests should play a secondary role.

A careful analysis of the special issues posed by female offenders suggests that while factors such as the incidence of coercion or abuse of female offenders and the lesser roles that female offenders tend to play can and should be accommodated, special sentencing rules to accommodate pregnancy or parental responsibilities are more difficult to justify. While compelling arguments support the view that guidelines should reflect gender impacts on criminality and sentencing, statutory directives and important penological interests will make it difficult. Moreover, any rules designed to account for the special circumstances of female offenders create the risk of reinforcing the negative gender stereotypes that underlay the paternalistic approach to sentencing that prevailed in the 1960s and 1970s. These competing policy considerations have posed, and will continue to pose, difficult challenges to the Sentencing Commission.

III. Women and Guidelines Sentencing: A Brief Empirical Overview

This section examines data for three broad categories of offenses within which female offenders are especially prominent: drug offenses, embezzlement, and fraud. These data suggest that the real-world consequences of the shift to ostensibly gender neutral guidelines have not been as dramatic as might have been expected, given the difficult policy issues discussed in the previous section. In effect, it appears that the considerable discretion in plea bargaining and sentencing that remains in the guidelines scheme limits the sentence exposure of female offenders and reintroduces some of the gender-based leniency of pre-guidelines sentencing.

Drug Offenses

More females are sentenced in the federal system for drug offenses than for any other type of offense.[165] More than one-third of all women receiving guidelines sentences in 1991 and 1992 committed drug offenses.[166] Thus, sentencing patterns for drug offenses reveal much about the sentencing of females under the federal guidelines scheme. An analysis of aggregate statistical data collected by the Commission regarding sentencing of federal drug offenders reveals that female offenders benefit disproportionately from each of the principal discretionary components in the guidelines scheme: downward departure for substantial assistance to authorities;[167] downward departure due to atypical facts or circumstances;[168] and selection of a sentence from within the low end of the applicable sentencing range.

Substantial Assistance. The Sentencing Reform Act instructs the Commission to consider a defendant's assistance to authorities in the prosecution of others as a mitigating factor.[169] Furthermore, the Act specifically empowers sentencing judges to depart below the guidelines or otherwise applicable mandatory minimum sentences upon motion by the prosecution certifying the substantial assistance of the defendant in the prosecution of others.[170] The Commission implemented Congress' substantial assistance directive through 5K1.1 of the guidelines. 5K1.1 provides that a court may, upon motion of the government, depart from the otherwise applicable guidelines range to reflect the defendant's substantial assistance.

Substantial assistance departures under 5K1.1 involve the exercise of considerable discretion by both the prosecution and the sentencing judge. As the Supreme Court has explained, 5K1.1 "gives the Government a power, not a duty, to file a motion when a defendant has substantially assisted."[171] A sentencing judge may also decline to grant a substantial assistance motion filed by the government.[172]

The Commission's data indicate that female drug offenders are considerably more likely to receive substantial assistance departures than their male counterparts. In fiscal year 1992, for example, 44.8% of female drug offenders received downward departures for substantial assistance, compared to just 28.1% of male drug offenders.[173] The fiscal year 1991 data reveal a similar pattern, although the gender difference is not quite as marked.[174]

Researchers do not know enough about the underlying cooperation practices of male and female offenders to conclude that equally cooperative male and female offenders are treated dissimilarly. Nevertheless, this pattern is notable, given the belief that female offenders, who play minor roles in drug offenses, often lack sufficient information to provide legally adequate substantial assistance.[175] Extensive field research on plea bargaining practices under the guidelines, conducted by Commissioner Ilene Nagel and Professor Stephen Schulhofer, provides a plausible explanation for the substantial assistance figures.[176] Their data, derived from extensive case record reviews and field interviews with judges, probation officers, prosecutors, and defense attorneys, suggest that factors other than the value of the defendant's cooperation influence prosecutors' decisions to file 5K1.1 motions. Specifically, they find that prosecutors often file 5K1.1 motions to reduce the guidelines sentence for sympathetic defendants, or defendants whose guidelines sentence exceeds prosecutors' view of what the defendant deserves.[177] The disproportionate share of substantial assistance departures received by female drug offenders may reflect prosecutors' and judges' greater sympathy for female offenders.[178]

Other Downward Departures. Still another mechanism for the exercise of discretion under the guidelines scheme is the authority granted sentencing judges to depart from the applicable guidelines range in atypical cases. The Sentencing Reform Act instructs judges to impose a sentence from within the range specified by the applicable guidelines unless there are aggravating or mitigating circumstances, not adequately considered by the Commission in adopting the guidelines, which warrant a different sentence.[179] Departures are subject to appellate review.[180] The power to depart is, however, discretionary in the sense that a judge's decision not to depart from the guidelines range is not subject to appellate review.[181]

As was the case with substantial assistance, female drug offenders receive downward departures more often than male drug offenders. In 1991, the rate of downward departure was 10.3% for females and 7.2% for males. That disparity increased in fiscal year 1992. In that year, 14.3% of female drug offenders received downward departures, compared to only 6.7% of males—a ratio of more than 2 to 1.

Points Within the Range. Sentencing judges also have discretion to select any sentence from within the applicable guidelines range. This authority is both broader and narrower than the authority to depart. It is broader in the sense that the selection of the point within the guidelines range is not subject to appellate review; it is narrower in the sense that the impact on the defendant's sentence is circumscribed by the outer points of the range, which may not exceed the greater of six months or twenty-five percent.[182]

The Commission's data suggest a modest correlation between gender and the selection of the point within the range used in imposing a sentence. For purposes of analysis, the Commission data divide the sentencing range into quartiles. A comparison of defendants receiving sentences at the bottom of the range (the first quartile) reveals the same pattern of preferential treatment of female offenders. In fiscal year 1991, the percentage of women at the bottom of the range exceeded that of men by only a one percent margin, 44.5% to 43.5%. However, in 1992, that margin increased to almost sixteen percent, 58.0% to 42.2%.

In short, the data indicate that female drug offenders benefit from sentencing mitigation at every turn—in plea bargaining, substantial assistance motions, departure from the applicable guidelines range, and selection of the sentence from within the applicable guidelines range.[183] While some of this undoubtedly reflects underlying differences in male and female criminality in drug cases, the pervasiveness of the pattern, along with the research findings of Nagel and Schulhofer,[184] suggests that females are treated more leniently than similarly situated males. The discretion that remains in the guidelines scheme seems to provide a mechanism through which courts and prosecutors revert to pre-guidelines sentencing patterns. These patterns are replicated, to a lesser extent, in sentencing for embezzlement and fraud.

Embezzlement Offenses

Females convicted of embezzlement are more likely than males to receive downward departures for reasons other than substantial assistance. In 1992, the rate of downward departure was 9.8% for female embezzlers and 7.5% for male embezzlers. Similarly, in 1991 the downward departure rates for females and males were 10.0% and 6.6% respectively.

Similarly, Commission data establish that females convicted of embezzlement are more likely than males to receive sentences at the bottom of the applicable guidelines range. In 1992, the percentages in the first quartile were 74.1% and 67.6%, respectively. In 1991, the figures were 75.0% and 65.0%, respectively.

Given the nature of the offense of embezzlement, substantial assistance departures were comparatively rare, 3.4% in 1992 and 2.4% in 1991.[185] Curiously, men were somewhat more likely than women to receive departures for substantial assistance under 5K1.1.[186] As noted, the opposite is true in drug offenses. The reason for this is unclear.

Larceny

Finally, the patterns for defendants convicted of larceny resemble those for offenders convicted of embezzlement. In both 1991 and 1992, females were substantially more likely to receive a sentence at the bottom of the range (79.5% to 56.3% in 1992, 75.0% to 56.2% in 1991); females were somewhat more likely than males to receive downward departures under the general departure provisions of 5K2.0 (3.0% to 2.5% in 1992, 3.8% to 3.1% in 1991); and females were less likely to receive departures for substantial assistance (6.7% to 3.9% in 1992, 7.5% to 3.2% in 1991).

Conclusion

The transition from a sentencing system featuring virtually unlimited judicial discretion to a system in which that discretion is structured and limited through presumptively binding guidelines, which delineate the factors to be taken into account at sentencing and specify the weight to be accorded those factors, is a difficult one. Tough policy choices previously made on an ad hoc basis, and therefore hidden from public view, must now be articulated and incorporated into guidelines applied to the vast range of offenders and offenses.

The difficulties of this transition are especially acute with respect to female offenders, who differ from male offenders in a number of ways and who traditionally received lenient treatment in the pre-guidelines era. Analysis of the policy questions posed by the sentencing of female offenders under the guidelines suggests that the desire to avoid a disparate impact on female offenders through facially neutral guidelines must not eclipse the principles of desert and crime control that animate our sentencing policy, or the fact that the lenient treatment of women in the criminal justice system may have macro-level social costs which must be weighed against any micro-level benefits to individual offenders.

In any event, the federal sentencing guidelines have not eliminated the favorable treatment of female offenders. Special treatment, not equal treatment, persists. The extent to which this differential treatment reflects differences in male and female criminality is not clear. To the extent that these findings reflect a continuation of the pre-guideline pattern of paternalistic treatment of female offenders, however, they highlight the difficulty of full implementation of sentencing reform, as well as the complexity of the issues involved.

Endnotes

[1] See, e.g., Rita J. Simon & Jean Landis, The Crimes Women Commit, the Punishments They Receive xv–xx (1991).

[2] See Lawrence M. Friedman, Crime and Punishment in American History 213 (1993) (noting that the relative paucity of female offenders has been a "constant, throughout American history" and that "the more serious the crime, the less likely. . . women commit it").

[3] The percentage of females among convicted offenders in U.S. District Courts rose from 7.0% in 1963 to 10.8% in 1979. See Admin. Office of the U.S. Courts, Federal Offenders in the United States District Courts 1963 10 (1964); Admin. Office of the U.S. Courts, Federal Offenders in United States District Courts 1979 75 (1980). Females represented 16.4% of offenders sentenced under the Federal Sentencing Guidelines in fiscal year 1992. See U.S. Sentencing Comm'n, Annual Report Table 13 (1992).

[4] Simon & Landis, supra note 1, at xv.

[5] See infra notes 9–50.

[6] See infra notes 34–50.

[7] See infra notes 53–73.

[8] Cf. *United States v. Quintero*, 937 F.2d 95 (2d Cir. 1991) (discussing the use of uncharged conduct in determining the guidelines sentencing range). As the Second Circuit noted: "for all the criticism the guidelines have attracted, one of their virtues is the illumination of practices and policies that were applicable in the pre-guidelines era, but that received less attention when sentences were only a generalized aggregation of various factors, many of which were frequently unarticulated." Id. at 97.

[9] Pub. L. No. 98–473, tit. II, ch. 2, 98 Stat. 1987 (1984) (codified at 18 U.S.C. 3551–3673; 28 U.S.C. 991–998.

[10] Rehabilitationism in American penal thought can be traced to the National Congress of Prisons' 1870 Declaration of Principles, which stated that the "supreme aim of prison discipline is the reformation of criminals and not the infliction of vindictive suffering." American Correctional Association, Transactions of the National Congress of Prisons and Reformatory Discipline (1870). See also *United States v. Grayson*, 438 U.S. 41, 46 (1978).

[11] 337 U.S. 241 (1949).

[12] Id. at 248.

[13] Id. at 247 (citations omitted) (emphasis added).

[14] See Francis A. Allen, The Decline of the Rehabilitative Ideal 5–7 (1981). See also Herbert L. Packer, The Limits of the Criminal Sanction 12–13 (1968) (explaining that the "behavioral" view of crime associated with the rehabilitative ideal was so widely accepted by psychiatrists, criminologists, and corrections professionals that it was absorbed by the popular culture).

[15] Allen, supra note 14, at 6 ("Almost all of the characteristic innovations in criminal justice in this century are reflections of the rehabilitative ideal: the juvenile court, the indeterminate sentence, systems of probation and parole, the youth authority, and the promise (if not the reality) of therapeutic programs in prisons, juvenile institutions, and mental hospitals."). For example, by the 1960s, every state in the nation had some form of indeterminate sentencing. Ilene H. Nagel, Structuring Sentencing Discretion: The New Federal Sentencing Guidelines, 80 J. Crim. L. & Criminology 883, 894 (1990).

[16] Andrew von Hirsch, Doing Justice 12 (1976).

[17] *Williams*, 337 U.S. at 247 (emphasis added).

[18] Willard Gaylin, Partial Justice 162–65 (1974). See also S. Rep. No. 225, 98th Cong., 1st Sess. 41 & n.18 (1983), reprinted in 1984 U.S.C.C.A.N. 3182, 3224 (citing evidence that federal judges disagree about the purposes of sentencing and noting that this disagreement is a cause of sentencing disparity).

[19] See John Hagan, Extra-Legal Attributes and Criminal Sentencing: An Assessment of a Sociological Viewpoint, 8 Law & Soc'y Rev. 357, 358 (1974). See also Ilene H. Nagel, The Legal/Extra-Legal Controversy: Judicial Decisions in Pretrial Release, 17 Law & Soc'y Rev. 481 (1983).

[20] See Hagan, supra note 19, at 358; Nagel, supra note 19, at 481.

[21] See infra notes 23–50.

[22] Thus, Rita Simon and Jean Landis concluded in a 1991 review of studies on gender and sentencing:

> Most observers feel that women receive preferential treatment, which in operational terms means that they are less likely than men to be convicted for the same type of offense; if they are convicted, they are less likely to be sentenced [to prison]; and if they are sentenced, they are likely to receive milder sentences. (Simon & Landis, supra note 1, at 57)

[23] See, e.g., Ilene H. Nagel & John Hagan, Gender and Crime: Offense Patterns and Criminal Court Sanctions, in 4 Crime and Justice: An Annual Review of Research 91, 129 (Michael Tonry & Norval Morris eds., 1983).

[24] See, e.g., Darrell J. Steffensmeier, Assessing the Impact of the Women's Movement on Sex-Based Differences in the Handling of Adult Criminal Defendants, 26 Crime & Delinq. 344, 346 (1980) (suggesting that apparent link between sentencing outcomes and gender may be an artifact of inadequate control for offense seriousness and prior record).

[25] Id. at 344–49.

[26] See, e.g., Candace Kruttschnitt & Donald E. Green, The Sex Sanctioning Issue: Is it History?, 49 Am. Soc. Rev. 541, 550 (1984). See also William Wilbanks, Are Female Felons Treated More Leniently by the Criminal Justice System?, 3 Just. Q. 516, 521–28 (1986); Hagan, supra note 19, at 375 (finding effect of gender on sentencing to be negligible).

[27] See, e.g., William M. Rhodes, A Study of Sentencing in Hennepin County and Ramsey County District Courts, 6 J. Legal Stud. 333, 350 (1977); John Hagan et al., Ceremonial Justice: Crime and Punishment in a Loosely Coupled System, 58 Soc. Forces 506 (1979); Ilene H. Nagel et al., Sex Differences in the Processing of Criminal Defendants, in 1 Women and the Law: A Social Historical Perspective 259, 266–69 (D. Kelly Weisberg ed., 1982); John Hagan et al., The Differential Sentencing of White Collar Offenders in Ten Federal District Courts, 45 Am. Soc. Rev. 802, 811–15 (1980) [hereinafter Hagan et al., White Collar Offenders].

[28] See Hagan et al., White Collar Offenders, supra note 27, at 811–15.

[29] See Nagel et al., supra note 27, at 272–73.

[30] Simon & Landis, supra note 1, at 59 (quoting Debra Anthony, Judges' Perceptions of Women Offenders and Their Own Actions Toward Women Offenders (1973) (unpublished Master's Thesis, University of Illinois)).

[31] Id. at 62 (citing Angela Musolino, Judge's Attitudes Toward Female Offenders, at 15 (1988) (unpublished manuscript)).

[32] As Nagel and Hagan concluded: "clearly, the research on sentencing produces the strongest evidence for the thesis that gender does affect court outcome decisions and that women receive preferential treatment." Nagel & Hagan, supra note 23, at 134.

[33] See Darrell Steffensmeier et al., Gender and Imprisonment Decisions, 31 Criminology 411 (1993). Their literature review reveals that

> a fairly persistent finding has been that adult female defendants are treated more leniently than adult male defendants. . . . The studies substantiate the widely held belief that female defendants receive more lenient treatment (apparently) because of judicial paternalism, the social costs to children and families of sending women

> to prison, or the view that female defendants are less dangerous and more amenable to rehabilitation than male defendants. (411–12)

Steffensmeier et al., note, however, that some of these studies have significant methodological weaknesses (413–16).

[34] Nagel & Hagan, supra note 23, at 134.

[35] See, e.g., Simon & Landis, supra note 1, at 11 (a "theme running through much of the women and crime literature in the past fifteen years has been the issue of chivalry").

[36] See Kathleen Daly, Structure and Practice of a Familial-Based Justice in a Criminal Court, 21 Law & Soc'y Rev. 267, 268 n.2 (1987).

[37] See Steffensmeier, supra note 24, at 350–51.

[38] Id. at 351–52.

[39] Simon & Landis, supra note 1, at 62 (citing Angela Musolino, Judges' Attitudes Toward Female Offenders, at 16 (1988) (unpublished manuscript)).

[40] See Cassia Spohn et al., Women Defendants in Court: The Interaction Between Sex and Race in Convicting and Sentencing, 66 Soc. Sci. Q. 178, 182 (1985).

[41] See Christy A. Visher, Gender, Police Arrest Decisions, and Notions of Chivalry, 21 Criminology 5, 22–23 (1983), who found that

> in encounters with police officers, those female suspects who violated typical middle-class standards of traditional female characteristics and behaviors (i.e., white, older and submissive) are not afforded any chivalrous treatment during arrest decisions. In these data, young, black, or hostile women receive no preferential treatment, whereas older, white women who are calm and deferential toward the police are granted leniency.

See also Clarice Feinman, Women in the Criminal Justice System 28 (2d ed. 1986) ("Chivalry is reserved for white middle- and upper-class women, except those who flout culturally expected behavior for ladies.")

[42] Nagel & Hagan, supra note 23, at 114.

[43] Elizabeth F. Moulds, Chivalry and Paternalism: Disparities of Treatment in the Criminal Justice System, in Women, Crime, and Justice 277, 283 (Susan K. Datesman & Frank R. Scarpitti eds., 1980).

[44] Id. at 282.

[45] See Nagel & Hagan, supra note 23, at 135–36.

[46] See Matthew Zingraff & Randall Thomson, Differential Sentencing of Women and Men in the U.S.A., 12 Int'l J. Soc. Law 401, 410 (1984).

[47] See Kathleen Daly, Rethinking Judicial Paternalism: Gender, Work-Family Relations, and Sentencing, 3 Gender & Soc'y 9 (1989); Daly, supra note 36, at 282–84; Candace Kruttschnitt, Sex and Criminal Court Dispositions: The Unresolved Controversy 21 Res. Crime & Delinq. 213, 224–27(1984).

[48] Daly, supra note 36, at 282–83.

[49] Id.

[50] Indeed, even Daly, who concluded that family concerns motivate much of the lenient treatment of women, acknowledged that the judicial decisionmaking in her study was "not completely devoid of female paternalism." Id. at 283. Moreover, the majority of probation officers and attorneys in her study believed that judicial leniency was based on paternalism. Id.

[51] It is troubling from more traditional perspectives as well. See infra notes 74–86 and accompanying text.

[52] See, e.g., Steffensmeier et al., supra note 33, at 413.

[53] See, e.g., infra notes 53–73 and accompanying text.

[54] See Stephen Breyer, The Federal Sentencing Guidelines and the Key Compromises upon Which They Rest, 17 Hofstra L. Rev. 1, 4 (1988).

[55] Id. at 4–5.

[56] S. Rep. No. 225, supra note 18, at 52, reprinted in 1984 U.S.C.C.A.N. at 3225.

[57] See, e.g., Edward M. Kennedy, Toward a New System of Criminal Sentencing: Law With Order, 16 Am. Crim. L. Rev. 353, 353–54 (1979).

[58] 28 U.S.C. 994(d) (1988) (emphasis added).

[59] See, e.g., Kate Stith & Steve Y. Koh, The Politics of Sentencing Reform: The Legislative History of the Federal Sentencing Guidelines, 28 Wake Forest L. Rev. 223, 250–51, 284 (1993) (language and legislative history of the Act demonstrate Congress' skepticism about the appropriateness of considering the offender's personal characteristics in sentencing); Ellsworth A. Van Graafeiland, Some Thoughts on the Sentencing Reform Act of 1984, 31 Vill. L. Rev. 1291, 1293 (1986) (Congress' instructions "have led the Commission to concentrate more on the nature and extent of the injury or harm resulting from the defendant's acts than on . . . the defendant's character and mental processes."). See also *United States v. Vela*, 927 F.2d 197, 199 (5th Cir.), cert. denied, 112 S. Ct. 214 (1991) ("One of the primary goals of the Sentencing Guidelines is to impose a sentence based on the crime, not the offender."); *United States v. McHan*, 920 F.2d 244, 247 (4th Cir. 1990) ("One of Congress' primary purposes in establishing the Guidelines was to reduce sentencing disparities and to rest sentences upon the offense committed, not upon the offender.").

[60] See 18 U.S.C. 3553(a)(2) (1988) (instructing courts to consider all four traditional purposes of sentencing—just punishment, deterrence, incapacitation, and rehabilitation). See also S. Rep. No. 225, supra note 18, at 67–68, reprinted in 1984 U.S.C.C.A.N. at 3250–51 (explaining that the Act generally does not explicitly "favor one purpose of sentencing over another").

[61] See, e.g., Steven P. Lab, Potential Deterrent Effects of the Guidelines, in The U.S. Sentencing Guidelines: Implications for Criminal Justice 32, 32–33 (Dean J. Champion ed., 1989).

[62] See S. Rep. No. 225, supra note 18, at 52, reprinted in 1984 U.S.C.C.A.N. at 3235 ("A primary goal of sentencing reform is the elimination of unwarranted sentencing disparity.").

[63] See, e.g., von Hirsch, supra note 16.

[64] See Nagel, supra note 15, at 916.

[65] According to Senator Phil Gramm who is a long-time supporter of mandatory minimum sentences, Congress passed mandatory minimums to accomplish the dual grounds of incapacitating hardened criminals and giving them their just punishment. Phil Gramm, Mandatory Minimums for Sentencing?, Washington Times, October 18, 1993, at B4.

[66] 18 U.S.C. 3553(b) (1988).

[67] 18 U.S.C. 3742 (1988).

[68] See United States Sentencing Commission, Guidelines Manual 5H1.1 (age), 5H1.2 (education and vocational skills), 5H1.3 (mental and emotional conditions), 5H1.4 (physical condition), 5H1.5 (employment), and 5H1.6 (family and community ties) (Nov. 1993) [hereinafter U.S.S.G.].

[69] See U.S.S.G. Ch. 1, Pt.A, intro. comment., at 5–6.

[70] See U.S.S.G. 5H1.10.

[71] See U.S.S.G. 4B1.1 (Career Offender), 4B1.4 (Armed Career Criminal).

[72] This also reflected, in part, desert-based concerns that white collar criminals were receiving more lenient sentences than property offenders of lower socioeconomic status. See S. Rep. No. 225, supra note 18, at 77, reprinted in 1984 U.S.C.C.A.N. at 3260 ("Some major offenders, particularly white collar offenders and serious violent crime offenders, frequently do not receive sentences that reflect the seriousness of their offenses.").

[73] See, e.g., Myrna S. Raeder, Gender and Sentencing: Single Moms, Battered Women, and Other Sex-Based Anomalies in the Gender-Free World of the Federal Sentencing Guidelines, 20 Pepp. L. Rev. 905 (1993).

[74] See, e.g., Wendy W. Williams, The Equality Crisis: Some Reflections on Culture, Courts and Feminism, 7 Women's Rts. L. Rep. 175, 196–200 (1982).

[75] Deborah L. Rhode, Justice and Gender 319 (1989). See also Wendy W. Williams, Equality's Riddle: Pregnancy and the Equal Treatment/Special Treatment Debate, 13 N.Y.U. Rev. L. & Soc. Change 325, 363 n.144 (1984–85) ("The history of governmental regulation and private practice with respect to femaleness, female sexuality and female reproductive capacity justifies treating such classifications as suspect.").

[76] See, e.g., *Califano v. Goldfarb*, 430 U.S. 199 (1977); *Craig v. Boren*, 429 U.S. 190 (1976); *Kahn v. Shevin*, 416 U.S. 351 (1974); *Frontiero v. Richardson*, 411 U.S. 677 (1973); *Reed v. Reed*, 404 U.S. 71 (1971).

[77] See, e.g., Christine A. Littleton, Reconstructing Sexual Equality, 75 Cal. L. Rev. 1279 (1987); Elizabeth H. Wolgast, Equality and the Rights of Women 14–15 (1980).

[78] Wolgast, supra note 77, at 14–15. "Equal treatment" and "special treatment" are, as Littleton explains, rather inapt terms, in that both strive for more equitable treatment of women. In that sense, the "special" treatment is designed to be equalizing at some level. Littleton, supra note 77, at 1286–87. Moreover, the equal/special treatment dichotomy fails to capture the nuances and complexity of the approaches to gender equity appearing in the literature. There has emerged a number of variations of these approaches, which are catalogued by Littleton. These variations include "accommodationist" approaches, which call for equal treatment except in certain defined circumstances. Littleton, supra note 77, at 1297. See, e.g., Sylvia A. Law, Rethinking Sex and the Constitution, 132 U. Pa. L. Rev. 955, 1007–13 (1984) (calling for equal treatment except with respect to reproduction, where biology demands differential treatment); Herma Hill Kay, Equality and Difference: The Case of Pregnancy, 1 Berkeley Women's L.J. 1, 27–37 (1985) (calling for equal treatment except for the duration of a woman's pregnancy). Littleton herself advocates an "acceptance" approach, which she categorizes as a type of special treatment approach. Under this approach, the "function of equality is to make gender differences, perceived or actual, costless relative to each other." Littleton, supra note 77, at 1297.

In practice, the differences among these approaches are relatively subtle. All, including the equal treatment approach, acknowledge the need to account for gender differences, but place varying emphasis on the presumption of formal, legal neutrality, and differ on the circumstances under which the law should recognize gender differences to foster more equitable treatment of women.

[79] Also, the value one attaches to leniency influences whether equal treatment or special treatment is appropriate. See supra notes 74–77.

[80] Williams, supra note 75, at 357 (second emphasis added).

[81] Antonin Scalia, The Rule of Law as a Law of Rules, 56 U. Chi. L. Rev. 1175, 1178 (1989).

[82] See, e.g., Joel Feinberg, The Expressive Function of Punishment, in Sentencing 23, 24–26 (Hyman Gross & Andrew von Hirsch eds., 1981).

[83] See von Hirsch, supra note 16, at 71–73.

[84] See, e.g., S. Rep. No. 225, supra note 18, at 46, reprinted in 1984 U.S.C.C.A.N. at 3229 ("Sentences . . . disproportionate to the seriousness of the offense create a disrespect for the law.").

[85] Cf. Elizabeth Rapaport, The Death Penalty and Gender Discrimination, 25 Law & Soc'y Rev. 367, 368 (1991).

[86] See, e.g., Samuel H. Pillsbury, The Meaning of Deserved Punishment: An Essay on Choice, Character and Responsibility, 67 Ind. L.J. 719, 740 (1992).

[87] 902 F.2d 133, 138–39 (1st Cir.), cert. denied, 498 U.S. 943 (1990).

[88] Id. at 139. ("We think the Commission was fully aware that some convicted felons are pregnant at the time of sentencing. If it had thought that pregnancy was a sentencing factor to be considered, the Commission would have said so.")

Commentators have criticized the court for construing the Commission's silence as an implicit rejection of pregnancy. See Raeder, supra note 73, at 947. Nevertheless, the First Circuit's conclusion about the Commission's views was accurate.

[89] Pozzy, 902 F.2d at 139.

90 Id. The court explained:

> It must also be noted that defendant became pregnant after she and her husband were arrested and charged with drug trafficking. We agree . . . "that to allow a departure downward for pregnancy could set a precedent that would have dangerous consequences in the future, sending an obvious message to all female defendants that pregnancy 'is a way out.'" (139)

While the use of pregnancy to thwart criminal justice aims might strike some as farfetched, experience suggests otherwise. In the course of its deliberations over the pregnancy issue, the Commission was presented with informal testimony that a well-established pattern of sentencing leniency for pregnant offenders in some states had prompted drug dealers to actively recruit poor, pregnant women as drug couriers. See also *United States v. Arize*, 792 F. Supp. 920, 921 (E.D.N.Y. 1992) (acknowledging risks in granting downward departures from the guidelines for pregnant drug couriers because "the general deterrence effect of punishment would be reduced if drug couriers were routinely sentenced leniently").

91 For example, the Supreme Court struggled with the issues of pregnancy and gender discrimination in the context of employment benefits in the landmark discrimination cases of *Geduldig v. Aiello*, 417 U.S. 484 (1974) and *General Electric Co. v. Gilbert*, 429 U.S. 125 (1976). These cases and others dealing with pregnancy stimulated extensive academic commentary, much of which was critical of the Court's analysis. See, e.g., Kay, supra note 78, at 30–31; Law, supra note 78; Littleton, supra note 77, at 1305–06, 1326–30; Williams, supra note 74.

92 450 U.S. 464 (1981). In *Michael M.*, the Court upheld California statutory rape legislation that imposed penalties on males convicted of having sexual intercourse with underage females, but left unpunished female intercourse with underage males. It noted that the differential treatment of males and females served the statute's purpose of preventing teenage pregnancy. Id. at 474 n.10.

93 See, e.g., *United States v. Maltese*, No. 90 CR 87–19, 1993 U.S. Dist. LEXIS 8403 (N.D. Ill. June 18, 1993) (downward departure under 5H1.4 based on the defendant's liver cancer); *United States v. Velasquez*, 762 F. Supp. 39 (E.D.N.Y. 1991) (downward departure based on defendant's cancer).

94 See *Arize*, 792 F. Supp. at 921 (recognizing potential reduction in general deterrence if lenient treatment of pregnant drug couriers became routine).

95 See U.S.S.G. 5H1.4 (physical condition not ordinarily relevant in decision to depart from guidelines).

96 Of course, this raises the question of whether incarceration unduly interferes with the bond between mother and child after birth, and whether such interference would justify sentence mitigation. This problem is, however, more appropriately characterized as one of parenthood or family ties, rather than pregnancy, and it is addressed in the next section.

97 Bureau of the Census, U.S. Dep't of Commerce, Marital Status and Living Arrangements xi (1992).

98 Raeder, supra note 73, at 951–53.

99 U.S.S.G. 5H1.6. By using the words "not ordinarily relevant," rather than "never relevant," the Commission left to the courts the discretion to determine, on a case-by-case basis, whether unusual family ties or circumstances would justify a sentence below that applicable to otherwise similarly situated offenders.

100 Some courts have interpreted this provision strictly, placing significant restrictions on the ability of district courts to depart downward on the basis of family circumstances. See, e.g., *United States v. Thomas*, 930 F.2d 526, 529 (7th Cir.), cert. denied, 112 S.Ct. 171 (1991) (holding that family circumstances are never relevant where probation or a fine is not a sentencing option authorized by the guidelines).

Others, while acknowledging the availability of departures under 5H1.6, have interpreted its scope fairly narrowly. See, e.g., *United States v. Shortt*, 919 F.2d 1325, 1328 (8th Cir.

1990) (impact of defendant's incarceration on family farm and wife's history of drug and alcohol abuse insufficiently extraordinary to warrant downward departure); *United States v. Goff*, 907 F.2d 1441, 1446 (4th Cir. 1990) (mother of 3 minor children ineligible for downward departure).

Finally, other courts have been more permissive in interpreting 5H1.6. See, e.g., *United States v. Alba*, 933 F.2d 1117 (2d Cir. 1991) (upholding downward departure for defendant with 2 young children and a disabled father); *United States v. Handy*, 752 F. Supp. 561 (E.D.N.Y. 1990) (downward departure for single mother of minor children).

101 See, e.g., *United States v. Johnson*, 908 F.2d 396, 398–99 (8th Cir. 1990) (single mother of infant not entitled to downward departure); *Goff*, 907 F.2d at 1446 (mother of minor children ineligible for downward departure); *United States v. Sailes*, 872 F.2d 735, 739 (6th Cir. 1989) (same). See generally Roger W. Haines, Jr. et al., Federal Sentencing Guidelines Handbook 522 (1992) ("But generally, the courts have held that it is improper to depart downward based on a defendant's responsibilities for the care of her children.").

102 S. Rep. No. 225, supra note 18, at 174–75, reprinted in 1984 U.S.C.C.A.N. at 3357–58.

103 See, e.g., Eleanor Bush, Considering the Defendant's Children at Sentencing, 2 Fed. Sent. Rptr. 194 (1990); Theresa Walker Karle & Thomas Sager, Are the Federal Sentencing Guidelines Meeting Congressional Goals?: An Empirical and Case Law Analysis, 40 Emory L.J. 393, 437–38 (1991); Charles J. Ogletree, Jr., The Death of Discretion? Reflections on the Federal Sentencing Guidelines, 101 Harv. L. Rev. 1938, 1953–54 (1988); Raeder, supra note 73, at 953; Stephen J. Schulhofer, Assessing the Federal Sentencing Process: The Problem is Uniformity, Not Disparity, 29 Am. Crim. L. Rev. 833, 858–61 (1992); Susan E. Ellingstad, Note, The Sentencing Guidelines: Downward Departures Based on a Defendant's Extraordinary Family Ties and Responsibilities, 76 Minn. L. Rev. 957 (1992).

104 Raeder, supra note 73, at 962.

105 *Johnson*, 908 F.2d at 398–99; *Goff*, 907 F.2d at 1446; *Sailes*, 872 F.2d at 739.

106 *United States v. Brand*, 907 F.2d 31, 33 (4th Cir.), cert. denied, 498 U.S. 1014 (1990).

107 Raeder, supra note 73, at 955–56.

108 See Marc Miller, Purposes at Sentencing, 66 S. Cal. L. Rev. 413, 458–63 (1992).

109 Even though the guidelines do not permit downward departures for single parents, they permit consideration of family ties in determining a sentence within the guidelines sentencing range. See, e.g., *United States v. Brady*, 895 F.2d 538, 543 (9th Cir. 1990).

110 28 U.S.C. 994(e) (1988).

111 See, e.g., Schulhofer, supra note 103, at 859–61.

112 See Stith & Koh, supra note 59, at 283–87.

113 See S. Rep. No. 225, supra note 18, at 175, reprinted in 1984 U.S.C.C.A.N. at 3357 ("It should be emphasized, however, that the Committee decided to describe [the factors in section 994(e)] as 'generally inappropriate,' rather than always inappropriate . . . in order to permit the Sentencing Commission to evaluate their relevance, and to give them application in particular situations found to warrant their consideration.").

114 See, e.g., Bush, supra note 103; Karle & Sager, supra note 103, at 437–38; Raeder, supra note 73, at 953; Ellingstad, supra note 103, at 980–81.

115 See, e.g., Adela Beckerman, Women in Prison: The Conflict Between Confinement and Parental Rights, 18 Soc. Just. 171, 180 (1991); Bush, supra note 103, at 194.

116 Bush, supra note 103, at 194.

117 See, e.g., Lionel Robbins, Interpersonal Comparisons of Utility: A Comment, 48 Econ. J. 635 (1938). See generally Kenneth J. Arrow, Social Choice and Individual Values 9 (2d ed. 1963).

118 See, e.g., von Hirsch, supra note 16, at 89–90.

> The assessment of severity. . . should be standardized: the focus should be on how unpleasant the punishment characteristically is. Such standardization is necessary as a limit on discretion. . . . It is also needed as a safeguard against class justice. Judges sometimes impose different penalties on persons convicted of similar crimes, in the hope of producing equivalent amounts of discomfort: the

middle-class person is put on probation and the ghetto youth jailed for the same infraction, on the theory that the former's sensitivities are greater.

[119] See, e.g., Edward M. Kennedy, Criminal Sentencing: A Game of Chance, 60 Judicature 208, 210 (1976) (characterizing sentencing system as "a national scandal").

[120] Raeder, supra note 73, at 953.

[121] Id.

[122] Id. at 959. Raeder emphasizes both the direct social costs of imprisonment of single parents (i.e., foster care) and the more speculative indirect social costs (future criminality). Id. at 953, 959. In short, she concludes that the "disadvantage to children who may have less supervision and care has societal costs which can outweigh any sentencing advantage." Id. at 961.

[123] Id. at 959 (footnotes omitted).

[124] See supra notes 10 to 15 and accompanying text.

[125] Cf. *United States v. Arize*, 792 F. Supp. 920, 921 (E.D.N.Y. 1992) (acknowledging reduction in deterrent effect if pregnant drug couriers were routinely sentenced leniently).

[126] See U.S.S.G. 5H1.1 (downward departure appropriate for elderly and infirm offenders "where a form of punishment such as home confinement might be equally efficient as and less costly than incarceration").

[127] See, e.g., *United States v. Sailes*, 872 F.2d 735, 739 (6th Cir. 1989) (upholding district court's refusal to depart downwardly under 5H1.6, noting the lower court's "apparent belief that the proper development of Mrs. Sailes' younger children might be facilitated by the children's removal from her direct influence for a time.").

[128] See Bureau of Justice Statistics, Department of Justice, Sourcebook of Criminal Justice Statistics—1992 459 (1993).

[129] Obviously, male defendants may be subject to coercion, but physical, psychological, and social differences between men and women make female crime more likely than male crime to be the result of coercion. See Raeder, supra note 73, at 973.

[130] U.S.S.G. 5K2.12.

[131] 956 F.2d 894 (9th Cir. 1992).

[132] Id. at 898 (citing *United States v. Cheape*, 889 F.2d 477, 480 (3d Cir. 1989)).

[133] Id. at 901–02.

[134] Id. at 902.

[135] Id. at 898.

[136] See, e.g., *United States v. Mickens*, 977 F.2d 69, 72–73 (2d Cir. 1992).

[137] 976 F.2d 1216, 1217–18 (9th Cir. 1992).

[138] See, e.g., Angela Browne, When Battered Women Kill (1987).

[139] In fiscal year 1992, these offenses accounted for just 1.2% of cases sentenced under the federal guidelines. See U.S. Sentencing Comm'n, supra note 3, Table 13.

[140] 956 F.2d 857 (8th Cir. 1992).

[141] 891 F.2d 650 (8th Cir. 1992).

[142] Id. at 654.

[143] Id.

[144] 963 F.2d 1523, 1528 (D.C. Cir. 1992).

[145] See also *United States v. Frazier*, 979 F.2d 1227, 1230 (7th Cir. 1992); *United States v. Desormeaux*, 952 F.2d 182, 185 (8th Cir. 1991); *United States v. Vela*, 927 F.2d 197, 199 (5th Cir. 1991), cert. denied, 112 S. Ct. 214 (1991).

[146] Cf., supra notes 10–15 and accompanying text.

[147] Raeder, supra note 73, at 977.

[148] Id. at 977–78.

[149] The guidelines permit adjustment of up to eight offense levels—four up and four down—to reflect the offender's role in the offense. See U.S.S.G. 3B1.1 (Aggravating Role), 3B1.2 (Mitigating Role). It could be argued, however, that the four-level mitigating role adjustment is insufficient to reflect the culpability of a female who played a minimal role in the offense and whose participation in the criminal scheme may have resulted from her

romantic involvement with a more culpable co-conspirator. See, e.g., Raeder, supra note 73, at 977–78.

150 No. CR-88–0720–AAH-1 (C.D. Cal. 1989), rev'd on other grounds, 925 F.2d 1472 (9th Cir. 1991).

151 See Miss America Bandit Crowned With Light Sentence, Oregonian May 11, 1989, at C7.

152 Id.

153 Note how the judge emphasized the defendant's "good" family background. Query whether a poor, minority defendant would have received the same downward departure as this attractive, former cheerleader. See supra notes 39–40 and accompanying text.

154 See U.S.S.G. 3B1.2.

155 735 F. Supp. 928 (D. Minn. 1990).

156 See U.S.S.G. 3B1.2.

157 On the other hand, plea-related manipulation of guidelines factors, such as role, sometimes results in unwarranted sentence mitigation. See infra notes 165–86 and accompanying text.

158 See, e.g., *United States v. Pofahl*, 990 F.2d 1456, 1484–85 (5th Cir. 1993), cert. denied, 114 S. Ct. 266 (1993) (defendant acted as a drug courier on several occasions); *United States v. Tabares*, 951 F.2d 405, 410 (1st Cir. 1991) (continued presence of drugs and money in apartment defendant shared with boyfriend prevented finding of minimal role). See U.S.S.G. 3B1.2, comment. (n.2) (stating that minimal role adjustment be used infrequently, for example, where the defendant was a courier or offloader involved in a single shipment or transaction).

159 See infra notes 160–64 and accompanying text.

160 Of course, this is true of some male offenders as well. However, the impact arguably is greater on female offenders, due to their typically lesser roles. See supra notes 1–4.

161 See Schulhofer, supra note 103, at 853–54. For example, one convicted of distributing five kilos of cocaine is subject to a mandatory minimum sentence of 10 years (120 months). The guidelines build on the mandatory minimum by fixing the distribution of five kilos of cocaine at offense level 32 (121–51 months). Similarly, the guidelines account for the five year (60 month) mandatory minimum associated with trafficking in 500g or more of cocaine by pegging the offense level for offenses involving 500–2000g of cocaine at offense level 26 (63–78 months). Intermediate drug amounts result in intermediate sentences—thus, an offense involving between 2 and 3.5 kg of cocaine result in an offense level 28 (78–97 months). See U.S.S.G. 2D1.1 (drug quantity table), 5A (sentencing table).

162 The Anti-Drug Abuse Act of 1988, Pub. L. No. 100–690, 102 Stat. 4181 (1988), extended the mandatory minimums to conspiracies to close a major disparity-producing loophole in the statutory scheme; the ability of defendants and prosecutors to avoid mandatory minimum sentences by plea bargaining to conspiracy charges. Unfortunately, the 1988 provisions dramatically increased the sentencing exposure of minor players in drug trafficking conspiracies, by holding all participants in a drug conspiracy liable for the total quantity of drugs involved in the conspiracy. See, e.g., *United States v. Rivera*, 971 F.2d 876, 892 (2d Cir. 1992) (total quantity of conspiracy's drug sales properly attributed to defendants working at only one sales location). As a result, those with peripheral roles in drug operations became subject to the same mandatory minimum penalties that Congress had earlier reserved for leaders or direct participants in trafficking.

163 See Proposed Amendment 8 (on file with authors).

164 See infra part III.

165 For example, fiscal year 1992 data reveal that 2127 females were sentenced for drug offenses, 1,863 of these for drug trafficking. See 1992 Annual Report, supra note 3, Table 13. Over 1,900 females were sentenced for drug offenses in fiscal year 1991. See U.S. Sentencing Comm'n, Annual Report, Table 17 (1991). In both 1991 and 1992, fraud accounted for the next largest number of female sentences, 958 and 1,176, respectively. See 1992 Annual Report, supra note 3; 1991 Annual Report, supra.

166 1991 Annual Report, supra note 165, Table 17; 1992 Annual Report, supra note 3, Table 13.

167 U.S.S.G. 5K1.1.

168 U.S.S.G. 5K2.0.

169 28 U.S.C. 994(n) (1988) provides:

> The Commission shall assure that the guidelines reflect the general appropriateness of imposing a lower sentence than would otherwise be imposed, including a sentence that is lower than that established by statute as a minimum sentence, to take into account a defendant's substantial assistance in the investigation or prosecution of another person who has committed an offense.

170 See 18 U.S.C. 3553(e) (1988), which provides:

> Upon motion of the Government, the court shall have the authority to impose a sentence below a level established by statute as minimum sentence so as to reflect a defendant's substantial assistance in the investigation or prosecution of another person who has committed an offense. Such sentence shall be imposed in accordance with the guidelines and policy statements issued by the Sentencing Commission . . . .

171 *Wade v. United States*, 112 S. Ct. 1840, 1843 (1992).

172 See *United States v. Damer*, 910 F.2d 1239, 1241 (5th Cir. 1990), cert. denied, 498 U.S. 991 (1990).

173 See U.S. Sentencing Comm'n. 1992 Data File, MONFY92.

174 In fiscal year 1991, 30.5% of female drug offenders received downward departures, compared to 24.6% of males. See U.S. Sentencing Comm'n 1991 Data File MONFY91.

175 See, e.g., Raeder, supra note 73, at 981–82.

176 See Ilene H. Nagel & Stephen J. Schulhofer, A Tale of Three Cities: An Empirical Study of Charging and Bargaining Practices Under the Federal Sentencing Guidelines, 66 S. Cal. L. Rev. 501 (1992); Stephen J. Schulhofer & Ilene H. Nagel, Negotiated Pleas Under the Federal Sentencing Guidelines: The First Fifteen Months, 27 Am. Crim. L. Rev. 231 (1989).

177 See Nagel & Schulhofer, supra note 176, at 550.

178 Female drug offenders appear to benefit from prosecutorial and judicial discretion in the form of charge bargaining as well. See Raeder, supra note 73, at 980 ("statistics reveal the likelihood of significant charge bargaining by female drug offenders"). Drug trafficking offenses under 21 U.S.C. 841 and 846, which carry substantial mandatory minimum sentences, are particularly prone to charge bargaining. Defendants can reduce their statutory exposure significantly by pleading to use of a communication facility in committing a drug offense, 21 U.S.C. 843(b) (1988) (48 month maximum); simple possession, 21 U.S.C. 844 (1988) (12 month maximum); or misprision of a felony, 18 U.S.C. 4 (1988) (36 month maximum).

Female drug offenders are more likely than male offenders to successfully plead to these lesser offenses. In fiscal year 1991, females accounted for 12.6% of offenders sentenced for substantive drug trafficking offenses, but 28.6% of those guilty of a communications facility offense, 18% of those guilty of simple possession, and 30.6% of those guilty of misprision offenses involving drugs. The 1992 data reveal a similar pattern. Females accounted for 11.9% of trafficking sentences in that year. But females received 25.5% of communications facility sentences, 25.1% of simple possession sentences, and 31.2% of drug-related misprision sentences. See Data File, supra notes 173–74.

179 See 18 U.S.C. 3553(b) (1988).

180 See 18 U.S.C. 3742 (1988).

181 See, e.g., *United States v. Morales*, 898 F.2d 99, 100 (9th Cir. 1990).

182 See 28 U.S.C. 994(b)(2) (1988). For example, the guidelines sentencing range of an offender with an offense level of 10 and a criminal history category of I is 6–12 months, a difference of 6 months; an offender whose offense level is 27 and whose criminal history category is IV, has a guidelines sentencing range of 100–125 months, a range of 25%.

183 Female drug offenders also are twice as likely as males to receive mitigating adjustments for playing a minimal or minor role in the offense. See, Data File, supra notes 173–74.

[184] See Nagel & Schulhofer, supra note 176.

[185] The crime of embezzlement, unlike drug trafficking or racketeering offenses, typically does not involve an extensive organization, but tends to be committed by individual employees with easy access to the embezzled funds. Thus, the opportunity for cooperation in the investigation of others is comparatively rare.

[186] The rates of substantial assistance departure for men and women respectively were 4.4% and 3.4% in 1992, 3.4% and 2.4% in 1991. It is important to emphasize, however, that the absolute numbers of such departures were quite small—17 men and 15 women in 1992, 12 men and 10 women in 1991. See Data File, supra notes 173–74.

9

The War on Drugs and the Incarceration of Mothers

Stephanie Bush-Baskette

Introduction

With the passage of the Anti-Drug Abuse Acts of 1986 and 1988, the "War on Drugs," first declared in 1972 by President Nixon and then *re*-declared 10 years later by President Reagan, began in earnest. In the years since the U.S. has seen unprecedented increases in incarceration rates and "exponential growth" in prison populations (Blumstein, 1998). The costs of the war, both social (Tonry, 1995) and fiscal (Horowitz, 1996), have been great, and the harms done to families and communities affected by increasing incarceration rates are well-documented (Lowenstein, 1986; Fishman, 1990; Carlson and Cervera, 1991; Gabel, 1992; Lynch and Sabol, 1992; King, 1993; Tonry, 1995; Rose and Clear, 1998). While the costs and harms associated with the increased incarceration of young black males remain important and salient issues for policy-makers to consider, those associated with the increased incarceration of young women may have even greater long-term effects and dire consequences.

It may be argued that social costs accrue with the imprisonment of any person. These costs include the building and maintenance of prisons and result in a diversion of more public funds from other important needs, such as health, education, and welfare, to meet these costs. Families and communities are impacted when the individuals incarcerated for felony offenses lose their right to vote, are removed from their families and communities, and

Reprinted with permission of the FSU School of Criminology and Criminal Justice from *Journal of Drug Issues* vol. 30, no. 4, pp. 919–928, 2000.

experience difficulties in securing legitimate and worthwhile employment upon their release from prison. One factor that is perhaps unique to women, however, is the effect of their incarceration on their children. More than 70% of incarcerated women have children under the age of 18, and most were responsible for their children at the time of their incarceration (Barry, 1985). In comparison, while 65% of incarcerated men *have* children, fewer than 50% of them were the primary caregivers of their children prior to imprisonment (Barry). The costs of incarcerating a woman who has children extend beyond the disruption to her life and the expenditure of public funds required to imprison her. These include the effect her incarceration has on her children and on those people who become the guardians, as well as the financial costs related to the supervision of her children while she is incarcerated.

This article has two purposes: The first is to present an overview of the historical and contemporary involvement of women with drugs and drug abuse, and the effects of the current War on Drugs on the incarceration of women and their children. A second concern is to call attention to the need to understand the social costs involved in imprisoning mothers for drug offenses and to urge researchers and policy makers to consider these when evaluating the efficacy of drug-war policies and initiatives.

Women and Drugs

Women in the United States have long been major consumers of both legal and illegal drugs. When the Harrison Act was passed in 1914, approximately one [million] of the 10 million people then living in the U.S. were addicted to drugs. Most of them were housewives who were addicted to opiates that could be legally purchased in over-the-counter medicinal remedies (Horowitz, 1993). Throughout the twentieth century, drugs such as sedatives and tranquilizers have been prescribed for women at a much greater rate than for their male counterparts. Women also outnumber men in emergency room treatment for overdoses of prescription drugs (Inciardi, Lockwood, & Pottieger, 1993). This gender differential has also been observed among recipients of Medicaid. Inciardi, Lockwood, and Pottieger report that although females use illegal drugs at much lower rates than males, their use is much greater than was previously assumed.

Despite the fact that drug use is common among women, until recently, research focused on male use. Some researchers have gone so far as to treat drug abuse as a male problem because they believed the sociocultural factors leading men to abuse narcotics actually protected females from doing so. This position prevailed for nearly 50 years. During the 1970s however, the women's movement and the "American drug crisis" of the previous decade had drawn attention to the use of drugs by females (Horowitz, 1993). Since then, processes and patterns common to female users have been uncovered, regularities that cut across class and substance of choice categories. Researchers have discovered that suburban, middle-class women with drinking problems and their inner-city counterparts who use heroin or crack are likely to experience a similar process at the onset of their drug use (Inciardi et al., 1993). Both groups of women articulate similar motives for taking drugs and share many of the same experiences [as] they progress from experimentation to addiction. Depression often precedes the use of drugs by women, although various drug types may be used to deal with the depression. Some women use drugs as a means of self-medication to cope with their own devaluation and low self-esteem. Personal traumas, such as rape, incest, and other sexual abuse, as well as economic pressures, may also contribute to drug abuse by women. The combination of being devalued because she is a woman, a minority, and poor is also posited as an underlying cause for drug abuse by some women (Inciardi, et al.).

Drug use often leads to the psychological, social, and cultural experience of stigmatization, a negative influence that can exacerbate drug use. Nearly any known drug use, and especially that of banned substances, violates the gender expectations established for women in society. Revelations of use can lead to social isolation, cultural denigration, and feelings within the woman that help to perpetuate the problematic behavior. Researchers have found that women are more likely than men to continue their use of drugs after initial experimentation as a means of coping with situational factors, life events, or general psychological distress (Inciardi et al., 1993).

Poor women who use illicit drugs on the street experience additional stigmatization. They do not have the protective societal buffer enjoyed by those who are insulated by family, friends, and a privileged economic status. Women using on the streets suffer criticism, denigration, and a loss of healthful relationships (Inciardi et al., 1993; Maher, 1997). These women are also the most likely to become prisoners of the "War on Drugs" because of their high visibility (Horowitz, 1993).

Much research has been directed at drug sales and the methods of users and dealers. Once again, drug dealing is most commonly seen as a male activity. However, with the advent of crack cocaine, women have become more involved in the drug's distribution. They also often buy the firearms or rent the residences that will be used to support the crack cocaine business. In Miami alone, 12% of young crack dealers are females (USSC, 1995, pp. 84–85).

The tactics most often employed in the War on Drugs focus on street-level drugs, such as cocaine, crack, and heroin, and street-level offenses, such as possession and trafficking. Contemporary policies require the same punishments for persons involved in a conspiracy to commit a crime as for the perpetrator of the substantive crime. The combined effects of these initiatives is that women who use these drugs in highly policed or visible places (i.e., urban markets) and/or who are associated with males involved in the drug market comprise the greatest portion of women convicted of and incarcerated for criminal offenses (Van Wormer & Bartollas, 2000).

Women, Imprisonment, and the War on Drugs

While drug abuse may have been common among women prior to the War on Drugs, incarceration for offenses related to the use of drugs was not. The War on Drugs fosters a policy shift that contributed greatly to the increase in the imprisonment of women in the United States (Feinman, 1994). The drug policies reflected in the Acts of 1986 and 1988 were directly responsible for the growing incarceration of female drug offenders, generally, and especially for low-level drug offenses (Bush-Baskette, 2000).

The number of women incarcerated in state prisons for drug offenses increased by 433% between 1986 and 1991, compared to an increase of 283% for men during the same period (Bloom, Lee, & Owen, 1995). In 1991, 1 of every 3 women confined to prison facilities in the U.S. in 1991 had been incarcerated for a drug offense; this figure was only l in 10 in 1979. Drug offenses represented 55% of the national increase in women prisoners from 1986 to 1991 (BJS, 1994). Accompanying these increases was a dramatic change in the composition of female prison populations. In the federal system, 1981 figures indicate that 7.1% of incarcerated females were sentenced for violent offenses, 28.2% for property offenses, and 26.1% for drug offenses. By 1991, as a result of the War on Drugs effort, those percentages had shifted to 2.0% for violent offenses, 6.3% for property offenses, and 63.9% for drug offenses (Kline, 1992). Seven years later, in 1998, the percentage of incarcerated females imprisoned in federal prisons for violent and property offenses had increased to 7% and 12%, respectively, and to 72% for drug offenses (BJS, 1999(c)).

Two initiatives stand out as possible explanations for the differential impact of the War on Drugs on the incarceration of women and men. The first included the provisions written into the Anti-Drug Abuse Acts for penalties specifically linked to small amounts of drugs and sanctions for conspiracy equivalent to those for the actual commission of the substantive crime. These provisions effectively shifted the focus of drug control efforts from trafficking activities by major dealers and treatment for users to the actions of street-level dealers, particularly those involved in crack cocaine, and to the prosecution of users. The second concerned the return to mandatory sentencing for drug law violations, also provided for in the Anti-Drug Abuse Acts of 1986 and 1988. Passage of the 1986 Act provided mandatory minimum sentences for drug trafficking offenses that were gauged to the amount of drugs involved (21 USC § 841 (B)(1)(A)). The Omnibus Anti-Drug Abuse Act of 1988 (21 USC § 844 as amended) singled out crack from other forms of cocaine, requiring a term of five years' imprisonment for the simple possession of an amount greater than five grams of crack cocaine and doubled the mandatory penalties for participating in a continuing drug enterprise from 10 to 20 years (21 USC § 848(a)).

These mandatory minimum sentencing standards have had a major impact on the sentencing of women (Feinman, 1994; Chesney-Lind,

1995). The actual role the offender plays in the crime can no longer be considered in the determination of the sentence, except for sentence enhancement. Furthermore, family situations, such as being the sole caretaker of minor children, can no longer be considered for sentencing purposes. These changes have resulted in increasing numbers of women being placed in state and federal prisons, which in turn lead to increasing numbers of dependent children being left to the care of relatives, guardians, and the state.

Having a Mother in Prison

In most instances, the incarceration of a woman affects many other people. More than 70% of incarcerated women have children under the age of 18 (Barry, 1985), and the majority of these mothers were the primary caretakers of their minor children prior to their imprisonment. The rate of primary caretaking for female inmates greatly exceeds that for male inmates (Snell, 1991). Consequently, whenever women are locked up, it is very likely that children will also be displaced (Phillips & Harm, 2000).

For example, taxpayers are forced to bear the added costs of foster care (Van Wormer & Bartollas, 2000). Perhaps more importantly, however, locking up these women places emotional, psychological, and social burdens on both the children left behind and on those entrusted with their care. Given that there are only a small number of prisons acceptable for female offenders and the fact that they are often located in remote areas, minor children are seldom able to visit their mothers while they are incarcerated. In fact, only 9% of the women in state prisons are visited by their minor children (Van Wormer & Bartollas).

We know too that the emotional toll on children whose mothers are incarcerated may be severe. Bloom and Steinhart (1993) report that when mothers and children are separated due to imprisonment, the children often grieve as if the parent has died. These children experience fear, anxiety, grief, and sadness and, if they are not helped, may display verbal or physical aggression, withdrawal, hyper vigilance, or sexualized behavior (Johnston, 1996). The emotional strain affects the mothers while they are in prison. Interaction between mother and child is important for the psychological and emotional well being of both parties, and facilitating these contacts may have implications for the success of the mother after her release (Hairston, 1995).

The trauma of separation from a mother due to her imprisonment also has long-term effects on the life chances of these children. Children of incarcerated women have a greater chance of being involved in the juvenile justice system (Gaouette, 1997; Phillips & Harm, 2000), and children of inmates of either sex are five times more likely than other children to be incarcerated as adults (Van Wormer & Bartollas, 2000). Substance abuse and gang membership are common reactive behaviors of children whose mothers are imprisoned (Johnston, 1996). These deleterious effects are not byproducts of the women's behavior towards their children, as the rate of abusive behavior among incarcerated mothers is no more than it is for other women. Consequently, it is the severe trauma experienced by these children of living in impoverished conditions and experiencing the arrest and incarceration of their mothers that makes it difficult for them to cope (Johnston, 1994).

It seems clear that the imprisonment of mothers has immediate as well as long-term effects that are very destructive, both to the women involved and to their children. These harms must be considered and investigated whenever social policies are being developed that may lead to the incarceration of large numbers of women. Much of the legislation associated with the War on Drugs has had these "unintentional" effects.

Summary and Implications for Research and Policy

At the end of 1999, the number of women held in state or federal prisons had risen to 90,668, an incarceration rate of almost 60 per 100,000 or 1 out of every 1,695 U.S. females (BJS, 2000). More than 10% (9,913) of the female prison population had been sentenced to federal institutions, and most women incarcerated in the federal system were there for drug offenses. The majority of these women had little or no prior criminal record and were directly involved in dealing or possessing only a relatively small amount of drugs. More than 80% were sentenced under mandatory minimum sentencing laws provided by the Anti-Drug Abuse Acts of 1986 and 1988 (Bush-Baskette, 2000). Approximately 70% of these women were mothers of one or more children under the age of 18.

Because crime and incarceration are primarily male phenomena, research to date has focused mainly on the effects of incarcerating males on their families and communities (Lowenstein, 1986; Fishman, 1990; Carlson & Cervera, 1992; King, 1993; see Gabel, 1992, for the exception). Given the greater rate of increase in the incarceration of women than men in recent years (BJS, 1999), driven almost exclusively by the War on Drugs, this focus should be widened to include the effects of incarcerating females, with special attention to the displacement of their dependent children. The effect of the mother's incarceration on herself and, particularly, on her children and their caretakers is necessary information for evaluating and understanding the impact of crime policies that mandate the imprisonment of any person convicted of a drug offense, regardless of their parental status. It is only by building upon our knowledge of the effects of the drug policies on individuals, families, and communities that the efficacy of the War on Drugs can be determined.

References

Barry, Ellen

1985 Children of prisoners: Punishing the innocent. *Youth Law News.* March/April.

Belenko, Steven R.

1993 *Crack and the evolution of anti-drug policy.* Westport, CT: Greenwood Press.

Bloom, Barbara, Lee, Cheoleon, & Owen, Barbara

1995 *Offense patterns among women prisoners: A preliminary analysis.* Paper presented at the American Society of Criminology Annual Meeting, November 1995, Boston, MA.

Bloom, Barbara, & Steinhart, Dorothy

1993 *Why punish the children? A reappraisal of the children of incarcerated mothers in America.* San Francisco, CA: NCCD.

Blumstein, Alfred

1998 U.S. criminal justice conundrum: Rising prison populations and stable crime rates. *Crime and Delinquency, 44,* 127–135.

Bureau of Justice Statistics

2000 *Prisoners in 1999.* Washington, DC: USGPO.

1999(a) *Correctional populations in the United States, 1996.* Washington, DC: USGPO.

1999(b) *Compendium of Federal justice statistics, 1996.* Washington, DC: USGPO.

1999(c) *Prisoners in 1998.* Washington, DC: USGPO.

1996 *Federal criminal case processing, 1982–1993.* Washington, DC: USGPO.

1995 *Correctional populations in the United States, 1993.* Washington, DC: USGPO.

1994 *Women in prison.* Washington, DC: USGPO.

Bush-Baskette, Stephanie

1999 *The war on drugs and the Black female: Testing the impact of the sentencing policies for crack cocaine on Black females in the federal system.* Unpublished doctoral dissertation, Rutgers University, Newark, NJ.

Carlson, Bonnie, & Cervera, Neil

1992 *Inmates and their wives.* Westport, CT: Greenwood Press.

Chesney-Lind, Meda

1995 Rethinking women's imprisonment: A critical examination of trends in female incarceration. In Barbara Raffel Price & Natalie J. Skoloff (Eds.), *The criminal justice system and women.* New York: McGraw-Hill.

Feinman, Clarice

1994 *Women in the criminal justice system.* Westport, CT: Praeger.

Fishman, Laura

1990 *Women at the wall.* Albany, NY: SUNY Press.

Gabel, Stewart

1991 Children of incarcerated and criminal parents: Adjustment, behavior and prognosis. *Bulletin of American Academic Psychiatry Law, 20,* 33–45.

Gaouette, N.

1997 Prisons grapple with rapid influx of women—and mothers. *Christian Science Monitor,* May 19, 1997: 1 ff.

Hairston, C.

1995 Family views in correctional programs. In *Encyclopedia of Social Work.* Washington, DC: NASW Press.

Horowitz, Craig

1996 The no-win war. *New York Magazine,* February 5, 1996, 22–33.

Hurling, Tracy

1996 Prisoners of war: Woman drug couriers in the United States. In Martin D. Schwartz & Dragan Milovanovic (Eds.), *Drug couriers: A new perspective.* London: Quartet Books Unlimited.

Inciardi, James A., Lockwood, Dorothy, & Pottieger, Anne E.

1993 *Women and crack-cocaine.* New York: Macmillan Publishing.

Jensen, Eric, & Gerber, Jurg

1998 The social construction of drug problems: An historical overview. In Eric L. Jensen & Jurg Gerber (Eds.), *The new war on drugs: Symbolic politics and criminal justice policy.* Cincinnati, OH: ACJS/Anderson.

Johnston, D.

1996 Interventions. In Gabel, K. & Johnston, E. (Eds.), *Children of incarcerated parents.* New York: Free Press.

1994 What we know about children of offenders. *Family and Corrections Network, Issue 3.* Palmyra, VA: Family & Corrections Network.

King, Anthony E. O.

1992 The impact of incarceration on African American families: Implications for practice. *Journal of Contemporary Human Service, 73,* 145–153.

Kline, Sue

1993 A profile of female offenders in state and federal prisons. *Female offenders: Meeting needs of a neglected population.* Baltimore, MD: United Book Press.

Lowenstein, Ariela

1986 Temporary single parenthood—The case of prisoner's families. *Family Relations, 35,* 79–85.

Lynch, James P., & William J. Sabol

1992 *Macro-social changes and their implications for prison reform: The underclass and the composition of prison populations.* Paper presented at the American Society of Criminology, New Orleans, November 5.

Maher, Lisa

1997 *Sexed work.* Oxford: Clarendon Press.

Mann, Cora Mae Richey

1995 Women of color and the criminal justice system. In Barbara Raffel Price & Natalie J. Skoloff (Eds.), *The criminal justice system and women.* New York: McGraw-Hill.

Maxfield, Linda Drazga, & Kramer, John H.

1998 *Substantial assistance: An empirical yardstick gauging equity in current federal policy and practice.* Washington, DC: USSC.

McCoy, Candace

1993 *Politics and plea bargaining.* Philadelphia: University of Pennsylvania Press.

National Council on Crime and Delinquency

1991 *National drug statement.* Hackensack, NJ: NCCD.

Phillips, Susan, & Harm, Nancy

2000 *Responding to the needs of children of incarcerated mothers.* National Association for Family Based Services.

Rafter, Nicole Hahn

1993 Equality or difference? *Female offenders: Meeting needs of a neglected population.* Baltimore, MD: United Book Press.

Rasmussen, David W., & Benson, Bruce L.
1994 *The economic anatomy of a drug war.* Lanham, MD: Rowman and Littlefield Publishers, Inc.
Rose, Dina R., & Clear, Todd R.
1998 Incarceration, social capital, and crime: Implications for social disorganization theory. *Criminology, 36,* 441–450.
Snell, Tracey
1994 *Women in prison: Survey of state prison inmates, 1991.* Washington, DC: BJS.
Tonry, Michael
1995 *Malign neglect: Race, crime, and punishment in America.* New York: Oxford University Press.
United States Sentencing Commission
1995 *Special report to the Congress: Cocaine and federal sentencing policy.* Washington, DC: US Government Printing Office.
1991 *Special report to the Congress: Mandatory minimum penalties in the federal criminal justice system.* Washington, DC: US Government Printing Office.
United States Department of Justice
1996 *Federal criminal case processing, 1982–1993.* Washington, DC: GPO.
Van Wormer, Katherine Stuart, & Bartollas, Clemens
2000 *Women and the criminal justice system.* Boston, MA: Allyn and Bacon.

Statutes

18 USC 924(1)
18 USC 3561 (b) (1)
21 USC 13 (I) (D) 841
21 USC 13 (I) (D) 844
21 USC 13 (I) (D) 846
21 USC 13 (I) (D) 848
21 USC 13 (I) (D) 859
21 USC 13 (I) (D) 860
21 USC 13 (I) (D) 861

10

The Wrong Race, Committing Crime, Doing Drugs, and Maladjusted for Motherhood
The Nation's Fury over "Crack Babies"

Enid Logan

Introduction

During the 1990s, women who use illicit drugs during pregnancy became the subject of intense public attention and social stigmatization. They are regarded as incapable of responsible decision-making, morally deviant, and increasingly, unfit for motherhood. In recent years, the civil courts have terminated the parental rights of thousands of women whose infants tested positive for drug exposure at birth (Beckett, 1995). Women have also faced criminal prosecution for prenatal drug use, under statutes including criminal child abuse, neglect, manslaughter, and delivering substances to a minor. For the most part, the women targeted by the courts and the media have been black, poor, and addicted to crack cocaine (Roberts, 1991; Krauss, 1991; Beckett, 1995; Neuspiel et al., 1994; Greene, 1991).

I argue here that the phenomenon of the "crack-baby" is not produced simply by a tragic interaction between illicit substances and a growing fetus. The "crack-baby," rather, has resulted from a broader conjunction of practices and ideologies associated with race, gender, and class oppression, including the war on drugs and the discourse of fetal rights. In the late 1980s and early 1990s, the image of trembling, helpless infants irrevocably damaged by their mothers' irresponsible actions became a potent symbol of all that was wrong with the poor, the black, and the new mothers in the post-women's movement, post-civil rights era. Crack-babies provided society with a powerful iconography of multiple social deviance (nonmarital sexuality, criminality, drug addiction, aberrant maternal behavior), perpetrated upon the most innocent, by the least innocent: women who are in fact "shameless" and "scandalous" (Irwin, 1995).

Below I will discuss the issue of prenatal substance abuse, focusing on women addicted to crack and their children. As I will illustrate, the social, legal, and political trends that comprise the nation's response to this problem have been largely inspired by racial, gendered, and socioeconomic imperatives, rather than by the blind hand of justice.

The Media and the Crack-Baby in the Popular Imagination

In the 1980s, a crack cocaine epidemic exploded in the United States, sweeping through low-income black communities with a vengeance (Roberts, 1991). Perceiving a dramatic rise in the number of boarder babies and children born to women abusing drugs, the media began to present the public with reports on a drug like no other, crack, and on the appearance of a "different" kind of child—the crack-baby. The narrative of the crack-baby interwove specific messages about crack, pregnant addicts, and crack-exposed children. Crack cocaine, journalists wrote, was a drug like no other previously on the streets. Crack was more potent, more addictive, and more likely to lead its users to acts of violence, crime, and desperation.

Among its most desperate and debased users were pregnant women. One of the most harmful effects of crack was said to be that it literally destroyed the maternal instinct in the women who used it (Irwin, 1995; Hopkins, 1990; Appel, 1992; Elshtain, 1990; Debettencourt, 1990). Utterly irresponsible and incompetent, addicted mothers were seen as "inhumane threats to the social order" who willingly tortured their helpless fetuses (Irwin, 1995: 635). One California doctor was quoted as saying, "with every hit the mother plays Russian roulette with the baby's brain" (Hopkins, 1990: 108). Only concerned with feeding their addictions, mothers on crack were said to be incapable of taking care of their children or even caring about the irreparable harm that smoking crack would do to their unborn fetuses. A *Rolling Stone* article reported that the crack epidemic had left some social service workers "nostalgic" for the heroin mothers who "could buy groceries occasionally and give the kid a bath." "Crack," on the other hand, "leaves nothing to chance. It makes babies that only a mother could love, and wipes out that love as well" (Ibid.: 71).

The press often spoke of the frustration or anger that many health care workers felt toward pregnant addicts. *The Economist*, for example reported that:

> Heartbreaking as it is for the doctors and nurses who care for the babies [to see them suffer] . . . they find it even more distressing to return the babies to mothers for whom drugs remain the dominant feature of life. (*Economist*, April 1, 1989: 28)

In a 1990 *People* magazine interview, Katherine Jorgensen, head nurse in the neonatal intensive care unit at Boston City Hospital, explained that the hardest part of her job "is when new mothers come to look in on their children." Seeing women come to visit their babies "with their pimps" or "while they are high," she said, made her "want to slug them" (Plummer and Brown, 1990: 85).

In the eyes of the media, the inhumane actions of addicted mothers often produced children who were almost beyond the pale of humanity. Crack-exposed babies were "supposedly doomed to a life of suboptimal intelligence, uncontrollable behavior, and criminal tendencies" (Neuspiel et al., 1994: 47). According to *People*, some crack-babies "shake so badly they rub their limbs raw" (Plummer and Brown, 1990: 85). In *Rolling Stone* we read, "During a crying jag their rigid little arms flap about, which makes them even more frantic: They seem to believe their arms belong to someone else, a vicious someone who relentlessly flogs them" (Hopkins, 1990: 71). Pictures of children who tested positive for exposure to drugs at birth most often showed them crying, "shrieking like cats" or staring, bug eyed into space for hours. According to the logic of the crack-baby narrative, the variety of physical and emotional problems faced by these children could be attributed to a single cause: prenatal exposure to crack cocaine (Greider, 1995; Griffith, 1992).

Children exposed to crack in the womb, it was reported, were likely to suffer from any number of serious medical conditions. Among the most frequently cited were cerebral hemorrhaging and intercranial lesions, prematurity, birth defects, genitourinary and cardiac abnormalities, prenatal strokes, heart attacks or death, fine motor disorders, low birth weight, and neonatal growth retardation (Hopkins, 1990; Sexton, 1993; Hoffman, 1990; Plummer and Brown, 1990; Langone, 1988; Zitella, 1996). Fetal exposure to cocaine was also said to greatly increase the risk of postnatal neurological complications, such as extreme sensitivity to external stimuli, unpredictable mood swings, high-pitched "cat-like" crying, tremulousness, and difficulty interacting with others (Appel, 1992; Sexton, 1993; Hopkins, 1990; *Economist*, April 1, 1989). Even in the mildest cases, crack-exposed children would likely suffer grave emotional and cognitive abnormalities.

Crack babies, we read, were generally unable to concentrate, prone toward violence and destructive behavior, and were averse to light, touch, and affection (Zitella, 1996; Hopkins, 1990).

From the inner cities, a new breed of child was being produced, one that was loveless, tortured, and demented. In the words of one pediatric researcher, "You can't tell what makes these children happy or sad. *They are like automatons*" (Hopkins, 1990: 72; emphasis added). Even in the "best case scenario" crack-exposed children were somehow fundamentally "different" from the rest of us—somehow less human. As Doctor Judy Howard told *Newsweek*, "in crack-babies the part of the brain that makes us a human being, capable of discussion or reflection has been wiped out" (Greider, 1995: 54). Similarly, another piece asserted that crack cocaine "robbed [exposed] children of 'the central core of what it is to be human'" (Irwin, 1995: 633).

Worst of all, the damage done to these children by their crack-smoking mothers was believed to be permanent and irreparable. In the chilling words of one journalist, "crack damages fetuses like no other drug . . . [and] the damage the drug causes . . . doesn't go away" (Hopkins, 1990: 68). Though the press was generally sympathetic to the plight of crack-exposed children, it typically portrayed them as damaged goods, largely beyond hope or salvation, and damned by the actions of their irresponsible mothers. One article read "for [some] people this is truly a lost generation, and neither love nor money is ever going to change that. . . . Love can't make a damaged brain whole" (Ibid.: 68–69).

State Response to Prenatal Cocaine Use: Prosecute and Terminate

The moral indignation, shock, and pity that such media imagery aroused in the American public were accompanied by an aggressive state response. Policy initiatives addressing the crack-baby phenomenon have been concentrated in the legal and social service arenas.

Legal Prosecution of Pregnant Addicts

In the later part of the 1980s, the country witnessed the emergence of a new and unprecedented legal strategy: the criminal prosecution of pregnant drug addicts. Due to the successful lobbying of the ACLU and medical, health, and women's organizations, no state has passed laws that make prenatal substance abuse an independent crime (Beckett, 1995; Lieb and Sterk-Elifson, 1995; Neil, 1992). Therefore, prosecutors have used "innovative" applications of existing laws to bring cases against pregnant addicts. Women have been charged under statutes for child abuse, neglect, vehicular homicide, encouraging the delinquency of a minor, involuntary manslaughter, drug trafficking, failure to provide child support, and assault with a deadly weapon (Mariner, Glantz, and Annas, 1990; Beckett, 1995; Sexton, 1993; Paltrow, 1990; Roberts, 1991; Greene, 1991).

In July 1989, Jennifer Johnson, a poor, 23-year-old African-American woman, became the first person convicted in the U.S. for giving birth to a drug-exposed infant. She was charged and found guilty of delivery of a controlled substance to a minor. Florida prosecutor Jeff Deen argued that this had taken place in the 30 to 90 seconds after the birth of the infant and before the cutting of the umbilical cord (Dobson and Eby, 1992).

Johnson received a 15-year sentence, including 14 years of probation, strict supervision during the first year, mandatory drug treatment, random drug testing, and mandatory educational and vocational training (Sexton, 1993; Logli, 1990; Neil, 1992). Johnson was further prohibited from "consuming alcohol, socializing with anyone who possessed drugs, and going to a bar without first receiving consent from her probation officer" (Sexton, 1993: 413). The court also ruled that if Johnson ever intended to again become pregnant, she must inform her probation officer and enroll in an intensive "judicially approved" prenatal care program (Logli, 1990; Sexton, 1993). Under Florida state law, she could have received a 30-year prison sentence (Curriden, 1990). Prosecutor Deen believed that prosecution "was the only way to stop her from using cocaine" and that Johnson "had used up all her chances" (Ibid.: 51). The case, Deen claimed, served to send the message "that this community cannot afford to have two or three cocaine babies from the same person."

Another highly publicized case was that of Kimberly Ann Hardy, also a poor, single young black woman addicted to crack cocaine. Hardy's case first came to the attention of the Department of Social Services in Muskegon County, Michigan, when the local hospital reported that her newborn had tested positive for cocaine at birth. Hardy's urine was tested for drugs because she had been identified as a "high-risk pregnancy" upon admission to the hospital: she had received no prenatal care and delivered six to eight weeks early (Hoffman, 1990).

Eleven days after she left the hospital, county prosecutor Tony Tague ordered Hardy arrested on the charge of delivering drugs in the amount of less than 50 grams—one generally used in prosecuting drug dealers (Ibid.). Though Hardy's case did not result in a conviction, district attorney Tague felt that the prosecution served to fulfill several important goals: it got Hardy into treatment and gave other pregnant crack addicts a strong warning to get clean or face jail and the loss of their children. Muskegon County Sergeant Van Hemert stated that adopting the hard line in prosecuting mothers is "a form of caring." Speaking with anger that many seem to hold toward pregnant addicts, he adds: "If the mother wants to smoke crack and kill herself I don't care. *Let her die, but don't take that poor baby with her*" (Ibid.: 34; emphasis added).

These two cases are fairly typical. The prosecutors are white males, the defendants are young black women, the drug is crack, and the rationale is safeguarding the health of babies. By 1992, 24 states had brought criminal charges against women for use of illicit drugs while pregnant. All of the defendants in these cases were poor and most were nonwhite (Beckett, 1995; Lieb and Sterk-Elifson, 1995). Nearly all of the convictions obtained in criminal prosecutions for perinatal substance abuse have been overturned (including Jennifer Johnson's), on the grounds that the charges against the defendants were not congruent with legislative intent (Beckett, 1995; Logli, 1990). Despite this fact, district attorneys continue to bring pregnant women up on criminal charges for substance abuse. As Beckett (1995: 603) has stated, "the continuation of these efforts reflects their political utility in our cultural climate."

Polls taken in the last few years have found that a large and growing proportion of the American public (71% in one survey) believes that women who use drugs while pregnant should be held criminally liable (Curriden, 1990; Sexton, 1993; Hoffman, 1990). The prosecutions of Johnson, Hardy, and others have boosted the careers of the attorneys who put them on trial; some have heralded them as "crusaders" in the war against drugs.

"Protective Incarceration"

Protective incarceration is another legal tactic that is becoming increasingly popular (Appel, 1992). In these cases, judges send pregnant women convicted of charges unrelated to their drug use to jail to "protect" their fetuses. At the 1988 sentencing of a pregnant addict convicted of writing bad checks, the judge stated:

> I'm going to keep her locked up until that baby is born because she's tested positive for cocaine. . . . She's apparently an addictive personality, and I'll be darned if I'm going to have a baby born that way. (Roberts, 1991: 1431, fn. 55)

Other addicts have been sent to jail for violations of their probation, in lieu of a probationary sentence, or for longer periods than is standard (Lieb and Sterk-Elifson, 1995; Schroedel, Reith, and Peretz, 1995; Appel, 1992).

Hospital Policy

Currently, at least 13 states require that public hospitals test women "suspected" of drug abuse and that they report those who test positive to social services or the police (Sexton, 1993). As in the Hardy case, mandatory reporting is often what triggers prosecution. Yet, drug screening conducted at public hospitals regularly takes place without women's consent or their being informed of possible legal ramifications.

In South Carolina, one hospital's testing and reporting policy (which stipulated that the police be notified of positive prenatal drug toxicologies) landed it a three million dollar lawsuit on the grounds that it violated patients' civil rights and discriminated on the basis of class and color. At the Medical University of South Carolina in Charleston, six lower-income women (five black and one white) who tested positive for drug use were "taken out of their hospital beds, handcuffed, and sent to jail without their babies" within days or hours after delivery (Furio, 1994: 93). At least one of the women "arrived at the jail still bleeding from the delivery; she was told to sit on a towel" (Paltrow, 1990: 41). The white woman was "detained for three weeks, put into a choke hold, and shackled by police during her eighth month of pregnancy . . . then placed against her will in a psychiatric hospital" (Furio, 1994: 93).

In September 1994, the case ended with a settlement and the requirement that the hospital abandon its practices. By that time, however, several hundred women had faced criminal prosecution under the reporting policy. Further, many other states continue to bring criminal or civil charges against women on the basis of drug tests performed without their consent.

Social Services—Unfit for Motherhood

The most frequent penalty for a mother's prenatal drug use is permanent or temporary removal of the newborn and/or other children. Based upon the results of drug screening, infants may be removed from their mothers right after birth, often without trial or hearing (Young, 1995). In today's political climate "positive neonatal toxicologies raise strong presumption of parental unfitness" (Roberts, 1991: 1431). Increasingly, civil courts agree that prenatal use of drugs constitutes neglect and is sufficient evidence for termination of parental rights (Beckett, 1995). In the last decade, literally thousands of women have permanently lost custody of their children as a result of their addiction. Upon appeal, the lower and appellate family courts have generally upheld these decisions (Ibid.).

Representative Kerry Patrick of Kansas introduced legislation that would require female addicts to have Norplant capsules inserted in their arms or else go to jail. Patrick says of his plan: "I've gotten a lot of support from nurses who deal with crack-babies. Once you see one, you don't care about the rights of the mother" (Willwerth, 1991: 62). Others echo his anger. One employee of the Los Angeles County Department of Health says: "Damn it, babies are dying out there! . . . You get someone with a terrible family history, stoned, no parenting skills—and we keep giving back her babies because we don't want to look racist or sexist" (Ibid.: 62).

Assumptions Behind the Crack-Baby Narrative and Punitive Treatment of Addicted Women

The intensity of legal, civil, and journalistic activity centering on babies born addicted to crack cocaine has been undergirded by three main sets of assumptions: about the effects of crack cocaine on fetal and child development, about the pregnant addicts targeted by the courts and the press, and about the efficacy of prosecution and punishment. The following section explores each of these assumptions and shows that despite their power, they are not substantiated by empirical evidence. Their tenacity comes not from their basis in fact, but from their ideological resonance with popular beliefs about drugs, crime, race, and motherhood.

The Medical Effects of Crack Cocaine on Fetal Health

The first assumption fueling the crack-baby scare is that crack is far more dangerous to fetal health than any other drug. As new evidence has emerged in the last five to six years, it has become apparent that early reports as to the impact of crack cocaine on fetal development were grossly exaggerated, and that what was painted as the norm is most likely the worst-case scenario. Perhaps the primary shortcoming of the early research was that it failed to disentangle the effects of cocaine from the effects of other chemical and environmental factors (Appel, 1992; Greider, 1995; *Science News*, November 19, 1991; Gittler and McPherson, 1990; Neuspiel, Markowitz, and Drucker, 1994). This was a particularly serious flaw given the population of drug users under study. Women who use crack are more likely to smoke cigarettes, drink alcohol, use other drugs, and to be malnourished; they are also less likely to obtain adequate prenatal care (Greider, 1995; Feldman et al., 1992; Griffith, 1992; Appel, 1992; Debettencourt, 1990; Neuspiel, Markowitz, and Drucker, 1994). Each of these factors has been documented to seriously impair fetal development—in the *absence* of cocaine (Appel, 1992; Neuspiel, Markowitz, and Drucker, 1994; *Science News*, November 19, 1991; *American Journal of Nursing*, May 1995).

Moreover, the presence of post-natal risk factors has also confounded the results of many studies. Cocaine-exposed children, like many poor black American children, are exposed to a higher-than-average level of violence, neglect, and abuse in their daily environments. Some scientists claim that "the social context of crack cocaine use, or more commonly polydrug use, is *more likely* to be related to the poor medical and developmental outcomes than to the actual drug exposure of the fetus" (Lieb and Sterk-Elifson, 1995: 690; emphasis added).

Despite these and other shortcomings, it was fairly easy for researchers to get this type of research published; conversely, it has been difficult to publicize findings that crack's effects on fetal development were minimal or nil (Greider, 1995; Pollitt, 1990; Beckett, 1995). Scientists whose work refuted the alarmist findings of the earliest published reports on crack cocaine and fetal development were often confronted with the disbelief, censure, and anger of their colleagues. In the words of one researcher, "I'd never experienced anything like this. . . . I've never had people accuse me of making up data or being an incompetent scientist or believing in drug abuse" (Greider, 1995: 54).

Dr. Ira Chasnoff has been a leading scientist in the field of prenatal cocaine exposure research since 1985. When Dr. Chasnoff recognized that his research was primarily being used to stigmatize and punish the women and children for whom he considered himself an advocate, he was appalled. In 1992, he stated that on average, crack-exposed children "are no different from other children growing up." Indicating his disgust with the popular rhetoric on "crack-babies," Dr. Chasnoff added, "they are not the retarded imbeciles people talk about. . . . As I study the problem more and more, I think the placenta does a better job protecting the child than we do as a society" (Sullum, 1992: 14).

Developmental psychologist Dan Griffith (formerly a member of Chasnoff's research group) has also sought to rectify the misimpressions concerning "crack-babies" so prevalent in the public imagination. Griffith notes that the most common assumptions about crack-kids—"(1) that all cocaine-exposed children are severely affected, (2) that little can be done for them, and (3) that all the medical, behavioral, and learning problems exhibited by these children are caused directly by their exposure to cocaine"—are false. Dr. Griffith cautions that far too little research has been conducted to allow scientists "to make any firm statement about the long-term prognosis" for cocaine-exposed children (Griffith, 1992: 30). However, his own research indicates that with early intervention and the reduction of other risk factors, most coke-exposed children "seem completely normal with regard to intellectual, social, emotional, and behavioral development through age three" (Ibid.: 31).[1]

Recent studies, which attempt to "smoke out" crack's unique impact on fetal development, tend to agree that cocaine increases the risk of low birth weight and prematurity in infants (Greider, 1995; Feldman et al., 1992; Barone, 1994; Beckett, 1995). Scientists have also found that receiving adequate prenatal care and curtailing drug usage significantly improves developmental outcomes for cocaine-exposed infants (Appel, 1992; Griffith, 1992). The extent to which cocaine alone causes neurobehavioral and other abnormalities is still up for debate. However, the consensus is that the average harm posed to infants by cocaine is far less than previously feared. Prematurity and low birth weight are indeed dangerous conditions for an infant, and each significantly contributes to the high rates of infant mortality and morbidity among African-Americans.[2] Yet these two primary effects are a far cry from the cranial hemorrhages, severe retardation, and lack of "human" qualities said to be typical of children born exposed to crack cocaine.

Current evidence also suggests that the effects of crack are *not* so different from those of tobacco or some other common street drugs. Comparison of scientific data on the effects of several chemical factors on fetal development demonstrates that the selection of pregnant crack-addicts in particular for censure and prosecution "has a discriminatory impact that cannot be medically justified" (Roberts, 1991: 1435). It may make no more sense, then, to speak about "crack-babies" than it does to speak of "cigarette-babies," "pot-babies," or "speed-babies." Most crack-exposed children will not suffer permanent pharmacologically induced brain damage and are not, medically speaking, beyond "hope." Whatever developmental delays or antisocial behavior they appear to express in later life may have more to do with poisons in their postnatal environment than in the fetal one.

Pregnant Addicts Targeted by Courts

The crack-baby mythology is also powerfully buttressed by a set of assumptions and stereotypes concerning the pregnant addicts who have been targeted by the courts and the media. Despite popular mythology to the contrary, empirical evidence shows that rates of prenatal drug use are consistent across race and class lines (Neuspiel et al., 1994; Lieb and Sterk-Elifson, 1995; Beckett, 1995; Appel, 1992). Stated otherwise, white middle-class women are no less likely to abstain from the use of illicit substances during pregnancy than are poor minority women. Ira Chasnoff's 1989 study of patterns of prenatal drug use and reporting policies in Pinellas County, Florida, clearly documented this trend.

In a toxicological screen for evidence of alcohol, marijuana, cocaine, and/or opiate use, 14.8% of women in the study tested positive overall. Chasnoff found that "there was little difference in the percentage of drug detection between women seen in public clinics (16.3) and those seen in private offices (13.1), or between blacks (14.1) and whites (15.4)" (Neuspiel, 1996: 48). There were, however, significant racial differences in the drug of choice. A higher percentage of pregnant black women (7.8) used cocaine than did pregnant white women (1.8); and pregnant white women (14.4) evidenced significantly higher usage of marijuana than their black counterparts (6.0). A more striking finding of the study concerned the discrepancy in the rates of reporting. In the state of Florida, health care providers are required by law to report both marijuana and cocaine use to authorities. Chasnoff discovered that "despite similar levels of use, black women were reported at *10 times* the rate for white women" and that poorer women were reported more often than middle-class women were (Ibid.: 48; emphasis added).

If not substance abuse rates themselves, then what explains the overwhelming race/class discrepancy in reporting and prosecution of prenatal drug use? This discrepancy has its roots in the fact that "the process in which pregnant women are suspected of substance abuse, diagnosed, and prosecuted is suffused with enormous discretion" (Lieb and Sterk-Elifson, 1995: 691). As the data indicate, this discretion quite often translates into pernicious discrimination along lines of race and class.

The Health Care Profession: Should We Test? Should We Report?

There are many loci where discretion is exercised and discrimination occurs. It begins with the decision whether to test a woman for substance use. State guidelines for mandatory reporting and testing are often vague and underspecified, leaving the implementation of policies up to individual doctors, clinics, or hospitals. The criteria for determining likelihood of prenatal drug use vary tremendously, but most "risk factors" are associated with socioeconomic status (Beckett, 1995) and race. Physicians often decide whether to order a newborn urine screen based upon whether the mother received timely and adequate prenatal care. Since black women as a group "are twice as likely as white women to begin prenatal care late or not at all" (Krauss, 1991: 528), and poor women are often unable to afford adequate prenatal care, this testing criterion tends to discriminate by both race and by class.

Health care providers also may act upon the basis of straightforward prejudice. As Krauss (Ibid.: 527) writes,

> suspicions of substance abuse may be informed by stereotyped assumptions about the identities of drug addicts. . . . [These stereotypes are] reinforced by studies in medical journals which list, with questionable accuracy, the characteristics of those presumed to be at risk.

Florida's reporting policy "does not require documentation of maternal drug use, but only a 'reasonable cause to suspect it'" (Ibid.: 527). Therefore, regardless of actual drug history, all women who appear to "fit the profile" are at risk of being subjected to particular scrutiny by social services and the police.

The fact that most testing is conducted at public hospitals that service low-income communities also means that poor women of color are more likely to face drug screening than are women protected by race and class privilege. In private hospitals, pregnant women are usually *not* tested for drug use, even if drug use is suspected (Beckett, 1995). Furthermore, even if they present a positive drug toxicology or admit drug use to their physicians, most women seen in private facilities are not reported to the authorities. Prenatal drug use by women who are affluent and/or white may often be viewed by private and public physicians as an exception, a lapse in judgment, or as incidental. Prenatal drug use by poor black women, however, is often viewed as endemic, typical, and evidence of their unfitness for motherhood.

Prosecutorial Discretion

Once prenatal drug use is reported, the authorities must then decide what, if any, course of action to take. Dwight Green argues that the unchecked discretion of prosecutors, who are overwhelmingly white and male, means that prenatal drug cases are often based not upon "unbiased law enforcement," but on "pluralistic ignorance" and race, gender, and class discrimination (Greene, 1991). Prosecutors must first decide what statutes, if any, apply to the offense at hand. As mentioned, prosecutors brought prenatal drug abuse trials into existence by stretching the interpretations of existing laws.

Having found an appropriate statute under which to press charges, prosecutors then decide whether to take a given case to trial. There are many intervening factors that go into this decision, often colored by considerations of race and class. Women who drink alcohol or ingest marijuana are quite unlikely to face criminal sanctions for prenatal drug use, even when they are reported to the police (Hoffman, 1990). Greene (1991: 745, fn. 28) writes,

> If long-term harm to children was the triggering event, this would present the unlikely image of affluent pregnant white women being subject to arrest at their country clubs or in the suburban home of a friend for having a drink.

The relative influence of a potential defendant may also influence the decision whether to press charges. Suspects in "white collar" crimes, for example, are often able to:

> hire well-paid criminal defense lawyers with social, political, and professional access to the prosecutor's office to argue at case screening conferences against instituting criminal charges or to lessen the seriousness of the crimes to be charged. (Ibid.: 755)

Even after initiating a criminal case, the prosecutor still has the option to discontinue prosecution. Although prosecuting a poor black crack-addict can boost a district attorney's reelection chances, taking an expectant socialite to trial for popping a handful of barbiturates with a glass of wine may only bring him embarrassment or ridicule.

The Efficacy of Criminal Punishment

The oft-repeated rationales for taking punitive action against pregnant substance abusers are to force them to enter drug treatment and to safeguard the health of their fetuses. The reality is that taking such action does not ensure, and may often be counterproductive to, the realization of these goals.

Threatening women with jail time in no way ensures that treatment services appropriate for pregnant addicts will be available (Beckett, 1995). One of the great ironies of the criminalization of prenatal drug use is that as a "general rule," substance abuse programs do not accept pregnant women (Sexton, 1993). A 1989 study of 78 treatment programs in New York City found that 54% refused all pregnant women, 67% refused pregnant women on Medicaid, and 87% would not accept pregnant women on

Medicaid who were addicted to crack (Appel, 1992; Hoffman, 1990; Roberts, 1991). Few addiction programs provide prenatal or obstetrical care and therefore most turn women away rather than risk treatment without these services (Lieb and Sterk-Elifson, 1995; Roberts, 1991).

Drug treatment programs designed primarily to serve men can also be alienating and ineffective for women. Appel (1992: 141) writes, "most treatment approaches are based on the characteristics and dynamics among male populations and comparatively little has been done to define the unique nature of addiction to women." Many female addicts, for example, "turned to drugs because they were sexually abused or raped as children, and they need help repairing the damage" (Willwerth, 1991: 63). According to one estimate, *80 to 90%* of female alcoholics and drug addicts have been victims of rape or incest (Paltrow, 1990). A program that does not address the special issues facing pregnant addicts will doubtlessly have high rates of withdrawal and relapse. Yet the focus on punishment has generally *not* been accompanied by a correspondingly intense drive to increase the availability of services geared toward the needs of pregnant addicts.[3]

Instituting criminal sanctions for perinatal substance abuse is also counterproductive to the goal of helping women and children because it serves to deter pregnant addicts from seeking medical attention. Medical evidence (cited above) indicates that receiving adequate prenatal care and/or curtailing drug consumption can significantly improve developmental outcomes for cocaine-exposed infants. Yet many women will avoid seeking the information and treatment they need if they realize that a positive urine screen could result in their children being placed in foster care or land them in jail (Krauss, 1991).[4]

Putting women in jail for evidence of drug use upon delivery will not undo whatever harm was done to their newborns in utero. Sending women to prison while pregnant is unlikely to ensure the health of their fetuses either. While incarcerated, pregnant women "face conditions hazardous to fetal health, including overcrowding, poor nutrition, and exposure to contagious disease" (Ibid.: 537). Prison health facilities generally provide little or no prenatal care and are ill-equipped to handle the medical needs of pregnant women, especially those with drug histories. Like other inmates, pregnant addicts may also be able to obtain illegal drugs while imprisoned (Paltrow, 1990; Schroedel and Peretz, 1995). Moreover, if the supply of drugs is suddenly cut off, the physiological changes that immediate withdrawal brings about in the mother and the fetus can be dangerous to the health of both (Schroedel and Peretz, 1995; Appel, 1992).

Criminalizing prenatal substance abuse punishes women for failing to obtain treatment that is generally unavailable and may prevent them from seeking prenatal care. Because of the harm that it is likely to cause, prominent sectors of the medical community have taken a stand against this policy. In a paper published in 1988, the American Medical Association stated that:

> the current policy of prosecuting women who use drugs during pregnancy is irrational because it does not further the state's purpose of preventing harm to infants. . . . [D]rug addiction is an illness, which like any illness, is not due simply to a failure of individual willpower. (Lieb and Sterk-Elifson, 1995: 693)

Similarly, in 1991, the American Nurses Association characterized the imposition of criminal sanctions against pregnant addicts as "extreme, inappropriate, and ineffective" (Sexton, 1993: 420–421).

Race, Crime, Drugs, Motherhood

If, as I have argued, the three primary sets of assumptions that have rationalized prosecuting crack-addicted mothers are false, then what is this really about? If not the neutral exercise of justice, what is the driving force behind the imposition of criminal sanctions for prenatal drug use? Why are prosecutors, judges, the press, and much of the American public now so eager to demonize and imprison drug-addicted mothers? Why is it that crack addicts and poor black women are targeted for reproach and condemnation? If it does not help mothers or protect their babies, what societal goal does punishing pregnant addicts serve?

The crack-baby phenomenon, it seems, has arisen from a particular confluence of contemporary ideas about race, crime, drugs, and motherhood. These ideas and practices have their most proximate roots in the Reagan/Bush era "war on drugs" and the discourse on "fetal rights." In each of these discourses, the civil rights of "offenders" (pregnant women or drug users/dealers) are increasingly seen as an impediment to the realization of social justice (Mariner, Glantz, and Annas, 1990; Willwerth, 1991; Krauss, 1991).

War on Drugs: War on Communities of Color

The late 1980s witnessed the emergence of an aggressive anti-drug crusade, waged on several fronts. This crusade defined as criminal the use and sale of illicit substances. The federal government appropriated millions of dollars in public monies for the pursuit, arrest, and conviction of dealers and users (Beckett, 1995; Irwin, 1995). In response to federal initiatives, state legislatures wrote tougher drug laws and imposed stiffer penalties for their violation. The courts, in turn, sent more and more drug offenders to jail, for longer terms. Currently, one-third of the state prison population is composed of individuals convicted on drug-related charges (Beckett, 1995). The United States now has the highest incarceration rate in the world, with .4 percent of its population behind bars at any given time (Neuspiel et al., 1994).

Besides law enforcement, special interest groups, politicians, and news agencies turned their attention to the evils of illicit substances (Irwin, 1995). Through the popular press, these groups articulated "a language of intolerance and a rhetoric of contempt" for those who used drugs (Ibid.: 632). Pregnant addicts were subject to special scorn in the media and viewed as particularly deficient in morals (Ibid.; Lieb and Sterk-Elifson, 1995). According to the discursive arm of the war on drugs, increasing rates of drug usage were somehow responsible for much of the social disorder, moral decay, poverty, and decadence of the late twentieth century.

Not all drugs received equal attention in the war on drugs: crack most firmly captured the nation's imagination. With crack's emergence in the mid-1980s, journalists "bombarded the public with frightening images of crack cocaine as a unique 'demon drug' different from any other . . . highly potent, instantly addictive, and conducive to systemic violence and moral decadence" (Lieb and Sterk-Elifson, 1995: 687). Crack cocaine was declared *Time* magazine's "issue of the year" in 1986 (*Time*, September 22, 1986). According to *Newsweek*, the devastation wrought by crack was "as newsworthy as the Vietnam War, the fall of Nixon's presidency, and the American civil rights movement" (Irwin, 1995: 633). With the issue of crack-babies, the war on drugs and the media's sensationalistic stories reached new heights.

Despite the sudden burst of alarmist press and the appearance of the war on drugs, the overall prevalence of drug use in the United States did not increase in the 1980s (Beckett, 1995). What did occur during this period was that "the practice of smoking cocaine, formerly restricted to the middle and upper-classes, spread into the inner-city with the increased availability of [crack], a new, less expensive form of smokable cocaine" (Ibid.: 599). The war on drugs received its greatest intensity and its moral urgency from the fact that a new drug had found its way to the "lower colored classes."

Periods of public alarm over the drug use of nonwhites have occurred repeatedly throughout the social history of the United States. During these drug scares, "'moral entrepreneurs' seek to blame a wide variety of social problems on chemical substances and those who imbibe them" (Ibid.: 597). In the 1870s, whites in California claimed that the state's economic depression could be attributed to the presence of Chinese immigrants and, in particular, to their usage of opium. The image of opium-smoking Chinese in this period "became synonymous with immorality and depravity" (Ibid.: 598). Such racist scapegoating led to the passage of laws that made the use of opium illegal for Chinese-Americans, but not for those defined as white (Neuspiel et al., 1994).

In the 1930s, anti-Mexican sentiment was successfully exploited in the campaign to criminalize marijuana. Many whites in this period believed that "reefer mad Mexican bandits" were largely to blame for the era's skyrocketing rates of unemployment and general social upheaval (Ibid.; Beckett, 1995). Several decades earlier, Jews and Italians were believed to be threats to the moral character of the nation due to their predisposition toward drug addiction (Neuspiel et al., 1994). At the turn of the century, the fear of "the cocainized black" coincided with Southern attempts to strip African-Americans of the political and social gains of the Reconstruction era. The racially motivated anti-drug crusades of the previous 100-odd years share much in common with the war on drugs of the 1980s and 1990s. As in the past,

> customary use of a certain drug [has come] to symbolize the difference between [a minority group] and the rest of society. . . . [It is thought that] eliminating the drug might alleviate social disharmony and preserve the old order. (Musto, 1973, as quoted in Neuspiel et al., 1994: 52)

In many respects, the Reagan/Bush-era war on drugs has been a war on communities of color. Racism in current U.S. drug policy is reflected in several arenas. Most notable are the rates of arrest and conviction for drug trafficking and drug usage. Concordant with the Reagan administration's mandate to combat "street crime," law enforcement officials have placed greatest emphasis upon the arrest and conviction of "low-level street dealers," who are disproportionately African American (Beckett, 1995; Neuspiel et al., 1994). Further, though 80% of drug users are white, the majority of those arrested and convicted for drug use are African American (Beckett, 1995). Increased police presence in inner-city neighborhoods, "ostensibly for the drug war—has resulted in a general increase of arrests and terror directed against people of color" (Neuspiel et al., 1994: 49). The rhetoric of "warfare" and portrayal of those who use and sell drugs as immoral social scum has legitimized the escalation of police brutality and harassment in inner-city communities, as well as the abrogation of the civil rights of suspected drug offenders.

Lastly, the tremendous discrepancy in federally mandated minimum sentences for the sale of powder cocaine and for crack (rock cocaine) is a clear manifestation of the targeting of black drug offenders by the U.S. legal system. In 1986, Congress amended the Comprehensive Crime Control Act (CCCA) of 1984, such that gram for gram, mandatory sentences for possession or sale of crack are 100 times greater than those for offenses involving powder cocaine (Neuspiel et al., 1994; Lieb and Sterk-Elifson, 1995). A federal defendant currently faces five years in prison for the sale of 500 grams of powdered cocaine, 100 grams of marijuana, or only five grams of crack. As one scholar has noted, the CCCA constitutes "an excellent example of institutional racism" (Beckett, 1995: 599).

The war on drugs has helped to legitimize the dismantling of the welfare state and the government's abandonment of the poor and the non-white. During the 1980s, the polarization of wealth in the United States reached an all time high; while the rich got richer, the poor only got poorer. With the restructuring of the economy and the disappearance of industrial wage labor, unemployment rates soared in urban communities. The income gap was further exacerbated by the Reagan administration's attempt to stimulate the economy by giving tax breaks to businesses while slashing social service programs that might have provided a safety net for disadvantaged Americans (Irwin, 1995).

At this time, anti-drug rhetoric "provided the ideological explanation of why certain segments of the population experienced hardship [while] select privileged groups were amassing more and more wealth" (Ibid.; 632). The message that increasing drug use was responsible for the declining economic and social welfare of the black community diverted attention from the role of factors such as global economic transformations, domestic social policy, and institutional racism (Roberts, 1991; Irwin, 1995; Neuspiel et al., 1994). Politicians found that "criminalizing the poor" was more "politically expedient" than examining the deep social roots of urban problems, creating a national health care system, or investing in the public school system (Beckett, 1995; Neuspiel et al., 1994). Through increased police surveillance and violence, discrimination in drug arrests and sentencing, and locking up pregnant addicts, the U.S. government has waged a war on communities of color and has been able to exert a powerful mechanism of social control over those most likely to rebel against it (Neuspiel et al., 1994).

Fetal Rights—Rescuing Fetuses from Pregnant Women

The second political current that has deeply influenced the nation's response to the problem of prenatal drug use is the fetal rights movement. Improvements in scientific knowledge and technology provided the medical foundation for the development of a discourse of fetal rights. In the mid-1800s, doctors began to position themselves as pregnancy experts, wresting control of that domain away from female midwives and pregnant women themselves (Krauss, 1991; Beckett, 1995). As the status and power of the medical profession has increased, so has its tendency to distrust the ability of women to make childbirth and pregnancy decisions on their own (Krauss, 1991). Major advances in biomedical technology in the last 40 years have made it possible to view fetuses in the womb and greatly improved our understanding of fetal developmental needs (Boling, 1995). Yet these developments have also legitimated a vision of the fetus as a "second patient" and reanimated the old patriarchal notion of the mother as "vessel," who merely provides a host environment for the growing embryo (Beckett, 1995; Boling, 1995). Pro-life ideology has contributed considerably to fetal rights discourse as well. The argument that abortion is murder rests upon the notion that the unborn are human beings who should be accorded a moral and legal status equal to that of the mother (Beckett, 1995).

The language of fetal rights implies that pregnancy is an adversarial relationship involving a "conflict of rights between a woman and her fetus" (Ibid.: 593). Advocates of fetal rights assert that the state has an affirmative duty to protect the unborn from potential (or likely) harm at the hands of the mother, and that once a woman has made the decision to carry a pregnancy to term, she should be legally liable for actions that could result in harm (Krauss, 1991; Pollitt, 1990). The image of women as the loving protectors of their unborn has been supplanted by "the image of the negligent mother whose willingness to support her fetus must be enforced by medical and legal professionals" (Beckett, 1995: 597). Once models of self-sacrifice, pregnant women are now believed to be selfish, confused, potentially violent, and incapable of making responsible choices (Pollitt, 1990). In addition, while women are being sent to prison for their alleged crimes against the unborn, "doctors, judges, prosecutors, and politicians are lining up as fetal advocates and authorities" (Beckett, 1995: 588).

Scholars have observed that as the rights of fetuses have expanded, those of mothers have diminished (Pollitt, 1990; Sexton, 1993). Both in and out of the courtroom, fetal rights are seen to take precedence over those of pregnant women. In some cases, the needs or wants of the mother are treated as an impediment to the more legitimate needs of the fetus.

In addition to legitimizing the imprisonment of pregnant drug addicts, fetal rights arguments have been used to force or coerce women into medical treatment. In the name of their unborn children, women have been made to undergo cesarean sections and other obstetrical interventions. The great majority of pregnant women forced to undergo unwanted medical treatment have been poor, nonwhite, or foreign born. According to a national study of women subjected to court-ordered cesarean sections, intrauterine transfusions, or detained in hospitals against their will, 81% were of black, Asian American, or Latin American descent, and 25% were non-native speakers of English (Krauss, 1991). Doctors and judges may decide whether to override a pregnant woman's medical wishes based in part upon their assessments of her competency. This assessment of competency (like the assessment of likelihood of prenatal drug usage) may often be based upon racial, cultural, and class stereotypes. In one case, when a Bedouin woman, believing that she would die, objected to cesarean delivery, a team of physicians explained that the woman's refusal "resulted from the mother's ignorance and prejudice, which prevented her from arriving at an intelligent decision" (Ibid.: 532).

The concept of fetal rights has been attacked from many angles. The most basic critique is that it violates women's rights during pregnancy, and specifically the right to bodily integrity (in the case of court-ordered medical treatment) and the right to privacy, which includes the decision to bear a child (in the case of pregnant drug addicts) (Krauss, 1991; Garcia and Segalman, 1991; Neil, 1992). During pregnancy, it is argued, fetal rights reduce women to "second-class citizen[s] with constitutional rights inferior to those of men and non-pregnant women" (Krauss, 1991: 539).

Other critiques have been leveled at the very concept of granting rights to fetuses. The centerpiece of the theory of fetal rights is the notion that from the time a woman decides to carry her pregnancy to term, she has a special "duty of care" to her fetus. She must act in such a manner as to ensure the health of her unborn child, or risk legal punishment. The danger in this increasingly prevalent line of argumentation is that, potentially, a pregnant woman could be held legally responsible for any behavior that could harm her fetus. As Lynn Paltrow (1990: 42) of the ACLU points out, "prosecutions of pregnant women cannot be restricted to illegal behaviors because many legal behaviors cause damage to developing babies." In 1980, the Michigan Supreme Court ruled that "a mother who had taken prescription medication for her own health could be held criminally liable for failing to provide 'proper prenatal care'" (Beckett, 1995: 594). Other pregnant women have faced charges for consumption of alcohol, failing to follow doctor's orders, and taking non-prescription valium (Paltrow, 1990; Pollitt, 1990). As long as the rights of fetuses are believed to be morally superior to, and in fundamental conflict with, those of their mothers, pregnant women who are obese, who take aspirin, travel by air, smoke cigarettes, change their cats' litter boxes, eat junk food, have sex, or fail to stay off their feet "could all be characterized as fetal abusers" (Pollitt, 1990; Schroedel and Peretz, 1995; quote from Paltrow, 1990: 42). In calling for increased governmental regulation of prenatal behavior, the "duty of care" standard seriously threatens to undermine women's reproductive autonomy.

There are many reasons to suspect that "fetal rights" is driven not by a concern for healthy children, but by a desire to control women (Pollitt, 1990). A universe of factors other than maternal behavior can jeopardize fetal health outcomes; but curiously, fetal rights activists have no interest in them. Outrage at pregnant women who use crack has not been accompanied by a corresponding level of outrage at the fact that many do not have health insurance, or that their children will be forced to live in roach-infested housing, or about the fact that many businesses have abandoned the inner cities. Fetal rights advocates have not campaigned for the building of day care centers in low-income communities, to increase the availability of prenatal care to poor mothers, or to expand eligibility for the WIC food vouchers program.

Fetal rights theorists also ignore male behavior. Though a woman's duty to her fetus may be "virtually limitless," the men in their lives have no corresponding duty of care. This is true despite the fact that a partner or spouse's drug abuse may itself contribute to neonatal mortality, low birth weight, learning disabilities, and abnormal newborn behavior (Krauss, 1991; Schroedel and Peretz, 1995).[5] Male battering is also a common and serious threat to fetal health. Approximately one out of 12 women are beaten during pregnancy and pregnant women as a group are more likely than non-pregnant women to be beaten by their partners or spouses (Pollitt, 1990; Schroedel and Peretz, 1995).

Furthermore, men who beat pregnant women often aim their assault directly at the woman's abdominal region, perhaps out of anger at, or jealousy of, the fetus. Battering can cause stillbirths, miscarriages, and other complications. In 1981, Lancet cited a case in which a baby was born "with bruises on its arms, neck, and shoulder, a swollen eye, and intraventricular hemorrhaging," as a result of prenatal battering (Schroedel and Peretz, 1995: 94). The baby subsequently died from its injuries. In 1990, Dianne Pfannenstiel, a pregnant woman from Laramie, Wyoming, went to the police to file a claim against her husband after being beaten severely. The police brought no charges against her husband, yet Pfannenstiel herself was charged with child abuse upon admitting that she had been drinking (Pollitt, 1990; Paltrow, 1990). As Pollitt (1990: 416) writes, "the threat to newborns is interesting only when it can, accurately or fancifully, be laid at the women's doorstep. . . . If the mother isn't to blame, no one's to blame." Male violence, malnutrition, lead paint, poverty, and racism, are immaterial to fetal rights advocates because they lie outside of the implicitly patriarchal and racist parameters of the fetal rights discourse.

Devaluation of Black Children and Degradation of Black Motherhood

In evaluating the motivations behind fetal rights actions, we must also consider the history of interactions between the government and their most preferred objects of salvation: poor black children. The record of "overwhelming state neglect" of African-American children casts doubt upon the sincerity of claims that the state is only looking out for their best interests in prosecuting their mothers (Roberts, 1991). Until the 1930s, black children were routinely excluded from eligibility for most child welfare services, including adoption and foster care (Hill, 1977). Currently, the slashing of social service programs, lack of concern about the notoriously high rate of black infant mortality (unless it can be attributed to black women's prenatal drug consumption), and the underfunding of the public school system are indicators of the U.S. government's continuing disregard for black children. Furthermore, the drive to incarcerate rather than to educate black youth and the iconography of fear of black males that dominates popular imagery reveal society's disgust for the teenagers that these children will become.

Implied in the extreme demonization of crack-addicted mothers is the unlikely presumption that in-utero exposure to drugs is the greatest harm that drug-exposed children will face in their lives. Prenatal drug prosecutions allow the government to appear concerned about the welfare of black children "without having to spend any money, change any priorities, or challenge any vested interests" (Pollitt, 1990: 410–411). These prosecutions place the blame for the plight of black children and the black community at the feet of African-American women and absolve the white middle class of responsibility or guilt.

Fetal rights discourse champions the rights of the black unborn, but not those of black children, adolescents, or adults. It is particularly not a discourse of empowerment for black mothers. Fetal rights, in fact, "seeks to punish women who fail to act according to idealized concepts of motherhood" (Beckett, 1995: 589). Women who are poor and nonwhite (or homosexual) are the least able to conform to white middle-class standards of motherhood (Roberts, 1991).

The tendency to blame black women for the problems of the black community has a long history in American society. The most notable example in recent years is the infamous "Moynihan Report." In this 1965 essay, sociologist Daniel Patrick Moynihan argued that domineering, matriarchal black mothers created emasculated black men who would fail in school, abandon their families, and be unable to succeed economically. Patricia Hill Collins writes that the black matriarchy thesis:

> allows the dominant group to blame Black women for the success or failure of Black children . . . diverts attention from the political and economic inequality affecting Black mothers and children, and suggests that anyone can rise from poverty if he or she only received good values at home. (Collins, 1990: 74)

The image of the black matriarch has lately been supplanted by that of the single black mother. With his 1984 book, *Losing Ground*, sociologist Charles Murray helped to validate stereotypical perceptions of the black "welfare mother" who "breeds" babies in order to increase the size of her government check and to avoid having to work. At the close of the 1990s, such images of black motherhood are as prevalent as ever. Patricia Williams argues that "the signifying power of the black single mother . . . as poor, drug addicted, and natally absent . . . is integral to the public articulation of fetal harm and abuse" (Bower, 1995: 144). On television talk shows such as Ricki Lake, Jenny Jones, Richard Bey, and Jerry Springer, young women of color are routinely characterized as irrational, immature baby machines, who practice irresponsible sexuality and are scarcely fit for parenthood. Their multiple illegitimate children, it is frequently claimed, place a severe drain on the welfare system and thus heavily burden the nation's economy. According to contemporary imagery, the fertility and sexuality of poor black women are "unnecessary and even dangerous" to the nation (Collins, 1990: 76), and associated with disease, "pollution," and the downfall of Western civilization (Bower, 1995).

In this vein, scholars have argued that what many poor black women are being punished for is not any actual harm done to fetuses, but the crime of getting pregnant while addicted (Paltrow, 1990; Roberts, 1991; Krauss, 1991). It is the addict's decision to carry her pregnancy to term that results in criminal liability (Young, 1995). If she obtained an abortion, or had never been pregnant, there would be no case against her. Further, women who do not habitually engage in prenatal behaviors deemed actionable by the state do not face the prospect of jail upon conception. What appears as outrage that pregnant women use crack, then, is in fact outrage that crack addicts bear children.

According to Roberts (1991: 1472), "the value we place on individuals determines whether we see them as entitled to perpetuate themselves in their children." Like enforced sterilization, fetal endangerment prosecutions reflect society's judgment that poor, addicted African-American women do not deserve to become mothers (Ibid.). American society stigmatizes the pregnancies of all poor black women and it criminalizes those of poor black crack-addicts. In selecting crack-addicts for special punishment, the courts, health care providers, and the press are saying: "We don't particularly need any more of these people or their offspring. They are utterly unfit for motherhood and the damaged, subhuman children they produce will most likely become the nation's financial burden and later its criminal element."

It is curious to note that many of those who lament the tragedy of drug-exposed children apparently care nothing about the tragedy of their mothers. Yet,

> pregnant women who are drinking excessively, abusing drugs, smoking, or eating inadequately are first and foremost hurting themselves. . . . In our rush to blame women for their failure to take care of others we are missing the point that they have never been encouraged to "selfishly" care for themselves. (Paltrow, 1990: 45)

In deciding that the best way to deal with the problem of drug-addicted babies is not to empower, but to punish their mothers, society is blind to the fact that their fates are inextricably intertwined. Locking a woman behind bars and castigating her in the press does little to prevent her child from having to face the same conditions (poverty, racism, gender oppression, and sexual violence) that likely contributed to her addiction. Who is to say that the addict's daughter will not have the same fate and become a scorned and degraded pregnant addict herself? When and why does that black girl child change from being among the most innocent to among the most guilty?

The primary utility of stigmatizing and punishing poor drug-addicted black women lies not in the prevention of fetal harm, but in the defense of normative standards of gender and motherhood, the resuscitation of public innocence concerning the plight of the black poor, and the legitimization of a status quo characterized by continuing oppression and inequality. With reflection upon the real imperatives driving the criminal prosecution of crack-addicted mothers, policymakers might begin to devise programs that empower pregnant addicts and allow them to be good mothers to their children. The policies pursued thus far have done little good for crack-exposed babies and have only helped undermine the fragile world into which they were born.

Notes

[1] All mothers in the study used cocaine and most also used other drugs during their pregnancies. Griffith's recent research was conducted with a study population in which several prenatal risk factors had been eliminated: while pregnant, expectant mothers received prenatal care, nutritional counseling, and therapy for chemical dependency.

[2] Infants born prematurely have increased risk of breathing difficulties, brain hemorrhage, and mental defects. Babies born underweight are 40 times more likely to die than are normal-weight babies and 10 times more likely to have cerebral palsy (Appel, 1992). The black infant mortality rate in 1987 was 17.9 deaths out of 1,000, compared to a white infant mortality rate of 8.6 per 1,000 (Roberts, 1991).

[3] As of 1993, the states of Georgia and New York had instituted mandatory reporting requirements, yet had allocated no funding for treatment of perinatal addiction (Sexton, 1993).

[4] In 1988, Minnesota became the first state to include perinatal drug use in its legal definition of child abuse. Since that time, observers have claimed that despite the fact that the revised law does not call for criminal sanctions against prenatal drug abusers, it has deterred pregnant addicts from seeking drug treatment and from disclosing their drug use to their doctors (Sexton, 1993; Paltrow, 1990).

[5] This is primarily by adversely affecting the quality of the sperm and through the mother's inhalation of second-hand smoke from cigarettes or illegal drugs.

References

Appel, Deborah

1992 "Drug Use During Pregnancy: State Strategies to Reduce the Prevalence of Prenatal Drug Exposure." *University of Florida Journal of Law and Public Policy 5* (Fall): 103–148.

Barone, Diane

1994 "Myths About 'Crack Babies.'" *Educational Leadership 52* (October): 67–68.

Beckett, Katherine

1995 "Fetal Rights and 'Crack Moms': Pregnant Women in the War on Drugs." *Contemporary Drug Problems 22* (Winter): 587–612.

Boling, Patricia

1995 "Introduction." Patricia Boling (ed.), *Expecting Trouble: Surrogacy, Fetal Abuse, and New Reproductive Technologies.* Boulder: Westview Press.

Bower, Lisa

1995 "The Trope of the Dark Continent in the Fetal Harm Debates: 'Africanism' and the Right to Choice." Patricia Boling (ed.), *Expecting Trouble: Surrogacy, Fetal Abuse, and New Reproductive Technologies.* Boulder: Westview Press.

Collins, Patricia Hill

1990 *Black Feminist Thought: Knowledge, Consciousness, and the Politics of Empowerment.* Boston: Unwin Hyman.

Curriden, Mark

1990 "Holding Mom Accountable." *ABA Journal* (March): 50–53.

1986 "Crack: A Cheap and Deadly Cocaine Is a Spreading Menace." *Time* (September 22).

Debettencourt, Kathleen B.

1990 "The Wisdom of Solomon: Cutting the Chord That Harms." *Children Today 19* (August): 17–20.

Dobson, Tracy and Kimberly K. Eby

1992 "Criminal Liability for Substance Abuse During Pregnancy: The Controversy of Maternal v. Fetal Rights." *Saint Louis University Law Journal 36*, 3 (Spring): 655–694.

1986 "Drug Treatment in City Is Strained by Crack, a Potent New Cocaine." *New York Times* (May 16).

Elshtain, Jean Bethke

1990 "Pregnancy Police: If You're an Addict It's Now a Crime to Give Birth." *The Progressive 54* (December): 26–28.

Feldman, Joseph G., Howard L. Minkoff, Sandra McCalla, and Martin Salwen
1992 "A Cohort Study of the Impact of Perinatal Drug Use on Prematurity in an Inner-City Population." *American Journal of Public Health 82* (May): 726–728.
1995 "Fetal Harm Greater from Cigarettes than Cocaine." *American Journal of Nursing 95* (May): 56.

Furio, Joanne
1994 "Women Fight Civil Rights Abuse in South Carolina." *Ms. 5* (November/December): 93.

Garcia, Sandra Anderson and Ralph Segalman
1991 "The Control of Perinatal Drug Abuse: Legal, Psychological, and Social Imperatives." *Law and Psychology Review 15* (Spring): 19–64.

Gittler, Josephine and Dr. Merle McPherson
1990 "Prenatal Substance Abuse." *Children Today 19* (July/August): 3–7.

Greene, Dwight L.
1991 "Abusive Prosecutors: Gender, Race, and Class Discretion and the Prosecution of Drug-Addicted Mothers." *Buffalo Law Review 39*, 3 (Fall): 737–802.

Greider, Katherine
1995 "Crackpot Ideas." *Mother Jones 20* (July/August): 52–56.

Griffith, Dan R.
1992 "Prenatal Exposure to Cocaine and Other Drugs: Developmental and Educational Prognoses." *Phi Delta Kappan 74* (September): 30–34.

Hill, Robert B.
1977 *Information Adoption Among Black Families.* Washington, D.C.: National Urban League, Research Department.

Hoffman, Jan
1990 "Pregnant, Addicted—and Guilty?" *The New York Times Magazine* (August 19): 32–35.

Hopkins, Ellen
1990 "Childhood's End." *Rolling Stone* (October 18): 66–69; 71–72; 108–110.

Irwin, Katherine
1995 "Ideology, Pregnancy, and Drugs: Differences Between Crack-Cocaine, Heroin, and Methamphetamine Users." *Contemporary Drug Problems 22* (Winter): 613–637.

Krauss, Deborah K.
1991 "Regulating Women's Bodies: The Adverse Effect of Fetal Rights Theory on Childbirth Decisions and Women of Color." *Harvard Civil Rights Civil Liberties Law Review 26*, 4 (Summer): 523–548.

Langone, John
1988 "Crack Comes to the Nursery: More and More Cocaine-Using Mothers Are Bearing Afflicted Infants." *Time 132* (September 19): 85.

Lieb, John J. and Claire Sterk-Elifson
1995 "Crack in the Cradle: Social Policy and Reproductive Rights Among Crack-Using Females." *Contemporary Drug Problems 22* (Winter): 687–705.

Logli, Paul A.
1990 "Drugs in the Womb: The Newest Battlefield in the War on Drugs." *Criminal Justice Ethics* (Winter/Spring): 23–29.

Mariner, Wendy K., Leonard H. Glantz, and George J. Annas
1990 "Pregnancy, Drugs, and the Perils of Prosecution." *Criminal Justice Ethics* (Winter/Spring): 30–41.

Moynihan, Daniel Patrick
1971 "The Tangle of Pathology." Robert Staples (ed.), *The Black Family; Essays and Studies.* Belmont, California: Wadsworth Publishing.
Murray, Charles
1984 *Losing Ground—American Social Policy, 1950–1980.* New York: Basic Books.
Musto, David F.
1973 *American Disease: Origins of Narcotic Control.* New Haven: Yale University Press.
Neil, Benjamin A.
1992 "Prenatal Drag Abuse: Is the Mother Criminally Liable?" *Trial Diplomacy Journal 15*: 129–135.
Neuspiel, Daniel R.
1996 "Racism and Perinatal Addiction." *Ethnicity and Disease 6* (Winter/Spring): 47–55.
Neuspiel, Daniel R., Morri Markowitz, and Ernest Drucker
1994 "Intrauterine Cocaine, Lead, and Nicotine Exposure and Fetal Growth." *American Journal of Public Health 84* (September): 1492–1495.
Paltrow, Lynn M.
1990 "When Becoming Pregnant Is a Crime." *Criminal Justice Ethics* (Winter/Spring): 42–47.
1986 "The Plague Among Us." *Newsweek* (June 16).
Plummer, William and S. Avery Brown
1990 "Children in Peril." *People Weekly 33* (April 16): 82–91.
Pollitt, Katha
1990 "'Fetal Rights': A New Assault on Feminism." *The Nation 250* (March 26): 409–411; 414–416.
Roberts, Dorothy E.
1991 "Punishing Drug Addicts Who Have Babies: Women of Color, Equality, and the Right of Privacy." *Harvard Law Review 104*, 7 (May): 1419–1482.
Schroedel, Jean Reith and Paul Peretz
1995 "A Gender Analysis of Policy Formation: The Case of Fetal Abuse." Patricia Boling (ed.), *Expecting Trouble: Surrogacy, Fetal Abuse, and New Reproductive Technologies.* Boulder: Westview Press.
Sexton, Patricia A.
1993 "Imposing Criminal Sanctions on Pregnant Drug Users: Throwing the Baby out with the Bath Water." *Washburn Law Journal 32* (Spring): 410–430.
1991 "Smoking Out Cocaine's in Utero Impact." *Science News 140* (November 19): 302.
Sullum, Jacob
1992 "The Cocaine Kids." *Reason 24* (August/September): 14.
Willwerth, James
1991 "Should We Take Away Their Kids?" *Time 137* (May 13): 62–63.
Young, Iris Marion
1995 "Punishment, Treatment, Empowerment: Three Approaches to Policy for Pregnant Addicts." Patricia Boling (ed.), *Expecting Trouble: Surrogacy, Fetal Abuse, and New Reproductive Technologies.* Boulder: Westview Press.
Zitella, Julia J.
1996 "Protecting Our Children: A Call to Reform State Policies to Hold Pregnant Drug Addicts Accountable." *John Marshall Law Review 29*, 3 (Spring): 768–798.

11

Bringing Back Shame
Women, Welfare Reform, and Criminal Justice

Amy E. Hirsch

Introduction

The right wing drive to "bring back shame" has dramatically affected the legal systems poor women interact with most often—welfare, the criminal justice system, and family courts. In each of these areas, poor women are increasingly stigmatized; their behavior is viewed with rising suspicion and hostility; and efforts to control their sexual and maternal behavior are ever more punitive. The connections between welfare law and family law have been recognized for decades, with a different, more onerous set of family law rules for poor women than for everyone else.[1] There are also numerous historical connections between welfare and criminal justice systems—ranging from 16th century laws simultaneously regulating relief-giving and criminalizing unauthorized begging to the expansion of workhouses in 1834 described by Disraeli as "announc[ing] to the world that in England poverty is a crime."[2] Despite these historical connections, relatively little attention has been paid in recent years to the interaction of the welfare and criminal justice systems.

However, welfare "reform" in the 1990s has linked the welfare system more closely and more explicitly with the criminal justice system, reflecting an increasingly punitive attitude towards low-income mothers. Denial of welfare benefits because of a woman's criminal record is one of an ever-increasing list of civil consequences of criminal offenses—loss of public housing (and often of private housing as well), denial of student loans, loss of employment, loss of child custody or parental rights, loss of immigrant status, and loss of the vote.

Disenfranchisement from subsistence benefits means not only material loss, but loss of a connection to civil society. For women with drug convictions, who are stigmatized as drug addicts, as criminals, as unfit mothers, becoming welfare recipients would mean a step up the social ladder, a return to normal life. The recent attacks on welfare mothers and their children as illegitimate and undeserving of social support dovetail all too well with the right wing portrayal of women with criminal records as irredeemable. This article uses recent research on women with drug convictions in Pennsylvania to examine the intersection of the war on drugs and the war on poor women.

The federal *Personal Responsibility and Work Opportunity Reconciliation Act of 1996* ("PRWORA"),[3] along with state welfare legislation, denies welfare benefits on the basis of certain types of criminal history, as well as requiring state welfare systems to interact with state and federal penal records systems. PRWORA bars fleeing felons and parole or probation violators (regardless of the charge they are fleeing from, or the condition of probation or parole violated) from receiving *Temporary Assistance for Needy Families* ("TANF") benefits.[4] The federal law also denies assistance for ten years to a person convicted in federal or state court of having fraudulently misrepresented her residence in order to obtain TANF, Food Stamps, SSI, or Medicaid benefits.[5] The most draconian welfare reform provision based on criminal records is a *lifetime* bar on benefits for individuals with felony drug convictions.

The Lifetime Ban on Benefits for Women with Felony Drug Convictions

The federal welfare statute requires states to deny TANF benefits[6] and food stamps to anyone who has been convicted of a drug felony,[7] unless the state legislature affirmatively decides to provide benefits to those individuals in state legislation passed after the effective date of the federal bill.[8]

Congress passed the lifetime ban on benefits for individuals with felony drug convictions after a total of two minutes of debate in the Senate, and no debate at all in the House of Representatives. Although at least thirty states have eliminated or modified the ban in order to reduce recidivism, ensure that drug and alcohol treatment services remain available,[9] encourage family reunification, and support women in recovery, the ban remains fully in effect in the remaining twenty states.[10]

At the time the ban on benefits was passed, relatively little was known about women with felony drug convictions, and most people's image of "drug felons" focused on men, not on women.[11] I conducted research to begin painting a picture of women with drug convictions and to start answering some basic questions about them: How many women have felony drug convictions? What offenses did they commit? How old are they? Do they have children? What have their lives been like? Did they have prior criminal records? What are their employment and educational backgrounds? When and how did they begin using drugs? Had they experienced abuse, as children or as adults? Did they have stable housing? What difference will it make to them, to their families, and to their communities if they are forever barred from getting cash assistance and food stamps?

The research was conducted in Pennsylvania, one of the states where the ban remains in effect,[12] and included three related projects. The main project, which is discussed in this article, consisted of interviews of women with drug convictions[13] and of staff in the criminal justice system. A total of twenty-six women (twenty-three women with drug convictions and three women with pending felony drug charges) were interviewed about their lives, their life histories, and their hopes and plans for the future.[14] They were found in drug treatment programs and half-way houses in four different counties in Pennsylvania, in the Philadelphia county jail, and by word of mouth. In addition, thirty professional staff working in drug treatment programs across the state, in the state and city departments of health, in other health care and social service programs, in the county jail, and in other parts of the criminal justice system were interviewed. The two other projects involved review of data from the Philadelphia Criminal Court system and from a well-respected women's residential drug treatment program.[15]

Each of these sources provided different types of data, and a different window through which to view issues around women's drug usage and criminal activities. Yet they also provided a surprisingly consistent picture of the women themselves, of their life histories and criminal histories, and of the barriers they have faced and continue to face in their struggles to recover from their addictions and from the abuse they have survived, to develop and maintain healthy relationships with their children, families, and friends, and to move forward with their lives. The picture that emerges is quite striking:

- The overwhelming majority of the women had no prior drug convictions, and their felony convictions are for very small quantities of drugs (often only five dollars or ten dollars worth).
- They began their drug usage as young children or as teenagers, often in direct response to sexual and/or physical abuse they were experiencing, or when they ran away to escape the abuse.
- They have limited educations, limited literacy, employment histories in short-term low-wage jobs, histories of homelessness and prostitution, multiple physical and mental health problems needing

treatment, and have survived repeated and horrific violence as children and as adults.

- They have children about whom they care very much, and with whom they have had very troubled relationships as a result of their drug addictions.
- Jail is the first place they have been offered drug treatment, and the first context in which the abuse they have survived has been addressed.

This article is based on a longer report detailing the results of the research.[16]

Women with Drug Convictions

According to data collected by the Pennsylvania Commission on Sentencing, in 1996, 1,104 women were convicted of drug felonies in Pennsylvania. Since the ban is life-long, the numbers of women affected will continue to increase cumulatively. National data on the number of women with felony drug convictions are not easily available. Only a small proportion of women whose addictions result in criminal behavior are actually charged with drug crimes—the offenses for which they are arrested are more likely to be prostitution, retail theft, or other non-drug charges. However it appears from data collected by the federal Bureau of Justice Statistics that approximately 61,000 women were convicted of felony drug offenses in state and federal courts in the U.S. during 1996.[17] Of those 61,000 women, approximately 26,000 (forty-three percent) were convicted of possession of drugs, rather than sales.[18] The Legal Action Center surveyed seventeen drug and alcohol treatment programs for women with children around the country, and found that twenty-one percent of the AFDC recipients in those treatment programs had felony drug convictions.[19]

All twenty-six of the women I interviewed had drug addictions, and their criminal offenses were closely connected to their addictions. For example, eighteen (sixty-nine percent) of the twenty-six women interviewed disclosed having prostituted to get cash for drugs, or traded sex for drugs.

> I didn't have to buy drugs because I could get them that way. I started doing everything I said I never would do. I had drug dealers to come over. I wound up selling my body to the drug dealers to trade for drugs. I danced strip for guys. Everything I said I'd never do, I did it. I started taking and stealing from my mother. I knew I was getting bad when I wanted to sell my food.[20]

Their drug offenses were also driven by their addictions—none of the twenty-six women who were interviewed were selling drugs but not using them; and all of the women who were selling drugs were doing it to get drugs for themselves. "All my women drug clients are users—none have been sellers unless they were using. If a woman is charged with a drug felony she's usually in really bad shape."[21]

Twenty-three of the women who were interviewed had drug convictions, and three had pending cases. The majority of the women interviewed had no prior convictions at all, and most of the women with prior convictions had been convicted of prostitution or other non-drug offenses. A few of the women had prior misdemeanor drug convictions. Of all twenty-six women who were interviewed, only one (four percent) had two felony drug convictions. These numbers are similar to the results from the Philadelphia Criminal Court data, in which none of the nine women convicted of felony drug offenses had prior drug convictions, and six (sixty-seven percent) of the nine women had no prior convictions at all.[22]

What Counts as a Felony Drug Conviction?

Under the federal law, for purposes of the ban on benefits, a conviction counts as a felony drug conviction if:

1. the conviction is for a felony (as defined by the jurisdiction involved) and
2. the offense "has as an element the possession, use, or distribution of a controlled substance . . ."[23] and
3. the conviction is for *conduct* after August 22, 1996.[24]

There is enormous variation as to what constitutes a drug felony in different states. Each state has its own criminal code that determines whether a particular crime is a felony or not. Under the federal ban, a woman may be barred from benefits in Pennsylvania for an offense which occurred in another state, and which, had it occurred in Pennsylvania, would not have been a felony.

In Pennsylvania, simple possession of a controlled substance is a misdemeanor. The usual misdemeanor drug charge is "K&I"—knowingly or intentionally possessing a controlled substance.[25]

In Pennsylvania, the most common felony drug charge is "PWID"—possession with intent to deliver, or actual delivery, of a controlled substance.[26] A woman could be convicted of PWID if she attempts to sell (or give) drugs to an undercover police officer, makes a sale or transfer of drugs which is directly observed by a police officer, or is found to possess a large enough quantity of drugs that a court is convinced she must have intended to give or sell some drugs to someone else.

There is no requirement that money be exchanged—if a woman shares drugs with a friend, that constitutes "delivery" whether or not a sale is involved. Similarly, the quantity or street value of the drugs involved is irrelevant if a woman has attempted to deliver drugs to an undercover officer, or if an officer has directly observed her hand drugs to someone else.

Many of the women who were interviewed were convicted of felonies for very small amounts of drugs—five dollars or ten dollars worth. This is consistent with other studies of women and drug sales. A study of women serving prison terms in Colorado for felonies also found that their drug sales tended to be "small trades (i.e. transactions of less than $10)."[27] A study of women drug users in Bushwick, New York found that "to the limited extent that they participated in drug selling, women were overwhelmingly concentrated at the lowest levels."[28] Although the quantity of drugs involved is not relevant to the conviction in Pennsylvania, it is relevant to sentencing.[29]

While a verdict of guilty entered by a judge or a jury, or a plea of guilty or no contest counts as a conviction, a disposition of "ARD" (accelerated rehabilitative disposition) or "§17" (probation without a verdict) does not. ARD and §17 are programs that allow a first time offender to agree to a term of probation (which can include drug or alcohol treatment) without having been convicted. If the individual successfully completes the probation, the underlying charges are dismissed, and no criminal record results. An individual whose case is disposed of through ARD or §17 does not have a conviction. Similarly, the Pennsylvania Department of Public Welfare has recognized that juvenile offenses do not count as convictions for purposes of the federal ban.[30]

These complicated criteria result in significant confusion, and the mistaken denial of benefits to individuals who are not barred by federal law. Welfare caseworkers often erroneously assume that *any* felony conviction is a bar to benefits, or that any *drug* conviction (including a misdemeanor) is a bar to benefits, or that what matters is the date of conviction, or the date of arrest.

For many women, the date of arrest is the same as or quite close to, the date of the illegal conduct. However Philadelphia Criminal Court data concerning individuals who were arraigned in September 1996 included several individuals whose date of alleged illegal conduct was weeks or months earlier than the date of arrest.[31] Similarly, I attended a court hearing in 1998 for one of the women in the study whose alleged illegal conduct was in 1993. Even if the welfare caseworker understands the rule correctly, it can be quite difficult for a woman to prove that her conviction is not covered under the ban because her conduct occurred on or before August 22, 1996, even if her conviction occurred after August 22, 1996.[32]

Life Histories of the Women: "The drugs I used when things really hurted me, so I wouldn't feel the hurt."[33]

All of the women were in recovery at the time of the interviews. Their histories of drug usage ranged from two years to fifty-three years, with the median being thirteen and a half years of drug usage. Tanya's story was typical:

> When I was a child, my father used to rape me. It started when I was nine. . . . After I ran away, I wanted somebody to want me. I ran into this guy, he was older, and I wanted him to want me. He gave me cocaine. I was thirteen.[34]

Most of the women were abused in many different ways, at different times and by different men in their lives—brothers, fathers, stepfathers, boyfriends, husbands, and strangers. They responded to that violence with drug usage as self-medication:

> They don't understand how she could have used drugs; they don't understand how much physical and emotional pain she was in—she had broken ribs, broken arms. The abuse this woman endured from her husband, I would have written prescriptions for myself too—she was in such pain.[35]

They also have multiple physical and mental health problems, including ongoing medical problems as the aftermath of trauma. Their injuries included lung and liver damage from a stabbing, severe headaches suffered by a woman with a metal plate in her head from being beaten in the head with a hammer, arm, shoulder and head injuries from shootings, and broken bones from beatings.

"Twenty-three (88%) of the twenty-six women interviewed had either been homeless or lived in very unstable housing before being arrested."[36] For many of the women, housing conditions most people would find appalling were a source of pride, because they were better than being on the street:

> I had been homeless in the past, but right before I was arrested, I wasn't homeless. I had my own room. I paid with money and with drugs. It was a crack house, but I had my own lock on the door of the room.[37]

Almost all of the twenty-six women identified the need for safe housing as a major concern facing them when they completed treatment.[38] "They saw housing as an overwhelming issue in maintaining recovery, in protecting their children, in extricating themselves from abusive relationships, and in reuniting their families."[39]

Lack of education was also a major barrier identified by the women. "Of the twenty-six women interviewed, nineteen (73%) had less than a high school education; fourteen (54%) of the women interviewed had less than a tenth grade education."[40] Abuse affected their ability to concentrate in school, and many left school when they ran away to escape abuse.

> I was afraid to go to sleep at home, because my mom's boyfriend came in and messed with me. I thought if I could just go to sleep—I only felt safe sleeping at school. So I went to sleep at school every day, and they yelled at me. . . . So I started taking Valiums, drinking cough syrup. I told my mom—it was her boyfriends who tried to mess with me—she didn't want to believe me, it happened with her uncles in her childhood. So I ran away. I went downtown and started getting locked up.[41]

Twenty-two (eighty-five percent) of the twenty-six women had work histories, but most had worked at short-term, low-wage jobs that they lost because of drug usage. The remaining four (fifteen percent) had only worked as prostitutes. Many had worked in fields that would now be closed to them as a result of their convictions (as nurse's aides, other health care workers, child care workers),[42] or in settings that would likely interfere with their recovery (as barmaids, strippers, dancers in topless bars). A few had held longer term jobs, but only one thought that she would be able to return to her former job, doing janitorial work. Most had lost their jobs well before they were arrested, as a result of their drug addictions.[43]

Twenty-two (eighty-five percent) of the twenty-six women interviewed had children, and those twenty-two women had a total of sixty-five children among them.[44] Sixty (ninety-two percent) of the sixty-five children were under age eighteen at the time of the interviews; of the women with children, only one woman (who was sixty-eight years old) had a grown child and no minor children.[45] Of the four women who did not have children of their own, three (seventy-five percent) had taken care of nieces, nephews, and friends' children for extended periods.

All of the women loved and worried about their children. Some had custody of their children and had their children with them in residential treatment programs. Others were in treatment programs that did not allow children, but had regular visits with their children. Others were in touch with their children who lived in other states by telephone or mail. Some were estranged from some or all of their children, because of the children's anger at their mothers, or the anger of the family members who were caring for the children. Some had children in foster care; some women with children in foster care were in contact with their children, had visits with their children, and hoped to get their children back shortly. Others were trying to locate their children with the help of program staff. Still others had lost their children to the child welfare system permanently because of their addictions. All of the women talked about their children with tremendous longing, and with enormous guilt and shame for the ways that they had failed their children during their addictions.[46]

The women who had children with them in treatment talked of their efforts to learn to be better parents, to rebuild their relationships with their children.[47] The women whose children were not with them, talked of their efforts to maintain connections and rebuild relationships with their children.[48] The lack of welfare benefits makes family reunification much more difficult, if not impossible. Criminal justice staff predicted that denial of benefits would result in children being placed in, or remaining in, out-of-home placements:

> If they don't get any help, kids will stay in foster care or with relatives. I'm a mother . . . well if I don't have food for my children, I'm going to steal or give them up. You don't want your kids hungry and if you can't provide for them that's what's going to happen.[49]

The impact on mothers and children of the loss of benefits also worries staff in the child welfare system:

> If a mother is not able to support her child, we would take the child; and at the end of twelve months of placement, we have to terminate

> parental rights unless there are compelling circumstances. If you've ever made a mistake in your life, it's very punitive. I imagine it would come into play as more and more women lose their benefits. Convictions will rise as women don't have places to live, then we will take the child while the woman is in jail. Women will lose their kids, will lose everything in their lives—cash assistance, kids, jobs. Employers won't hire them with felony drug convictions. The Department would say we will do everything in our power to provide necessary services to enable women and children to stay together, but that doesn't include cash assistance or housing.[50]

"Welfare Helps Us Stay In Touch With Society"[51]

In addition to making physical survival and family reunification more difficult for the women, the ban has a particularly damaging psychological effect: it denies women membership in civil society. Although welfare receipt carries tremendous stigma as a result of the right-wing attack on poor women, for women struggling to maintain recovery from addiction and avoid arrest and incarceration, welfare is often something to aspire to. The women who were interviewed spontaneously brought up the ways in which welfare helps them feel connected to society:

> We still need welfare until we are strong enough to get on our feet. Trying to stay clean, trying to be responsible parents and take care of our families. We need welfare right now. If we lose it, we might be back out there selling drugs. We trying to change our lives. Trying to stop doing wrong things. Some of us need help. Welfare helps us stay in touch with society. Trying to do what's right for us.[52]

The women's comments were echoed by drug treatment and public health staff. The director of a health project working with injecting drug users talked about the impact of losing benefits on the women she sees:

> There's a general sense of helplessness engendered by losing benefits. Helplessness at not being able to advocate for themselves, a sense of the overwhelming inability to move through the system. We see a lot of people having to scrounge to get money—collecting cans, shoplifting, sex work—there seems to be more of that when women lose benefits. They're not happy in their addiction. They're not reveling in their 30-year heroin habit. Addiction is a devastating condition.
>
> I think that for folks who are trying to get away from their addiction—when we think of what it takes for someone to pay bills, maintain a residence, feed oneself, you need such a network of support—families, friends. For people in addiction who never had, or have lost those supports, to regain their functioning, they need those supports. There is no other place to turn for support. I find [the ban] to be very cruel and unrealistic. I think that the cost of those minimal benefits is the least we can do as a society for people who have been ravaged by addiction . . . or this whole class of people will never be able to function.[53]

Criminal justice staff agreed as well. An experienced probation office supervisor explained:

> It seems grossly unfair to me. It's tantamount to saying you're just looking for a reason to deny people benefits. These women live life on the margins—to take that safety net away increases drug use, criminality... it's a set of dominoes in someone's life. You lose one thing, then another; lose benefits, then everything. If someone is in a job program or a drug treatment program I would restore benefits.... I wouldn't penalize them for their background.[54]

The women were also clear about the psychological impact of the ban: "I feel like [an] outcast."[55]

Welfare as a Source of Independence: "I wouldn't have to ask nobody for anything."[56]

The women interviewed also stressed that getting welfare would make them *independent*, in contrast to mainstream depictions of welfare receipt as dependency. "If I could get welfare, it would make a lot of difference to me. I wouldn't have to ask nobody for anything. I'd have something of my own."[57] The women most often didn't want to have to turn to an abusive man. Almost all of the women interviewed had been physically and sexually abused, in multiple ways, often by men they depended upon financially.[58] One woman said:

> My husband, we were together for eighteen years. He gave me drugs, that was how I started using, when I was fifteen. He was taking care of me. He was hitting me a lot, off and on the whole time we was together, but he took care of me.[59]

Fear of being homeless as a result of losing benefits was also a recurring theme in women's comments.[60] Over and over, women expressed fear that lack of alternatives would force them to go back to abusive relationships and unsafe living arrangements, and that they will relapse into active addiction as a result.[61]

> My baby's father wants me to go back with him to live at his mother's house. I don't want to go back there. The last time I was in treatment I went back there and stopped making meetings and relapsed and went back to selling drugs and went back to jail.[62]

Many of the women talked about the ways in which being denied benefits makes it harder for them to stay in treatment, and to maintain recovery. Treatment programs, half-way houses, and shelters depend on the women's food stamps and a portion of their cash assistance checks to support the program.[63] None of the programs in this study planned to discharge individual women because of welfare denials, but all of them described it as a significant loss of funds that would make it harder to keep the program operating. The women often worried about whether they would be able to stay in treatment programs, or go to a transitional housing or follow-up program afterwards, without benefits.

> I'm hoping I can still stay here in rehab—I've been borrowing money. I'm supposed to give $15 of each check to the program, and I can't because I don't have a check. I have no way to buy clothes or personal stuff. I need to stay here and get together. I need six to nine months here. I would die out there if I have to go back on the Avenue. I was selling myself to get money because of drugs. I've come a long way from what I was. People that are getting theirself clean deserve a chance to start all over again. I pray and hope they'll do something. I need rent, personal needs, food. Do you know if they'll let me stay here without a check?[64]

The women worried that lack of alternatives would drive them back to abusive relationships, back to drug usage, back to prostitution, or back to other criminal activity.

> I think [welfare] helps a lot. Some people need it—to have somewhere to stay, for positive things, for clothing and sheltering. If they take welfare from people, the crime rate will go up higher, because people will rob people or prostitute to get money. People need help. It makes a big difference.[65]

Other research has shown that access to public assistance is important in enabling women to leave prostitution.[66] As a child welfare agency supervisor explained:

> If you don't have adequate housing and adequate therapy there's nothing else but the street and on the street there's nothing else but drugs. You and I have so many resources—if I lost my job today I would not be on the street. These parents don't have resources.[67]

Self Sufficiency is Overrated: The War on Welfare Mothers

One of the mantras of the current wave of welfare reformers, whether they identify as liberal, moderate, or conservative, is that welfare recipients suffer from "dependency" and need to become "self-sufficient." While much debate takes place over the correct mechanism for "weaning" welfare mothers from their "addiction" to welfare—should they be forced to go cold turkey after a limited period of benefits, or should employment and training programs be provided—hardly anyone is publicly questioning the underlying assumption. Even those who defend the need for a safety net are quick to decry "dependence" on welfare.

Social interaction necessarily involves dependence. Whether "dependence" is identified and denounced has much more to do with who is being considered dependent than what they have or have not done. And, of course, the presentation of women, of poor people, and of people of color as "dependents" has a long history.[68] For many years now, some observers have pointed out that welfare allows women to be *independent* of violent relationships, of bad marriages, and of abusive employers.[69]

> One of the many ways in which "the 1960s" began in the 1950s, welfare-claiming was a part of the civil rights movement. We need to understand this in order to avoid the mistaken assumption that being "on welfare" always connotes dependency and despair. . . . The 1960s welfare rights movement was also a women's movement. Claiming welfare was a strategy for upward mobility and especially for benefiting one's children, a move away from poverty and resignation.[70]

One of my colleagues, Gloria Browne, argues that low-income communities, and especially communities of people of color, have been forced to be too independent, isolated from the mainstream economy, from decent jobs and housing, effective schools, good health care, subsidized transportation, and denied much of the benefits of most government spending.[71] Similarly, the women in this study have been isolated from the mainstream economy, from social supports, and the benefits of civil society. Shame, the response they have most often encountered, simply acts as a trigger for relapse into addiction and recidivism into crime.

After years of isolation, and struggle with addiction, the women know that successful recovery requires connections to society and support, and can't be sustained alone.

> Drugs are one of the worst things that can happen to anyone. It's a trap and you need help to stop and you got to stay with it. It takes time and someone to help. You got to have a group to go to and someone to talk to and it's hard. It's wrong to take them off welfare—if they can't get jobs, what they are going to do?[72]

The women's plans for building a new, productive life had three parts: rebuilding relationships and taking care of their children, maintaining recovery, and looking for work. Access to welfare benefits is a critical factor for all three pieces. As one woman said, "now it matters because I'm trying to do the right thing."[73]

Conclusion

The lifetime ban on benefits for women with felony drug convictions is clearly counter-productive. The women who were interviewed were very clear that the ban on benefits would not have acted as a deterrent. The realities of life in active addiction make the ban irrelevant in determining behavior. "I was too much into the addiction to care about anything."[74] "If my daughter didn't nothing would."[75] An experienced prosecutor echoed the women's belief that the ban on benefits is not an effective deterrent: "I think that if the policymakers looked into the lives of these women and if they understood the implications they might conclude that the impact of it is not as a deterrent. It's purely punitive. It isn't thoughtful."[76]

The women interviewed in this study experienced pervasive violence, and responded to battering and rape with drug usage as self-medication. They acquired their felony drug convictions by way of sexual and physical assault, mental illness, and homelessness. We should not be socially disenfranchising women for the rest of their lives for drug crimes they committed in response to physical and sexual abuse, mental illness, or homelessness. Nor should jail be the first place a woman is offered drug treatment or help responding to physical or sexual assault.

Public discussion on criminal justice, like public discussion on welfare, has been dominated by punitive rhetoric based in myths and stereotypes and driven by fear. No one exemplifies those fears more than drug addicted welfare mothers. The women I interviewed are trapped at the intersection of the war on drugs and the war on poor women. During the attacks on welfare that led up to the 1996 law, there were numerous comments about welfare mothers being addicted to "the narcotic of welfare."[77] Banning women with drug convictions from receiving welfare benefits was a manifestation of that convergence. In a decade when prisons are virtually the only new public housing being constructed for poor people, and jails have replaced psychiatric hospitals, the closer interaction of the welfare and criminal justice systems isn't surprising. However, the implications for low-income women and their children are frightening, and demand a more thoughtful response.

Valuing interdependence and recognizing that individuals and communities cannot survive without interaction and assistance from each other would produce a different approach to thinking about welfare and welfare reform. Similarly, paying serious attention to the violence that women who are defendants in criminal cases have experienced would produce a different response to their situations. "We need to ask why a thirteen-year-old girl runs away to the street because it's safer."[78]

Appendix A
List of States Choosing to Eliminate or Modify the Ban

States that have eliminated the ban:

Connecticut
Idaho
Michigan
New Hampshire
New York
Ohio
Oklahoma
Oregon
Vermont

States that have modified the ban:

Arkansas
Colorado
Florida
Hawaii
Illinois
Iowa
Kentucky
Louisiana
Maryland
Massachusetts
Minnesota
Nevada
New Jersey
New Mexico
North Carolina
Rhode Island
South Carolina
Texas
Utah
Washington
Wisconsin

Source: Legal Action Center, National Governors' Association, Center on Budget and Policy Priorities and calls to states. Updated January 2002.

Notes

[1] See Amy E. Hirsch, *Income Deeming in the AFDC Program: Using Dual Track Family Law to Make Poor Women Poorer*, 16 N.Y.U. Rev. L. & Soc. Change 713 (1987–88); Herma Hill Kay & Irving Philips, *Poverty and the Law of Child Custody*, 54 Cal. L. Rev. 716 (1966); Jacobus tenBroek, *California's Dual System of Family Law: Its Origin, Development and Present Status* (pts. 1, 2, & 3), 16 Stan. L. Rev. 257 (1964), 17 Stan. L. Rev. 614 (1965).

[2] Francis Fox Piven & Richard A. Cloward, *Regulating the Poor: The Functions of Public Welfare* 35 (2d ed. 1993).

[3] P.L. 104–193.

[4] 42 U.S.C. § 608(a)(9) (1996). Similar provisions exist for food stamps. See 7 U.S.C. § 2015(k)(1). See David A. Super, *Food Stamps and the Criminal Justice System* (March 6, 2001) (manuscript on file with the author) for a more detailed discussion of interactions between the Food Stamp Program and the criminal justice system. Pennsylvania law also denies TANF and General Assistance (state-funded benefits for individuals not eligible for TANF) benefits to any individual with an outstanding warrant or fine, from any jurisdiction, for any charge, no matter how old the warrant or how minor the offense, until the warrant is resolved or the individual demonstrates compliance with an approved payment plan for the fine. See 62 P.S. § 432(9). Other states' laws vary. See e.g. Legal Action Center, *Welfare As We Know It Now: What New York's New Welfare Laws Mean for People with Criminal Records, Substance Abuse Histories and HIV/AIDS* (1998).

[5] See 42 U.S.C. § 608(a)(8) (1996).

[6] TANF is the block grant which replaced the 60-year old Aid to Families with Dependent Children program. It ends any federally based individual entitlement to benefits, sets a five

year lifetime limit on federally funded assistance, and limits recipients' access to education and job training. It is governed by Title I of PRWORA. See 42 U.S.C. § 601 et seq. (1996).

[7] The federal law bars TANF assistance and food stamps to any individual "convicted of any offense which is classified as a felony by the law of the jurisdiction involved and which has as an element the possession, use or distribution of a controlled substance. . . ." 21 U.S.C. § 862a. The ban, as modified by the *Balanced Budget Act of 1997*, P.L. 105-33, applies to convictions for *conduct* after August 22, 1996, rather than applying to all convictions entered after that date. 21 U.S.C. § 862a(d)(2).

[8] The state may pass legislation to completely opt out of the ban or to modify it. See 21 U.S.C. § 862a(d)(1).

[9] Many treatment programs depend on the food stamps and cash assistance that women receive to help pay for treatment.

[10] Connecticut, Idaho, Michigan, New Hampshire, New York, Ohio, Oklahoma, Oregon, and Vermont have completely opted out of the ban. At least 21 other states have modified the ban. A list of states that have eliminated or modified the ban as of January 2002, is attached as *Appendix A*, based on information compiled by the Legal Action Center, the National Governors' Association, the Center on Budget and Policy Priorities and calls to states.

[11] Although an excellent, small but growing literature exists on women drug users, including Sheigla Murphy & Marsha Rosenbaum, *Pregnant Women on Drugs* (Rutgers U. Press, 1999); Claire Sterk, *Fast Lives: Women Who Use Crack Cocaine* (Temple U. Press 1999); Lisa Maher, *Sexed Work* (Clarendon Press 1997); and Stephen R. Kendall, *Substance and Shadow* (Harvard U. Press 1996), most general discussions of drug addiction and of drug policy pay little attention to women, and no attention to the connections between women's drug usage and sexual and physical violence against women. If women are discussed at all in the general literature it is in the context of drug usage by pregnant women. See e.g. Franklin E. Zimring & Gordon Hawkins, *The Search for Rational Drug Control* (Cambridge U. Press 1992).

[12] The State Department of Public Welfare has also unilaterally extended the ban to General Assistance ("GA"), without authorization from the state legislature, despite a state statute providing for time limited GA benefits for individuals in drug or alcohol treatment.

[13] All of the women's names used here have been changed in order to protect their privacy.

[14] "In general, studies have shown that data obtained from drug users tend to be both reliable and valid." Susan K. Datesman & James A. Inciardi, *Female Heroin Use, Criminality, and Prostitution*, 8.4 Contemporary Drug Problems, 455–72 (Winter 1979).

[15] The study of Philadelphia Criminal Court data is discussed in greater detail in Amy E. Hirsch, *Drug Charges in Philadelphia: Who Gets Charged? Who Gets Convicted?* (unpublished manuscript on file with the author of article) [hereinafter Hirsch, *Who Gets Charged?*]. The study of women in drug treatment is discussed in greater detail in Amy E. Hirsch, *Women in Residential Drug Treatment: Survivors of Violence* (unpublished manuscript on file with the author of article).

[16] See Amy E. Hirsch, *"Some Days Are Harder Than Hard": Welfare Reform and Women With Drug Convictions in Pennsylvania*, Center for Law and Social Policy (1999) [hereinafter Hirsch, *Some Days Are Harder Than Hard*]. The results concerning physical and sexual abuse are reported in Amy E. Hirsch, *"The World Was Never A Safe Place For Them": Abuse, Welfare Reform and Women With Drug Convictions*, 7 Violence Against Women 159–75 (Feb. 2001), and policy recommendations resulting from the research are reported in Amy E. Hirsch, *Welfare Reform and Women With Felony Drug Convictions: Research Results and Policy Recommendations*, 33 Clearinghouse Review: Journal of Poverty Law & Policy 587–96 (Jan.–Feb. 2000).

[17] These estimates were derived from data in two reports from the Bureau of Justice Statistics: Jodi M. Brown, Patrick A. Langan & David J. Levin, *Felony Sentences in State Courts, 1996,* Tables 1 & 5 (May 1999, revised, July 30, 1999), and Jodi M. Brown & Patrick A. Langan, *Felony Sentences in the United States, 1996*, Table 2 (July 1999).

[18] See id. (indicating that in some jurisdictions, simple possession of drugs is a felony).

[19] See Legal Action Center, *Making Welfare Reform Work. Tools for Confronting Alcohol and Drug Problems Among Welfare Recipients* 40–41 (Sept. 1997).

[20] Interview with Tanya (July 7, 1998).

[21] Interview with Cristi A. Charpentier, Asst. Defender, Defender Assn. of Phila. (Nov. 24, 1998).

[22] See generally Hirsch, *Who Gets Charged?*

[23] Although each jurisdiction gets to decide whether a particular offense is classified as a felony, the definition of "controlled substance" is set by federal law. See 21 U.S.C. § 862a(a).

[24] See 21 U.S.C. § 862.

[25] See *Pennsylvania Controlled Substance, Drug, Device and Cosmetic Act*, § 13(a)(16), 35 Pa. Consol. Stat. § 780-101.

[26] See *Pennsylvania Controlled Substance, Drug, Device and Cosmetic Act*, § 13(a)(30).

[27] Kim English, *Self-Reported Crime Rates of Women Prisoners*, 9 J. Quantitative Criminology 357, 372 (1993).

[28] Lisa Maher & Kathleen Daly, *Women in the Street-Level Drug Economy: Continuity or Change?*, 34 Criminology 465, 472 (1996).

[29] Pennsylvania's criminal code provides for a mandatory two-year prison sentence if at least two grams of drugs are involved; a mandatory three-year prison sentence if at least 10 grams are involved, and a mandatory five-year prison sentence if at least 100 grams are involved. 18 Pa. Consol. Stat. § 7508. Two grams is approximately $200 worth of cocaine or heroin according to routine police estimates in Philadelphia. There are 28 grams in an ounce. Ten dollars worth of drugs (an amount for which many women are convicted of felonies) is 1/280 of an ounce. For comparison, spices are often sold in one-ounce jars in the supermarket. Under Pennsylvania state law, unlike under federal criminal law, no distinction is made between crack and powder cocaine. However, Pennsylvania law does distinguish between cocaine and narcotics (including heroin), with longer maximum sentences provided for narcotics than for cocaine. See *Pennsylvania Controlled Substance, Drug, Device and Cosmetic Act*, § 13(f), 35 Pa. Consol. Stat. §780-101, et seq.; Cmmw. of Pa. Commn. on Senten., *Sentencing Guidelines Implementation Manual*, 5th ed., 175 (June 13, 1997).

[30] See Pa. Dept. of Pub. Welfare Off. of Income Maint., Policy Clarification: *Juvenile Court/ Criminal History Provisions* (Oct. 27, 1997).

[31] See Hirsch, *Who Gets Charged?*

[32] When a woman is released from jail after serving her sentence, she usually has no proof as to whether her conviction was for a felony or not, let alone whether it counts as a drug offense or what date her illegal conduct occurred.

[33] Interview with Lynette (Aug. 27, 1998).

[34] Interview with Tanya (July 9, 1998).

[35] Interview with non-urban county jail staff member (Dec. 15, 1998).

[36] Hirsch, *Some Days Are Harder Than Hard*, at 39.

[37] Interview with Laura (Nov. 24, 1998).

[38] Hirsch, *Some Days Are Harder Than Hard*, at 41.

[39] Id.

[40] Id. at 27.

[41] Interview with Wendy (Apr. 28,1998).

[42] Under state law in Pennsylvania, as in many other states, individuals convicted of drug felonies are barred from employment in child care, public or private schools, home health care agencies, nursing homes, or personal care homes. 23 Pa. Consol. Stat. Ann. § 6344(c)(2); Debbie A. Mukamal, *Confronting the Employment Barriers of Criminal Records: Effective Legal and Practical Strategies*, 33 Clearinghouse Rev.: J. Poverty L. & Policy 597 (Jan.–Feb. 2000).

[43] Hirsch, *Some Days Are Harder Than Hard*, at 30.

[44] See id. at 42.

[45] See id.

[46] Hirsch, *Some Days Are Harder Than Hard*, at 42.

[47] See id.

[48] Id.

[49] Interview with urban criminal justice staff person (Mar. 27, 1998).

[50] Interview with Rita Urwitz, Supervisor at the Phila. Dept. of Human Servs. (Dec. 15, 1998). The federal *Adoption and Safe Families Act of 1997* requires child welfare agencies to move to terminate parental rights very quickly. See P.L. 105-89.
[51] Interview with Tanya (July 9, 1998).
[52] Id.
[53] Interview with Julie Parr, Exec. Dir. of Prevention Point Phila. (Dec. 3, 1998).
[54] Interview with Joseph M. Harrington, Supervisor, Drug/I.S.P. Unit, First Judicial Dist. of Pa. (May 14, 1998).
[55] Interview with Wendy (Apr. 28, 1998).
[56] Interview with Linda (June 25, 1998).
[57] Id.
[58] See Hirsch, *Some Days Are Harder Than Hard*, at 6.
[59] Interview with Julie (June 19, 1998).
[60] See Hirsch, *Some Days Are Harder Than Hard*, at 39.
[61] See id. at 6.
[62] Interview with Laura (Nov. 24, 1998).
[63] Since these interviews were completed, some treatment programs have stopped the practice of taking a portion of women's cash assistance, instead putting the funds into a mandatory savings program. Half-way houses and shelters still require the women to pay part of their income as rent. All of the programs still require women to contribute their food stamps towards the cost of food.
[64] Interview with Donna (Feb. 4, 1998).
[65] Interview with Lynette (Aug. 27, 1998).
[66] Nabile El-Bassel et al., *Sex-Trading and Psychological Distress among Women Recruited from the Streets of Harlem*, 87.1 Am. J. Pub. Health 66–70 (Jan. 1997).
[67] Interview with Rita Urwitz, Supervisor at the Phila. Dept. of Human Servs. (Dec. 15, 1998).
[68] See e.g. Gwendolyn Mink, *The Lady and the Tramp: Gender, Race, and the Origins of the American Welfare State*, Women, the State, and Welfare 92 (Linda Gordon ed., U. of Wisconsin Press 1990); Nancy Fraser & Linda Gordon, *"Dependency" Demystified: Inscriptions of Power in a Keyword of the Welfare State*, 1 Social Politics 4 (1994).
[69] See e.g. Mimi Abramowitz, *Regulating the Lives of Women: Social Welfare Policy From Colonial Times To The Present* 352 (South End Press 1988); Frances Fox Piven, *Ideology and the State: Women, Power, and the Welfare State*, Women, the State, and Welfare 250, 254 (Linda Gordon, ed. 1990); June M. Axinn & Amy E. Hirsch, *Welfare and the "Reform" of Women*, 74 Families in Society 563, 571 (Nov. 1993).
[70] Linda Gordon, *Welfare Reform: A History Lesson*, Dissent 323, 326 (Summer 1994).
[71] Gloria Browne, (speech) *Training for Students Participating in the Interdisciplinary Health Project* (U. of Pa., Summer 1992); John Pucher, *Discrimination in Mass Transit*, APA J. 315 (Summer 1982); Stephanie Coontz, *The Way We Never Were: American Families and the Nostalgia Trap*, Ch. 4 (Basic Books 1992).
[72] Interview with Rose (July 21, 1998).
[73] Interview with Sharon (Apr. 28, 1998).
[74] Interview with Maria (Feb. 25, 1998).
[75] Interview with Sharon (Apr. 28, 1998).
[76] Interview with Mimi Rose, Chief, Family Violence and Sexual Assault Unit, D.A.'s Off., Philadelphia, Pa. (Dec. 17, 1998).
[77] Dan Quayle, quoted in Laura E. Gomez, *Misconceiving Mothers* 118 (Temple U. Press 1997).
[78] Interview with Elaine Lord, Warden of Bedford Hills Maximum Sec. Correctional Facility, N.Y. State (Nov. 13, 1998).

SECTION IV

Programming for Women Offenders

As mentioned in the beginning section of this text, traditional criminological theories were essentially founded on negative images of female offenders. Further, these theoretical perspectives focused on biological or psychological explanations of female offending rather than appreciating women's economic, social, and political reality. These limited perspectives also have influenced programming deemed essential to meet the needs of these women. Feminist theory, however, has provided critical frameworks that allow scholars and practitioners to re-think, re-assess, and re-structure programming for women offenders. This section illustrates how scholars and practitioners have re-examined such programming for incarcerated women. The first two articles explore general issues related to program implementation such as women-centered prisons and correctional administrators' perceptions of gender. The remaining two articles specifically focus on two types of programs for women—substance abuse treatment and boot camps.

In her article, "Feminine Fortresses: Women-Centered Prisons?" Kelly Hannah-Moffat explores issues surrounding Canada's efforts to develop a woman-centered model of corrections. She outlines various problems, or paradoxes, associated with Canada's approach to incorporating feminist ideals in the restructuring and rethinking of women's incarceration. The concerns related to such a vision include failing to depart from traditional conceptualizations of punishment; using a broader definition of "woman" by excluding social, economic, political, and cultural relations of power; and differing interpretations of empowerment between reformers and the state. Moffat concludes her discussion by emphasizing that feminist knowledge should not attempt to alter an existing institution of social control. Rather, feminist knowledge should attempt to challenge institutions of confinement and consider different approaches to sanctioning women offenders.

In article 14, Merry Morash and Amanda Robinson explore how correctional administrators' construction of gender influences their perceptions of programming for women in prison. Content analysis of data from telephone and mail surveys reveals that the correctional administrators viewed women offenders and their programming needs from four perspectives. Morash and Robinson identify these perspectives as (1) gender irrelevant—no difference between men and women prisoners; (2) gender maintenance—women prisoners are different and traditional gender roles should be maintained; (3) gender issues—women prisoners are different and traditional gender roles are problematic; and (4) gender challenge—women prisoners are different and traditional gender arrangements must be challenged. Their findings reveal that many correctional administrators acknowledged the family-related concerns of women in prison. These concerns, however, are reflected in programs that continue to reinforce traditional gender stereotypes. The researchers note that a few correctional administrators emphasize the importance of empowering these women and challenging gender arrangements.

In her article "Women in Prison: Approaches in the Treatment of Our Most Invisible Population," Stephanie Covington provides a compelling argument concerning substance and alcohol abuse treatment programs for women offenders. She begins by noting the increasing number of women offenders in the criminal justice system since the 1980s; this increase is primarily due to drug-related offenses. Further, these women differ from men in numerous ways including their parental responsibilities, history of physical and sexual abuse, and addiction issues. When these women are incarcerated, very few correctional facilities have adequate treatment programs to address their addictions. It is in this context that Covington argues that effective treatment programs for women offenders need to be developed. These programs should incorporate a framework that not only addresses their addiction issues but also addresses the realities of their lives including their histories of emotional, physical, and sexual abuse as well as their social, political, and economic marginalization.

Susan Marcus-Mendoza, Jody Klein-Saffran, and Faith Lutze illustrate the problems associated with applying feminist therapy with boot camp ideology in article 16. They maintain that the goals and methods of the boot camp are considerably different than the goals and methods of feminist therapy. First, boot camp ideology assumes that all women offenders have similar issues that can be addressed with similar types of treatment; these women need to be more disciplined and responsible. Second, the power structure of boot camps may be harmful for women offenders, especially those who are survivors of sexual and physical abuse. Third, boot camps are essentially punishment; this punishment not only includes a loss of freedom but also entails drilling and yelling. This type of punishment is contrary to feminist, and other forms of, therapy. Marcus-Mendoza, Klein-Saffran, and Lutze conclude that feminist therapists need to realize the difficulties inherent in working with women incarcerated in boot camps. Therapists should encourage women to identify and express their feelings in a way that will not be punished. Ideally, correctional departments should implement short-term programs in community-based settings without the punishment context of boot camps.

12

Feminine Fortresses
Woman-Centered Prisons?

Kelly Hannah-Moffat

> Like all habitual patterns of social action, the structures of modern punishment have created a sense of their own inevitability and of the necessary rightness of the status quo. Our taken-for-granted ways of punishing have relieved us of the need for thinking deeply about punishment, and what little thinking we are left to do is guided along narrowly formulated channels. (Garland, 1990, p. 3; also see Douglas, 1986)

> The prisons built for women today will incarcerate the daughters of tomorrow. Prisons are not left empty and social definitions about crime are not easily changed. (Mayhew, 1994, p. 43)

Theorizing about an ethic of care and alternative visions of justice and punishment have remained, by and large, at the level of philosophy. Few scholars have explored the compatibility of feminist ideals and institutional practices of imprisonment. However, contemporary feminist criticisms of the male-based models of punishment governing women's prison regimes have led to the construction of an alternative model of woman-centered corrections. The woman-centered correctional model can be interpreted as a version of a feminist "ethic of care." Recent Canadian efforts to develop an operational model of a woman-centered prison have been regarded as innovative, progressive, and revolutionary.[1] In its 1990 report, *Creating Choices*, the Canadian Task Force on Federally Sentenced Women explicitly notes that feminist knowledge has provided a basis for restructuring women's prisons. *Creating Choices* assumes that Corrections

Canada can manage the difficult task of merging two objectives: the protection of the public, through security and control, and the empowerment and social reintegration of the offender. Notwithstanding the changes this report represents and the practical/managerial logic of the prison, there are several difficulties associated with an uncritical embrace and integration of selected feminist ideals.

This article raises some of the complicated questions associated with recent efforts to reconstruct women's prison regimes and reflects some of the contradictions, trade-offs, and frustrations experienced by reformers and feminists within and outside of the state. By outlining the recent Canadian effort to define and operationalize woman-centered corrections, I argue that current regimes and proposed visions of woman-centered corrections often fail to depart from traditional conceptualizations of punishment. The definition and constitution of a woman-centered regime is troublesome for the following reasons: It relies on the problematic category of "woman"; it is insensitive to wider social, economic, political, and cultural relations of power; it sets up a false dichotomy between the woman-centered and the male-centered regimes; and it denies the legal and material realities of imprisonment. Further, I argue that woman-centered reforms rely on a flexible rationality of empowerment. The language of empowerment is used to legitimate both correctional and feminist[2] strategies. The difficulty is that reformers and the state are working with different interpretations of empowerment. The following section briefly outlines the main tenets and recommendations of the Task Force on Federally Sentenced Women and the current efforts to implement and interpret the report's "vision for change."

Creating Choices

For more than 50 years, advocates have been arguing for the closure of the Prison for Women and for programs that accommodate the needs of women. The context of this reform initiative is shaped by a long history of struggle and survival. Tragic conditions and overt discrimination in the Prison for Women,[3] Canada's only federal institution for women prisoners (*federally sentenced* prisoners are those serving 2 years or more) has been a source of frustration for feminists, researchers, bureaucrats, and advocates since the Prison for Women opened in 1934 (Adelberg & Currie, 1987, 1993; Bernzies & Copper, 1982; Cooper, 1993; Moffat [Hannah], 1991; Shaw, 1991b). These concerns have led to numerous task forces, commissions, and recommendations calling for the closure of the Prison for Women. Each report cites similar concerns about sexism, the absence of institutional and community programming, geographic dislocation, overclassification, and cultural insensitivity. However, the recent report notes clearly that "there is urgent need for action *now* to respond to the needs of federally sentenced women" and that "there is urgent need *now* to create choices which reflect the experiences and meet the needs of women" (Task Force on Federally Sentenced Women, 1990, p. 105; emphasis in original).

The most recent report[4] of the Task Force on Federally Sentenced Women, *Creating Choices*, seems to have broken the cycle of apathy and neglect. Although the content of this report is similar to that of previous reports, the organization, philosophy, and aftermath of this report marks a fundamental shift in thinking and responding to women in prison.

The Task Force on Federally Sentenced Women[5] was established nearly 10 years after the last committee specifically set up to "settle" the issue of federal women's imprisonment had faded into obscurity (Shaw, 1993, p. 50). It was the consequence of immense social and political pressure on the government by reformers, feminists, Aboriginal organizations, and the media. This pressure for change came from a variety of sources,[6] all of whom emphasized the long history of apathy and neglect of the federal government with respect to federally incarcerated women. These groups and the revelation of sensational cases and tragedies[7] at the Prison for Women exposed the prison and the government to increased public scrutiny (Moffat [Hannah], 1991, p. 191). The government responded to the concerns and criticisms of the public by setting up a joint community and government task force (March, 1989).

From its inception, the task force committee was unlike any previous government committee in Canada or elsewhere (Shaw, 1993, p. 53). The Steering Committee of the task force was cochaired by the Canadian Association of Elizabeth Fry Societies and a deputy commissioner of the Correctional Service of Canada. Two thirds of the task force members were women. Two of these women had served federal sentences, and more than half of the members were from nongovernment and/or voluntary organizations. As Shaw (1993) indicates, "No previous government inquiry into women's imprisonment had included so many voluntary sector representatives, or Aboriginal or minority groups, and certainly no women who had personal experience of prison" (p. 53). Further, many of the task force members held a feminist perspective and a passionate commitment to change. The report states unequivocally that it adheres to a feminist philosophy and it clearly acknowledges the plight of Aboriginal women prisoners.

There were a number of struggles and sacrifices made by the task force participants in their efforts to cooperatively produce a vision for change. For example, many of the voluntary organizations expressed their concerns about having to work within the existing legislative and penal structure when they believed that a community-based correctional approach was more appropriate (Shaw, 1993, p. 54). There were also concerns about whether the voices of the Aboriginal women and prisoners would be heard and respected. Despite these reservations, the government and the community worked together to design a prototype for woman-centered corrections. The recommendations of *Creating Choices* are currently being implemented, and the Canadian government is planning to close the Prison for Women and replace it with four new woman-centered facilities (prisons) and an Aboriginal "healing lodge."[8]

The task force indicated that, by rejecting the traditional male approach to correctional programming and management, it has had

> to formulate a plan which would respond to the needs and risks represented by women themselves, which would respond in a way reflective of women's perceptions of, and interactions with, each other and society generally. However, it should be noted that the work to build a correctional system, based on women's reality rather than sexual and racial stereotypes, was made more difficult by the fact that a comprehensive, coherent female correctional model does not exist, particularly one that is also responsive to Aboriginal perceptions. (Task Force on Federally Sentenced Women, 1990, p. 91)

The report of the task force, *Creating Choices*, envisions that the new women-sensitive correctional model will be characterized by five guiding principles: empowerment, meaningful and responsible choices, respect and dignity, supportive environment, and shared responsibility.[9] It was expected that these principles would "provide a strong direction for immediate action" and "light the way as we walk further down the path towards our ideal" (Task Force on Federally Sentenced Women, 1990, p. 105). Empowerment, in *Creating Choices* (pp. 105–106), is clearly aligned with the structural inequities experienced by women prisoners. It is noted that the "research and the words of federally sentenced women have repeatedly stressed the connections between women's involvement in the criminal justice system and the inequalities, hardships, and suffering experienced by women in our society." In addition to structural inequality, empowerment is connected to perception that women prisoners lack self-esteem and, as a result, they are believed to have little power to direct their lives. In short, "they feel disempowered, unable to create or make choices, unable to help create a more rewarding, productive future, even if realistic choices are presented to them" (Task Force on Federally Sentenced Women, 1990, p. 105). The task force locates the disempowerment of women in two sites: in the structural arrangements of society and in the woman herself (with an emphasis on the latter).

Meaningful choices, the second guiding principle of the woman centeredness, is defined as the need to provide women "choices which relate to their needs and make sense in terms of their past experiences, their culture, their morality, their spirituality, their abilities or skills, and their future realities or possibilities" (Task Force on Federally Sentenced Women, 1990, p. 108). These choices are necessary if women are to have a sense of control over their lives, raise their self-esteem, be empowered, and make meaningful and responsible choices (p. 107). The construction of a meaningful choice in this report suggests that there are two types of meaningful choice: the choices offered to the prisoner by the institution in terms of programming and the choices (or decisions) made by the woman while residing in the institution and on her release.

The third principle, respect and dignity, is "based on the assumption that mutuality of respect is needed among prisoners, among staff, and between prisoners and staff if women are to gain the self-respect and respect for others necessary to take responsibility for their futures" (Task Force on Federally Sentenced Women, 1990, p. 109). The task force indicates that it feels this principle is important because Canadian correctional institutions "have often been criticised for their tendency to encourage dependent and child-like behaviour among women" (p. 109). Further, it is acknowledged that many of the rules in the prison have been administered in an arbitrary and humiliating way. These practices are said to have contributed to the prisoners' sense of powerlessness (or disempowerment).

Supportive environment, the fourth principle, is understood in terms of the "constellation of many types of environments . . . political, physical, financial, emotional/psychological, and spiritual, especially for Aboriginal women" (Task Force on Federally Sentenced Women, 1990, p. 110). *Creating Choices* suggests that "a positive lifestyle which can encourage the self-esteem, empowerment, dignity and respect for self and others so necessary to live a productive and meaningful life can only be created in an environment in which all aspects of environment are positive and mutually supportive" (p. 110). The notion of a supportive environment is closely linked to the objective of empowerment, to interdependence of all aspects of the correctional environment, and to notions of equality for women prisoners. With respect to equality, *Creating Choices* indicates that it is through the interdependent nature of all aspects of the environment that equality of programming and security can be achieved. The report explicitly notes that "equality of treatment is not defined in terms of *sameness* of treatment" but "instead a sensitivity to needs and experiences which ensures equality in terms of meaningful outcome" (p. 110).

The final guiding principle of woman-centered corrections outlined in the task force report is shared responsibility. Similar to other principles, the conceptualization of shared responsibility emphasizes the responsibility of the prisoner, the government, and the community. The report notes that

> governments at all levels, correctional workers, voluntary sector services, businesses, private sector services and community members generally must take responsibility as inter-related parts of society. This is essential in order to foster the independence and self-reliance among federally sentenced women to allow them to take responsibility for their past, present and future actions. To make sound choices, women must be supported by a coordinated comprehensive effort involving all elements in society. This, as Aboriginal teachings instruct us, is a holistic approach. (Task Force on Federally Sentenced Women, 1990, p. 111)

Further, the principle is said to be important because

> the holistic programming and multifaceted opportunities which support an environment in which women can become empowered can only be built on a foundation of responsibility among a broad range of community members. Currently, because the Correctional Service of Canada has legal obligations for federally sentenced women, *responsibility for federal women is too narrowly assigned to correctional systems*. (p. 111; emphasis added)

Under the heading "supportive environment," the task force clearly emphasizes the responsibility of the community in the empowerment of the women prisoner while simultaneously redefining the responsibilities of the Correctional Service of Canada. According to correctional administrators, these principles of woman centeredness have been extended beyond *Creating Choices* to guide future institutional approaches and planning for female offenders.

Implementation of *Creating Choices*

The implementation of the recommendations of the task force was expected by its membership to be inclusive and to adhere to the principles set out in *Creating Choices*. However, the implementation process has been marred by exclusions and redefinitions of the meaning of woman-centered corrections. Whereas Shaw (1993) and others are quite right in noting that "the involvement of feminists and prison activists in a task force cannot always be dismissed as incorporation or legitimation" (p. 66), as discovered by the participants, there are limits to their power and ability to fundamentally alter institutional structures. Many feminists and activists were included and successful in having their philosophies reflected (as least in part) in the report of the task force. However, the outcome of their involvements was largely unanticipated and underestimated. Nonstate feminist and community groups have been systematically alienated from much of the task force implementation process. The activity of "rethinking" women's incarceration has been informed by feminist knowledge and expertise and the reemergence of therapeutic regimes, specifically feminist therapy. Perhaps one of the most profound difficulties is that feminists have failed to adequately define the meaning and criteria of woman centeredness. The implementation of the task force's recommendations and the definition of *woman centered* have been left to Corrections Canada with little external (feminist) input. At present, the operationalisation and definition of woman-centered corrections is in the hands of the Correctional Service of Canada.

The Federally Sentenced Woman Program of the national headquarters of the Correctional Service of Canada and the wardens of the five "new" institutions are controlling the implementation process. Wardens continue to selectively draw on "volunteer" community resources to define the types and content of programming in the institutions. They have retained a monopoly on the power to define and redefine the recommendations of the community. The present involvement of the community in the planning process for the new prisons is subject to the discretion of individual wardens. By and large, feminists and activists are no longer being included in the process of defining the meaning and content of the new penal regimes. In spite of these exclusions, the Correctional Service of Canada continues to maintain that it is adhering to a woman-centered approach as defined by the task force. While struggling for inclusion in the planning processes, activists continue to attempt to hold the government accountable for their treatment of federally sentenced women and diversions from *Creating Choices*.

Recent efforts by Correctional Service of Canada to define and operationalize woman centeredness selectively emphasize some aspects of *Creating Choices* while minimizing other components. Correctional Service of Canada (1994a) operational documents have stated that a woman-centered approach means "that programs must reflect the social realities of women and respond to the individual needs of each woman" (p. 3). To implement the woman-centered philosophy, the government has outlined the following five "operational" principles,[10] what they call "contextual analysis," "cooperative," "challenging," "connection," and "agency." These operating principles selectively incorporate feminist analysis and ideals outlined in the guiding principles of *Creating Choices*.

The principle of contextual analysis draws on the premise that the lives and actions of federally sentenced women have to be placed in a wider social, political, and economic context and on the belief that programs must reflect the social realities of women while responding to the individual needs of each woman. The second principle, cooperative, argues in favor of a correctional model not based on hierarchical relations of power. Women are said to be valued as experts on their own needs and, thus, are to be afforded some decision-making autonomy. The third principle, challenging, is expected to promote "the most effective interaction between women and the facilitator in a supportive, encouraging, empathetic, accepting, *challenging*, and nonconfrontational manner" (Correctional Service of Canada, 1994a, p. 10). The principle, challenging, is vague, but it seems to imply that penal regimes should encourage prisoners to question their life choices and promote change. The fourth principle, connection, invites women to learn from one another through a dialogue and sharing process designed to promote trust. The final principle of woman centeredness is agency, which envisions women as

> active agents rather than passive victims. While they are accountable for their actions, including criminal activities, all activities are understood in relation to the context in which they occur. Though many women have been victimized, they have also survived violence even when their options were very limited. The strength and creativity employed by

> women demonstrates their potential power to effect change. This strength can be used and refocused towards empowerment. (p. 10)

The preceding principles have been identified by Corrections Canada as guidelines for the development of a woman-centered penal regime. Overall, the woman-centered approach is perceived as empowering federally sentenced women.

Paradoxes of Woman-Centered Corrections

When these developments are placed in a wider historical context, the proposed changes become particularly disconcerting. Canadian histories of women's imprisonment reveal that building an institution based on the perceived needs and experiences of women prisoners; employing only female staff and administrators; and integrating feminist, maternal, and therapeutic discourses with a penal regime is not original or radical.[11] Strange's (1983) discussion of the Andrew Mercer Reformatory, the first separate institution for women in Canada, illustrates that in the past women's penal regimes have been based on variations of the woman-centered philosophy. Strange illustrates clearly that although maternal regimes ameliorated some of the pains of imprisonment, they also induced their own pains. This comparison is not intended to suggest that past and current regimes are the same; they are not. However, it does illustrate that certain institutional dynamics have continually undermined the successful implementation of woman-centered reforms irrespective of the way in which they are conceptualized. All reform efforts are historically contingent; failures of the past should not inhibit plans for the future. However, past experiences should be taken into consideration.

The language of woman-centered corrections incorporates problematic assumptions and overlooks certain material experiences of incarcerated individuals. The language that defines the new woman-centered regime is not being contested, even though it is increasingly apparent that feminists and correctional officials have conflicting interpretations of terms such as empowerment. Feminist uses of the term empowerment and correctional uses of the term are different and are perhaps irreconcilable in the current institutional context. Unlike Corrections Canada, feminists do not believe that the woman-centered model is contingent on the construction of new institutions. The following analysis outlines some of the difficulties associated with these assumptions. I address four problems: the category "woman," false dichotomy of woman- and male-centered prisons, legal/material "reality" of women's imprisonment, and the problematic of empowerment.

The Category "Woman"

Corrections Canada notes that one important influence on corrections has been a feminist critique of women's criminality and inequality. Recent government reports have adopted the same assumptions as have many feminist criminologists. That is, "women in prison have more in common with other women than they do with male inmates, and . . . programs and services should be designed to meet their local needs and circumstances, or planned individually, not on the basis of some centralized blueprint" (Task Force on Federally Sentenced Women, 1990, p. 68). One female member of the task force explicitly noted: "We need to think in terms of a safe place for women. Women offenders are not different from any other woman in this room" (p. 23). Until recently, there has been little "association between women's opportunities and their criminal acts. However, it is now acknowledged that there is "a clear link between crimes women commit and their disempowered positions" (Kendall, 1993, p. 14). Reformers and feminists have tended to emphasize the commonalities shared by women as a disempowered and marginalized group. Although this assumption of common disempowerment illustrates some of the undeniable experiential and demographic similarities between women prisoners and "free" women, it fails to articulate the heterogeneity that exists among women. The experiences of women in prison are much more than a microcosm of the experience of all women.

Recent postmodern (Howe, 1994, chaps. 4–6) attacks on the analytic category, woman, reveal that "woman" is a shifting subject, multiply organised across variable axes of difference" (de Lauretis, 1990, p. 116; cited in Howe, 1994, p. 167). Women's experiences are reflective of a number of different subject positions. Race, class, sexual orientation, employment status, education, and motherhood define some aspects of this heterogeneity. However, the crucial difference between "other women" and women prisoners is freedom. Women prisoners are not free. They have and continue to experience the dehumanizing pains of imprisonment—a unique experience shared by a small portion of Canadian women (and men). The construction of women prisoners as "no different from other women," or as "having more in common with other women than male prisoners," denies the involuntary and unique aspects of their experience of incarceration. An emphasis on the commonalities of women results in an insensitivity to the differences among women and, subsequently, the experiences of women as prisoners are trivialized. This lack of attention to difference leads to many flawed assumptions such as a belief that if women are employed as guards, run programs, and administer prisons, women in prison will be cared for better.[12]

The women-centered prison is a manifestation of this oversight. Although the woman-centered model acknowledges that women suffer injustices because of their sex, it fails to see how a feminist vision of justice can reproduce different kinds of injustices by denying the problematic experiences of incarceration and by viewing women as a homogeneous group. This underlying assumption creates a climate of reform that fails to recognize relations of power among women in different social sites. The governance of women by women can be as problematic as the governance of women by men, particularly when the relations among the "keepers" and the "kept" are shaped by the institutional dynamics of imprisonment.

A related point is that the language of *woman centered* has the capacity to deny other forms of oppression experienced by women prisoners. An emphasis on gender-based oppression minimizes and obscures other forms of oppression such as race and class. The woman-centered prison and the expectations placed on women prisoners are informed by White, middle-class sensibilities.[13] *Creating Choices* expends considerable effort discussing the importance of cultural sensitivity; however, most of these sensitivities are limited to Aboriginal women's experiences.[14] Such an awareness is crucial because Aboriginal women are disproportionately overrepresented in Canadian prisons (Adelberg & The Native Women's Association of Canada, 1993). Nevertheless, it overlooks the needs of other minority women. This oversight has left Black women inmates "feeling slighted because they have not been asked for their opinions on any of the proposed facilities of programs" (Stewart & MacKay, 1994, p. 37). Issues of systemic racism[15] tend to be limited to a discussion of Aboriginal culture. Even though the issues of Aboriginal women appear to be a priority, Aboriginal prisoners have expressed some discontent. Some Aboriginal women prisoners feel that they have been alienated from the development process for the healing lodge (prison). Native women prisoners reportedly want to know more about the prison being built for them (Stewart & MacKay, 1994, p. 37).

Cultural sensitivity is limited to the content and not the structure of the regime. Some of the frustrations expressed by the Aboriginal women involved in the wider *Creating Choices* process articulate a similar concern. They note that the rhetoric of inclusion and cultural sensitivity does not resonate with the current government's actions and approach (Adelberg & The Native Women's Association of Canada, 1993). Although the importance of race is acknowledged through the inclusion of Aboriginal voices, Aboriginal women reformers are not fully empowered to explore carceral alternatives consistent with their abolitionist philosophies. Adelberg and the Native Women's Association of Canada's (1993) discussion of the *Creating Choices* process describes some of the frustrations Aboriginal women experience in engaging with "federal correctional officials and other organizations said to represent women in cages which had already conducted study upon study" (p. 77). For many women, the bureaucratic discourse had little relevance and connection to the "reality" they had experienced. Adelberg and the Native Women's Association of Canada (1993) note,

> No amount of tinkering with prisons can heal the before-prison lives of the Aboriginal women who live or have lived within their walls. Prison cannot remedy the problem of poverty on reserves. It cannot deal with immediate or historical memories of genocide that Europeans worked upon our people. It cannot remedy violence, alcohol abuse, sexual assault during childhood, rape and other violence Aboriginal women

> experience at the hands of men. Prison cannot heal the past abuse of foster homes, or the indifference and racism of the Canada's justice system in its dealings with Aboriginal people. However, the treatment of Aboriginal women within prisons can begin to recognize that these things are realities of the lives that Aboriginal women have led. By understanding this, we can begin to make changes that will promote healing instead of rage. (p. 79)

However, Adelberg and the Native Women's Association of Canada also maintain that although prisons have been problematic in the past, they still have within them the capacity to "promote healing instead of rage." Although I acknowledge that recognition by correctional officials of the abuses suffered by women and particularly minority women is crucial, what is equally important is that prison regimes are not safe places for healing. What remains to be seen is the extent to which diverse cultural goals can be integrated in the forthcoming healing lodge (prison).

False Dichotomy of Woman- and Man-Centered Prisons

The construction of two separate and distinct models of corrections—woman centered and male centered—sets up a false dichotomy. The woman-centered approach tends to be juxtaposed to its obvious counterpart, the male-centered approach. Some feminist critics argue that women's penal regimes have epitomized male-centered corrections with an emphasis on security, discipline, and control. The woman-centered approach is conversely characterized as caring, empowering, supportive, respectful, and meaningful. This split reproduces and reinforces normative standards of femininity in the correctional discourse. This dualism does not adequately reflect the diversity or complexity of either women's or men's prisons.

The woman-centered trope reproduces male-centered views about what women need and want. The image of a woman-centered prison as benevolent, caring, therapeutic, and supportive denies the existence of similar relations in men's prisons. Conversely, dominant conceptualizations of the therapeutic nature of woman-centered prisons tend to minimize and obscure the oppressive aspects of involuntary treatment and disciplinary regimes. It is assumed that woman-centered punishment will be experienced by women prisoners as less oppressive than previous male-centered approaches. The potentially coercive nature of therapeutic regimes is well documented in many correctional histories (Dobash, Dobash, & Gutteridge, 1986; Foucault, 1977; Strange, 1983). Whereas debates about treatment versus punishment are not likely to be resolved, it is worthwhile to consider the limitations of both options.

The ability to achieve the ideals of the woman-centered approach in a prison setting is generally assumed. To date, reformers have tended to embrace feminist-based therapies for women without clearly acknowledging and articulating the limits of this approach in prisons. The feminization of penal regimes does not absolve these regimes of their punitive and oppressive tendencies, particularly when the subjects of the regimes are involuntary. For example, Kendall (1994) notes that whereas

> feminist therapy is premised on helping the woman see their own power so they can resist harm and take self-determined action, prisons generally remove whatever autonomy women have in their lives by enforcing rigid control over inmates, restrictions on movement, scheduling of activities and communication. Such control, coupled with arbitrary enforcement and application of rules, merely reproduces a sense of powerlessness and unpredictability present in the lives of women prior to their imprisonment. (p. 21)

Kendall (1993, 1994) further notes that it is this control that women prisoners identify as most damaging. Nonexistent opportunities and choices make it almost impossible for women to make what they regard as "meaningful choices." Women in prison lack the power and autonomy to make even the most mundane decisions and choices such as when to get up and go to sleep, when and what to eat, when and whom to visit. This paradox frames women's experiences as prisoner and the experiences and frustrations of many well-intentioned therapists and correctional staff.

Arguably, therapeutic ideals are compromised by the preexisting structure and discipline that require correctional authorities to be accountable and legally responsible for those in their charge. After all, the main priority of Corrections Canada is the protection of the public, not healing the offender. Frequently, therapy is aligned with control and security. Women prisoners who are believed to be dangerous or violent are often defined as needing "more structure and more intensive therapeutic programming" (Correctional Service of Canada, 1995, p. 42). If we are to learn anything from correctional histories, we should be cautious when embracing ideological shifts away from punishment and toward healing and treatment in prison settings. Woman-centered ideals uncritically embrace therapeutic notions of healing and holistic regimes. Caution is warranted when one recalls the tragedies and abuses that led to the demise of the rehabilitative ideal in Canada and elsewhere (Culhane, 1979; Ekstedt & Griffiths, 1988; Gosselin, 1982; McNeil & Vance, 1978).

Advocacy of woman-centered prisons fails to challenge the use of prisons. Most feminists have discussed penal policy in ways that accept the current institutional framework rather than question it. The woman-centered approach assumes that whereas "male models of corrections" are not suitable for women, prisons are suitable as long as they are based on a feminist vision of justice, punishment, and care. The restructuring of women's imprisonment based on a feminist vision of justice, care, or punishment is problematic because there is no uniform or essential "female approach." Drawing on the work of Gilligan (1982), many feminist criminologists and legal theorists have argued that the law and the criminal justice system are based on a male system of norms that, when applied to women, are inappropriate. Male-based norms and rules are said to deny the experiences and social situations of women offenders. Male-based justice is often taken for granted in feminist efforts to document the deficiencies of the law and criminal justice policy and practice. To encourage a female-based approach to justice, some feminists (see Heidensohn, 1986) have argued that the emphasis needs to be placed on the differences between men and women to produce a uniquely feminine approach. Interestingly, in spite of the criticisms by many feminists (Daly, 1989) that question the possibility of a "woman's" law or criminal justice system, some feminists still maintain that the woman-centered model can be achieved in prisons (Heidensohn, 1986, p. 297).

Although it is acknowledged that it is impractical to expect that the law and the criminal justice system will be restructured to reflect a feminine approach to justice, there remains a commitment to and a belief in the reconstruction of women's prisons. This logic is distressing in that it decontextualizes women's prisons. They are portrayed as somehow separate from the wider criminal justice system. A woman's prison is not a separate entity. The prison is tied into wider networks of social action and meaning (cf. Garland, 1990). Simply changing the content of a penal regime to reflect a woman-centered approach leaves the wider institutional framework unchallenged. Currently, the way we think about and define punishment is derived from the wider criminal justice context. The feminizing of women's penal regimes reinforces and to some extent legitimates the incarceration of women. Rather than presenting a viable alternative to the problems faced by incarcerated women in the prison setting, feminist discourses, informed by therapeutic ideals, are selectively mobilized. The selective integration of some feminist ideas and not others contributes to the production of a feminized social control talk dressed up in therapeutic and feminist language. In some ways, these "woman-centered reforms" only replace the discredited regimes with a less overt but nonetheless oppressive exercise of power.

The reform of women's prisons emphasizes a shift in the content of the regime without challenging the wider system of sanctioning. The sanction of imprisonment remains at the extreme end of the carceral continuum in a retributive system of justice. The woman-centered prison ironically uses the same structures, institutions, relations, and values that have created the initial problem to resolve the more general problem of women's incarceration. Reform in certain institutional contexts will be influenced by the structure of the institution. Given the implicit and explicit relations of power in prisons, reforms that occur in these institutions retain disciplinary and repressive components irrespective of their discursive construction. The new forms of power that emerge and coexist with the old disciplinary regimes must be questioned and analyzed for their impact. It should not be assumed that the relations of power in the new woman-centered prison are any less problematic.

Material/Legal "Reality" of Women's Imprisonment

Another concern with the woman-centered prison is its denial of the material and legal reality of carceral relations embodied in the prison. The use of incarceration in a liberal state assumes the loss of certain rights and freedoms. The explicit intention of imprisonment is to punish and to limit the freedom and autonomy of individuals subject to this sanction. As noted, reforming the content of a regime tends to obscure and to some extent silence or minimize the oppressive aspects of prisons and the unequal relations of power that characterize this sanction. Prisons are governed by material structures, cultural sensibilities, and mentalities that limit the extent to which the content of a regime can be changed. Regardless of the form and content of a woman-centered regime, it is still, in many respects, about punishment, security, and discipline. The following discussion highlights the contradictions that emerge when state agents of social control, feminists, and reformers attempt to operationalize the ideals of woman centeredness in a disciplinary context.

Efforts to make the new "regional facilities" (prisons) more women-centered include modifying the architecture and security barriers to less intrusive technologies. *Creating Choices* proposes the construction of five regional facilities for women. These institutions are expected to be "community orientated, holistic, woman-centered, culturally sensitive, supportive of autonomy and self-esteem, and orientated towards release" (LeBlanc, 1994, p. 12). Accordingly, *Creating Choices* (Task Force on Federally Sentenced Women, 1990, p. 115) states that the design of the "new" facilities should use "environmental factors known to promote wellness." These factors include natural light, fresh air, color, space, privacy, and access to land. The design will also incorporate small cottages, independent living areas, and nonintrusive security measures. However, in at least one instance, it seems that Corrections Canada has not modified its approach to prison architecture, and in another the architectural design has been changed to address public and state concerns about security and protection of the public.

A Correctional Service of Canada (1994b) document describing a proposed regional facility in Kitchener, Ontario, notes that

> the entire facility will be enclosed by an eight foot chain link security fence. In addition, a four foot fence with state of the art electronic detection devices will form the interior perimeter surrounding the living area. There will be alarms on all the exit doors and windows of the living units. The architectural design has been changed to allow the community access to the gymnasium without any contact with the *inmates*. (p. 2; emphasis added)

The same document notes that the public need not be fearful of these women because "*the number one priority of the correctional system is the protection of society* as recognized by the Mission Statement of the Correctional

Service of Canada and the Corrections and Conditional Release Act" (p. 3). This description of the new woman-centered facility refers to women prisoners as inmates instead of the popular terms such as "the women," "consumer," "client," or "resident." The term inmate and the claim that the main priority of Corrections Canada is the public and not the woman prisoner reinforce a commitment to public safety, security, and discipline. They clearly situate the prisoner as a threat and object of control. The needs of the community are a priority. These concerns refocus the rhetoric and ideals of woman-centered prisons. By placing this ideal in a wider penal context, the contradictions are more apparent, thus stressing the importance of examining the relations and practices of surveillance and discipline that determine the nature and experiences of incarceration.

A good example of how woman-centered ideals are compromised is illustrated in Karleen Faith's description of one of the new federal facilities, the Burnaby Correctional Centre in British Columbia. Although Burnaby was not built as specified by *Creating Choices,* the institution was modified to house federally sentenced women and will continue to do so after the Prison for Women is closed. In addition, programming and staffing are expected to conform to the spirit of *Creating Choices*. Faith describes Burnaby as a replica of Bentham's panopticon, which reproduces the same security and classification problems for which the Prison for Women is criticized. Faith (1993) notes that

> technically, the institution is a medium security facility, but for all practical purposes, due to the architectural design and high level technological security systems, and because women from every classification are locked up together, they must all abide by the maximum custody rules intended for the few women who are perceived as security risks. The immense rotunda in the centre of the prison recalls and structurally manifests the Panopticon design, conceived by the English utilitarian reformer, Jeremy Bentham in 1787 as the ideal architectural design for (male) penitentiaries or, for that matter schools or factories. (p. 146)

Ironically, *Creating Choices* (Task Force on Federally Sentenced Women, 1990, pp. 31–32) documents the same concern to justify calls for the closure of the Prison for Women. The report quotes the *Ouimet Report* (Canadian Committee on Corrections, 1969), the report of the Royal Commission on the Status of Women (1970), the *MacGuigan Report* (Subcommittee on the Penitentiary System, 1977), and the *Daubney Report* (Standing Committee on Justice and Solicitor General, 1988), all of which indicated the problematic nature of incarcerating women in "facilities which provide much higher security than most of them require and than most of them would be subject to if they were men" (Task Force on Federally Sentenced Women, 1990, pp. 31–32).

Faith's discussion of Burnaby documents clearly the continued presence of intrusive, static models of security. Irrespective of the institutional rhetoric to the contrary, "the impression imparted by the new Burnaby prison is that this highly secure institution has been constructed for the precise purpose of protecting 'the public' from dangerous, unruly criminals, when in reality very few of the women who are sent here represent a threat to anyone at all" (Faith, 1993, p. 147). Further, some of the most coercive and repressive aspects of confinement can be reproduced in new architectural settings (Brown, Kramer, & Quinn, 1988, p. 300; Dobash et al., 1986). The development of plans for the more "disruptive" prisoners reveals, in their starkest form, some of the contradictions of a woman-centered prison. Faith's discussion points to additional, forceful representations of power such as institutional rules and regulations and staff/inmate relations. Women who breach the rules of the prison continue to be "punished with segregation from the main prison population, or, if in the opinion of the staff they are suicide risks or otherwise require 'medical observation,' they are placed in solitary confinement in top security 'strip' cells in isolated locations, where total twenty-four hour a day surveillance is achieved by both cameras and the direct and constant gaze of guards who sit behind protective glass" (Faith, 1993, p. 147). Similar practices are occurring in the Prison for Women, where a special handling unit has recently emerged in the prison's segregation facility. The characteristics of this prison within the prison include additional mesh fencing on windows, 24-hour surveillance cameras, no activity, sensory deprivation, minimal contact with significant others in the institutions, and the shackling and handcuffing of women while being showered and during recreation. These descriptions fail to support the previously outlined general principles of empowerment, meaningful and responsible choices, respect and dignity, supportive environment, and shared responsibility or the operational principles of "cooperation," "challenging," and "connection" originally conceived to provide the philosophical foundations of the woman-centered regime. The continued use of such facilities for some women reveals the naiveté of a vision of a woman-centered prison that denies the sometimes extreme realities of prison life.

Current classification strategies in the Prison for Women are being intensified, and the new prisons are making changes to accommodate problem prisoners. These practices suggest that an increasing number of women are being classified by institutional staff as risky despite the fact that 4 years ago many of the same women were believed to present more of a risk to themselves than to anyone else (Task Force on Federally Sentenced Women, 1990, pp. 41–42, 89–91). According to *Creating Choices*, traditional means of risk management and individual planning are limited by a number of problematic assumptions, one of which being the "assumption that federally sentenced women are a risk to society. . . . Most federally sentenced women are not a risk to society" (p. 89). Further, *Creating Choices* notes that "a very small number of women have come to rely on violence in order to survive overwhelming abuse throughout their lives. It is believed that these women will respond well to a supportive environment" (p. 90).

And, finally, *Creating Choices* argues that "punishment, such as segregation, whether in response to disciplinary offenses, to the *good order of the institution*, or whether in response to an individual being victimized by other prisoners, is inappropriate when the aim is to empower women to accept responsibility and make good choice for themselves" (p. 91; emphasis in original). None of the new security developments discussed previously are perceived by Corrections Canada as being in contradiction with its wider philosophy of empowerment and woman centeredness.

Other aspects of the material reality of prisons are highlighted in the relations between the existing and proposed dynamic, supportive, and cooperative relations between the guards and the prisoners. According to the new mandate of Corrections Canada and *Creating Choices*, the institutional staff, including the guards, are expected to engage in meaningful, respectful, and supportive relations with the prisoners under their charge. Traditions of discipline, security, and coercion are to be placed in a new context. With respect to staffing and surveillance, a current warden notes that

> the facility will have a 21 bed capacity (phasing up to 31), and the security practises will always be a balance of supervision and sound programming within a supportive environment. Security will be essentially dynamic; *therefore all staff will be correctional staff.* In general, the security will be based on the fact that few of these women are high risk offenders. (LeBlanc, 1994, p. 12; emphasis added)

Creating Choices and planning documents emphasize the important role played by staff in the new institutions and the importance of training all staff to be sensitive to gender and cultural issues. *Creating Choices* notes that the primary responsibility of the staff will be to provide positive interaction, to be

> role models, and to support women's efforts to develop self-esteem and self-reliance. Staff will have a high level of responsibility for identifying problems, providing support, and developing and utilising effective intervention techniques for women who are in crisis. (Task Force on Federally Sentenced Women, 1990, p. 117)

The staff are involved in all aspects of the women's treatment and discipline. The role and objectives outlined for the staff at the new prisons are similar to the goals and objects set out for other women's institutions except that in the new prisons the punitive and disciplinary role of the guards has been redefined as "caring," "supportive," and "challenging." As one incarcerated woman notes, even though guards are now *program deliverers* and newly classified under case management, "they still wear the uniform of guards" (Horii, 1994, p. 14). It is difficult to envision the development of meaningful, respectful, and supportive relationships when guards continue to perform strip searches, open women's mail, monitor their relations with others within and outside the institution, and at times punish the prisoners for infractions against institutional order.

One could claim that these descriptions characterize a small and insignificant part of the women's carceral regime and that the punishments noted were directed at a small number of disorderly inmates. However, "orderly" women, in the general prison population, are uninformed and confused about the pending changes. Advocates for the women are equally perplexed. Corrections Canada, however, continues to maintain that it is working toward empowerment in partnership with the community. At best, these relations can be characterized as a reporting: Corrections Canada dutifully reports on program development and on the progress of the new institutions. Consultation with the prisoners and the commitment to the principle of "cooperation" (Correctional Service of Canada, 1994a), which *favors a nonhierarchal model and values women as experts on their own lives*, seems to have ended before it began. The material experiences of the prisoners and the disempowerment of advocates who are trying to ameliorate the current situation are informative. These examples offer a few illustrations of the existing gap between the state's current and emerging notion of an empowered, woman-centered prison, designed to foster self-esteem, and advocates' notions of empowerment and woman-centered institutions. Rather than blaming individuals for these emergent discrepancies, one needs to look more generally at the types of relations that characterize institutions of social control and the objectives being sought by state, nonstate, and quasi-state reformers. The governance of risky women by women through feminized carceral strategies is perhaps no less problematic than is the governance of risky women by men and patriarchal strategies.

Imprisonment defines a certain set of relations between those imprisoned against their will and their keepers. These relations are structured by unequal power relations that do not facilitate supportive environments, self-respect, or empowerment. These relations are contingent on the institutional culture, which is the product of accumulated knowledge, techniques, normative rules, and working procedures that have developed over time (Garland, 1990, p. 283). The institutional culture is reciprocally affected by wider social networks that extend beyond the narrow parameters of the prison. For the most part, correctional systems are in the business of assessing and minimizing risk while maximizing the public's security. Given that such tasks will occur in conjunction with the described woman-centered reforms, the contradictory nature of these goals will likely result in compromises that mystify most observers. For example, Corrections Canada has recently suggested that "the many interpretations of the *special needs* [of women] have led to confusion in roles, policies and practises within the institution" (Correctional Service of Canada, 1995, p. 43). The "dual personality of corrections" (i.e., the promotion of conflicting objectives such as therapy and discipline; see Ekstedt & Griffiths, 1988) can limit the best intentions of guards and/or administrators. As Garland (1990) notes, "Members or personnel of the institution are generally guided by this institutional logic whenever they function within it, and they are obliged to frame any problem or issue in the terms dictated by the institutional framework" (p. 283). Although the coercive and oppressive powers of the keepers may be downplayed in the woman-centered model, unequal relations of power and the legal responsibilities of the prison remain and will continue to shape the institutional response to women in prison. Increasingly, it is unclear as to whom or what is being empowered: the prisoner or the prison.

Problematic of Empowerment[16]

Young (1994), in her article on the treatment and punishment of female drug addicts, notes that "empowerment is like democracy: everyone is for it, but rarely do they mean the same thing by it" (p. 49). Young's comments capture some of the difficulties associated with the current emphasis placed on empowerment in women's penal and treatment regimes. Whereas some feminists have begun to think about the meaning of empowerment as it relates to punishment (Snider, 1994), most of these analyses have emphasized the empowerment of the victim rather than the offender. For feminists, empowerment (ideologically, politically, and economically) has been traditionally embraced as a way of transforming the lives of women by limiting gender oppression. The language of empowerment emerging out of social movements has provided a base for many reform efforts. Empowerment strategies have been used by many activists to reorganize relations of power and effect organizational and policy changes.

Feminist criticisms of empowerment strategies, for the most part, have been limited to a concern with the individual rather than the collective character of empowerment programs and the perceived abandonment of the political for the personal (Cruikshank, 1993, p. 327). Feminist concerns with the individualizing and pathologizing potential of strategies such as battered women's syndrome are good examples of this critique. Many feminists are apprehensive because current structural arrangements are not able to empower marginalized women. Criminal justice institutions tend to stress that women need to take ownership of and responsibility for their problems without simultaneously acknowledging wider systemic barriers. Further, as Young (1994) notes cogently, programs for women "often operate to adjust women to dominant gender, race, and class structures" (p. 33) while depoliticizing and individualizing their situations. Canadian feminists have similar concerns about the Corrections Canada implementation process for the new woman-centered prisons. Marxist and socialist critiques of empowerment are concerned with the operationalization of empowerment rather than with the concept and construction of empowerment.

These critiques are limited in that they do not show how empowerment is part of a wider technology of self-governance[17] and how empowerment discourse has produced a self-to-self relation that is governable. They fail to acknowledge the political nature of personal relations. Moreover,

Cruikshank's (1993) Foucauldian critique of the "American self-esteem enterprise"[18] argues that even collective strategies of empowerment are problematic because they leave wider strategies of governance unchallenged. Cruikshank (1993, p. 327) notes that whereas strategies of empowerment, self-help, and democratic participation can enhance the subjectivity of women and the poor, they are also practical techniques for the subjection of individuals.[19] She also argues that the movement toward empowerment or self-esteem seeks "to forge a new terrain of politics and a new mode of governing the self, not a new government" (p. 328). For Cruikshank, the question of governance is a question of self-governance through a discourse on self-esteem. Canadian women's prison reform can be placed within a similar framework by asking how the question of governing women in prison has been transformed into a question of self-governance in the discourse of empowerment.

Empowerment is a flexible rationality that resonates with several governmental technologies to create strategies for reform. These strategies can be employed to regulate many marginalized groups. Recently, this language of empowerment has been incorporated into state discourses of punishment and women's prison reform. The incorporation of a language of empowerment signifies a transformation in the strategy for the governance of women prisoners. The difficulty is that strategies of empowerment resonate with multiple and conflicting objectives. Such a situation is apparent in the most recent reform effort. Although the strategy of empowerment coincides with the feminist objectives and intentions of the reformers, it is also compatible with the goals and objectives of correctional officials. The use of a language of empowerment by feminists to endorse the use of woman-centered prisons is problematic. As I have argued previously, the concept of a woman-centered prison is fundamentally flawed and arguably incapable of empowerment.

The objective of Corrections Canada is to "empower women to accept responsibility and make good choices for themselves" (Task Force on Federally Sentenced Women, 1990, p. 91). Empowerment in this context has a different meaning from empowerment in a wider feminist discourse (which seeks to redistribute power and link women's oppression to wider structural inequalities). For Corrections Canada, empowerment is individualized and clearly linked to responsibility and self-esteem. It is noted that

> the inequalities and reduced life choices encountered by women and experienced even more acutely by federally sentenced women have left them with little self-esteem and belief in their power to control their lives. . . . Low self-esteem can contribute to the inability to plan for the future, take responsibility for one's actions and to violence against others. Improving self-esteem increases the ability of each FSW [federally sentenced woman] to make choices and gain more control in her life. Empowerment is a process through which women gain insight into their situation, identify their strengths, and are supported

> and challenged to take positive action to gain control of their lives. (Correctional Service of Canada, 1994a, p. 2)

Here it is implied that empowerment strategies should be linked to improving the low self-esteem of women prisoners and to the promotion of responsible decision making.

Corrections Canada indicates that its empowering process "acknowledges and holds FSW [federally sentenced women] accountable for their actions, but also recognizes their actions in a wider social context" (Correctional Service of Canada, 1994a, p. 9). However, concerns about accountability tend to override concerns about the prisoner's self esteem on the wider context of her offending. This construction of empowerment is consistent with recent discontent reflected in the following statement by Corrections Canada:

> There are conflicting philosophies influencing the Prison for Women. These are the Mission Statement of the Correctional Service of Canada and the belief that female inmates are victims of violence and therefore not responsible for their actions. The Management of the Prison for Women appears to have been forced into a balancing act between the two. The media, non-governmental agencies such as the Elizabeth Fry Society of Canada, and Government policies affecting Natives have all contributed to this influence. (Correctional Service of Canada, 1995, p. 40) . . . The philosophy governing treatment and management of inmates at the Prison for Women appears to assume that women are victims and therefore not responsible for their behaviour. This assumption results in confusion of treatment and no clear goals for inmates. The operational framework should integrate the Mission Document's first Guiding Principle under Core Value 2, namely that *offenders are responsible for their actions and must bear the responsibility for giving up their criminal behaviour.* (p. 42)

This Correctional Service of Canada document continues to note that because of the inconsistencies in the management of the women, there has been a "diminished level of control and feeling of powerlessness among the staff" (p. 41), suggesting that the staff as well as prisoners require some empowering.

Empowerment for Corrections Canada is clearly about "responsibilizing" (cf. O'Malley, 1992; Rose & Miller, 1992; Singh, 1994) the prisoners and having them become accountable for their actions. Individuals become responsible for carrying out the activities that were previously state functions. This new discourse is integrated with an old correctional discourse that emphasizes reforming the irresponsible deviant. The new solution to the "crisis of governability" that exists in women's prison regimes is "relocated in the capacity of women prisoners to act on themselves guided by the expertise of social science[20] and social service professionals" (Cruikshank, 1993, p. 328). This "new science of the self places the hope of liberation in the psychological state of the people" to whom the social problems are attributed (p. 328).

Empowerment is used to justify, rationalize, and legitimate a variety of disciplinary techniques through a parallel discourse of responsibility. Having the offenders take responsibility or ownership for their actions is a paramount concern for correctional institutions. The expectation for women to make "meaningful and responsible choices" is affected by the social and political structure that informs penal cultures and society more generally. When evaluating the choices made by prisoners in the new prison, a pressing question comes to mind about the determination of what Corrections Canada calls "responsible and meaningful choices": For whom are these choices meaningful and responsible—the prisoner, the social worker, or the parole board? The discourse of empowerment is a technology of self-government that requires a woman to take responsibility for her actions to satisfy the objectives of the authorities and not her own.[21] Even though woman-centered regimes may emphasize treatment over punishment, they still retain their punitive tendencies. At times, women are coerced into programs or into situations where overt power is exercised over them that somehow compels them to participate in programs and to behave in a particular way (Cruikshank, 1993, p. 331). For example, women prisoners may participate in institutional programs so that they are in a better position when they have a parole hearing, or a woman prisoner could be paroled on her agreement to participate in a required community treatment program. However, Cruikshank notes that, just as often, women are convinced to participate in their own empowerment without threats (p. 331). Women prisoner's contributions to and willingness to participate in the prison reform process, and their requests for particular types of program options, can be viewed as participation in the empowerment process. However, it can also be viewed as governance. Governance, "in this case, is something that we do to ourselves rather than something that is done to us by those in power" (Rose, 1990, p. 213; cited in Cruikshank, 1993, p. 331).

The responsibilizing agenda of the Correctional Service of Canada blends with reformers because feminist demands for the integration of women's experiences and a strategy of empowerment do not imply or necessitate the displacement of offender accountability or "agency." Feminists have fully acknowledged that the negation of personal accountability or responsibility often results in the "disempowerment of women by rendering them harmless victims, thus stripping them of self-determination" (Allen, 1987; Shaw, 1991b; cited in Kendall, 1993, p. 14). It is this particular facet of feminist notions of empowerment that resonates with the agenda of the Correctional Service of Canada. One of the guiding principles of woman-centered facilities, "agency," clearly constructs the offender as accountable and responsible for her actions irrespective of victimization and structural impediments. Corrections by virtue of their legal role and responsibility in the criminal justice process attempt to make the offender accountable and responsible for her criminal behaviors, regardless of structural and/or situational limitations. It is this process that Corrections Canada terms empowerment. This individualistic approach contradicts the feminist approach, which places the woman's actions into a wider social, political, and economic context.

The woman-centered prison and its capacity for empowerment is constructed as a challenge to the hegemony of punitive carceral regimes and oppressive technologies of surveillance and discipline. Woman-centered prisons and the ethics of empowerment have not significantly challenged this hegemony; rather, they have softened some of the rough edges of incarceration. Despite the influx of "empowerment discourse," woman-centered corrections is about responsibilizing the prisoner and not empowerment as defined by some feminists. Corrections Canada's acknowledgment of the structural barriers facing women and their attempt to remove some of the "pains of imprisonment" are compatible with a liberal notion of individual responsibility. This emphasis on responsibility decontextualizes feminist constructions of women's resistance, and it disregards feminist analysis of the social, economic, and political barriers experienced by women—and, in particular, by marginalized women.

Conclusions

As Garland (1990) notes, "The penal system's very existence helps us forget that other answers to these problems are possible: that institutions are based upon convention rather than nature" (p. 4). Instead of attempting to append feminist knowledge and women's experience to an existing institution of social control, feminists need to challenge this institutional base and consider alternative systems and meanings of sanctioning.[22] This article has documented some of the problems associated with woman-centered models of corrections and with Corrections Canada's appropriation and misuse of some feminist ideals. Feminist strategies such as empowerment and penal strategies are fundamentally different projects. Although changes have occurred, they do not represent a significant departure from traditional male-centered approaches to punishment. The current trend toward woman-centered corrections reproduces normative standards of femininity and individualized constructions of deviance. Further, woman-centered models are exclusionary and limited in their construction of the category "woman." Although the woman-centered model appears to be less intrusive and less punitive, it is not; these qualities of incarceration are simply obscured by a feminized social control talk that tends to deny the legal and material realities of imprisonment.

Notes

[1] Corrections Canada and federal officials were the first in Canada to promote and operationalize a woman-centered model of corrections with the Task Force on Federally Sentenced Women (1990). However, at least two provincial governments, Nova Scotia and

Ontario, have demonstrated an interest in the woman-centered model. The reports *Blueprint for Change* (Province of Nova Scotia, 1992) and *Women's Voices, Women's Choices* (Women's Issues Task Force, 1995) outline reforms that are based on the woman-centered criteria included in the report of the Task Force on Federally Sentenced Women, *Creating Choices*.

[2]The feminist strategies discussed in this article are specific to the reform initiative being analyzed.

[3]For a more detailed history of the Prison for Women, see Cooper (1993).

[4]For a detailed background to the current debates on federal women's incarceration in Canada, see Shaw (1991a).

[5]The task force's mandate was to examine the "correctional management of federally sentenced women from the commencement of their sentence to the date of final warrant expiry and to develop a plan which will guide and direct this process in a manner that is responsive to the unique and special needs of this group" (Task Force on Federally Sentenced Women, 1990, p. 1).

[6]For a more detailed description of the events that led to the development of the Task Force on Federally Sentenced Women, see Shaw (1993) and Moffat (1991).

[7]During the few years prior to the development of the task force and during the task force meetings, there were several suicides and attempted suicides at the Prison for Women. Many of the inmates who committed or attempted suicide during this time were Aboriginal women. These events, in addition to the inadequate living conditions at the prison, led to an increased public awareness of federally sentenced women.

[8]The emphasis of this article is on the four regional facilities (prisons) for women and the current situation at the Prison for Women. Although the healing lodge is mentioned briefly, it is not addressed in detail. The healing lodge has specific cultural characteristics that are unique to the facility. A separate analysis of the healing lodge is required. The comments on "cultural sensitivity" and racial oppression contained in this article refer more generally to the exclusion of non-Aboriginal prisoners and to the regimes in the other facilities. Whereas the other facilities have noted the importance of cultural sensitivity, their regimes and processes are substantially different from those of the healing lodge.

[9]More detailed descriptions of these terms can be located in *Creating Choices* (Task Force on Federally Sentenced Women, 1990) and the *Draft Correctional Program Strategy for Federally Sentenced Women—Abridged Version* (Correctional Service of Canada, 1994a). Shaw (1993, pp. 55–56) provides a more detailed summary of these principles.

[10]The operational principles do not appear to replace the original guiding principles outlined in *Creating Choices* (Task Force on Federally Sentenced Women, 1990, pp. 104–112). Instead, these operational principles are further elaborations and modifications of the guiding principles. In some correctional documents, both sets of principles are referenced.

[11]Strange's (1983) master's thesis, *The Velvet Glove: Maternalistic Reform at the Andrew Mercer Reformatory for Females, 1874–1927*, and Oliver's (1994) essay, "To Govern With Kindness: The First Two Decades of the Mercer Reformatory for Women," document Canadian efforts during the 1870s to design a separate and unique institution for women, run by women, and staffed by women. Likewise, Dobash, Dobash, and Gutteridge's (1986) "Therapy and Discipline" in *The Imprisonment of Women* illustrate that new regimes often focus on the perceived needs and characteristics of women offenders. Although the regime being discussed in this article is different in that it has been informed by feminist ideas, the concept of woman-centered penal regimes is not new.

[12]Howe (1994), in her book *Punish and Critique: Towards a Feminist Analysis of Penality*, discusses some of the possibilities for addressing the discredited category of "woman" on a political level. For example, she cites the efforts of political prisoners and others who have sought to develop "new bases for affiliation" with fellow inmates and other political detainees (Harlow, 1986, pp. 508–520; cited in Howe, 1994, p. 169).

[13] The reference to a White, middle-class sensibility is not meant to suggest that the category "White, middle-class individual" is homogeneous.

[14] The experiences of Aboriginal women prisoners are different from those of non-Aboriginal women prisoners. This article does not articulate the breadth and content of these differences and experiences. For further information on Aboriginal women prisoners, see Sugar and Fox (1990a, 1990b), and Adelberg and the Native Women's Association of Canada (1993).

[15] More recently, the Commission on Systemic Racism in the Ontario Criminal Justice System (1994) has begun to consider the experiences of racism in a wide variety of communities. However, the recent report of the commission, *Racism Behind Bars: The Treatment of Black and Other Racial Minority Prisoners in Ontario Prisons*, does not provide a detailed or systemic account of the experiences and problems of minority women prisoners.

[16] This discussion of empowerment will be addressed in greater detail in my forthcoming Ph.D. thesis titled *The Governance of Risky Women: Maternalism, Feminism, and Empowerment in Women's Prison Reform* (Hannah-Moffat, in press).

[17] This analysis of empowerment is based on a Foucauldian critique of power and the literature on governmentality.

[18] In particular, Cruikshank is responding to the general "contemporary self-esteem movement" and is responding specifically to criticism of Gloria Steinem's best-seller, *Revolution From Within: A Book of Self Esteem*, calling for a feminist retreat to personal life from the collective political front, and to the California Task Force on Self-Esteem spearheaded by legislator John Vasconcellos.

[19] Perhaps one limitation of the approach offered by Cruikshank (1993) is that it tends to overstate the "social control" qualities of self-esteem technologies while understating alternative interpretations of these technologies.

[20] Cruikshank's (1993) article, "Revolution Within Self-Government," further elaborates on how social science and social service professionals contribute to and produce the discourse of self-esteem.

[21] This statement is not meant to suggest that the objectives of the women prisoners are always, or even generally, incompatible with the objectives of the correctional authorities. Rather, what is important here is that the woman prisoner is expected to conform to certain standards and criteria that are defined and evaluated primarily by the correctional authorities.

[22] Perhaps the most significant problem that the debate on the woman-centered prisons in Canada highlights for me is the absence of a parallel debate about how we limit the number of women being sent to prison. It is necessary to rethink the questions we are asking and why they are being asked. For example, rather than asking how we reform the prison—a question that presupposes the appropriateness and utility of this sanction—we could instead proceed with a question about how current structures and relations of power facilitate the incarceration of an increasingly high number of nonviolent women.

References

Adelberg, E., & Currie, C. (1987). *Too few to count: Women and the Canadian justice system.* Vancouver: Press Gang.

Adelberg, E., & Currie, C. (1993). *In conflict with the law.* Vancouver: Press Gang.

Adelberg, E., & the Native Women's Association of Canada. (1993). Aboriginal women and prison reform. In E. Adelberg & C. Currie (Eds.), *In conflict with the law* (pp. 76–94). Vancouver: Press Gang.

Allen, H. (1987). Rendering them harmless: Professional portrayal of women charged with serious violent crimes. In P. Carlen & A. Worrall (Eds.), *Gender, crime, and justice* (pp. 81–94). Milton Keynes, England: Open University Press.

Bernzies, L., & Cooper, S. (1982). Political economy of correctional planning for women. *Canadian Journal of Criminology, 24,* 399–416.

Brown, D., Kramer, H., & Quinn, M. (1988). Women in prison: Task force reform. In M. Findlay & R. Hogg (Eds.), *Understanding crime and criminal justice* (pp. 273–308). Sydney: Law Book.

Canadian Committee on Corrections. (1969). *Report of the Canadian Committee on Corrections (Ouimet Report).* Ottawa: Queen's Printer.

Commission on Systemic Racism in the Ontario Criminal Justice System. (1994). *Racism behind bars: The treatment of Black and other racial minority prisoners in Ontario prisons* (interim report). Toronto: Queen's Printer for Ontario.

Cooper, S. (1993). The evolution of federal women's imprisonment. In E. Adelberg & C. Currie (Eds.), *In conflict with the law* (pp. 33–49). Vancouver: Press Gang.

Correctional Service of Canada. (1994a). *Draft correctional program strategy for federally sentenced women—Abridged version.* Ottawa: Author.

Correctional Service of Canada. (1994b). *Proposed women's prison—Kitchener.* Ottawa: Author.

Correctional Service of Canada. (1995). *Board of Investigation—Major disturbances and other related incidents—Prison for Women from Friday, April 22, to Tuesday, April 26, 1994.* Ottawa: Author.

Cruikshank, B. (1993). Revolutions within self government and self esteem. *Economy and Society, 22,* 327–343.

Culhane, C. (1979). *Barred from prison: A personal account.* Vancouver: Pulp.

Daly, K. (1989). Criminal justice ideologies and practises in different voices: Some feminist questions about justice. *International Journal of the Sociology of the Law, 17,* 1–18.

de Lauretis, T. (1990). Eccentric subjects: Feminist theory and historical consciousness. *Feminist Studies, 16,* 115–150.

Dobash, R., Dobash, R., & Gutteridge, S. (1986). Therapy and discipline. In R. Dobash, R. Dobash, & S. Gutteridge (Eds.), *The imprisonment of women* (pp. 124–158). Cambridge, England: Basil Blackwell.

Douglas, M. (1986). How institutions think. Syracuse: State University of New York Press.

Ekstedt, J., & Griffiths, C. (1988). *Corrections in Canada: Policy and practise.* Toronto: Butterworths.

Faith, K. (1993). *Unruly women: The politics of confinement and resistance.* Vancouver: Press Gang.

Foucault, M. (1977). *Discipline and punish: The birth of the prison* (A. Sheridan, Trans.). New York: Vintage.

Garland, D. (1990). *Punishment and modern society.* Oxford, England: Clarendon.

Gilligan, C. (1982). *In a different voice.* Cambridge, MA: Harvard University Press.

Gosselin, L. (1982). *Prisons in Canada.* Montreal: Black Rose.

Hannah-Moffat, K. (in press). *Governance of risky women: Maternalism, feminism and empowerment in women's prison reform.* Ph.D. thesis, University of Toronto, Centre of Criminology.

Harlow, B. (1986). From the woman's prison: Third World women's narratives of prison. *Feminist Studies, 12,* 501–524.

Heidensohn, F. (1986). Models of justice: Portia or Persephone? Some thoughts on equality fairness and gender in the field of criminal justice. *International Journal of the Sociology of the Law, 14,* 287–298.

Horii, G. (1994). Disarm the infamous thing. *Journal of Prisoners on Prisons, 5*(2), 10–23.

Howe, A. (1994). *Punish and critique: Towards a feminist analysis of penality.* London: Routledge.

Kendall, K. (1993). *Literature review of therapeutic services for women in prison—Companion Vol. 1 to program evaluation of therapeutic services at Prison for Women.* Ottawa: Correctional Service of Canada.

Kendall, K. (1994). Creating real choices: A program evaluation of therapeutic services at the Prison for Women. *Forum on Corrections Research, 6*(1), 19–21 (special issue).

LeBlanc, T. (1994). Redesigning corrections for federally sentenced women in Canada. *Forum on Corrections Research, 6*(1), 11–12 (special issue).

Mayhew, J.-A. (1994) . . . Seeking minimum facilities 4 women. *Journal of Prisoners on Prisons, 5*(2), 40–44.

McNeil, G., & Vance, S. (1978). *Cruel and unusual: The shocking reality of life behind bars in Canada.* Ottawa: Deneau & Greenberg.

Moffat (Hannah), K. (1991). Creating choices or repeating history: Canadian female offenders and correctional reform. *Social Justice, 18*(3), 184–203.

Oliver, P. (1994). To govern by kindness: The first two decades of the Mercer Reformatory. In J. Phillips, T. Loo, & S. Lewthwaite (Eds.), *Essays in the history of Canadian law* (Vol. 5, pp. 516–571; Crime and Criminal Justice series). Toronto: University of Toronto Press.

O'Malley, P. (1992). Risk, power and crime prevention. *Economy and Society, 21,* 252–275.

Province of Nova Scotia. (1992). *Blueprint for change: Report of the Solicitor General's Special Committee on Provincially Incarcerated Women.* Halifax: Author.

Rose, N. (1990). *Governing the soul: The shaping of the private self.* London: Routledge.

Rose, N., & Miller, F. (1992). Political power beyond the state: Problematic of government. *British Journal of Sociology, 43,* 173–205.

Royal Commission on the Status of Women in Canada. (1970). *Report of the Royal Commission on the Status of Women in Canada.* Ottawa: Supply and Services.

Shaw, M. (1991a). *The federal female offender: A preliminary study.* Ottawa: Solicitor General of Canada.

Shaw, M. (1991b). *Paying the price: Federally sentenced women in context.* Ottawa: Solicitor General of Canada.

Shaw, M. (1993). Reforming federal women's imprisonment. In E. Adelberg & C. Currie (Eds.), *In conflict with the law* (pp. 50–75). Vancouver: Press Gang.

Singh, A.-M. (1994). *Will the real community please stand up? "Community" in community policing.* Unpublished master's thesis, University of Toronto, Centre of Criminology.

Snider, L. (1994). Feminism, punishment and the potential of empowerment. *Canadian Journal of Law and Society, 9,* 75–104.

Standing Committee on Justice and Solicitor General. (1988). *Report of the Standing Committee on Justice and Solicitor General on its review of sentencing, conditional release, and related aspects of corrections (Daubney Report).* Ottawa: Supply and Services.

Stewart, M., & MacKay, J. (1994). Anxious women await prison closing. *Journal of Prisoners on Prisons, 5*(2), 37–39.

Strange, C. (1983). *The velvet glove: Maternalistic reform at the Ontario Mercer Reformatory, 1874–1927.* Unpublished master's thesis, University of Ottawa, Department of History.

Subcommittee on the Penitentiary System in Canada. (1977). *Report to the Parliament by the Subcommittee on the Penitentiary System in Canada (MacGuigan Report).* Ottawa: Supply and Services.

Sugar, F., & Fox, L. (1990a). Nistum Peyako Seht'wawin Iskwewak: Breaking the chains. *Canadian Journal of Women and the Law, 3,* 465–482.

Sugar, F., & Fox, L. (1990b). *Survey of federally sentenced Aboriginal women.* Ottawa: Correctional Service of Canada.

Task Force on Federally Sentenced Women. (1990). *Creating choices: Report of the Task Force on Federally Sentenced Women.* Ottawa: Correctional Service of Canada.

Women's Issues Task Force. (1995). *Women's voices, women's choices: Report of the Women's Issues Task Force.* Toronto: Ministry of the Solicitor General and Correctional Services.

Young, I. (1994). Punishment, treatment, empowerment: Three approaches to policy for pregnant addicts. *Feminist Studies, 20,* 33–57.

13

Correctional Administrators' Perspectives on Gender Arrangements and Family-Related Programming for Women Offenders

Merry Morash
Amanda L. Robinson

Introduction

As the population of women in prison and jails has grown, there has been increased but, depending on the correctional system or program, uneven and varied attention to programmatic needs that relate to the families of women offenders. The rate of imprisonment for women has quadrupled in the 1990s (Bureau of Justice Statistics, 1995), and correctional policies continue to focus primarily on punitive rather than rehabilitative goals. Due to current drug laws, mandatory minimum sentencing, and the removal of family circumstances as a mitigating factor in federal cases, researchers have concluded that the national trend for women offenders is "equality with a vengeance" (Chesney-Lind & Pollock, 1995; Pollock, 1999). Despite the overriding social forces which seem to be pushing increased numbers of people into prisons and jails, correctional institutions

"Correctional Administrators' Perspective on Gender Arrangements and Family-Related Programming for Women Offenders," by Merry Morash and Amanda L. Robinson, from *Marriage & Family Review*, Vol. 32(3/4), pp. 83–109, 2001. Permission granted by The Haworth Press Inc.

are rarely able to address the criminogenic needs of women offenders, and punitive approaches are relied on to the exclusion of potentially successful alternatives (Morash, Bynum, & Koons, 1995). At least three aspects of family life are relevant to women offenders' pathways to crime and their immediate circumstances: sexual and other abuse of women offenders in their families of origin, abuse by husbands or other male partners, and relationships with and responsibilities for children. These negative aspects of family life create many of women offenders' unique dilemmas and needs. The gendered nature of these family-related concerns therefore constitutes the focus of our research.

The literature provides empirical evidence of the characteristics of women offenders' family experiences and relations. Studies using survey and self-report methods have found that a high proportion of incarcerated women self-report prior sexual or physical abuse in routine inmate surveys (Bureau of Justice Statistics, 1991; Snell, 1994). A Bureau of Justice Statistics Special Report (1999) indicated that "nearly 6 in 10 women in state prisons had experienced physical or sexual abuse in the past; just over a third of imprisoned women had been abused by an intimate in the past, and just under a quarter reported prior abuse by a family member" (p. 1). Some research that has used in-depth interviews has produced estimates that up to 80% of women offenders were abused as children (Richie, 1996). When women commit violent acts, the victim is frequently a family member or intimate. For example, "of the 60,000 murders committed by women between 1976 and 1997, just over 60% were against an intimate or family member, among the 400,000 murders committed by men over the same period, 20% were against family members or intimates" (Bureau of Justice Statistics, 1999, p. 4). Many women killed an intimate or family member in response to being abused. Finally, an estimated two-thirds of women in prison and in jail have children under 18 years old, and 4 out of 5 women had children living with them before coming to prison (Bureau of Justice Statistics, 1999; Snell, 1994).

Aside from the obvious pressures and negative emotional outcomes that can be created by domestic and sexual abuse and by separation from children, theories of the etiology and the context of women's criminality have identified a link between gender-related oppression in the family and the etiology and continuation of women's illegal behavior. Chesney-Lind and Sheldon (1992) have postulated that girls running from families in which they experience physical and/or emotional abuse become involved in prostitution and drug use (sometimes as a way to dull the pain resulting from the realities of their lives), criminal activity to support themselves, and eventually the adult justice system as incarcerated women. Research has also provided evidence of the negative relationships that women have with men as a factor supporting involvement in the drug trade, which, again, can lead to incarceration (Maher, 1992; Maher & Daly, 1996; Pollock, 1999). Consistent with the current perspective on rehabilitation (Andrews, Bonta

& Hoge, 1990), effective correctional programs must address criminogenic needs in order to reduce recidivism and produce other positive outcomes. Thus, correctional programs would need to address prior and ongoing abuse within the family and the realities of motherhood in order to produce positive outcomes. Consistent with feminist theories of female criminality (Chesney-Lind & Sheldon, 1992; Daly, 1992; Daly & Chesney-Lind, 1988; Maher, 1992; Maher & Daly, 1996; Pollock, 1999), effective intervention would require empowering women to escape gender arrangements that maintain criminality or actually altering these arrangements.

This article considers how administrators with responsibility for correctional programming for women offenders view family-related programming and the related picture they have of women offender's location in a gendered society. Correctional administrators include those who head state correctional departments and local jails, prison wardens, and directors of programs for women offenders. At a deeper level, we were interested in understanding whether women's gender-based disadvantage is recognized, reproduced, or challenged in administrators' perceptions. This interest builds upon the social constructionist perspective on gender that emphasizes that the purpose of the gender order is to make men and women feel and act differently from one another (Lorber, 1994, 1998). Past gender research emphasized the dichotomous nature of male/female or masculine/feminine by treating behavior as originating from biology rather than as a social interaction. Gender has since come to be viewed in a very different light. For example, Connell (1985) states that "social gender relations do not *express* natural patterns; they *negate* the biological statute" (p. 269). This conceptualization of gender has allowed the analysis to move away from biology or sex role differences (often an essentialist perspective) and into a realm that realizes that gender relations affect the levels of power, resources, and opportunity available to individuals (the social constructionist perspective) (Lorber, 1994; West & Zimmerman, 1987).

The social constructionist perspective has been used to understand many aspects of social life, including the division of labor (Connell, 1987; Messerschmidt, 1993), gendered work organizations (Acker, 1990; Kanter, 1977), sexuality (Coltrane, 1994; Kimmel, 1994; Rich, 1993), race-ethnicity (Baca Zinn & Thornton Dill, 1996; Hill-Collins, 1986; West & Fenstermaker, 1995), education (Connell, 1997; Thorne, 1992), violence and crime (Bowker, 1998; Collier, 1998), and women in the criminal justice system (Martin & Jurik, 1996). Using this framework to guide our analysis of the data, we posited that the discourse of people involved in the correctional enterprise is more than just talk—it would reveal how they construct gender and the degree to which these constructions maintain (or challenge) the gendered social order. We also proposed that how correctional administrators construct gender would influence what they viewed as appropriate programming for women offenders, whether their needs were unique from those of male inmates, and how this translated into the correctional services received by women. We chose to make gender central to our analysis because researchers "seldom if ever consider the possibility that patriarchal and gender-based assumptions might have played a role in the development of the modern prison" and how this subsequently affects the correctional experiences of women offenders (Dobash, Dobash, & Gutteridge, 1986, p. 9).

The effect of the constructions of gender on perceptions of appropriate family-related programming for women offenders would be relevant to program design and interactions that staff have with women offenders in correctional settings. There is a tension between programming that seeks to empower women offenders by enabling them to break from traditional gender constructions and programming that practitioners or offenders find acceptable because it is consistent with traditional gender ideologies. Specifically, correctional programs that focus on the unjust exercise of male power through childhood sexual abuse or partner abuse directly challenge a gender order in which women are oppressed. Programs that emphasize women's right to child custody similarly can empower women. Programming that has a sole emphasis on preparation of women to parent and on the importance of this activity, alternatively, is consistent with the existing gender order. However, at all times we must keep in mind that the ultimate limitation of even the most "empowering" programs in jails, prisons, or community settings is that they exist within the confines of mandated supervision or correctional institutions, which, by their very nature, are disempowering, debilitating, and destabilizing.

Methodology

Data used to examine correctional experts' perceptions of gender and family-related correctional programming for women offenders were gathered through a combined mail and phone survey of correctional administrators. This survey was one part of a larger study of contemporary thinking about best practices in management and effective programming for female offenders (see Koons, Burrow, Morash, & Bynum, 1997).

Sample of Correctional Administrators with Responsibility for Women Offenders

Correctional administrators work in prison, jail, and community settings. Prisons and (in some states) community programs such as parole supervision, halfway houses, and boot camps are centrally administered by a state correctional department, and in each state one or more prisons for women is administered by a warden. Jails serve metropolitan areas, counties, or multi-county regions and hold women who have not yet had a court hearing or who are sentenced for comparatively short periods, which is normally less than a year. Most prisons hold only women, though a small number house both men and women, whereas jails typically hold both women and men, except in approximately 15 high-population areas where there is a separate facility for women. The sampling frame of correctional staff with responsibility for women offenders included top state-level correctional administrators, administrators of prisons and jails, and administrators of programs focused on women offenders in jails, prisons, and the community.

There were several steps in the selection of a sample of correctional administrators (for a full description of the sampling process, see Morash et al., 1995). The head of each state's correctional department was asked to respond to a mail and telephone survey or to designate a person at the state level who could knowledgeably address questions regarding women offenders from the perspective of the leadership of the state department of corrections. Additionally, all wardens in the 65 prisons housing women were surveyed by mail. Because we did not want to have a sample that over-represented large states, prison wardens were excluded from the follow-up telephone survey if their facility was in the same state and served the same population of offenders as another facility (e.g., offenders classified at the same security level or offenders from the same geographic location). This reduced the sample of prison wardens who were surveyed by phone to 56. The sample also included all administrators of jails that housed only women and a sample of administrators of other jails that were stratified by region of the United States and size of the population served. Jails that held less than 10 women were not included in the follow-up telephone interview. Finally, the sample included directors of a purposively selected set of programs considered to be effective for women offenders. These programs were identified through the other interviews, a review of the literature, a review of materials provided by programs, and supplementary phone calls to individuals knowledgeable about community corrections programs. The list was stratified according to type of program (e.g., substance abuse treatment, parenting, multi-purpose) and geographic location, and programs were purposively selected from a range of locations and with a range of foci.

Response rates were quite high.

- A state correctional administrator responded to a mail survey and a subsequent phone interview in every state.
- Of 70 wardens in the sample, 93% (65) completed a mailed survey. For the phone interviews, 96% (54 of 56) of wardens asked to complete a phone interview did this.
- Of the 61 jail administrators sampled, 89% (54) returned a mailed survey; and, of 54 asked to respond to a telephone interview, 93% (50) participated.
- Of 71 sampled program administrators, 87% (62) completed a phone interview.

Except for the directors of programs for women, samples represent the different types of correctional administrator. The program director sample is restricted to those heading programs that either another administrator or the literature suggested were promising or effective for women offenders.

Specific Questions Asked of Administrators

Presented in summary form below are several questions that elicited information on administrators' perspectives on gender, family, and programming. Contained in brackets are the types of administrators to whom the question was posed.

- Given the national increases in the numbers of women in prison today, what are the most important management problems in processing these women through the system in your state? In operating the facilities? In maintaining the security of facilities? [state correctional, jail, and prison administrators]
- What are the unmet program needs of women in correctional facilities? Are some of these program needs more serious compared to others? Unique from those of men? [state correctional, jail, prison, and program administrators]
- What background or knowledge base do you find essential in managing an institution or program that handles women? [state correctional, jail, and prison administrators] or, What background or knowledge base do you find essential in the line staff who work in your program? [program directors]
- Do women offenders require a different type/style of management than men? What is the type/style of management? [state correctional, jail, and prison administrators, program directors]

Data Analysis

Responses to the questions about management and programming were coded into categories of response for the larger research project (Morash et al., 1995). Some of the analysis presented below provides a quantitative summary of various types of responses (also see table 1).

To more fully understand how administrators perceived gender and to reveal the connections of differing perceptions to their views on appropriate response to women offenders, we also carried out a qualitative analysis of the data, primarily using a content analysis technique. Content analysis is "any technique for making inferences by objectively and systematically identifying specified characteristics of messages" (Holsti, 1969 and Stone, 1966, cited in Ogilvie, Stone, & Kelly, 1982). In other words, it is a useful method for drawing conclusions about a topic of interest. In this case, we analyzed the content for references related to gender, gender roles, and any mention made of family-related concerns or the families of women

Table 1. Characteristics of Correctional Administrators

	State n = 63	Prison n = 56	Jail n = 52	Program n = 68
Gender				
Male	52% (33)	23% (13)	69% (36)	24% (16)
Female	48% (30)	77% (43)	31% (16)	75% (51)
Education				
No College	0	0	10% (5)	0
Some College	6% (4)	13% (7)	21% (11)	13% (9)
College Degree	33% (21)	23% (13)	62% (32)	34% (23)
Grad. Degree	60% (38)	59% (33)	0	50% (34)
Years at Job				
< 1 yr.	6% (4)	50% (28)	12% (6)	3% (2)
1–4 yrs.	40% (25)	41% (23)	48% (25)	51% (35)
5–9 yrs.	27% (17)	9% (5)	17% (9)	21% (14)
10 or more	5% (3)		15% (8)	12% (8)
Years in Corrections				
1–9 yrs.	11% (7)	< 7 yrs. 4% (2)	27% (14)	35% (24)
10–19 yrs.	25% (16)	7–20 59% (33)	46% (24)	34% (23)
20 or more	41% (26)	> 20 38% (21)	19% (10)	19% (13)
Top 5 programs in need of expansion	Subs. abuse 38% Ment. health 36% Parenting 32% Work 24% Aftercare 22%	Subs. abuse 24% Family-rel. 19% Vict./abuse 14% Ment. health 15% Work 13%	Subs. abuse 41% Education 30% Work 24% Parenting 17% Vict./abuse 9%	Family-rel. 13% Subs. abuse 11% Trans. hous. 11% Work 8% Aftercare 8%
Unique needs of women offenders	Family-rel. 36% Ment. health 28% Subs. abuse 14% Work 10%	Family-rel. 32% Ment. health 32% Subs. abuse 9%	Parenting 13% Vict./abuse 6%	Not asked

offenders. Analysis of the responses to these questions provided initial insight into administrators' perspectives on gender and allowed us to categorize these perspectives into a typology (see table 2).

For the qualitative analysis, we listed responses to questions about managing women offenders by respondent identity and by type of administrator. The responses reflected four general ways in which administrators described their perceptions of gender as it affected women offenders; we categorized responses according to these types. Also, responses included related recommendations for appropriate ways of interacting with women offenders and descriptions of women's "character" as it differed from men's "character."

After analyzing the data on management, we arranged the responses to questions about the program needs of women offenders and those

Table 2. Constructions of Gender and Correctional Programming

Gender Perspective	Definition	Program Emphasis	Management Style	Implications
Gender Irrelevant	No difference between male and female inmates	Lack of gender-specific programming	Focus on "quality" management; treat all offenders the same	Status quo; traditional female roles upheld by default; family issues ignored
Gender Maintenance	Female inmates are different; traditional gender roles should be maintained	Traditional programming that reinforces gender stereotypes—focus on parenting	Focus on paternalistic management; biological differences of women emphasized	Status quo; traditional female role maintained; traditional emphasis on family issues
Gender Issues	Female inmates are different; traditional gender roles are problematic	Programming to deal with emotional needs, self-esteem, abuse, victimization issues	Focus on more communication, interaction, sensitivity with female inmates	Identify and fix women's problems; hold the individual accountable; psychological focus; therapeutic emphasis on family issues
Gender Challenge	Female inmates are different; traditional gender arrangements must be challenged; structural inequality	Non-traditional vocational programming; emphasis on relationship independence and equality, "stand alone" woman	Focus on empowerment, independence of women	Avoid gender stereotypes; hold the system accountable; vocational focus; family issues deemphasized

concerning whether they were unique to women in a table format, with the respondent ID in the left column and responses relevant to the most frequently-mentioned program areas that were identified as unique to women in the columns to the right. Four frequently mentioned areas were identified: (1) prior sexual or domestic abuse, (2) parenting, (3) problems with negative relationships with men, and (4) employment. Additional program areas that were in need of expansion and that were less frequently identified as unique to women also were noted. We examined the responses for each person to get an understanding of how she or he viewed program needs in relation to offenders' gender, and we compared the answers within each of the frequently identified areas. Because the qualitative analyses were conducted at the response level, characterization of the administrators themselves as having a particular gender perspective is beyond the scope of the present analysis. Therefore, it is useful to remember that the categories contained in the typology are not mutually exclusive and that one should expect there to be some overlap or even inconsistency in how individual people view the relationship between gender and correctional programming for women offenders.

Findings

Correctional Administrators' Perceptions of Program Needs of Women Offenders

Characteristics of the different types of administrators surveyed (gender, education, years on the job, years in corrections) are contained in table 1. Administrators in the different settings have different demographic profiles, with women predominating in prison and program settings and men in jail settings.

Summary information about administrators' responses to the types of programs in need of expansion and the unique programming needs of women offenders is also presented in Table 1. If administrators in state correctional departments, prisons, and jails mentioned family circumstances as relevant to management or programming at all, they also highlighted women's skills and concerns as mothers. Responding to a question about the knowledge needed to manage a women's institution, for example, some state administrators described the importance of recognizing women's closer connections to their children and families, and some prison wardens pointed out that "the impact of family situations" should be covered in correctional training programs. Parenting programs were among the five types of programs that the highest proportions of state-level administrators felt should be expanded. Wardens had more diverse perceptions than did state administrators, but, similar to state correctional administrators, they most often identified substance abuse programming as in need of expansion, and family-related programming was mentioned by the next highest proportion. Smaller numbers of wardens said there was a need to expand programs to address prior victimization or abuse, mental health, and vocation or work preparation. Jail administrators followed a similar pattern, with the third-highest proportion identifying parenting programs as in need of expansion for women, and higher proportions identifying substance abuse programming and job training. Few saw a need to expand domestic violence programs, though sizable proportions did identify education and life skills as in need of expansion.

Perceptions of the types of programs that needed expansion were somewhat different among those directors of the programs thought to be effective for women offenders. The 62 program administrators listed 143 different program needs that were most in need of expansion for the populations that they served, and these were categorized. The following categories were mentioned most often: family-related programming (13% or 18 of the 143), transitional housing (11% or 16), vocational training or apprenticeships in the community (8% or 12), aftercare services (8% or 11), and substance abuse treatment (11% or 15).

Overall, if correctional experts saw a need for expanded family-related programming, it was for parenting programs that *maintain and support women's role as mother.* However, small proportions of prison wardens and jail administrators did identify program expansion needs in the areas of prior sexual abuse and domestic violence, respectively. It should be recognized that administrators' perceptions of which sorts of programming needed to be expanded are affected not only by their ideas about women, but also by the availability of programs. It is in their answers to questions about the unique needs of women offenders that we could isolate their reasoning about gender.

Responding to questions about whether the programs most needing expansion were unique to women, state correctional administrators mentioned four general types that were unique: the administrator in 36% of states (18) identified family-related programming; the administrator in 28% of states (14) identified mental health programming; the administrator in 14% of states (7) identified substance abuse programming; and the administrator in 10% of states (5) identified vocational programming. Administrators described some of the unique aspects of women inmates' family experiences, including the need for programming to overcome early socialization that limits women's independence and occupational choices and the need for parenting programs to strengthen nurturing and discipline skills. Also, frequently mentioned was a need for programs to address mental health problems, especially with regard to increasing self-esteem and countering the effects of abuse and victimization. Several administrators commented on the connection between low self-esteem, victimization, and other problems, like the lack of vocational skills and experience, drug abuse, and family issues. In general, there was emphasis on the degree to which women had unique needs for programming to address individual-level problems, or what based on qualitative analysis described later in this paper we came to call programming with a *gender issues* focus.

Similar to state correctional administrators, administrators in under one-third of the prisons viewed the needs for both mental health and for family-related programming as unique for women. In contrast, very few jail administrators said that the needs they reported for women's programming were unique and different from the needs of men. This could partly be a function of shorter incarceration periods in jails compared to prisons that reduced the likelihood that administrators became exposed to or aware of women's unique needs. The slight exceptions were in the area of parenting and domestic assault.

Deeper Analysis of Administrators' Perspectives on Gender and Correctional Responses

The quantitative analysis and selected examples that we have described provide a general picture of how different types of correctional administrators viewed programming for women offenders. It is not clear from this type of analysis, however, how administrators understood gender arrangements in the family or more broadly and how they tailored the correctional response, including attention to the offender's family history and circumstance, to their understanding of gender arrangements. The deeper qualitative analysis addressed these issues.

Four perspectives on gender. Overall, administrators' comments on background, knowledge, and style for effective management of women offenders reflected four general perspectives on (or constructions of) gender. We have termed these perspectives (1) *gender irrelevant,* (2) *gender maintenance,* (3) *gender issues,* and (4) *gender challenge*. The different perspectives and the implications of each for correctional response to women are summarized in table 2.

Especially jail administrators, but also some other correctional administrators, demonstrated what we called a *gender irrelevant* perspective. Just over one third (35% or 17) felt that there were no differences between male and female inmates, and nearly half (49%) of the 50 jail administrators felt that male and female inmates should be managed in exactly the same way. Some comments reflecting this perspective are listed below. We have provided contextual information about the respondents in brackets following the quotes, including: respondent's gender, type of correctional administrator, level of education, years tenure in current job, and years tenure in correctional field:

> Really, no. Staff and management need to treat all offenders the same—fairly, and I don't think that is different for men or women. [male jail administrator, BA, 5 yrs./current job, 18.5 yrs./corrections].

> Not really. We handle them just about the same as the men. The programs are about the same anyway [male jail administrator, some college, 3 yrs./current job, 5 yrs./corrections].

Many of the administrators' comments reflected a *gender maintenance* perspective. They identified character attributes that differed between men and women, and related styles of interacting with the women that "fit" the difference. Several administrators, for example, pointed out that "women require more attention, more communication, are more verbal, have more emotions" [female warden, some college, 2 yrs./current job, 21 yrs./corrections]. They went on to explain that it was necessary to communicate more with incarcerated women than with incarcerated men. Other less frequently described character differences included women's being more manipulative and more needy than men, and as a result requiring more skill in detecting their "games" as well as more support. One administrator explicitly attributed unique characteristics of women to their biology, for instance,

> There are definitely different issues here. For example, if you get 30 women in a housing unit on the same menstrual cycle, and that happens, you have real trouble. Those hormones can kill you. We have a lot more petty interpersonal problems with the women than with the men. All the women do is bitch and moan, scream, cry, fight, yell [male jail administrator, BA, 12 yrs./current job, 12 yrs./corrections].

Also reflecting a *gender maintenance* perspective, some administrators talked about the importance of adapting to the roles that women were "taught" and/or preparing them to hold particular roles assigned to women. One individual explained,

> Oftentimes female inmates respond better to male administrators because they have had a history of being subservient to males [female warden, some college, 12 yrs./current job, 28 yrs./corrections].

Another stated,

> It is a lot like a day care center. They respond to rewards and punishments much more than men [female jail administrator, BA, 3 yrs./current job, 18 yrs./corrections].

In the first administrator's view, by assigning male administrators to work with women, there was an advantage through the "fit" with women's previously socialized submissive response; the other recommended the use of reward and punishment as particularly effective with women. These comments reflect a belief that women offenders may be more easily managed by maintaining gender roles that construe them as subservient and even childlike.

Many program administrators took a *gender issues* perspective with regard to women inmates. The needs of women, including medical problems, their concerns for children, and history of abuse, were frequently called "women's issues." In the *gender issues* perspective, women are viewed as characterized by multiple, gender-related "women's issues." This *gender issues* view is represented in these statements:

> The person [correctional staff] must have insight on what women's issues are [male warden, MS, 3 yrs./current job, 14 yrs./corrections].

> Anyone can do it [manage a women's institution] but to do it well you must understand the women's background and their special needs, [such as] abuse, self-esteem [female warden, BA, 2.5 yrs./current job, 2.5 yrs./corrections].

> There is a need for formal training to work with women and their various problems [female warden, MS, 11 yrs./current job, 17.5 yrs./corrections].

The *gender challenge* perspective rejects the status quo in gender arrangements. Several study participants pointed to the need to correct the gender inequity when women's access to programming was more limited compared to men's within the jail or prison context. Examples of these statements include:

> The [jail] school system offers more of a variety of courses for males that are not available for females, such as printshop [female jail administrator, some college, 3 yrs./current job, 10.5 yrs./corrections].

> Women don't have nearly the opportunities available to male inmates in the [work program]. We can't and won't work females when there are male inmates unless there is heavy supervision [male jail administrator, BA, 2 yrs./current job, 3 yrs./corrections].

Less frequent were challenges to a gender order that disadvantages women outside of the correctional system. When such challenges did occur, they were typically in relation to work opportunities. For example, one administrator felt that it was important to reduce women's disadvantage in the workforce by providing nontraditional training opportunities and another sought to reduce the disadvantage by avoiding stereotyping traditional occupations along gender lines. However, as described below, few administrators challenged the gender order in the family context.

Perspectives on Gender and Family-Related Programming

The four perspectives on gender are apparent in correctional administrators' comments on women's families and family histories and on their related thoughts about appropriate management and programmatic response. It was fairly straightforward to look across each administrator's answers to questions about women's unique needs for programming and to categorize the responses that were pertinent to family as reflecting one of the four basic perspectives on gender. However, in some cases, it was unclear whether respondents saw needs relating to children as based on the importance of preparing women to be mothers (*gender maintenance* orientation) or to deal with the stresses and responsibilities of motherhood (*gender issues* orientation). Very few respondents reflected a *gender challenge* perspective, and when they did, consistent with the *gender issues* perspective, they also talked about special women's issues that programming should address.

Program administrators' responses were most difficult to categorize according to the different perspectives. Although the transcript of their answers included examples of each perspective, several of the study participants did not provide an indication of whether or not they felt that program needs were unique to women. They instead answered questions about unique needs by stating that their program focused only on women and women's needs. The relationship between the family-related concerns of women offenders and each of the four gender perspectives are explicated below.

Gender irrelevant orientation toward managing women offenders. Consistent with the quantitative analysis already described, for jail administrators, the modal response to the question about unique program needs was either to not answer this question, or to indicate that there were no differences between the program needs of women and men. Thus, many jail administrators felt gender was irrelevant to program needs or were blind to differences in needs or experiences based on gender. In contrast, only a few of each of the other types of administrators felt that gender was irrelevant to programming and that women did not have unique needs. In their comments, they sometimes explained that there were misperceptions that needs related to parenting and prior abuse were unique to women and that, in fact, these needs were just as frequently experienced by men who were offenders.

Gender maintenance: Reinforcing and reproducing existing gender arrangements. Many administrators identified the need for programming that would prepare women to adequately fulfill their roles as mothers. One exemplified this viewpoint in a statement that program needs of women are unique from those of men, because there "should be a focus on maintaining the bond with the family" through such activities as visitations and retreats with children [female state-level administrator, BA, 2 yrs./current job, 19 yrs./corrections]. Other administrators pointed out that program needs unique to women included areas such as the development of parenting skills and teaching women about nutrition so they could prepare adequate meals for children. As one respondent put it, "We do work to keep the family together" [female program director, MS, 4 yrs./current job, 5 yrs./corrections]. A characteristic of programming that would reinforce and/or reproduce existing gender arrangements is the acceptance of women's role as "primary parent." As one respondent indicated,

> [Women's] family orientation is different. . . . Men have no high desire to become involved. Mothers have a closer bond to their children and respond more to this type of programming [male state-level administrator, MS, 5 yrs./current job, 19 yrs./corrections].

Acceptance of the status quo in gender arrangements was often connected to the *gender maintenance* perspective. Explaining that women did not have unique needs for vocational training, one person commented that nontraditional training programs had been offered, but they had not been met with much enthusiasm by women inmates. In contrast to the *gender challenge* position regarding gender and jobs (which is described below), this individual presented women's lack of interest in nontraditional jobs as a constant to which programming would need to be adapted. Similarly, one administrator indicated that "the program needs of women are probably not different from those of men" [female state-level administrator, MS, 15 yrs./current job, 17 yrs./corrections]. But family needs are an issue (where there may be unique needs) in that many of the inmates are single. Another similar response was:

> Some parenting issues are unique. Nutritional counseling is very unique to women. I would like to know that the inmates with small children know how to feed them. The reality is that men will not be taking on these roles [female warden, some college, 4 yrs./current job, 15 yrs./corrections].

The *gender maintenance* perspective was closely linked to a perceived need for programming to make women better parents and to a singular emphasis in this as a need unique to women. In other words, in this perspective, women have unique needs by virtue of being mothers, and programming should be provided to support this role.

Gender issues focus with regard to female offenders. Another conceptualization of gender that is reflected by many of the responses was that women disproportionately suffer from various types of negative experiences and circumstances and that programming needs to address the results, including poor self-esteem, substance abuse, and stress. Negative experiences and circumstances included sole responsibility for children, prior childhood victimization through abuse, abuse by a partner, and involvement in relationships characterized by "codependency" that supported negative outcomes like substance abuse. As one warden put it, "women's issues" are the most serious problem.

> A response that demonstrates the gender issues perspective is that programs "must help the women from the position of being a victim" [female state-level administrator, MS, 5 yrs./current job, 10 yrs./corrections].

The administrator went on to say that women's parenting responsibilities were greater than men's, and as a result of these and other differences, the 12-step substance abuse programming was not as effective for women as for men, for it did not address self-esteem issues. More generally, "whenever planning for women, you need to ask, 'Are there special, different needs for women?'" [same female state-level administrator cited above]. Another administrator described the attention to *gender issues* as a "twist" that was put into programming.

In the *gender issues* perspective, an issue that was frequently mentioned was women's responsibility for the care of children. Comments describing this gender perspective are provided below:

> Dealing with becoming the primary support of children—a microcosm of what happens nationally. In a sense this is a unique need of women, because the children usually come back to women. More pressure is

> placed on the women [male state-level administrator, MS, 2 yrs./current job, 33 yrs./corrections].

> [You] get more bang for the buck out of females in comparison to males with regard to parenting skills programming. Female offenders are often the main figure in family situations. We support parenting skills through addressing other needs as well [male state-level administrator, MS, 1 yr./current job, 17.5 yrs./corrections].

> Eighty-five percent of the women report they are mothers and these women especially have difficulty with securing appropriate housing, which is oftentimes a stipulation of parole [female warden, MS, 2.5 yrs./current job, 18 yrs./corrections].

In the last example, having responsibility for children has been shown to result in housing problems for women. Several administrators noted that it was not necessarily a good thing that women disproportionately were responsible for children, but then went on to emphasize that programming must in some way address this reality through help to women. Different from the *gender maintenance* perspective, which emphasizes the need to better prepare women to be "good" mothers, the emphasis in the *gender issues* perspective is on the problems women experience because they are mothers. What is also different in the *gender issues* perspective is that there was not usually a singular focus on parenting, rather administrators identified one to several other problems that affected women.

Administrators holding both the *gender maintenance* and the *gender issues* perspectives saw women as responsible for parenting and took an individual level rather than a social structural view of the problems associated with parenting. That is, the focus was on improving the parenting skills of individual women rather than addressing societal factors that affect parents as a group (e.g., legislation, employment opportunities, health care, and welfare).

Other frequently mentioned *gender issues* were prior history of abuse, subjection to domestic violence, and the negative effects of "codependent" relationships with men. A few individuals also presented a deficit model of women as disproportionately lacking in vocational skills or in need of mental health care. Women were also seen as being unique in the degree to which they had problems of low self-esteem, in the proportion of female as opposed to male prisoners who had substance abuse problems, and in their needs for medical services. The specific deficit of low self-esteem was linked, by one administrator, to the need to alter the commonly used 12-step program to address substance abuse and to use instead an approach that improved self-esteem.

For all but the jail administrators, a focus on *gender issues* was the modal response to questions about women's unique program needs. At the program level, this translated into efforts to deal with either selected or multiple special problems of women. A program addressing a selected problem was described:

> Relationship based is the key issue. [This program] is different than similar programming for males. Have small groups, work on communication skills, personal relationships, decision-making skills (anger and passivity), human relationship skills. There are three parts [to the program]: life planning, life skills, and parenting [female program director, MS, 8 yrs./current job, 20 yrs./corrections].

A program that addressed multiple *gender issues* was described,

> The whole program is designed to address female needs. We are in a female prison, have female staff, and are all oriented to female offenders. We look at family violence, abuse, incest, everything. We work with their kids, their partners, individuals [female program director, BA, 2 yrs./current job, 2 yrs./corrections].

More general explanations of programming to address *gender issues* included statements such as

> All the services we provide are gender specific [female program director, BA, 3 yrs./current job, 5 yrs./corrections], and we try to do everything that is unique to female offenders [male program director, MS, 22 yrs./current job, 29 yrs./corrections].

Challenging gender arrangements. In speaking about the unique needs of women offenders, few of the higher level correctional administrators talked about the need for programming that would challenge traditional gender arrangements. When they did, it was usually not related to family but to preparation for employment. Examples of these comments are provided below:

> [We are] faced with many challenges in this area. For example, in the construction area women are not as strong and haven't had the experiences of men. This must be taken into account [but is] difficult as a result of the small population of women. [We are also] trying to recognize the fact of socialization. Women need a broader range of choices of occupation that they can access later. [We] must provide a window of opportunity [male state-level administrator, PhD, 5 yrs./current job, 5 yrs./corrections].

> Good job skills—most men can get jobs with less skills and make more, men's image as breadwinner affects this, women are often insecure in this area—[they] feel they don't deserve good jobs [male state-level administrator, MS, 9 yrs./current job, 25 yrs./corrections].

> Females are not getting the multiple certificates like the males. They are affected more by family dynamics. It is difficult to get around stereotypes. They are less independent. We are going to use a new test with job categories that are the same as in the "real world" [male state-level administrator, BA, 8 yrs./current job, 17 yrs./corrections].

> Caution should be taken to avoid using stereotypes to determine programming. [The specific caution was against stereotyping occupations

> along gender lines for work related programming] [male state-level administrator, PhD, 3 yrs./current job, 21 yrs./corrections].

Whereas the state correctional administrators cited above noted a combination of factors external to the prison (e.g., prior job experience, socialization, societal stereotypes) and internal to it (e.g., small population of women which, among other things, reduces access to a variety of programs), the small proportion of jail administrators who focused on gender inequity all spoke of a lack of access within their institution. They gave specific examples such as the jail school system offering less variety in courses for women than men, and restricting access to work related programs to just men. Each of the examples above includes claims that existing gender arrangements block women from desirable jobs, that there needs to be a "window of opportunity," that "men can get [good] jobs with less skills," and stereotypes (along with other realities of women's lives) that limit job preference programming. Perhaps the most consequential hurdle that women face in finding desirable jobs, yet one that was never mentioned, is the stigma from criminalization and incarceration itself. It is doubtful that the detrimental impact of serving time in prison or jail on employability can ever be completely overcome by involvement in a correctional program, no matter how "empowering" it may be.

> Challenges to exiting gender relations also occurred in a few accounts of programming on power within relationships, or apart from relationships. We also, for example, discuss negotiating sex, which is a really important issue for women in some cultures, particularly Latina [male state-level administrator, MS, 9 yrs./current job, 25 yrs./corrections].

> The program seeks to develop a stand alone woman, tries to make the women understand they do not need to live in a relationship that is not beneficial to them and helps them recognize and avoid codependency. [This] may not be unique to women but they certainly come from a different angle [male warden, some college, 2.5 yrs./current job, 24 yrs./corrections].

The notion of empowerment was also embedded in a response about a broader set of relationships. As one respondent stated,

> Empowerment skills and negotiating social service assistance. These things are unique to women offenders [female program director, MS, 1.5 yrs./current job, 8 yrs./corrections].

In each of the responses presented above, there is a statement that programming should increase women's limited power in relationships with men or, as in the last example, with institutions. However, it must be reiterated that the *gender challenge* perspective was most often advanced in discourse on vocational programming. Inequality within family or other relationships was mentioned rarely, although this is a significant factor related to women's criminality.

Summary and Conclusions

Overall, our findings suggest that many correctional administrators recognized the family-related concerns of women offenders. Our analysis of the quantitative data revealed that correctional administrators often mentioned programming related to family-related issues as in need of expansion. However, these programs tended to focus on parenting to the exclusion of many other important family-related issues of women offenders (e.g., domestic violence, childhood abuse, etc.). For example, when asked about the unique needs of women offenders, more of state-level prison and jail administrators mentioned parenting programs than domestic violence counseling or past victimization issues. Additionally, administrators often saw these family-related concerns as only unique to female offenders; male offenders were viewed as not wanting or needing any parenting or family-related programming. Thus, correctional administrators usually perceived women offenders' needs through a prism of traditional gender images that mirrored society at large, especially in relation to families. However, there was variance within our sample of administrators that was revealed through a deeper analysis of the data.

For the qualitative analysis, we utilized a social constructionist perspective to understand how prison administrators' perceptions of gender are related to their views of programs for women, including programming with a focus on the family. Administrators saw women and related correctional programming for them from four perspectives, which we labeled (1) *gender irrelevant,* (2) *gender maintenance,* (3) *gender issues,* and (4) *gender challenge*. How administrators constructed gender influenced what they viewed as appropriate programming for women offenders, whether their needs were considered unique from those of male inmates, and how this translated into types of correctional services provided. In short, we were able to shed some light on how constructions of gender in institutional settings maintained or challenged the gender social order.

One of our most important findings pertained to the relationship between gender perspectives and family-related issues (e.g., partner abuse, visitation with children, parenting skills, etc.). The administrators who took the *gender irrelevant* perspective tended to ignore the family-related issues of inmates, and there was a noted lack of gender-specific programming. On the other hand, *gender maintenance* administrators tended to focus on parenting issues to the exclusion of many other unique needs of women: female inmates were viewed solely as mothers. This finding suggests that particularly in jails, but also in some other correctional institutions, not much has changed since the inception of women's prisons, when administrators encouraged the "social organization of prisoners into small 'family' groups" because it "has been regarded as being in the *nature* of women to need such relationships" (Dobash et al., 1986, p. 183). An emphasis on parenting reflects the long-standing tradition of women's prisons to "encourage and ingrain 'appropriate' gender roles" (Belknap, 1996, p. 95), the most acceptable roles being those of wife and mother (Carlen, 1983; Dobash et al., 1986; Feinman, 1983; Freedman, 1981; Rafter, 1985).

Those administrators who subscribed to the *gender issues* perspective also emphasized the importance of family-related issues. However, they did not focus solely on parenting or even on issues related to family. Rather, these administrators were concerned with the many special needs and problems of female inmates. In contrast, the *gender challenge* perspective focused on programming aimed at developing good job opportunities and healthy relationships for female inmates. *Gender challenge* administrators did not ignore the family-related concerns of women offenders, but they focused on more than women's biological or social status as mothers and considered the need to empower women in the family and in other settings.

Elements of the *gender issues* and the *gender maintenance* perspectives are consistent with the therapeutic correctional model, which is based on three assumptions: (1) higher proportions of female inmates are mentally unstable compared to their male counterparts, (2) female inmates are not acting in accord with stereotypically female roles, and (3) female inmates are more difficult to manage because they respond to imprisonment in more "extreme and more neurotic" ways than male inmates (Dobash et al., 1986, p. 129). To medicalize women offenders is to accept the proposition that female criminality is "irresponsible and largely unintentional behavior . . . an individual maladjustment to a well-ordered and consensual society" (Smart, 1876, p. 145). The focus is placed on the individual rather than recognizing and holding repressive social structures accountable.

The *gender maintenance* perspective reflected early "theories about women's crime which stressed its bio-psychological and sexual basis" (Dobash et al., 1986, p. 6). Views of female inmates being emotionally and/or biologically driven were provided in comments regarding the management style of *gender maintenance* administrators. In contrast to *gender issues* administrators, who viewed women as different but equal to men in deserving to have gender-specific needs addressed, gender maintenance administrators tended to subscribe more negative or derogatory characteristics to the female inmates (e.g., manipulative, sneaky, crafty). "Manipulative" is a term that is "invariably attached to oppressed individuals, the powerless, and the frightened to whom it is often the only strategy available" (Dobash et al., 1986, p. 192). Staff tended to maintain traditional societal views that females are "emotional and manipulative and males are cool and aloof" (Pollock, 1984; Pollock-Byrne, 1990, p. 71).

Although only a small proportion of administrators subscribed to the *gender challenge* perspective, this perspective was important to explore if we wanted to understand how correctional programming might challenge the very traditional gender arrangements which, at least some have argued, contribute to women's criminality. This perspective is reminiscent of earlier reform efforts that targeted limited opportunities in terms of work and education (Belknap, 1996) rather than focusing on the psychological or moral problems of women offenders. Particularly for programs within prisons and jails, the ideal of empowerment may be impossible to attain, since incarceration is intrinsically debilitating to employability. Indeed, recognition of this contradiction could prove to be an enormous source of status conflict to administrators in institutional settings, if they want to help and empower female inmates. Administrators adopting the *gender challenge* perspective sought to address women's "dependent status in and out of prison" (Belknap, 1996, p. 107). They focused on empowering women within family and other relationships, though, as we have argued, this may be impossible in institutional settings.

Given women offender's status of powerlessness, the tendency to ignore women's unique needs and circumstances when they are a minority among offenders (the situation in most jails) and the sanctity of the patriarchal family, it is not surprising that the *gender challenge* perspective was rarely manifested and described in relation to correctional programming for women offenders. In many ways, our research confirmed concerns of the degree to which programming ignores women's needs or reinforces stereotypes and powerless roles. However, some evidence suggests that administrators were attempting to empower women and challenge traditional gender arrangements, albeit often within an extremely treacherous landscape (i.e., state-sponsored correctional confinement with limited resources serving the most educationally, economically, and socially deprived females in our society).

Our research suggests that the policy of increased reliance on incarceration for women offenders is highly questionable. In jails, it places women in settings where administrators are particularly unaware of the needs for programming responsive to the high prevalence of family-related violence and the needs of mothers. In prisons, the contradiction between the nature of incarceration and empowerment most likely accounts for the few examples of the *gender challenge* perspective in our data. Aside from the problems with increasing reliance on incarceration, this research further suggests a need for administrators to have training and education that prepares them to at least recognize the different perspectives as they relate to program design and decisions about what programs will be available. This might also enable them to see the limitations of programming that, on the surface, appears to be relevant to women's needs but that fails to address some of their most serious needs at the same time that it provides some basic assistance to them.

References

Acker, J. (1990). Hierarchies, jobs, bodies: A theory of gendered organizations. *Gender & Society, 4*, 139–158.

Andrews, D. A., Bonta, J., & Hoge, R. D. (1990). Classification for effective rehabilitation: Rediscovering psychology. *Criminal Justice and Behavior, 17*, 19–52.

Baca Zinn, M., & Thornton Dill, B. (1996). Theorizing difference from multiracial feminism. *Feminist Studies, 22*, 321–331.

Belknap, J. (1996). *The invisible woman: Gender, crime, and justice.* Belmont, CA: Wadsworth.

Bowker, L. H. (1998). *Masculinities and violence.* Thousand Oaks, CA: Sage.

Bureau of Justice Statistics. (1991). *Women in prison.* Washington, DC: U.S. Author.

Bureau of Justice Statistics. (1995). *Bulletin: Prisoners in 1994.* Washington, DC: U.S. Author.

Bureau of Justice Statistics (1999). *Women offenders.* Washington, DC: U.S. Author.

Carlen, P. (1983). *Women's imprisonment. A study in social control.* London: Routledge and Kegan Paul.

Chesney-Lind, M., & Pollock, J. (1995). Women's prisons: Equality with a vengeance. In A. Merlo & J. Pollock (Eds.), *Women, law, and social control* (pp. 155–177). Boston, MA: Allyn and Bacon.

Chesney-Lind, M. & Sheldon, R. G. (1992). *Girls, delinquency and juvenile justice.* Pacific Grove, CA: Brooks/Cole.

Collier, R. (1998). *Masculinities, crime and criminology.* Thousand Oaks, CA: Sage.

Coltrane, S. (1994). Theorizing masculinities in contemporary social science. In H. Brod & M. Kaufman (Eds.), *Theorizing masculinities* (pp. 39–60). Newbury Park, CA: Sage.

Connell, R. W. (1985). Theorizing gender. *Sociology, 19*, 260–272.

Connell, R. W. (1987). *Gender and power: Society, the person, and sexual politics.* Stanford, CA: Stanford University Press.

Connell, R. W. (1997). Disruptions: Improper masculinities in schooling. In M. Baca Zinn, P. Hondagneu-Sotelo, & M. A. Messner (Eds.), *Through the prism of difference: Readings on sex and gender* (pp. 418–430). Boston, MA: Allyn and Bacon.

Daly, K. (1992). Women's pathways to felony court. *Review of Law and Women's Studies, 2*, 11–52.

Daly, K., & Chesney-Lind, M. (1988). Feminism and criminology. *Justice Quarterly, 5*, 497–538.

Dobash, R. P., Dobash, R. E., & Gutteridge, S. (1986). *The imprisonment of women.* New York: Basil Blackwell,

Feinman, C. (1983). An historical overview of the treatment of incarcerated women: Myths and realities of rehabilitation. *Prison Journal, 63*, 12–26.

Freedman, E. (1981). *Their sisters keepers: Women's prison reform in America, 1830–1930.* Ann Arbor, MI: University of Michigan Press.

Hill-Collins, P. (1986). Learning from the outsider within: The sociological significance of black feminist thought. *Social Problems, 33*, 514–532.

Kanter, R. M. (1977). *Men and women of the corporation.* New York: Basic Books.

Kimmel, M. S. (1994). Masculinity as homophobia: Fear, shame, and silence in the construction of gender identity. In H. Brod & M. Kaufman (Eds.), *Theorizing masculinities* (pp. 119–141). Newbury Park, CA: Sage.

Koons, B. A., Burrow, J. D., Morash, M., & Bynum, T. (1997). Expert and offender perceptions of program elements linked to successful outcomes for incarcerated women. *Crime & Delinquency, 43*, 512–532.

Lorber, J. (1994). Night to his day: The social construction of gender. In J. Lorber (Ed.), *Paradoxes of gender* (pp. 13–36). Yale University Press.

Lorber, J. (1998). *Gender inequality: Feminist theories and politics.* Los Angeles: Roxbury.

Maher, L. (1992). Punishment and welfare: Crack cocaine and the regulation of mothering. *Women & Criminal Justice, 3*, 35–70.

Maher, L., & Daly, K. (1996). Women in the street level drug economy: Continuity or change? *Criminology, 34*, 465–498.

Martin, S. E., & Jurik, N. C. (1996). *Doing justice, doing gender.* Thousand Oaks, CA: Sage.

Messerschmidt, J. (1993). The state and gendered politics. In J. Messerschmidt (Ed.), *Masculinities and crime* (pp. 155–164). Lanham, MD: Rowman & Littlefield.

Morash, M., Bynum, T., & Koons, B. (1995). *Findings from the national study of innovative and promising programs for women offenders.* East Lansing, MI: Michigan State University Press.

Ogilvie, D. M., Stone, P. J., & Kelly, E. F. (1982). Computer-aided content analysis. In R. B. Smith & P. K. Manning (Eds.), *A handbook of social science methods* (Vol. 2) (pp. 219–246). Cambridge, MA: Ballinger.

Pollock, J. M. (1984). Women will be women: Correctional officers' perceptions of the emotionality of women inmates. *The Prison Journal, 64*, 84–91.

Pollock-Byrne, J. M. (1990). *Women, prison, and crime.* Pacific Grove, CA: Brooks/Cole Publishing.

Pollock, J. M. (1999). *Criminal women.* Cincinnati, OH: Anderson.

Rafter, N. (1985). *Partial justice: State prisons and their inmates, 1800–1935.* Boston: Northeastern University Press.

Rich, A. (1993). Compulsory heterosexuality and lesbian existence. In H. Abelove, M. A. Barale, & D. Halperin (Eds.), *The lesbian and gay studies reader* (pp. 227–254). London: Routledge.

Richie, B. E. (1996). *Compelled to crime.* New York: Routledge.

Smart, C. (1976). *Women, crime, and criminology: A feminist critique.* London: Routledge and Kegan Paul.

Snell, T. L. (1994). *Women in prison* (Bureau of Justice Statistics Special Report). Washington, DC: U.S. Department of Justice.

Thorne, B. (1992). *Gender play: Girls and boys in school.* New Brunswick, NJ: Rutgers University Press.

West, C. & Fenstermaker, S. (1995). Doing difference. *Gender & Society, 9*, 8–37.

West, C. & Zimmerman, D. (1987). Doing gender. *Gender & Society,* l, 125–151.

14

Women in Prison
Approaches in the Treatment of Our Most Invisible Population

Stephanie S. Covington

Overview

Some of the most neglected, misunderstood and unseen women in our society are those in our jails, prisons and community correctional facilities. While women's rate of incarceration has increased dramatically, tripling in the last decade, prisons have not kept pace with the growth of the number of women in prison; nor has the criminal justice system been redesigned to meet women's needs, which are often quite different from the needs of men.

There are many reasons for the growing numbers of women in the criminal justice system, but the primary one is the increase in drug-related convictions and the advent of mandatory sentences for these offenses. According to the Federal Bureau of Prisons, over 60% of the women in their custody are serving sentences for drug offenses. For many states the rate is even higher for alcohol and drug-related crimes.

In spite of this, the issues of addicted women are, for the most part, invisible in the criminal justice system. Historically, treatment, research and recovery have been based on the male experience, often neglecting women's needs. While this neglect has a serious impact on women and treatment programs in the free world, the problem is magnified for women in the criminal justice population.

"Women in Prison: Approaches in the Treatment of Our Most Invisible Population," by Stephanie Covington from *Breaking the Rules: Women in Prison and Feminist Therapy*, pp. 141–155. © 1998. Permission granted by The Haworth Press, Inc.

Statistics indicate that for women there is a high correlation between drug abuse and incarceration and parole/probation violations, and yet our society provides no comprehensive continuum of care for these women. This article will discuss a relational model of treatment that incorporates the multiple issues involved in women's recovery. Three theoretical perspectives—addiction, trauma, and women's psychological development—are interwoven to provide the foundation for a model based on the concept of a woman's journey to recovery. This model can be adapted for both the prison population and community-based programs.

In summation, the objectives of this article are:

1. To increase awareness of women's lives in the criminal justice system.
2. To discuss a comprehensive and integrated treatment model (theory of addiction, theory of trauma, theory of women's psychological development).
3. To examine the four areas that women report as being both most challenging, and their major triggers to relapse: self, relationships, sexuality, and spirituality.
4. To discuss twelve-step programs for women.

Rising Numbers of Women in the Criminal Justice System

Since 1980, the number of women in United States prisons has tripled. During this time, the rate of incarceration for women has surpassed the male rate during every year but one; and in 1996, the number of women imprisoned nationally was 69,028 (LeBlanc, 1996).

The war on drugs has inadvertently become a war on women, clearly contributing to the explosive increase in the number of women who are incarcerated. The 1986 mandatory drug sentencing laws, with their "get tough on crime" philosophy specifying that anyone caught with possession of a drug should automatically be sentenced, were designed to rid society of drug dealers and major players in the illegal drug trade. Unfortunately, this law backfired in the case of women. The assumption that this law was only sending dangerous males to prison was a false one. Between 1986 and 1991, the number of women in state prisons for drug offenses increased by 433%, compared to a 283% increase for men (LeBlanc, 1996). Currently, 35.9% of women serving time for drug offenses were charged solely with "possession." "Instead of a policy of last resort, imprisonment has become the first-order response for a wide range of non-violent and petty offenses and women have been disproportionately swept up in this trend" (Bloom, Chesney-Lind, & Owen, 1994, p. 2).

To keep up with the high costs of incarceration—it takes $50,000 per cell to build a new prison and $20,000 per person per year to house offenders—many states have cut vitally needed social service, educational, and drug/alcohol programs (Raspberry, 1991). Since there is a high rate of recidivism among women who are convicted for possession or use of drugs, curtailing drug and alcohol recovery programs has proven to be an expensive and illogical move.

One of the questions we must ask ourselves when faced with the issues surrounding the growing number of women in the criminal justice system is whether or not there is always a need for incarceration. In a private conversation, a warden at one of the largest women's prisons in the U.S. stated that 75% of the women in her custodial care would be better treated in the community (personal communication, May 1995). Clearly, this would be a more humane and economical solution to the overcrowding of our prisons by women who have committed nonviolent, petty offenses.

Profile of Women in the Criminal Justice System

Female prison populations differ from their male counterparts in several significant ways. First of all, they are less likely to have committed a violent offense and more likely to have been convicted of a crime involving alcohol, other drugs, or property. It is important to point out that many property crimes are economically driven, often motivated by the abuse/addiction of alcohol and other drugs and/or poverty (Chesney-Lind & Bloom, 1997; Watterson, 1996). A 1994 study done in California showed that 71.9% of women had been convicted on a drug or property charge versus 49.7% of men. Men also commit nearly twice the violent crimes that women do (Bloom, Chesney-Lind, & Owen, 1994). These statistics are consistent with national trends (LeBlanc, 1996). Women are significantly less violent than their male counterparts, and show more responsiveness to prison programs, although they have less opportunity to participate in them than male prisoners do. While men often deal with their anxiety by working their bodies constantly, women tend to fear the central yard, working out their anxieties with too much sleep, food, and prescription pills (LeBlanc, 1996).

Most female prisoners are poor, undereducated, unskilled, single mothers, and a disproportionate number of them are women of color. In a study of California prisons, over half of the women were African American (35%) and Hispanic (16.6%). One-third were Caucasian and the remaining 13% were made up of other racial groups. Of those who had been employed before incarceration, many were on the lower rungs of the economic ladder, with only 37% working at a legitimate job. Twenty-two percent were on some kind of public support, 16% made money from drug dealing and 15% were involved in prostitution, shoplifting or other illegal activities (Bloom, Chesney-Lind, & Owen, 1994). One of the things that these statistics clearly show is that there are issues of race and class involved in the criminal justice system. For example, there has been a law in the state of Minnesota (recently held unconstitutional) that says first-time users of crack cocaine will receive mandatory four-year sentences, but first-time users of cocaine in its powdered form will receive only probation. Since 92% of those arrested on charges for possession of crack in 1988 were African Americans and 85% of those arrested for possession of powdered cocaine were Caucasian, the law is clearly racist (Raspberry, 1991). When racial and economic factors drive the issue of who will be imprisoned, where is the "justice" in the criminal justice system (Belknap, 1996)?

One major health concern in prisons is AIDS. In a study done with 400 female volunteers in a Massachusetts prison, 35% of the women tested were HIV positive, compared with 13% of the men. In one California prison, women who tested positive were placed in a segregated AIDS unit, whether they showed signs of the disease or not (Salholz & Wright, 1990).

Two-thirds of incarcerated women have children under the age of 18 (Smith, 1991). Many feel enormous guilt about being absent from their children's lives and worry about whether they will still have custody of their children when they get out (Bloom & Steinhart, 1993). These and other concerns, including unresolved issues of physical and sexual abuse, lead female inmates to make requests for psychological counseling that far exceed those made by men. Penal experts agree that women would benefit from additional services (Salholz & Wright, 1990).

Many incarcerated women either abuse or are addicted to alcohol and/or other drugs. In a study done in the Las Colinas Detention Facility in California, 37% of the women said that alcohol was their drug of choice, 21% said heroin, 24% crystal meth, and 18% cocaine (Covington, 1991c). Unfortunately, drugs are readily available in prisons, usually brought in and sold by prison guards (Salholz & Wright, 1990).

Along with their history of alcohol/drug use, many women in prison also have a history of physical and sexual abuse. In California prisons, nearly 80% have experienced some form of abuse. Twenty-nine percent report being physically abused as children, and 60% as adults, usually by their partners. Thirty-one percent experienced sexual abuse as a child and 23% as adults; and 40% reported emotional abuse as a child and 48% as an adult (Bloom, Chesney-Lind, & Owen, 1994). Women are also abused *within* the prison system. An ongoing investigation by the Human Rights Watch Women's Rights Project documented custodial misconduct in many forms including verbal degradation, rape, sexual assault, unwarranted visual supervision, denying goods and privileges, and use or threat of force. "Male correctional officers and staff contribute to a custodial environment in state prisons for women which is often highly sexualized and excessively hostile" (Human Rights Watch Women's Rights Project, 1996, p. 2).

What Kind of Addiction Treatment Are Women Receiving in Prisons?

With nearly 60% of women in prison for a drug-related crime, and with the number of addiction and abuse issues that women bring with them, it would not be unreasonable to expect prisons to invest some resources in alcohol/drug recovery programs, support groups, and psychological counseling. Unfortunately, although the current programs we have in men's prisons are few and inadequate, there are even fewer for women (Salholz & Wright, 1990). Health care, especially prenatal care, education, job training and treatment for alcohol/other drug abuse are all missing from the women's prison system. Only 3% of California prisoners have any alcohol and/or drug treatment programs available to them, even if such voluntary programs as Alcoholics and Narcotics Anonymous are included (Bloom, Chesney-Lind, & Owen, 1994). In light of these facts, the term "correctional institutions" becomes a sad euphemism in a system that provides no programs to help redress the most basic needs and concerns that are shared by many women.

The lack of proper substance abuse treatment programs was recently confirmed by the National Criminal Justice Association. In a nationwide survey done under the U.S. Department of Justice, they found that "Virtually every survey respondent reported that there is too little funding for treatment services, that there are not enough drug treatment facilities or appropriate placements for drug dependent clients, and there is a lack of qualified personnel to staff treatment programs" (Zawistowski, 1991, p. 9).

There is also a wide gap between what our judicial system actually believes about the availability of health care and alcohol/drug recovery programs in prison, and the existence of such programs. In recent years, shrinking tax dollars for community based programs have led judges to believe that the best chance that pregnant, addicted women have for treatment is through sentencing and incarceration. Unfortunately, this belief is a myth, because the programs simply do not exist, often with tragic consequences for the high number of these women who enter the penal system. Although detoxification of pregnant, substance-dependent women can be accomplished safely, successfully and at low cost, many prisons force these women to go "cold turkey." Many times this results in the death of the fetus or serious damage to it. Nor do pregnant, addicted women in many prisons receive even the most basic of gynecological or maternity care. In addition, illegal drugs are often more readily available in prisons than they are on the street (Barry, 1991).

If we are to develop effective programs for women in prison and community corrections, we need to develop a theoretical approach to addiction treatment that is gender sensitive, addressing itself to the realities of women's lives.

Developing an Integrated Model of Addiction

To develop an integrated model for the treatment of addiction, it is important first to develop a sound theoretical framework, asking ourselves to what theory of addiction we are subscribing. The next step is to utilize a theory of women's psychological development, which refers to what is known about how women learn, grow and heal. Lastly, it is important to incorporate a theory of trauma since the majority of women who are chemically dependent, especially those in the criminal justice system, have experienced emotional, physical and sexual abuse in their childhood and/or adulthood. The definition of victimization and trauma also needs to be expanded to include racial prejudice, witnessing violence, and the stigma, stress, and abusiveness of incarceration.

Theory of Addiction

Traditionally, addiction treatment has been based on a medical model, which views addiction as a disease. The most commonly used analogy is that addiction is like diabetes, a physical disease that carries no moral or social stigma. This analogy is often useful because neither diabetes nor addiction can be managed by will power. They both require adherence to a lifestyle regimen for physical and emotional stability.

However, this analogy sees the disease/disorder rooted solely in the individual. As we move into the twenty-first century, health professionals in many disciplines are revising their concept of disease in general. Based on a holistic health model, we are now acknowledging not only the physical aspects of disease, but also the emotional, psychological, and spiritual aspects.

I believe we can best understand addiction as a disease/disorder if we understand it holistically and include cancer as an analogy. The diabetes model is useful, but too individualistic and simplistic to adequately explain addiction.

Like cancer, addiction has a physical component as well as emotional, psychological, and spiritual dimensions. I would argue that two other components of disease must also be added to a fully holistic model: the environmental and the sociopolitical dimensions. It's interesting that few people question that cancer is a disease even though some experts estimate that 80% of doctors link cancer to lifestyle choices (diet and exercise) and the environment (pesticides, emissions, nuclear waste, etc.) (Siegel, 1996). There are also sociopolitical aspects of cancer, especially when we realize the huge profits carcinogenic products make for powerful business interests. The same is true of addictive substances, both legal and illegal. For example, medical doctors prescribe 80% of the amphetamines, 60% of the psychoactive drugs and 71% of the antidepressants to women (Galbraith, 1991). Companies that produce and sell alcohol are indirectly responsible for over 23,000 deaths and three quarter of a million injuries each year—and these are only the figures reported to insurance companies (Zawistowski, 1991). Even though some women may have a strong genetic predisposition to addiction, an important treatment issue is acknowledging that many of them have grown up in an environment where drug dealing and addiction are a way of life.

Theory of Women's Development

The next important element for developing a treatment model is having a theory of women's psychological development. Traditional developmental psychology is based on a separation/individuation model. The Relational Model, developed by the Stone Center in Wellesley, Massachusetts, posits that the primary motivation for women throughout life is not separation, but establishing a strong sense of connection. When a woman is disconnected from others or involved in abusive relationships, she experiences disempowerment, confusion, and diminished zest, vitality and self-worth—fertile ground for addiction. Healthy, growth-fostering relationships create increased zest and vitality, empowerment, self-knowledge, self-worth and a desire for more connection. In a growth-fostering relationship, a woman develops a sense of mutuality that is "creative, energy-releasing and empowering for all participants," and fundamental to her psychological well-being (Covington & Surrey, 1997).

If we are trying to create treatment for women to help them to change, grow and heal from addictions, it is critical that we place them in programs and environments where relationship and mutuality are core elements. The system needs to provide a setting where women can experience healthy relationships with their counselors and each other. Unfortunately, the criminal justice system is designed to discourage women from coming together, trusting, speaking about personal issues or forming bonds of relationship. Women who leave prison are often discouraged from associating with other women who have been incarcerated.

If women are to be successfully reintegrated back into the community after serving their sentences, there must be a *continuum of care* that can connect them in a community after they've been released. Ideally, these community programs should have a relational basis.

Theory of Trauma

The last element we need in order to create a model for treatment is a theory of trauma. A vast majority of chemically dependent women have been physically, sexually and emotionally abused for much of their lives, and these numbers are even greater within the criminal justice population. Traditional addiction treatment often does not deal with abuse issues in early recovery, even though they are a primary trigger for relapse among women (Covington & Surrey, 1997). Therefore, we need a theory of trauma that is appropriate for women in early recovery.

Psychiatrist Judith Herman (1992) writes that there are three stages in the process of healing from trauma: safety, remembrance and mourning, and reconnection. "Survivors feel unsafe in their bodies. Their emotions and their thinking feel out of control. They also feel unsafe in relation to other people" (Herman, 1992, p. 160). Stage One (safety) addresses the woman's safety concerns in all of these domains. In the second stage of recovery (remembrance and mourning) the survivor tells the story of the trauma and mourns the old self that the trauma destroyed. In Stage Three (reconnection) the survivor faces the task of creating a future; now she develops a new self. As we have seen above, the difficulty is that many women are *not* safe in our criminal justice system where they are vulnerable to abuse and harassment from correctional staff.

Stage One recovery from trauma, safety, is the appropriate level of intervention for women in early recovery from addiction. If we want women to heal from addiction, we must set up a safe environment in which the healing process can begin to take place. Dr. Herman uses twelve-step groups as an example of the type of group appropriate for Stage One (safety) recovery because of their focus on present-tense issues of self-care, in a supportive, homogeneous environment.

Addiction Recovery for Women

The Center for Substance Abuse Treatment (1994, p. 178) has developed the following list of issues that should be reflected in a comprehensive treatment model for women:

- The etiology of addiction, especially gender-specific issues related to addiction (including social, physiological, and psychological consequences of addiction and factors related to onset of addiction)
- Low self-esteem
- Race, ethnicity and cultural issues
- Gender discrimination and harassment
- Disability-related issues, where relevant
- Relationships with family and significant others
- Attachments to unhealthy interpersonal relationships
- Interpersonal violence, including incest, rape, battering, and other abuse
- Eating disorders
- Sexuality, including sexual functioning and sexual orientation
- Parenting
- Grief related to the loss of alcohol or other drugs, children, family members, or partners
- Work
- Appearance and overall health and hygiene
- Isolation related to a lack of support systems (which may or may not include family members and/or partners) and other resources
- Life plan development
- Child care and child custody

When I interviewed women around the country who had recovered in twelve-step programs and asked them to describe both the things that had changed the most for them in their journey from using to recovery and the issues that contributed to relapse, they listed the self, relationships, sexuality and spirituality. It is interesting to note that these four issues incorporate the issues listed above. If we are going to create recovery programs for women in correctional settings, these four issues need to be understood and addressed. (For additional information, see *A Woman's Way Through the Twelve Steps*, Covington, 1994.)

The Self. The generic definition of addiction I use is "the chronic neglect of self in favor of something or someone else." Addiction can be conceptualized as a self-disorder. One of the first questions women in recovery need to begin to address is "Who am I?" Women in our culture are taught to identify themselves according to role: mother, professional, wife, daughter. One of the first tasks for women in recovery is to find words to describe who they are from a deep, interior place. In addiction, one loses the sense of oneself and, with it, the ability to have a real connection with others. Recovery is about expansion and growth of the self, both the inner and the outer self.

Many women enter the prison system with a poor self-image and a history of trauma and abuse. As we have seen, prisons actively discourage relationship. Creating the kinds of programs that help incarcerated women to develop a strong sense of self, an identification that goes beyond who they are in the criminal justice system, is vital to their recovery.

Relationship. Some women use addictive substances to maintain relationships with using partners, some use them to fill up the void of what is missing in relationship, and some use alcohol/other drugs to deal with the pain of being abused (Covington & Surrey, 1997). One of the tasks of any recovery program is to teach women self-soothing techniques in order to deal with the myriad of feelings that surface when abstinent.

Women in the prison system often have unhealthy, illusory or unequal relationships with spouses, partners, friends, and family members. For that reason, it is important for recovery programs to model healthy relationships, among both staff and participants, providing a safe place and a container for healing (Covington & Beckett, 1988). Our greatest challenge is to overcome the alienation that is fostered within prison walls, and replace it with a greater sense of relationship in community.

Sexuality. Sexuality is one of the most neglected areas in the treatment of addiction, and one of the major causes for relapse. Healthy sexuality is integral to one's sense of self-worth. It represents the integration of the biological, emotional, social, and spiritual aspects of who one is and how one relates to others (Covington, 1991a; Covington, in press; Kaplan, 1981; Schnarch, 1991). Addiction is often defined as a physical, emotional, social, and spiritual disease. Since healthy sexuality is defined as the integration of all these aspects of the self, we can see that addiction can have an impact on every area of sexuality. Therefore, addressing and healing all aspects of the sexual self is critical to a woman's recovery process (Covington, 1991a; Covington, in press).

Creating healthy sexuality is a developmental process that occurs over time. This normal developmental process is often interrupted by addiction. In addition, many women entering the early stages of recovery report the following sexual concerns: sexual dysfunction, shame and guilt, sexual identity, prostitution, sexual abuse, and the fear of sex clean and sober. These issues need to be addressed if we expect women to maintain their recovery (Covington, 1991a; Covington, 1993).

Few women in prisons have a positive view of sex. Some have been prostitutes, many have been abused, and most connect sex with shame and guilt. Even those who have been the most sexually active have little accurate information about sex. Developing programs that can work with this part of a woman's recovery can help to create a positive sense of self and a healthier image of relationship.

Spirituality. The root of the word psychology is "psyche," which means "the knowledge and the understanding of the soul." Although we live in a secular culture where traditional psychology does not focus on the spiritual, helping women to reconnect to their own definition of the spiritual is critical to their recovery process. Religion and spirituality are not the same—they may or may not be connected. Religion is about form, dogma and structure, and is institutionally based. Spirituality is about transformation, connection, wholeness, meaning, and depth.

Women connect with their spirituality in many different ways. Some have rejected the religion of their childhood and must find a new path for themselves. Some return to the religion of their youth. In recovery groups I have facilitated, I often find it useful to give women art history books to look at how, for thousands of years before the Patriarchy, the female was revered. Since the feminine has been so denigrated in our culture, it is often helpful to show women that they are a part of a long history of birthers, growers and caregivers, helping them to reconnect with the energy of the great goddess.

The design of the criminal justice system is antithetical to spiritual values, and it is essential that any recovery program designed for women in this system find a way to help each woman find her own definition of a "higher power."

Twelve Step Programs

In recent years, twelve-step programs have been critiqued in various ways and, as some feminists have pointed out, the language used is simplistic, sexist, and reductionist (Bepko, 1991; Berenson, 1991; Kasl, 1992;

Rapping, 1996). Feminists are particularly concerned about the twelve steps' emphasis upon powerlessness as liberating. In contrasting the recovery movement with the women's movement, Marianne Walters (1990) points out that "one movement encourages individuals to surrender to a spiritual higher power, where the other encourages people to join together to challenge and restructure power arrangements in the larger society" (p. 55). What is often missed in feminist analysis is the masculine "power over" is what is being relinquished in order to experience the feminine "power with," "power to be able," i.e., a sense of empowerment (Miller, 1982). "The process of recovery from addiction is a process of recovering a different, more feminine, sense of power and will" (Berenson, 1991, p. 74). There is also a confusion between surrender and submission. "When we submit, we give in to a force that's trying to control us. When we surrender, we let go of our need to control" (Covington, 1994, p. 48). Recovery encourages surrender and giving up the illusion of control. Feminist writer Marilyn French (1985) describes ". . . life is the highest value for 'feminine' people; whereas control is the highest value for 'masculine' people" (p. 93).

If we look at the underpinnings of Alcoholics Anonymous we can see that it was actually very radical for the 1930s, the time it was founded, and that this continues to be true even today. Twelve-step programs are free, a radical concept in a capitalistic society; they are non-hierarchical, a radical idea in a patriarchal society; and they are spiritual, a radical stance in a non-spiritual society. As previously stated, women grow and develop in relationship, and twelve-step programs can provide a growth-fostering relational context and offer their members social support through the creation of a caring community (Covington, 1991b; Covington & Surrey, 1997). These programs can also create a safe environment, which is an essential element for recovery from trauma (Herman, 1992). Although some critics have focused on the sexist language in which the twelve steps are couched, I have found that women are able to interpret the steps in ways that are distinctly personal, meaningful and useful to themselves (Covington, 1994).

Since we know that women grow and develop in relationship and connection, and that these programs are free and available in our communities, it would make sense to enable women to have access to them both while they are incarcerated and while they are making the transition back into community. The twelve-step programs also need to be incorporated into community correctional settings. These programs offer us an already existing "continuity of care" that we cannot afford to ignore.

Conclusion

With women being incarcerated for drug-related offenses at an alarming rate, it is imperative that treatment services be designed to reflect the realities of their lives. This means comprehensive, integrated programs that understand and address the intersection of race, class, gender, and addiction. Even though most professionals believe addiction is a disease/ disorder, societally we still respond to it chiefly as a crime. We can also no longer think only of individual addicts but must acknowledge that society fosters addiction.

On one level our task is to provide better services for the invisible women caught in our criminal justice system. These are women whose lives represent all women's issues—*magnified*. On a deeper level, we must question whether therapeutic, healing care can be provided in the ultimate system of oppression and domination.

Our criminal justice system is in desperate need of repair and revision. What changes would make a difference? The Human Kindness Foundation (1995) has suggested "Seven Ways to Fix the Criminal Justice System":

- Learn to recognize the influence of socially sanctioned hatred.
- Make drugs a public health problem instead of a criminal justice problem.
- Separate violent and nonviolent offenders right from the start.
- Regain compassion and respect for those who wrong us.
- Allow for transformation, not merely rehabilitation.
- Join and support the restorative justice movement.
- Take the issue of crime and punishment personally.

References

Barry, E. (1991, Winter). Pregnant, addicted and sentenced. *Criminal Justice*, 23–27.

Belknap, Joanne. (1996). *The invisible woman: Gender, crime and justice.* Belmont, CA: Wadsworth.

Bepko, Claudia (Ed.). (1991). *Feminism and addiction.* New York: The Haworth Press, Inc.

Berenson, D. (1991). Powerlessness—liberation or enslaving? Responding to the feminist critique of the twelve steps. In C. Bepko (Ed.), *Feminism and addiction* (pp. 67–80). New York: The Haworth Press, Inc.

Bloom, B., Chesney-Lind, M., & Owen, B. (1994). *Women in California prisons: Hidden victims of the war on drugs.* San Francisco: Center on Juvenile and Criminal Justice.

Bloom, B., & Steinhart, D. (1993). *Why punish the children? A reappraisal of incarcerated mothers in America.* San Francisco: National Council on Crime and Delinquency.

Center for Substance Abuse Treatment. (1994). *Practical approaches in the treatment of women who abuse alcohol and other drugs.* Rockville, MD: Department of Health and Human Services, Public Health Service.

Chesney-Lind, M., & Bloom, B. (1997). Feminist criminology: Thinking about women and crime. In B. MacLean & D. Milovanovic (Eds.), *Thinking critically about crime* (pp. 54–65). Vancouver: Collective Press.

Covington, S. (in press). Women, addiction, and sexuality. In L. Straussner & E. Zelvin (Eds.), *Gender issues in addiction: Men and women in treatment.* Dunmore, PA: Jason Aronson.

Covington, S. (1991a). *Awakening your sexuality: A guide for recovering women and their partners.* San Francisco: Harper San Francisco.

Covington, S. (1991b). Sororities of helping and healing: Women and mutual help groups. In P. Roth (Ed.), *Alcohol and drugs are women's issues* (pp. 85–92). Metuchen, NJ: The Scarecrow Press, Inc.

Covington, S. (1991c). Unpublished research. From Las Colinas Detention Facility for Women in San Diego County, California.

Covington, S. (1993). Alcohol, addiction and sexual dysfunction. In E. Freeman (Ed.), *Substance abuse treatment* (pp. 189–216). Thousand Oaks, CA: Sage Publications.

Covington, S. (1994). *A woman's way through the twelve steps.* Center City, MN: Hazelden Educational Materials.

Covington, S., & Beckett, L. (1988). *Leaving the enchanted forest: The path from relationship to intimacy.* San Francisco: Harper San Francisco.

Covington, S., & Surrey, J. (1997). The relational model of women's psychological development: Implications for substance abuse. In S. Wilsnak & R. Wilsnak (Eds.), *Gender and alcohol: Individual and social perspectives* (pp. 335–351). Piscataway, NJ: Rutgers University.

French, M. (1985). *Beyond power: On women, men, and morals.* New York: Ballantine Books.

Galbraith, S. (1991). Women and legal drugs. In P. Roth (Ed.), *Alcohol and drugs are women's issues* (pp. 150–154). New York: The Scarecrow Press, Inc.

Herman, J. (1992). *Trauma and recovery.* New York: Basic Books.

Human Kindness Foundation. (1995). *Can we do better than our present prison system?* Durham, NC: Human Kindness Foundation.

Human Rights Watch Women's Rights Project. (1996). *All too familiar: Sexual abuse of women in U.S. state prisons.* New York: Human Rights Watch.

Kaplan, H. S. (1981). *The new sex therapy.* New York: Brunner/Mazel.

Kasl, C. (1992). *Many roads, one journey.* New York: Harper Collins.

LeBlanc, A. N. (1996, June). A woman behind bars is not a dangerous man. *The New York Times Magazine*, 35–40.

Miller, J. B. (1982). *Women and power.* Work in Progress, No. 82-01. Wellesley, MA: Stone Center Working Paper Series.

Northrup, C. (1994). *Women's bodies, women's wisdom.* New York: Bantam Books.

Rapping, E. (1996). *The culture of recovery.* Boston: Beacon Press.

Raspberry, W. (1991, June 2). Why are so many people in prison? *Washington Post*, p. 57.

Salholz, E., & Wright, L. (1990, June). Women in jail: Unequal justice. *Newsweek*, 37–38, 51.

Schnarch, D. (1991). *Constructing the sexual crucible.* New York: Norton.

Siegel, B. (1996). Personal communication.

Smith, S. (1991, March). Women in prison. *Bureau of Justice Statistics Special Report.*

Walters, M. (1990, July–August). The co-dependent Cinderella who loves too much . . . fights back. *The Family Therapy Networker*, 53–57.

Watterson, K. (1996). *Women in prison: Inside the concrete womb* (Rev. ed.). Boston: Northeastern University Press.

Zawistowski, T. A. (1991, March/April). Criminal addiction/illegal disease. *The Counselor*, 8–11.

15

A Feminist Examination of Boot Camp Prison Programs for Women

Susan T. Marcus-Mendoza
Jody Klein-Saffran
Faith Lutze

Strict moral ideology has dictated the laws that govern women in the United States and the punishments that they receive. Consequently, correctional programming for women has reflected a punishment orientation, aimed at punishing the "fallen woman," and has not considered the needs and problems of women inmates. A recent example of such programming is shock incarceration (boot camps), which has been instituted in many states as a low-cost, short-term alternative to traditional prison programming. The purpose of boot camps is to teach discipline and responsibility, to "break down and build up" inmates so that they will no longer commit crimes. The use of a program to instill discipline and responsibility assumes that female offenders are lacking in these areas and that this is the reason for their criminal behavior. The current research on female offenders does not substantiate this assumption. In addition, boot camp practices are not consistent with feminist conceptualizations of effective clinical practice with women. This article will examine the theoretical basis and clinical implications of boot camps for women. The social context of female criminality and the resulting implications for prison programming

"A Feminist Examination of Boot Camp Prison Programs for Women," by Susan Marcus-Mendoza, Jody Klein-Saffran, and Faith Lutze, from *Breaking the Rules: Women in Prison and Feminist Therapy*, pp. 173–185, 1998. Permission granted by The Haworth Press, Inc.

for women will be discussed, and boot camp policies will be examined in the context of feminist therapy practices.

The Social Context of Female Criminality

The dominant moral codes and gender stereotypes of American society have dictated the laws used to incarcerate women and the correctional programming available to female inmates. Freedman (1981) examined the political climate of the early 1880s and suggested that the rise in female incarceration during that era was related to the increase in urbanization and the resulting moral reforms. Women were incarcerated for such "moral" crimes as disorderly conduct, vagrancy, drunkenness, and prostitution. Many women who were left without means of supporting themselves and their families during the wars of the 1800s were incarcerated for prostitution and stealing. Society considered them "fallen women," abnormal and unworthy of attention due to their deviance from the strict moral standards of the time. In prison, women were subjected to miserable living conditions and were largely ignored. What little programming was offered was just an adaptation of male-oriented programs. Most of society continued to shun these women upon release from prison.

Even the theories of criminality focused on men, ignoring criminal women as being unworthy of notice (Belknap, 1996). The notable exception was the work of Lombroso and Ferrero (1900), who developed a theory of criminology based on Social Darwinism. Lombroso theorized that women, nonwhites, and the poorer classes were less evolved than white, upper-class men. Therefore, they were more likely to commit crimes. Further, he stated that for a woman to commit crime and stray from the "normal" path of "maternity, piety, and weakness, . . . her wickedness must have been enormous . . ." (Lombroso & Ferrero, 1900, p. 150). This theory is reflective of the madonna/whore duality (Feinman, 1986) by which women of that era were judged; the good woman (madonna) is loyal and submissive and knows her place, and the bad woman (whore) steps out of prescribed roles and must be punished for being evil.

At the end of the nineteenth century, social reformers, who rejected the idea that women who committed crimes were moral deviants, began to explore such correlates of female criminality as mental ability, poverty, and lack of education (Freedman, 1981). These reformers espoused the idea of such preventative services as education and training to keep economically marginalized women from committing crimes. Prison staff began "to retrain women through sympathetic female staff, prayer, education, and domesticity" (Freedman, 1981, p. 90). However, women's prisons still valued discipline. Consequently, ". . . the tension between domesticity and discipline pervaded the internal life of the women's prison" (Freedman, 1981, p. 90).

Ultimately, reformers, who brought about the inclusion of programming for women, only partially met their goals of making women self-supporting.

Women inmates were taught to be submissive and feminine, and received training in such domestic skills as cooking and ironing. However, the training they received in domestic skills did not prepare them to be financially self-supporting. They found few jobs that required these skills upon release from prison. Therefore, they often found themselves back in prison (Freedman, 1981).

Female Inmates in the 1990s

By focusing on moral reform and using male correctional programming for women inmates, prison programming often fails to address the real problems and needs of women. Recent research on female inmates has helped to dispel the myth of the fallen woman, and increased our understanding of women in prison. Studies suggest that female inmates are typically young women (mid-twenties to mid-thirties) who have experienced many social, environmental, and personal problems (American Correctional Association, 1990; Belknap, 1996; Eaton, 1993; Marcus-Mendoza & Briody, 1996; Pollock-Byrne, 1990; Rafter, 1990; Sommers, 1995).

Although the incidence of violence against women is high in the United States, rates of sexual and physical abuse are even higher for female inmates. In a study of the incidence of sexual abuse of women in the general population, Russell (1984) found that 25% had been raped and one-third had been sexually abused as children. In her comprehensive review of the literature, Walker (1994) reported that approximately one out of every four adult women had been battered by a partner. Overall, she found that about 50% of women had experienced some form of physical, sexual, or psychological abuse. Research on psychiatric patients revealed that 50% to 80% of hospitalized male and female patients had experienced some form of physical, sexual, or psychological abuse, and 68% of female outpatients had experienced physical or sexual abuse (Walker, 1994). However, research on female inmates indicates that 80%–88% have experienced at least one type of physical, sexual, or emotional abuse (Gilfus, 1988; Marcus-Mendoza, Sargent, & Chong Ho, 1994; Owen & Bloom, 1995). Although statistics on abuse often vary due to differences in definitions of abuse and the types of measurements used, this demonstrates a high, consistent rate of abuse. The high percentage of abuse perpetrated against women in the United States is alarming. However, the fact that there is a higher incidence of abuse among psychiatric populations and inmates than among the general population of women clearly demonstrates the debilitating effects of violence against women.

Female inmates frequently report substance abuse, which is common among survivors of trauma (Herman, 1992). According to the Bureau of Justice Statistics (BJS), 41% of female inmates reported daily drug use in the month before their arrest (Bureau of Justice Statistics, 1991). Overall, according to BJS, the majority of female inmates have used drugs and alcohol, and close to half the inmates report having a drug or alcohol problem. In contrast, in a survey of women in the United States in 1995, only 8.7% reported using drugs within the past year, and 4.5% reported using drugs within the past month (U.S. Department of Health and Human Services, 1996).

Female inmates often face economic problems as well as personal and interpersonal problems. Many female inmates have children and are the sole providers for their families. As many as 70%–80% of female inmates have children, the majority of whom are under the age of 18 (American Correctional Association, 1990; Bureau of Justice Statistics, 1994; Gilfus, 1988; Marcus-Mendoza & Briody, 1996; Owen & Bloom, 1995). Gilfus (1988) found that of those inmates with children, 46.7% were single mothers. Nationwide, only 22% of families with children are headed by single mothers (U.S. Department of Commerce, 1995). And, in their study of female inmates in Oklahoma, Marcus-Mendoza and Briody (1996) found that 73% of the inmates who were mothers were not receiving any child support from their children's fathers.

Research reveals that just over half of female inmates were unemployed prior to their arrest (Bureau of Justice Statistics [BJS], 1991; Marcus-Mendoza & Briody, 1996; Owen & Bloom, 1995). The BJS (1991) study found that 53% of female inmates were unemployed prior to incarceration, as opposed to only 32% of male inmates. This statistic is particularly alarming given the high percentages of women inmates who, prior to their incarceration, were single mothers and received little or no child support. Fletcher, Shaver, and Moon (1993) reported that female inmates are also concerned about job prospects upon release. When asked about what they needed to be successful upon release, 80% of the female inmates wanted more education and training to get jobs.

Although the problems commonly faced by women before incarceration are being studied, researchers have largely neglected to study women's motivations for committing crimes, and have instead adapted theories from research on men (Belknap, 1996). The theories of male criminality include social control theory which suggests that the strength of a person's social bonds and the degree of their belief in society's rules determines whether a person will commit a crime, and power-control theory which posits that power dynamics in the home and workplace determine risk-taking, and therefore, criminal behaviors. However, Sommers (1995), in her qualitative study of 14 female inmates in Canada, found that women commit crimes for reasons unrelated to control theories or gender stereotypes. Some women commit crimes to maintain an adequate standard of living for their families, and others are looking for acceptance by trying to buy expensive gifts for others. Several women committed crimes as an expression of the pain that had been inflicted upon them. This study found that relational and economic needs were the pervasive primary motivators of women's crime, and that power was not generally a factor. Sommers concluded that researchers and therapists must consider the societal context of crime, and the individual experience of each woman in order to understand the motivation for crime.

The work of reformers has led to current programming that more accurately reflects some of the needs of female inmates. Many prisons offer education, vocational programs, life skills training, and psychological services. Despite recent progress, however, Morash, Haarr, and Rucker (1994) argued that programming for female inmates still reflects gender stereotyping. They point out that women learn horticulture, typing, and food preparation, while men learn more marketable skills. This still puts women at a disadvantage when they enter the job market. The skills they acquire in prison are more appropriate for full-time homemakers, whereas the majority of women in prison are single mothers. The gender-stereotyped vocational training also reinforces the attitude of the "fallen woman." By training inmates to be better at "women's work," correctional administrators are perpetuating the notion that if inmates can learn to assume gender-stereotyped roles, they will stay out of trouble. This is contrary to feminist therapy theory which encourages women to resist dominant role expectations so that they can formulate their own life goals. Prison administrators still set therapeutic goals rather than encouraging women to formulate their own.

Hannah-Moffat (1995) suggested that although changes have "softened some of the rough edges of incarceration" (p. 159), women's prisons do not empower women in the feminist sense of the word. For instance, the Canadian program, *Creating Choices*, was designed to empower women by offering programming designed to meet women's specific needs, rather than just adapting male programming for women. However, programs were not created by consultation with prisoners as originally intended, but by the government. In essence, as Hannah-Moffat commented, *Creating Choices* dictates certain programs designed to increase individual responsibility of the inmates, and "disregards feminist analysis of the social, economic, and political barriers experienced by women—and, in particular, by marginalized women" (p. 159).

Boot Camps

A relatively recent addition to prison programming for men, and subsequently for women, is the correctional boot camp. Since the first prison boot camp was started in 1983, more than 50 boot camps have opened in prisons and jails around the country. Prison and jail boot camps, modeled after military boot camps, are typically short-term programs which emphasize military drill and ceremony, discipline, physical training, and daily work assignments (MacKenzie, 1991; Parent, 1989). Some boot camps also offer educational programming, psychological services, substance abuse counseling and education, and life skills training. Inmates who are sentenced to boot camps are generally non-violent first offenders and non-violent juveniles.

The rationales for the development of boot camp programs vary from camp to camp. Parent (1989), in his study of the advent of shock programs, found that personal experience with the military and success stories by other prison administrators were the basis for most of the boot camps, and that there was little empirical data to support the utilization of boot camps. Prison administrators most often cited the goals of boot camps as improved discipline of offenders during and after incarceration, punishment, deterrence, incapacitation, reduction in recidivism, reduction in cost of housing inmates, and rehabilitation (Austin, Jones, & Bolyard, 1993; Osler, 1991; Parent, 1989).

The results of research on boot camps are mixed. Some studies have found positive results, such as reduction in recidivism (Marcus-Mendoza, 1995), and positive changes in attitude (Burton, Marquart, Cuvelier, Alarid, & Hunter, 1993). Women in one study reported that learning discipline would be helpful to them in negotiating life after prison (MacKenzie, Elis, Simpson, & Skroban, 1994). Others have found that the goals cited above are not being met or the results differ across camps (MacKenzie, 1991; MacKenzie, 1994; MacKenzie & Brame, 1995; MacKenzie, Brame, McDowall, & Souryal, 1995; MacKenzie, Shaw, & Gowdy, 1993; MacKenzie, Shaw, & Souryal, 1992; MacKenzie & Souryal, 1994). The short duration of the programs may help to reduce costs and relieve overcrowding, but this is only the case when programs are well designed (MacKenzie, 1994; Parent, 1994).

Questions have also been raised about the possible detrimental effects of boot camps. Critics claim boot camps are demeaning, poorly implemented, and a "quick-fix" (Morash & Rucker, 1990; Osier, 1991; Parent, 1989; Sechrest, 1989). They argue that the strict discipline and drilling is abusive in some instances (Osier, 1991), and may be traumatic for inmates who are survivors of abuse (MacKenzie et al., 1994; Marcus-Mendoza, 1995).

Currently, there are only six boot camps for female offenders in the United States, and several which are co-correctional—for men and women. Both the stated goals of the boot camps and the programming differ across camps for women. The common theme that seems to define the boot camp concept is the goal of improving self-concept and instilling discipline, which was given as a goal by all six camps. Some camps also have more pragmatic goals such as reducing overcrowding and protecting the public. Two camps list reducing recidivism as a goal. Only one program lists the seemingly conflicting goals of punishment and improved self-concept/discipline. Although they all have one goal in common (instilling discipline), the intents of the camps still seem to differ.

Differences in programming at the camps are reflective of the divergent beliefs about the purpose of the correctional boot camp. The programs are similar in that they are short-term programs that have a military drilling component, work, and physical fitness. However, they differ in the inclusion of educational, psychological, religious, vocational, and life skills programming. More extensive programming tends to be used in institutions where "reducing recidivism" is listed as a goal. To date, the most comprehensive camp for women is the six-month program at the Federal Prison Camp in Bryan, Texas, in which drilling is minimal, and a full range of programming exists. Inmates participate in programming three days a week, and most evenings.

Feminist Theory and Boot Camp Ideology

The goals and methods of the boot camp as described previously are very different from the goals and methods of feminist therapy. In fact, feminist therapy emerged as a reaction to similar ideas and practices in the fields of psychology and psychiatry. Many volumes have emerged to dispel the myths of women's frailty, incompetence, and dependence, and have put forth new, more accurate ideas about women and feminist therapy with women. In her synthesis of work on feminist therapy to date, *Subversive Dialogues*, Laura Brown (1996) describes a vision of therapy which is grounded in feminist political philosophy. Brown suggests that a therapist aids the client in resisting dominant cultural norms and attending to her own voice. Resistance is a positive and healthy endeavor given the social and political context, rather than a form of denial or misconduct. The therapist and client work "toward strategies and solutions advancing feminist resistance, transformation, and social change in daily personal life, and in relationships with the social, emotional, and political environment" (p. 22).

Such works as Brown's have created alternatives for women therapists and women clients. Women who are dealing with the issues that the female inmates are dealing with—poverty, abuse, domestic violence, and addiction—can seek out feminist therapy that will help them address such problems as low self-esteem, inability to trust others, and anger (Herman, 1992). The therapist and client address problems in the context in which they were created, and solutions provide movement toward personal and social change. Women can receive help in an environment that fosters resistance and personal integrity rather than infantilization, self-directedness rather than conformity, and self-esteem rather than self-doubt.

However, boot camps for women reflect a curious mixture of ideologies, goals, and programs which do not necessarily consider the problems and needs of female inmates. Utilization of boot camp programs presumes that all women offenders who qualify for boot camp have the same difficulties and need the same "treatment." The boot camp conceptualization of female offenders assumes that women who have committed crimes need a stronger sense of discipline and responsibility. This doctrine is reminiscent of the "fallen woman" ideology that feminists and reformers have been fighting for the last two centuries, and ignores our current knowledge about female offenders. As a form of social control, boot camps attempt literally to drill these missing attributes into the "fallen women" in an attempt to make them "disciplined," "respectable," or "socially acceptable."

This form of "treatment" is contrary to feminist therapy practice as conceptualized by Brown (1996). In boot camps, women are dressed alike, drilled, and worked in a regimented manner. Prison administrators assume that drilling and work (with no other programming in some cases) will instill discipline, thereby producing the desired positive changes in women. This is contradictory to Brown's conceptualization of feminist therapy in which women learn to attend to their own voice and resist dominant role expectations if these expectations conflict with their own goals. Although MacKenzie et al. (1994) found that some female inmates felt that learning discipline might help them better to negotiate life after prison, this premise has not been empirically validated. Further, the notion that improved discipline and responsibility are the proper therapeutic goals for all women in boot camps is inconsistent with the existing research on female inmates, especially Sommers' (1995) findings on women's motivation for committing crime. It ignores such social contexts of women's crime as poverty, violence, and substance abuse. Indeed, prison programs will probably best address social problems by helping women to confront prescribed social norms rather than drilling them into conformity.

Boot camp programs also set up a very definite and unhealthy power structure which may be detrimental to the female inmates, especially those who have been survivors of incest, acquaintance rape, and domestic violence. Such abuse, which occurs in the context of an "intimate" relationship, leaves the victim confused and traumatized (Herman, 1992). This confusing dynamic is the core of boot camps which try to habilitate but may further traumatize by sending conflicting messages to women. Boot camps in which a woman is marching and being inspected by a powerful other one minute, and in therapy with that same powerful other the next, may create a similarly warped environment to the one in which the woman was abused. This strategy institutionalizes and further sanctions the abuse dynamic, in which a parent or spouse is both a caring confidante and an abuser. It would be less confusing (to both inmates and staff) if the jailer and the counselor were different people, in different settings. Female inmates could learn that, contrary to much of their prior experience, intimidation and intimacy do not have to coexist in all relationships.

Finally, boot camps are first, and maybe foremost, punishment. The drilling and yelling that take place in all boot camps to a greater or lesser extent are punishment. In addition, Hannah-Moffat (1995) points out that in a society as liberal as ours, depriving a person of numerous rights by incarceration is a serious penalty. Since boot camp programs are housed in prisons, the assumption that female offenders should be punished is inherent to boot camps and any other prison-based programs. And this is, again, contrary to feminist and most other forms of therapy. It creates the same unhealthy tension that Freedman (1981) referred to in the nineteenth century prisons, where "fallen women" were being punished and taught to be domestic.

Conclusions

Feminist therapists employed in a boot camp must learn to work in a difficult environment. The therapist in a boot camp, as in other prison settings, has the difficult assignment of earning the trust and respect of the inmates in a context in which it is advisable for inmates to be cautious. Therapists must also find a way to separate themselves sufficiently from the power structure of the prison so that they do not engage in confusing dual relationships that would undermine the process of feminist therapy (i.e., acting as both therapist and disciplinarian). Maintaining confidentiality, acting as an advocate for the inmates, and treating the inmates with respect in an environment where others may treat the inmates with contempt may help the therapists' efforts. Negotiating clear boundaries with prison administrators that are conducive to providing a safe and respectful environment is also imperative.

In their practice with female inmates, whether in boot camps or in other prison settings, therapists face the challenge of working in a punishing environment. This poses a difficult balancing act for the feminist therapist who must somehow nurture personal growth in a situation where resistance may be punished by expulsion from the boot camp program and a longer and more unpleasant incarceration. The feminist therapist working in the boot camp or other prison must aid the clients in identifying and asserting their own needs while their clients are being denied their freedom in an environment that demands conformity. In addition, the therapist must find a way to help women identify and express their feelings, including those about their incarceration, in a way that will not be punished. It is incumbent upon the therapist to face these challenges successfully in order to help to counter the negative messages of the boot camp and prison, support the women and foster growth, and help their clients survive the confusion and trauma they are experiencing.

Unfortunately, it is not possible to separate punishment and habilitation of offenders as long as they are being sentenced to prison. It is important to try to find alternative methods of sentencing offenders, especially the non-violent first offenders who are typically sentenced to boot camps. The advent of the boot camp is an important one in that it does represent a willingness to institute short-term habilitative correctional programming as opposed to long-term warehousing of offenders. However, departments of corrections should institute short-term programs conducted on a community or "out-patient" basis, and without the punishment. Therapists who work in such programs could orient interventions toward helping women to identify and attain their own objectives rather than imposing other people's ideals upon them. Punishment need not be the focus of corrections. After leaving the bench when ordered by the Supreme Court of Pennsylvania to impose a mandatory five-year sentence that she felt was unjust, Judge Lois Forer (1994) observed, "The rage to punish is a costly American obsession. Punishment is defined as 'subjecting a person to pain for an offense or fault.' In any other context the desire to cause pain is considered sadism, a psychiatric disorder" (p. 10).

References

American Correctional Association. (1990). *The female offender: What does the future hold?* Arlington, VA: Kirby Lithographic Company, Inc.

Austin, J., Jones, M., & Bolyard, M. (1993). *The growing use of jail boot camps: The current state of the art.* Washington, DC: National Institute of Justice, U.S. Department of Justice, Office of Justice Programs.

Belknap, J. (1996). *The invisible woman: Gender, crime, and justice.* Belmont, CA: Wadsworth Publishing Co.

Brown, L. S. (1996). *Subversive dialogues: Theory in feminist therapy.* New York: Basic Books.

Bureau of Justice Statistics. (1991, March). *Special report: Women in prison* (Report No. NCJ-127855). Washington, DC: U.S. Government Printing Office.

Bureau of Justice Statistics. (1994, March). *Special report: Women in prison: Survey of state prison inmates* (Report No. NCJ-145321). Washington, DC: U.S. Government Printing Office.

Burton, V. S., Marquart, J. W., Cuvelier, S. J., Alarid, L. F., & Hunter, R. J. (1993). A study of attitudinal change among boot camp participants. *Federal Probation, 57* (3), 46–52.

Eaton, M. (1993). *Women after prison.* Buckingham, England: Open University Press.

Feinman, C. (1986). *Women in the criminal justice system* (2nd ed.). New York: Praeger Publishers.

Fletcher, B. R., Shaver, L. D., & Moon, D. G. (Eds.). (1993). *Women offenders in Oklahoma: A forgotten population.* New York: Praeger Press.

Forer, L. G. (1994). *A rage to punish: The unintended consequences of mandatory sentencing.* New York: W. W. Norton & Company.

Freedman, E. B. (1981). *Their sisters' keepers.* Ann Arbor: The University of Michigan Press.

Gilfus, M. (1988). *Seasoned by love/tempered by violence: A qualitative study of women and crime.* Unpublished doctoral dissertation, Brandeis University.

Hannah-Moffat, K. (1995). Feminine fortresses: Woman-centered prisons? *The Prison Journal, 75* (2), 135–164.

Herman, J. L. (1992). *Trauma and recovery.* New York: Basic Books.

Lombroso, C., & Ferrero, G. (1900). *The female offender.* New York: Appleton.

MacKenzie, D. L. (1991). The parole performance of offenders released from shock incarceration (boot camp prisons): A survival time analysis. *Journal of Quantitative Criminology, 7* (3), 213–236.

MacKenzie, D. L. (1994). Boot camps: A national assessment. *Overcrowded Times, 5* (4), pp. 1, 14–18.

MacKenzie, D. L., & Brame, R. (1995). Shock incarceration and positive adjustment during community supervision. *Journal of Quantitative Criminology, 11* (2), 111–142.

MacKenzie, D. L., Brame, R., McDowall, D., & Souryal, C. (1995). Boot camp prisons and recidivists in eight states. *Criminology, 33* (3), 327–357.

MacKenzie, D. L., Elis, L. A., Simpson, S. S., & Skroban, S. B. (1994). *Female offenders in boot camp prisons.* Washington, DC: National Institute of Justice, U.S. Department of Justice, Office of Justice Programs.

MacKenzie, D. L., Shaw, J. W., & Gowdy, V. B. (1993). *An evaluation of shock incarceration in Louisiana* (NCJ no. 140567). Washington, DC: National Institute of Justice, U.S. Department of Justice, Office of Justice Programs.

MacKenzie, D. L., Shaw, J. W., & Souryal, C. (1992). Characteristics associated with successful adjustment to supervision: A comparison of parolees, probationers, shock participants, and shock dropouts. *Criminal Justice and Behavior, 19* (4), 437–454.

MacKenzie, D. L., & Souryal, C. (1994). *Multisite evaluation of shock incarceration* (NCJ no. 142462). Washington, DC: National Institute of Justice, U.S. Department of Justice, Office of Justice Programs.

Marcus-Mendoza, S. T. (1995). A preliminary analysis of Oklahoma's Shock Incarceration Program. *Journal of the Oklahoma Criminal Justice Research Consortium, 2,* 1–6.

Marcus-Mendoza, & Briody. (in press). Female inmates in Oklahoma: An updated profile and programming assessment.

Marcus-Mendoza, S. T., Sargent, E., & Chong Ho, Y. (1994). Changing perceptions of the etiology of crime: The relationship between abuse and female criminology. *Journal of the Oklahoma Criminal Justice Research Consortium, 1,* 13–23.

Morash, M., Haarr, R. N., & Rucker, L. (1994). A comparison of programming for women and men in U.S. prisons in the 1980s. *Crime & Delinquency, 40* (2), 197–221.

Morash, M., & Rucker, L. (1990). A critical look at the idea of boot camp as a correctional reform. *Crime & Delinquency, 36* (2), 204–222,

Osler, M. (1991). Shock incarceration: Hard realities and real possibilities. *Federal Probation, 55* (1), 34–42.

Owen, B., & Bloom, B. (1995). Profiling women prisoners: Findings from national surveys and a California sample. *The Prison Journal, 72* (2), 165–185.

Parent, D. G. (1989). *Shock incarceration: An overview of existing programs.* Washington, DC: National Institute of Justice, U.S. Department of Justice, Office of Justice Programs.

Parent, D. G. (1994). Boot camps failing to achieve goals. *Overcrowded Times, 5* (4), 8–11.

Pollock-Byrne, J. M. (1990). *Women, prison, and crime.* Pacific Grove, CA: Brooks/Cole Publishing.

Rafter, N. H. (1990). *Partial justice: Women, prisons, and social control* (2nd ed.). New Brunswick, NJ: Transaction Publishers.

Russell, D. E. H. (1984). *Sexual exploitation: Rape, child sexual abuse, and sexual harassment.* Beverly Hills, CA: Sage.

Sechrest, D. K. (1989). Prison "boot camps" do not measure up. *Federal Probation, 53* (3), 15–20.

Sommers, E. K. (1995). *Voices from within: Women who have broken the law.* Toronto: University of Toronto Press.

U.S. Department of Commerce. (1995). *Statistical abstract of the United States 1995* (115 ed.). Washington, DC: U.S. Government Printing Office.

U.S. Department of Health and Human Services. (1996). *National household survey on drug abuse: Population estimates 1995* (DHHS No. SMA 96-3095). Rockville, MD: Author.

Walker, L. E. A. (1994). *Abused women and survivor therapy.* Washington, DC: American Psychological Association.

Index